Their Sisters' Keepers

Their Sisters' Keepers

Prostitution in New York City, 1830–1870

Marilynn Wood Hill

UNIVERSITY OF CALIFORNIA PRESS

Berkeley / Los Angeles / London

University of California Press
Berkeley and Los Angeles, California

University of California Press, Ltd.
London, England

© 1993 by
The Regents of the University of California

Library of Congress Cataloging-in-Publication Data

Hill, Marilynn Wood.
    Their sisters' keepers : prostitution in New York City,
1830–1870 / Marilynn Wood Hill.
        p.   cm.
    Includes bibliographical references and index.
    ISBN 0-520-07834-9 (alk. paper)
    1. Prostitution—New York (N.Y.)—History—19th century.
2.   Prostitutes—New York (N.Y.)—History—19th century.
I. Title.
HQ146.N7H55   1993
74'2'09747109034—dc20   92-6558
                                                              CIP

Printed in the United States of America
9   8   7   6   5   4   3   2   1

The paper used in this publication meets the minimum require-
ments of American National Standard for Information Sciences—
Permanence of Paper for Printed Library Materials,
ANSI Z39.48-1984. ∞

To John, Shannon, and Allison

Contents

Illustrations

Tables

Acknowledgments

In the course of this study I have received assistance from many individuals. Staff members at several libraries and archives were helpful as well as obliging in locating many sources. Especially important for this project were the New York Public Library, the county clerk's office in the Hall of Records, the New York State Library in Albany, and the Rockefeller Archives in Pocantico Hills. Individuals at other institutions also were very helpful: Robert Macdonald, director, and Marguerite Lavin and Terry Ariano of the Museum of the City of New York; Dale Neighbors, Patricia Paladines, and Diana Arecco of the New-York Historical Society; Evelyn Gonzalez and Kenneth Cobb of the New York Municipal Archives; and Calvin Otto, trustee, and Georgia Barnhill of the American Antiquarian Society. Rose Anne Burstein, Charling Fagan, and the wonderful staff at the Sarah Lawrence Library offered not only assistance but also a place to work and support as my project progressed.

Other individuals have contributed to this study in measurable and immeasurable ways. Early in my research I met Christine Stansell at the Hall of Records. She shared with me chapters of the dissertation she was finishing and names of other scholars who might be helpful, and she told me about the rich resource in the House of Refuge records. I have found her generosity as well as her historical scholarship outstanding. I profited from comments by members of Nondescript, before whom I presented a portion of the manuscript. Diana Zentay spent many hours turning poorly focused photographic negatives of crumbling newspapers into prints from which I could work. My nephew, Von Pilcher, took care of my children one summer while I did research. Dr. George Unis provided resource materials and advice on medical issues and also proofread one chapter of the study. The partners and staff of First Reserve Corporation generously and patiently shared work space as well as word-processing and photocopying equipment through several stages of my writing. Betty Dell'Orfano spent many days and many late hours typing and photocopying the various drafts of the manuscript and, with the help of Dorothy Mulcahy and Lisa Altomare, we finally produced a finished copy. Contributions of a more indirect nature came from several close friends and members of my family, who offered constant encouragement and were willing to forgo visits and vacations together while I did writing or research. In particular, I am grateful to my mother and father, Mary Mitchell Wood and the late Gordon Brannen Wood, for so many years and kinds of encouragement.

I have appreciated the comments of several individuals who read and criticized drafts of the manuscript: George Calcott, J. Kirkpatrick Flack, Claire Moses, and E. B. Smith. Claire Moses was especially helpful, with suggestions for reorganizing and rewriting some of the material. I also have profited from the assistance given by my editors at the University of California Press: Sheila Levine, Rose Vekony, Ellen Stein, and Monica McCormick. Paul Boller, as an undergraduate and graduate professor, shared his excitement for American history and his warm friendship. He has continued sharing both over many years and many miles, still offering sound advice and critiques of my writing.

The person most instrumental in causing this study to happen is my graduate adviser and mentor, David Grimsted. Beginning with his inspiring course on the middle period and continuing through years of guidance, criticism, encouragement, and patience, he has shown me, by his example, the true meaning of scholarship.

And finally, to Allison and Shannon who "grew up" with my study of prostitution, and to John who says he "grew old" with my study of prostitution, I dedicate this book. They did not know what home life or vacations were like without my project, but they never lost faith that someday it would be completed.

Introduction

This book is a study of the life and work of prostitutes in New York City between 1830 and 1870. During this period the New York City prostitute had to cope with the limited economic, social, and legal options available to women at the time, yet she managed to create a life for herself that, though fraught with difficulties, was open to possibilities. New York prostitution was at a unique juncture in its history during these years because some of the women involved were able to establish a significant degree of control over the business, and because the more fortunate ones were able to reap meaningful economic rewards.

The story of the New York prostitute is not easy to tell; it is filled with ambiguities, ironies, and even contradictions. Were these women's lives characterized by victimization or agency, dependence or independence, constraints or possibilities? There are no simple answers. There were limits to their lives, of course, for like all people, they made their choices in a world, as Marx put it, which they neither made nor controlled. Some prostitutes prospered and lived fruitful lives. Others experienced disappointment and heartbreak. The desire here, therefore, is to avoid talking about these women in any particular category, but to see them as the immensely varied group of human beings they were, drawn together by the way they earned money, whether as a temporary expedient or a long-range commitment.

Recent historians of American prostitution have done much to help us to understand these women within a theoretical framework stressing gender and class. My own research has led me to put greater emphasis on the role of gender than on class, though certainly the existence of the poor and the increase in New York's foreign-born population during these years were factors that exacerbated class issues and fostered restrictions in people's lives. But "limitations" were a fact for all women where gender largely truncated legal, economic, and social possibilities. In a society where women were subordinate to men, "class" became a function of the gender system, a reflection of the status of the male on whom a woman was dependent or from whom she inherited or was given economic independence. Without a connection to a male, a woman discovered that her socially structured powerlessness almost invariably left her in the lower part of the socioeconomic order. Although the American dream promised that class was not a hard-and-fast designation, upward mobility and economic success were more often bright dreams than achieved realities. And yet, in an environment where feminine and class identities were somewhat fluid, as they were in New York at this time, there were some promising possibilities for women.

Ironically, some of the possibilities offered by prostitution were the result of the profession's dubious socio-legal status. Prostitution's position at the fringes of the law and outside the realm of respectability allowed a woman freedom from many of the restrictions and conventions that circumscribed the activities and opportunities of other females. Furthermore, a successful prostitute gained a degree of economic and social independence from the constraints of a patriarchal, or male-controlled, structure, even though she worked in an occupation that was dependent on a male clientele. Thus, in spite of the limitations dictated by nineteenth-century America's socio-legal system, some prostitutes were able to manipulate the oppressions and dependencies inherent in the system more effectively than many other working or male-supported women, and they succeeded in creating opportunities for improving their lives and the lives of those they cared for.

Though the lives of the majority of nineteenth-century prostitutes have been obscure, there is a surprising array of sources that have helped to recover their history, offering us a deeper understanding of individual prostitutes and hence of their career sisterhood. By piecing together bits of information from contemporary sources such as newspapers, brothel guides, reformers' surveys and reports, along with data from public documents such as tax, census, court, and police records, it is possible to discern many hitherto unknown dimensions of the prostitutes' private and public lives. One of the most illuminating sources for the present study is a collection of prostitutes' letters not previously cited in other works on nineteenth-century prostitution.

This study considers New York City's prostitutes within a broad historical context. The first chapter discusses social changes in the nineteenth century that caused prostitution to become identified as a major social issue and attempts to determine the magnitude of this "problem" in New York by estimating the number of women who practiced prostitution. The second chapter presents collective and personal profiles that suggest the variety of women who chose the profession. The remaining seven chapters explore both the public and private dimensions of these women's lives. Despite a wide range of personal motives, most women chose prostitution from the limited occupational options available because they wished to provide as well as possible for themselves, their children, and other loved ones. In addition to economic rewards unavailable in other female occupations, prostitution offered social freedoms that traditional employments and familial restrictions did not allow. Prostitutes understood that most people judged their profession unrespectable, but theirs was not an unredeemable status: they might move on to other, respectable occupations, to marriage, and even to wealth.

Officially outside the law, New York's prostitutes were in a vulnerable position, constantly subject to legal harassment and discrimination. Nevertheless, many found that cooperative relationships with fellow citizens and with public officials facilitated their utilization of the workplace, the legal system, and the municipal structure to their advantage. In mid-century New York's rapidly changing urban environment, prostitutes were more often integrated into than ostracized from the daily lives of ordinary citizens. Furthermore, though most prostitutes practiced the trade as an occasional or part-time occupation, many of those who became long-term professional prostitutes were able to achieve economic goals and have managerial experiences that were not generally available to other women at the time.

But to note the ameliorating aspects of the prostitute's life does not negate the dangers and hardships—violence, disease, undesirable company, possible arrest, and incarceration. The degradation and difficulties inherent in the profession, widely recognized at the time, were real.

Only with the emotional support of family and especially close friends within the profession were many prostitutes able to function effectively in their often-difficult working situations.

Prostitutes, like other nineteenth-century women, were mothers, sisters, daughters, wives, lovers, and laborers, and they experienced the common cares, desires, and constraints of women of their time. Like other women with few resources, they had limited opportunities and faced daily difficulties that often necessitated hard and potentially debilitating choices. As women who needed to earn an income in the nation's largest and most dynamic urban center, prostitutes coped or failed to cope, as their personal strengths, weaknesses, and luck dictated, in a world never made easy for them.

This study, of course, owes much to the recent historiography of prostitution. Judith Walkowitz, through her research on nineteenth-century English prostitution, and Ruth Rosen, through her studies on American prostitution, have been instrumental in restructuring the discussion of this topic among historians. Their studies, and the works of others who have followed, have expanded our understanding not only of the lives of the women who chose to be prostitutes but also of the ways in which a society's response to prostitution reflects its social structure and cultural values. New research continues to explore different aspects of prostitution, enlarging both the chronological and geographical perimeters of the topic while offering a broadened perspective on the historical experiences of all women.[1]

Two of the recent works that discuss New York prostitution have been especially provocative for my study. Ruth Rosen's *The Lost Sisterhood* (1982), a study of prostitution in America's large cities in the early twentieth century, provides a continuation of the story I begin in the nineteenth century. In Rosen's study, the independent prostitution businesses of the mid-nineteenth century which I describe—businesses that were run predominantly by females and offered individual prostitutes a significant degree of freedom within the profession—were replaced in the twentieth century by a more commercialized and rationalized form of prostitution. Rosen's research picks up the thread of the narrative after late-nineteenth-century Tammany politicians incorporated prostitution into their tightly woven network of political-business interests, and control of the sex trade shifted to organized crime syndicates, pimps, and other third-party agents who made a living by exploiting the prostitutes. Rosen stresses the impact of gender and class biases in creating an environment that drew women into prostitution, allowed their exploitation, and inspired Progressive laws and reforms that were designed to abolish the trade. In spite of increasingly oppressive conditions surrounding the practice of prostitution in this period, however, Rosen emphasizes that prostitutes were making choices about their lives, albeit within a framework of limited and unattractive options. Furthermore, prostitutes were better able to cope with their difficult lives because they were given support, protection, and a sense of self-worth by other women in the subculture of urban prostitution.[2]

Christine Stansell's fine book, *City of Women: Sex and Class in New York, 1789–1860* (1987), describes how prostitution, especially casual prostitution, was interwoven with other aspects of New York City's working-class culture. Her study, like mine, emphasizes the structured dependencies of women in mid-nineteenth-century New York society: the "large oppressions but small freedoms" of these women, and the "possibilities" that poor women, including prostitutes, "traced out" for themselves, in large part because of networks of support and mutual assistance.[3] Because Stansell focuses on casual and street prostitution, as opposed to the more organized brothel-based forms of the profession, the prostitutes in her study are a part of a more homogeneous class structure than are those in my study.

My study places greater emphasis than do those of other historians on the positive appeal and rewards of prostitution, especially for women better situated in the profession, including long-term career prostitutes. There is some danger in this, as Stansell notes: "We are still too much influenced by the Victorians' view of prostitution as utter degradation to accept easily any interpretation that stresses the opportunities commercial sex provided to women rather than the victimization it entailed."[4] Of course, one should not "accept easily" positive appraisals of any career as fraught with difficulty, danger, and a potential for degradation as prostitution was, but it is perhaps time that Victorian prejudice ceases to blind us to the human possibilities in the lives of those it deemed fallen, just as we have come to see the human limitations for those women the Victorians declared wholly blessed and fortunate.

PART ONE

Nineteenth-Century Prostitution: Profiles and Problems

1

"The Terrible State of Society and Morals . . . in Unhappy New York"

Nineteenth-Century Moralism and the Prostitution Problem

On Monday, April 11, 1836, the *New York Herald* ran two lead articles side by side at the top of its front page. One story described the brutal murder of a young prostitute whose body had been found the day before; the second reported on efforts by local church leaders to dispose of a controversy involving a leading moral reformer who campaigned against prostitution. The murdered prostitute, virtually unknown except to her patrons, coworkers, and a few who recognized her in her neighborhood, would within days became a household name and would achieve considerable posthumous notoriety. The moral reformer, whose name was already widely familiar in New York and other states, would within a few months die in relative obscurity, broken in health and spirit.[1]

There is no evidence that the prostitute and the reformer had known one another or even been aware of one another, though both had been intimately involved with New York's prostitution community. The double lead billing for their stories evoked two sides of the same coin, two completely different images of the world of prostitution. Ironically, perhaps, from their vastly different perspectives and experiences, both individuals can be said to have played a role—symbolic, if not actual—in shaping issues and public discourse that would impact on the social fabric of mid-nineteenth-century New York City.

Under the title "A Most Atrocious Murder," the *Herald* described the brutal death of prostitute Helen Jewett in a brothel at 41 Thomas Street.

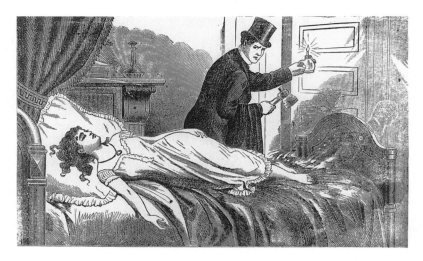

1. THE MURDER OF HELEN JEWETT.   On the night of April 9, 1836, Helen Jewett was murdered by an ax blow to her head. The murderer then set fire to her body and bed before escaping. A customer-lover who was with her that night was charged with the murder but was acquitted. (Courtesy of the New-York Historical Society, New York City)

Jewett had been found murdered in her bed, the victim of an ax blow to her head. Her room had been set on fire, apparently in an attempt to destroy evidence. An estranged lover, Richard P. Robinson, with whom she had last been seen the previous evening, was accused of the crime. Based on physical evidence and the testimony of other residents of the house, a coroner's jury bound Robinson over for trial, and he was sent to jail.[2]

News of the murder created an immediate sensation. For the two months between the April crime and the end of the week-long trial in June, New York newspapers devoted lengthy columns and even entire pages to daily coverage of the case. Reports were carried in newspapers as far away as Mississippi and Maine, and the murder-trial proceedings were the most widely covered of any in America to that time. The public seemed to have an insatiable curiosity about the event, the young victim, her prostitute associates, and their clients. For the week the trial was in session, spectators lined up outside the courtroom hoping to get seats or at least a glimpse of the characters involved. Although evidence pointed to Robinson's guilt, he was acquitted by a jury suspicious of the testimony of prostitutes, and the crime was left unsolved. For decades afterward, newspapers continued to make references to Jewett's murder, and the story became part of nineteenth-century New York legend and fiction. Jewett even appears briefly in Gore Vidal's 1973 historical novel, *Burr*.[3]

Publicity surrounding the incident fed an obvious public appetite for the lurid details of the murder, but it also revealed a deep uneasiness about the environment of the crime. The *Herald* termed Jewett's death the natural result of a "terrible state of society . . . and morals which ought to be reformed altogether in unhappy New York."[4] After 1830, the increasing presence of prostitutes on the city streets had caused New Yorkers to begin speaking much more publicly about a "prostitution problem," voicing their concerns in the press, the pulpit, and municipal forums. In language and rhetoric that was often more moralistic than realistic, prostitutes were depicted as either "innocent victims" or "corrupt denizens," and their brothels were "places of perdition" or "vile receptacles." This mode of discussion obscured deeper issues, deflecting attention from dramatic social changes then under way in economic and family lives as well as in attitudes and mores.[5] From the moralistic perspective, the Jewett murder was viewed as the inevitable result of an obvious decline in both private and public morality—the product of innocent lives gone astray, the fruition of urban social decay. But even many contemporary accounts of the case had to admit that Helen Jewett did not readily fit the moralistic prototype, and her divergence from contemporary notions of a prostitute's sorrowful existence no doubt contributed to the nineteenth-century public's fascination with her story. Contrary to moralistic expectations, Jewett appeared to have led an attractive and independent life, a life she had chosen for herself over more conventional options.

Many versions of Jewett's life exist. In the telling and retelling of her story at the time of the murder and later, authors have sometimes described her as the innocent victim of a licentious seducer, unable to avoid a certain doom, and sometimes presented her as a girl who may have been tricked into losing her virginity but who made the most of her subsequent life—a life that was glamorous and adventurous, though filled with risks.[6] Because Jewett has been the object of so much notoriety, it becomes difficult to separate the reality from the myth, but some information about her short life is available—a life that serves as an introduction to issues and events that this study will explore in telling the story of the diverse group of women who became prostitutes in mid-nineteenth-century New York City.

Jewett was born in Hallowell, Maine. Before taking the name Helen (Ellen or Nell) Jewett, she also went by Dorcas Doyen (or Dorrance), Maria G. Benson, Ellen Spaulding, Helen Mar, and Maria Stanley, the first probably being her real name. She was born in 1813, and at the time of her death she was twenty-three. One story of her background, based on what she told an enamored reporter from the *Transcript* in 1834, is that she was the daughter of a major general and had been seduced while at boarding school. Another version, more generally accepted, is that she was the daughter of Welsh immigrant parents, a mechanic father who drank and a mother who died when Jewett was about ten years old. At age thirteen Jewett went into service in the home of Judge Nathan Weston of Augusta, Maine, where she lived for four years. She was sent to school during that period and was said to have been a very proficient student with a taste for literature. One source stated she spoke several languages and enjoyed quoting lines of verse from French, Italian, and English poets.

At the end of her years of service in the Weston home, seventeen-year-old Jewett apparently had a liaison with a young man, an episode that preceded her move into a life of prostitution. She may have worked first as a prostitute in Portland, Maine, then moved to a Mrs. Bryant's in Boston, and then to New York, where she stayed for a short while at Mrs. Post's on Howard Street and then at the Laurence house on Chapel Street. Like other prostitutes of the time, Jewett was mobile, changing her place of employment periodically. In 1833 she went to Rosina Townsend's at 41 Thomas Street for about ten months, and in 1834 she moved to Mary Berry's at 128 Duane Street, where she lived until early 1836. Following a disagreement with Mrs. Berry she moved to Mrs. Cunningham's at 3 Franklin Street for a brief period, and finally, three weeks before her death, she moved back to Rosina Townsend's.[7]

Although Jewett was an ordinary prostitute, she lived and worked in well-situated houses, near the top of the prostitution hierarchy, and thus she cannot be considered representative of the majority of prostitutes, who were poor and practiced the trade on a casual basis. Because the documents concerning Jewett reveal no evidence of her plans for the future, it is unclear whether she aspired to make prostitution a lifelong profession or regarded it as a temporary option through which she might achieve upward mobility or possibly marriage.

Jewett was said to be "one of the most intelligent, beautiful and accomplished women to be found in her class of life," and "aside from her disreputable calling, was deemed a high minded and honorable woman."[8] The *Herald* described her as a "fascinating woman in conversation, full of intellect and refinement . . . with talents calculated for the highest sphere in life, had she had a happier destiny and steady moral principles." She was said to dress "splendidly," owning a variety of "elegant dresses." She also was rumored to be a good seamstress who enjoyed sewing for her friends and clients as well as herself.[9]

Jewett appeared to be popular with both colleagues and clients. She was described as a "star" of the Berry house, where she lived the longest, and she probably earned as much as $50 to $100 a week for the establishment, or between $1,000 and $2,000 in current dollars. Her earnings also provided her with sufficient personal economic resources to travel, attend the theater, dress elegantly, make generous gifts to her friends, and even lend money on occasion. When she fell in love with one of her clients, however, Jewett's value to her brothel declined, and the madam of her house warned her that fidelity to her lover would ruin her career—not to mention the madam's profits.[10]

Like most prostitutes, Jewett had contact with the local police. On one occasion, she was brought into police headquarters because the brothel was raided, but most of her dealings with the law came about because Jewett brought charges against other parties. She sued a client named Burke for cutting several of her dresses to pieces following an argument, and the court required that he reimburse her $100. She brought charges of assault against an overzealous suitor named Laraty, who had accosted her in the lobby of a public theater by throwing his arms around her and kissing her. She claimed that he also kicked her. With Mrs. Berry, her brothel madam at the time, she sued a client named Boyd who in turn countersued Jewett and Berry. Several newspapers reported that Jewett also brought charges against a young woman but "settled" the suit, and on one occasion she was brought before a grand jury to give testimony. Clearly, Jewett did not fear that notoriety as a prostitute would cause her problems with law officials, and in fact

2. **HELEN JEWETT AT THE THEATER.** On one of her many visits to the theater, Jewett was accosted by an overzealous customer in an incident that led her to file assault charges against the man. Like many mid-nineteenth-century prostitutes, Jewett was not shy about asserting her rights as a citizen before the courts. (Courtesy of the New-York Historical Society, New York City)

her frequent recourse to the legal system suggests that she was quite comfortable as a "public citizen" seeking justice from the court.[11]

One of Jewett's most interesting pastimes, and an activity that distinguishes her from the majority of prostitutes, was carrying on a vast correspondence with clients, friends, patrons, lovers, and former colleagues. One newspaper commented that she was seen frequently at the post office, where her postal bill was as great as that of some business firms in the city. After her death the police confiscated from her bedroom a trunk containing approximately ninety letters, some of which were introduced into evidence in the trial.[12] Revealed in the correspondence that became public are aspects of her personal life that are far more detailed than the information available about most other prostitutes: her joys and excitement, her gregariousness, generosity, loyalty, understanding, and affection, as well as glimpses of her jealousy, anger, insecurity, anxiety, sadness, and disappointments.

Jewett's correspondence was obviously important to her, both on a practical level, as a skill useful in recruiting and scheduling customers, and on an emotional level, as a means of fulfilling deeply felt needs for social ties. Communication with people from different cities or different stations in life brought new experiences to Jewett, allowing her to escape mentally the restrictions and debasements of the world of prostitution. Correspondence with men she admired and liked allowed her to enjoy their companionship without the sexual and physical considerations that would be invoked during a personal visit in the brothel. One customer, Edward, who wished for a closer relationship with Jewett, noted this distancing technique at the end of one of his letters: "You have often said write me, but never said call and see me."[13]

Jewett also received from her correspondence a degree of emotional sustenance and reinforcement—from both male and female friends whose responses reconfirmed their affection for and personal interest in her, and from acquaintances who complimented and admired her literary skills and considered them an indication of refinement unusual for "one of her station in life." Thus, Jewett's correspondence set her apart from other prostitutes and provided her with a sense of self-esteem and importance, but her writing ability and education were a double-edged sword. While her talent enabled her to communicate with interesting people on a level different from the sexual, it also made her aware of the limitations of the life she led: "I have often wished I had never been educated, but like those I every day meet, I could not read my name in print."[14]

By leaving Jewett's murder unsolved, authorities only added to the mystique surrounding the crime, its central figure, and the world of prostitution. The story also seemed to confirm the popular belief that a life of prostitution often led to an untimely death, though Jewett's death in fact was linked not so much to hapless fate as to the passion she aroused in clients and the independent spirit in which she conducted her brief life. The murder deprives us of the knowledge of how her full life might have been lived, of the public and private circumstances she would have faced and choices she would have made. We will return to her story for insights into the world of prostitution, but for a story of those missing years and missing experiences we must turn to the stories of many other New Yorkers—both the women who practiced prostitution and the other community members who interacted with them.

The New York City of the 1830s, the city deemed "unhappy" by the *Herald* editor, was already the leading city of the new nation, which by 1810 had surpassed other American cities in population and commerce, and, many believed, in problems as well. All of the social changes that were transforming an idealized agrarian nation, changes that were perceived by observers as disturbing the foundations of American society, were magnified in the country's most expansive urban setting. Unprecedented urban growth and industrialization had led to overcrowding, unemployment, and poverty on a scale previously unimagined. After the War of 1812, the increasing influx of European immigrants brought to American cities strange customs and sometimes different languages as well as new political influences that challenged the hegemony of the propertied classes. Urban housing for the poor was both scarce and wretched, and city dwellers became accustomed to large numbers of vagrants wandering the streets. Sanitation was primitive, and mortality high.[15]

These changes in American life were also transforming basic social institutions such as the family. The nineteenth-century industrial-commercial economy that replaced the traditional domestic economy of small farms and household industries forced breadwinners into new occupations and redefined women's roles. Marriage was no longer a self-contained economic partnership, as men, and often women and children, went to work outside the home. The change in family structure and functions was accompanied by a change in attitudes: woman's role as homemaker, mother, and transmitter of moral and cultural values was idealized in what has been called the "cult of true womanhood" or the "cult of domesticity," which both elevated women to a new level of veneration in the public's consciousness and relegated them to a sphere separate from the dominant and more significant world in which men operated. The nineteenth-century woman's sphere, defined by the activities and functions that men thought appropriate to women, involved a narrowed role and one which was obviously subordinate in power to the male sphere.

Many nineteenth-century women, however, were able to move beyond such a narrowly defined or idealized role. Some worked actively in voluntary and religious associations, groups that were vital to the social-reform movements of the early nineteenth century as well as to the development of the nineteenth-century women's rights movement. Such activities involved mostly women from the middle and upper classes, but the idealized view of woman in the home was even further from reality in the daily lives of working-class women, who by necessity went out to work to supplement their husbands' inadequate earnings or to provide in full for themselves or their families. With women's occupational options limited and wages low, employment often entailed a choice between unpleasant alternatives, including prostitution.[16]

Among the many social ills that marked life in a rapidly changing America after 1830—poverty, unemployment, inadequate housing, disease—prostitution often became the symbol of what was perceived as the social and moral disintegration of society. As a challenge to the idyllic view of woman as asexual, maternal, and pure, and as a threat to the stability of one of the most revered social institutions, the family, prostitution was dubbed the major nineteenth-century social problem, often called, for the rest of the century, "*the* social evil."[17]

The leading figure in bringing the issue of prostitution to the center of public debate in New York was John R. McDowall, the reformer featured alongside Jewett in the April 11, 1836, edition of the *Herald*. McDowall was the fulcrum around which New York's earliest major prostitution controversy swirled. He had arrived in New York in the summer of 1830, as a student intern working as a volunteer missionary for the American Tract Society. The son of a minister, McDowall was born in 1801 in Canada. He attended Amherst, Union (or Schenectady) College, and then Princeton for his theological studies. While at Princeton in 1828–1829, McDowall was active in a number of evangelical and missionary societies, and in 1830 he and his brother, also a divinity student, volunteered for missionary work among the lost souls in the poor districts of New York City. The brothers spent their summer in the Five Points area, visiting crowded tenements, lecturing inhabitants, and distributing tracts and Bibles. They also began visiting the many brothels of the neighborhood, leading prayers with inhabitants and customers and exhorting them to abandon their lives of sin. At the end of his internship, McDowall, feeling he could not leave the work he had begun, remained in New York to continue as a missionary on his own. He set up Sunday schools and Bible classes in the city's almshouses and prisons and visited hospitals, where he continued to meet prostitutes who seemed to be trapped in lives of dissipation, disease, and crime. McDowall's work among the unfortunate attracted the attention and support of a number of respectable New York women, and with the generous assistance of the evangelicals Arthur and Lewis Tappan, McDowall's female supporters were able to establish the New York Magdalen Society. The Society opened a House of Refuge where penitent harlots could be taught respectable ways and skills to support themselves in the community.[18] The Society women hired McDowall as their chaplain, missionary, and agent, and at the end of the first year in operation they published a report he wrote. This report, which claimed there were "not less than 10,000" prostitutes in the city, caused a great furor and focused attention not only on prostitution but also on the report's author. McDowall found himself in the middle of a controversy between reformers aroused by a problem of seemingly near-plague proportions and respectable New Yorkers outraged by statistics they considered preposterous about a subject they viewed as obscene—and by the report's implied criticism of New York and its many members of prominent families who were said to be regular clients at the brothels. Former Mayor Philip Hone wrote in his diary in the summer of 1831 that the report was a "disgraceful document." Several public meetings at Tammany Hall were held to protest the Magdalen Society and its report, and a grand jury was called to investigate the extent of prostitution. McDowall and the Magdalen Society were verbally assailed, and some members of the society, such as Arthur Tappan, received letters threatening mob destruction of their

3. REFORMER PREACHING TO PROSTITUTES.   Moral reformers like the Reverend John R. McDowall frequently visited brothels and other prostitution establishments, distributing tracts and Bibles and praying with the inhabitants, in hopes of reforming the wayward sisters. (Courtesy American Antiquarian Society)

homes. After several months of harassment, the society succumbed, its members disbanded, and the refuge was closed.[19] McDowall considered the response of reform leaders like Tappan a "cowardly betrayal," and he publicly accused them of having "dumped" the poor prostitutes into the streets. Refusing to retreat under pressure, McDowall published a second report, *Magdalen Facts*, which defended his actions, reaffirmed and enlarged upon statements and information in the original report, and attacked his critics. He also continued preaching on his own, even though he was officially reprimanded by the Presbytery, or church hierarchy. [20]

In January 1833, McDowall began issuing a monthly, *McDowall's Journal*, which encouraged the formation of reform societies and campaigned against illicit sex and licentious literature, art, and songs. He also alarmed some citizens by threatening to expose publicly the names of men who frequented brothels and seduced innocent girls. Either because the threat intimidated the opposition or because the list never materialized, McDowall managed to avoid another public outburst for a few months. [21]

Throughout the controversy McDowall had continued to receive the unofficial support of a group of women who in February 1833 formed the Female Benevolent Society, which hired McDowall as its agent and the manager of its house of refuge. After six months he retired from the society to devote his full time to publishing *McDowall's Journal*. [22] Shortly thereafter, McDowall's zealous approach to sin again put him at odds with respectable citizens of New York. A grand jury was convened to review *McDowall's Journal*, and it declared the journal a "public nuisance, calculated to increase the very evil it professes to prevent, [by] inciting the young to the gratification of criminal passions."[23] In spite of this finding, a number of New York women continued to believe that the publication could become an effective instrument in furthering their moral-reform work. This group of women, from several different reform societies, joined together to form the New York Female Moral Reform Society and took over *McDowall's Journal*, renaming it the *Advocate of Moral Reform*. McDowall was hired as the society's official missionary, and he reactivated his spirited crusade against prostitution by visiting brothels, almshouses, and hospitals. He and his followers especially enjoyed descending upon brothels in the early hours of the morning while the residents and their clients were still in bed, startling them with loud hymns and Bible recitations in the hope that by disrupting the activities of the houses they would eventually break up the brothels. [24]

Unhappy with McDowall's notoriety, financial management, and unconventional approach to ministering to the unfortunate, the Presbytery called him to trial and suspended him from the ministry. McDowall spent a year defending his actions in print and in person, until in 1836, following the Jewett murder, the synod reversed its sentence and reinstated him. But McDowall was a broken man. Exhausted and depressed from his conflict with the church and the pain of a lifelong knee ailment, he became sick with tuberculosis and died in poverty later that year, at the young age of thirty-five.[25]

Despite his early death, McDowall had significant impact. He had succeeded in focusing widespread public attention on an occupation the public had previously ignored or quietly accepted, and he had helped raise concern about the issue to the point that anti-prostitution and moral reform became a major thrust in the evangelical movement that swept New York and the Northeast for over a decade.

Moral reformers were not alone in rediscovering prostitution during the 1830s. The issue was broached by writers from several different perspectives. Whereas moral or religious exposés, much like McDowall's, related prostitution to sin, most often with substantial sympathy for the women who were its "victims," articles in the popular press took up the subject frequently, in voyeuristic detail, describing the institution as part of the social or criminal underground, society's dark netherworld. Short essays and book-length sketches guided readers on fictional tours through the streets of poverty and dens of vice of the urban underworld. They described the prostitutes' clothing, brothels, and haunts, and catalogued a social hierarchy said to exist among the "fallen."

Still another group of social critics, in both Europe and the United States, represented a new breed of researcher-writers who broached public problems in the manner of scientific investigators, though their writings were never totally devoid of moralistic overtones. These researchers noted the detrimental effects of prostitution on public health and the public economy, treating prostitution largely as an aspect of the filthy dehumanized world of the urban poor. Their studies included personal interviews with large numbers of prostitutes, supplemented by records from police, detention facilities, and hospitals. Statistics were compiled on the prostitutes' backgrounds, their reasons for entering prostitution, and their lives in the profession. Because prostitutes were associated with the rapid spread of the dreaded disease syphilis, most of these researchers argued that the best way to control venereal disease would be to regulate prostitution.[26]

Though all of the literary sources on prostitution provide information about the lives of nineteenth-century prostitutes and the society in which

FIFTH EDITION—WITH MANY ADDITIONS.

PROSTITUTION EXPOSED ;

OR, A

MORAL REFORM DIRECTORY,

LAYING BARE THE

Lives, Histories, Residences, Seductions, &c.

OF THE MOST CELEBRATED

COURTEZANS AND LADIES OF PLEASURE

OF THE CITY OF NEW-YORK,

Together with a Description of the Crime and its Effects,

AS ALSO, OF THE

Houses of Prostitution and their Keepers,

HOUSES OF ASSIGNATION,

THEIR CHARGES AND CONVENIENCES,

AND OTHER PARTICULARS INTERESTING TO THE PUBLIC.

BY A BUTT ENDER.

NEW-YORK :

PUBLISHED FOR PUBLIC CONVENIENCE.

1839.

4. 1839 "MORAL REFORM DIRECTORY." This title page from one of the earliest of the nineteenth-century brothel directories satirizes moral reformers' efforts to combat the "prostitution problem." Along with brief but dubious statistics on the numbers of prostitutes, as well as warnings of the dangers facing customers, the directory conveniently gives the names, addresses, and descriptions of more than one hundred prostitutes and brothels. (Courtesy New York Bound Bookshop)

they lived, the scientific studies offer especially fruitful data for investigating both the nature and extent of the practice in specific locations. One of the earliest such studies was that of A. J. B. Parent-Duchatelet, who published *De la prostitution dans la ville de Paris* in 1836 and whose research methodology became the model for later writers in Europe and the United States. Parent studied the police and hospital records of 12,000 French women who were "inscribed," or officially registered, as prostitutes over a twenty-year period. He also interviewed and further observed a smaller group of these women to develop a detailed profile of the typical French prostitute, including her reasons for entering the profession.[27]

Other European investigators, such as William Tait in Edinburgh and William Acton in London, attempted similar studies of prostitution in their respective cities. In the United States, physician Charles Smith wrote in 1847 on the causes and effects of prostitution in New York City, covering many of the same topics as Parent, but drawing conclusions only from impressionistic data he garnered in his medical practice among prostitutes rather than from hard data collected in surveys and interviews. A large part of Smith's study is a biography of the famous New York City abortionist, Madam Restelle, because he believed that abortion—"Restellism"—"may either cause or prevent prostitution."[28] Such ambiguous analysis, which reflected the moralistic thinking of many of his contemporaries, held that abortions saved the reputations of promiscuous women so they could avoid prostitution but also aided women in developing an appetite for lascivious living that led to prostitution. Smith argued that the overwhelming majority of New York's prostitutes were poor, ignorant, and untalented, and he described life in the profession as degraded. Because he believed prostitution was a proved necessity but a drain on the public economy, he called for a system of regulation.[29]

The most extensive study of nineteenth-century American prostitution was published in 1858 by Dr. William Sanger, chief resident physician of Blackwell's Island Hospital in New York City. In 1855 the Board of Governors of the Almshouse had appointed Sanger to examine the extent of venereal disease among the poor in New York City, but Sanger had enlarged his assignment into a history of prostitution and the resulting social pollution in New York. He directed the local police in administering a questionnaire to two thousand prostitutes throughout the city and submitted a questionnaire to the inspector of each police ward, or precinct, asking about the extent of prostitution in his district. Each inspector was asked for information on the number of brothels, assignation houses, dancing saloons, and liquor stores where prostitutes congregated, and the number of individual prostitutes in the district. Sanger also drew on data from hospital records; as chief resident physician at the city's contagious-disease hospital, he was familiar with many poor patients, especially prostitutes, who suffered from syphilis and other venereal diseases. At the conclusion of his study, Sanger, like Smith and their European counterparts, made a strong plea for state regulation of prostitution as a means of controlling the further spread of venereal disease.[30]

There are limitations to Sanger's study. The prostitutes interviewed, selected by the local police, were probably the most well known in each ward, and may not have represented a cross-section of New York City prostitutes.[31] Streetwalkers were given little attention, and child prostitution was virtually ignored. The 2,000 women surveyed included only two fifteen-year-old girls, and none who were younger, even though police and newspapers repeatedly noted that many female children were engaged in prostitution. Sanger's refusal to recognize the extent of childhood prostitution was evident when he scoffed at a report concerning the previous prostitution of some House of Refuge inmates: "We can not see very clearly what connection exists between the New York House of Refuge and prostitution considering the ages of children generally admitted to that institution; . . . we are rather dubious as to the acts of impurity alluded to, except in a very few exceptional cases."[32] Although Sanger's agents may have selected a broad community sample of adult prostitutes—prostitution seems to have been practiced quite openly at this time and local policemen would have known not only brothel residents but also many women who practiced independently in their neighborhoods—some of his data is probably inaccurate. Because Sanger used public officials to administer his survey, it is likely that some women gave false answers to certain questions or gave responses they thought the surveyors wanted to hear.[33] Furthermore, even though Sanger did his research with apparent earnest integrity, his results were interpreted within a moralistic and middle-class framework, with obvious biases against the mores of immigrants and the poor. Nonetheless, he offers data about nineteenth-century New York City's prostitutes that is both extensive and telling.

Sanger's study also is valuable because of its timeliness. Published in the 1850s, it presents information on the profession at mid-century, about halfway between the 1830s, when McDowall's report first focused widespread public attention on the problem, and the 1870s, when the city's political machine gained control of the trade, thus ending a brief but unique era when prostitution was managed predominantly by females. Sanger offered New Yorkers a methodical accounting of the numbers of prostitutes, and his data on the extent as well as the causes, conditions, and consequences of prostitution helped fuel the public debate on the merits of officially regulating the practice. Though the "prostitution problem" remained a public issue in New York City for several decades, seemingly involving more and more females of all ages in both its degraded street trade and its predominantly female-managed brothel businesses, efforts to pass laws regulating the practice were unsuccessful. In the 1870s state lawmakers abandoned efforts to control prostitution by legalizing it, and they returned New York City's municipal governance to the city's machine politicians, who thereafter incorporated the prostitution business into a political-economic structure that was firmly in their control.

Though Sanger's study offers a unique and important perspective on prostitution as a part of New York's mid-nineteenth-century urban culture, the life of the New York prostitute, in its private as well as public dimensions, has not yet been fully explored. Primary source material is limited, since prostitutes left few written records. Nonetheless, surprising quantities of personal and economic records exist that allow not only a critical analysis of the data and conclusions given by Sanger and other investigators but also a glimpse of the private lives of prostitutes. Contemporary sources such as brothel guides and newspapers, and tax, census, court, and police records reveal much about prostitution and the women who practiced that trade in the nation's largest city. Reformers' records, such as those from the House of Refuge, are also a fruitful source of information illuminating the backgrounds of young prostitutes and some of the reasons these women entered the profession. Especially in the first two and a half decades of the Refuge's operation (1825–1850), intake officers wrote long and detailed histories of the inmates and seemed very interested in whether or not young girls had ever "slept with a man." Though follow-up records are less complete, case notations were often made for a number of years after a woman had stayed at the Refuge, suggesting the long-term possibilities for women who had practiced prostitution at some point in their lives.[34]

Equally important for understanding the private lives of mid-nineteenth-century New York City prostitutes is Helen Jewett's correspondence: a collection of eighty-eight letters to and from Jewett and her clients, her madam, and her friends in the profession. Written over a period of two years, from early 1834 until a few weeks before her murder, the Jewett letters are a direct reflection of her personal and professional life while in the midst of it, offering information about her associations with and feelings about other women and her view of the practices and customs that governed relationships with clients in the prostitute community. In conjunction with other data, the letters deepen our understanding of the private lives, personal relationships, and sensibilities of New York City prostitutes in the nineteenth century.[35]

Who were New York's prostitutes, these women who elicited so much public interest? Although the term *prostitution* has sometimes been used so broadly as to encompass all extramarital sex, and the nineteenth-century data is not always clear about when sexual promiscuity becomes professional prostitution—a judgment that varies in different periods and in different societies according to legal and cultural determinations—in the more strict and common usage of the term a prostitute was a woman who sold sexual favors promiscuously to those who could pay.[36] This group would include women who worked at other trades or in families but who were occasional or part-time prostitutes. It might also include women "kept" for some financial consideration as non-conjugal sexual partners. In this study, a narrow definition of the term will be used, i.e., a woman who earned money by the promiscuous sale of sexual favors outside of marriage.

Extent of Prostitution in New York City, 1830–1870

There are no official censuses or registries of New York City prostitutes in the nineteenth century. Although several population censuses list some women as prostitutes, there are many reasons for concluding these figures are incomplete and incorrect. A woman was not likely to admit her profession to an official government representative, especially when she might practice another profession such as seamstress, milliner, or boardinghouse keeper that was a respectable—and legal—activity. At various times police officials were charged with keeping track of prostitutes and claimed to have records of all houses of prostitution and lists of names of public prostitutes.[37] If these records were kept, however, they no longer are available. There are several semi-annual reports by chiefs of police giving total numbers of prostitutes in the city, but these reports probably enumerate only the more well known of the occupation and omit occasional prostitutes. One suspects as well that police officials tended to underestimate prostitution in response to periodic public outcries about the extent of the vice, which encouraged the police to present themselves as keeping the problem under control. The only official survey of New York prostitution known to exist is that made by Sanger, which thus becomes the centerpiece for judging other figures.

Until 1830, prostitutes were not so much counted or studied as they were hidden away in the back streets of New York and other seaports and large urban centers. Legal pressure was applied to keep prostitutes and brothels obscure, contained in certain areas, and hence as invisible as possible. In New York the Common Council, courts, and groups like a short-lived Magdalen Society founded in 1812 periodically had to deal with issues involving prostitutes, but public references to prostitution were infrequent until the McDowall controversy of 1830–1831.[38] From that time on, discussion of prostitution would become interwoven into the fabric of everyday life, and estimates of the numbers of women involved would become in part a basis for evaluating the extent of corruption and vice in the city.

McDowall's 1831 report stated that there were at least 10,000 prostitutes in the city, amounting to one-tenth of the females of all ages in the total city population of approximately 203,000. McDowall estimated that about 5,000 of the prostitutes were full-time public prostitutes. He claimed his figures were conservative, but respectable New Yorkers considered them outrageously high and convened a grand jury to produce an independent estimate. The jury reported that even after enumerating every suspicious female in the city as a member of the Sisterhood only 1,438 prostitutes—one in seventy female New Yorkers—could be identified. The *Morning Courier and Enquirer* editorialized that even the grand jury's much lower estimate was "excessive."[39]

The discrepant estimates put forth by McDowall and the grand jury set the pattern for efforts at measuring the incidence of prostitution throughout the period: moral reformers, religious leaders, and politicians claimed the number of prostitutes was quite high, and scientific investigators and city officials consistently issued much lower figures. McDowall's estimate of 10,000 prostitutes, initially considered so outrageous, was nonetheless invoked frequently throughout the 1830s and into the 1840s, especially by politicians, ministers, reformers, and the

POLICE
OFFICE,
NOTICE.

The Landlords, Tenants, and Occupiers of all houses of ill fame, situated in and about the neighbourhood of East George-street, in the Seventh Ward, are hereby notified, that all houses of the above description, found west of Rutgers-street, from and after the first day of May next, will become the particular objects of the vigilance of the Police, until they are suppressed.

January, 1813.

Printed by Hardcastle & Van Pelt, 86, *Nassau-street.*

5. POLICE OFFICE NOTICE, 1813. In the late eighteenth and early nineteenth centuries, legal pressure was used to keep prostitutes confined to certain areas of New York City. This 1813 police warning to prostitutes and landlords in the area near the Hook illustrates this policy but indicates that the police were courteous enough to wait four months until May Day, New Yorkers' traditional moving day, before enforcing their threat. (Courtesy Museum of the City of New York)

popular press. Counterclaims that the majority of the owners of prostitution houses were pious, worthy, moral, respectable men also persisted. But by the mid-1840s, such discussion caused no outcry; the
public had become much more aware of the existence of prostitution
through the press, the work of reformers, and the frequent appearance
of prostitutes on the public sidewalks, at shops and theaters, and in many
neighborhood streets.[40]

Although claims that New York had large numbers of prostitutes no
longer surprised many citizens, New Yorkers still debated the figures. In
1847, Dr. Charles Smith wrote in his book on prostitution that the
numbers of New York harlots had been "absurdly" inflated. Remarking
that the truth was bad enough without any exaggeration, he presented
as "accurate returns" the statistics in the official report of the Chief of
Police for November 1846 through April 1847. This report lists the
number of public prostitutes as 2,483, or one of every seventy-seven
females in the city.[41]

In 1858, Sanger, too, expressed doubt about McDowall's estimate,
pointing out that in the nearly twenty years since McDowall's report,
"vice has not decreased in New York, but has steadily increased, and yet
the most diligent search can discover . . . only 7,860 public and private
prostitutes," even broadly defined.[42] Sanger based his estimate on a figure
of 5,000 given by Chief of Police George W. Matsell in 1856, which
he adjusted to reflect precinct-level police estimates, general population
growth, the "floating prostitute population," and those prostitutes who
were "effectively disguised." Sanger's conclusion was that New York had
one prostitute for every forty-seven females in the population.[43]

Three police reports in the 1860s put forth much lower estimates,
reporting as few as 2,100 prostitutes and no more than 2,700, working
at approximately 600 brothels. The highest of these figures, the count of
2,700 in 1866, identifies one of every 136 females, or less than one percent of the female population, as prostitutes.[44] Eight years earlier, Sanger
had actually interviewed almost that many *known* prostitutes, when New
York City's population was 100,000 less, suggesting that the police
calculations must have been on the low side. Just how low they were
is illustrated by arrest reports between 1866 and 1870, when prostitution
arrests numbered around 6,000 annually; the official police estimate of
2,700 prostitutes in the city could be accurate only if each prostitute had
been arrested an average of twice each year, which was certainly not the

Table 1 *Estimates of New York City Prostitutes, 1831–1872*

Source	No. Prostitutes	Female Population	
		Total No.	% Prostitutes
McDowall, 1831	10,000	101,295	9.9
Grand Jury, 1831	1,438	101,295	1.4
Aldermen's Report, 1844	10,000	190,751	5.2
Police Report, 1847	2,483	190,751	1.3
Chief Matsell, 1856	5,000	314,952	1.6
Sanger, 1858	7,860	365,815	2.1
Police Report, 1864	2,123	363,193	0.6
Police Report, 1866	2,670	363,193	0.7
Bishop Simpson, 1866	11,500	363,193	3.2
Police Report, 1867	2,562	363,193	0.7
Reverend Bellows, 1871	20,000	471,146	4.2
Police Report, 1872	1,223	471,146	0.3

SOURCES: Contemporary reports on the scope of prostitution are discussed in Chapter 1 and its notes. For New York City population figures, see U.S. and New York State censuses, 1830–1870.

case.[45] In 1872 police estimates were even less reliable; the 1,223 prostitutes said to be in New York that year amount to only three-fifths of the number of prostitutes interviewed by Sanger fifteen years earlier, despite population growth of almost 50 percent during that period.[46]

The police statistics did not go unchallenged. In keeping with the spirit of McDowall, two Protestant ministers declared to their congregations that prostitution's numbers were much greater than reports stated. In 1866, Methodist Bishop Matthew Simpson announced that there were 11,000 to 12,000 prostitutes in New York City, a population equal to the number of members of the Methodist Church. Five years later, the Reverend Dr. Henry W. Bellows estimated the number of "fallen" women had increased to 20,000, which amounted to one of every twenty-four females in the city (table 1).[47]

Understandably, police estimates of the prostitution population from 1830 to 1870 were extremely low, while ministers, reformers, and public commentators tended to give exaggerated estimates. As has been noted, Sanger used the most thorough method of determining the number of

Table 2 *Wards with Most Prostitutes, Brothels, and Assignation Houses,
as Identified by Sanger*

Ward	Prostitutes		Houses	
	No.	Rank	No.	Rank
4	750	1	48	3
5	420	3	70	1
6	228	7	58	2
8	300	4	58	2
16	500	2	10	12

SOURCE: William Sanger, *History of Prostitution*, 580.

prostitutes in New York City at any one time, though the accuracy of
his study can still be questioned. One approach to assessing the accuracy
and limitations of Sanger's figures is to check some of them against other
data suggesting the prevalence of prostitution in the mid-1850s.

Two wards of the city, the eighth and fifth, were home to a number
of noted brothels, though Sanger's study did not identify them as the
leading wards in prostitute population. Separated by Canal Street, the
two wards covered neighborhoods west of lower Broadway that included
several streets where prostitution houses were concentrated. New Yorkers repeatedly commented on the fact that prostitutes, as well as brothels
and assignation houses, were dispersed throughout all wards of the city,
in both the best and worst neighborhoods, but wards five and eight were
recognized as having a significant prostitution population (table 2).[48]

Using newspapers, brothel guidebooks, and city records, it is possible
to locate approximately 53 percent of the prostitutes said to be in ward
eight by the police inspectors' survey and more than 25 percent of those
said to be in ward five. A few more brothel keepers in these neighborhoods can be identified by city directories, newspapers, and other
sources. Using the 1855 census, the average number of residents of
prostitution houses in these wards can be calculated, providing a basis
for estimating the number of prostitutes likely to live in additional
houses known through other records. By this method, one can estimate
a brothel-based prostitute population that accounts for 83 percent of the
number Sanger found in ward eight and 52 percent of the number he
found in ward five (table 3).[49]

Table 3 *Estimated Number of Prostitutes in Wards 5 and 8 in 1855*

	Ward 5	Ward 8	Total
Identified in Census			
Prostitutes	106	158	264
Houses	14	28	42
Prostitutes per House (avg.)	7.57	5.64	6.29
Additional Known Houses	15	16	31
Additional Prostitutes (est., based on avg. per house)	114	90	204
Total Prostitutes (census + add'l. est.)	220	248	468
Sanger Estimate of Total	420	300	720
Total as % of Sanger Estimate	52	83	65

SOURCES: 1855 New York State Census, city directories, other contemporary sources; Sanger, *History of Prostitution*, 580.

Thus, over a century later, a high percentage of individual prostitutes—a population group not easily located in sources—can still be identified, leading to the assumption that Sanger's figures, particularly for the brothel-based rather than part-time prostitute population, are not significantly above the actual numbers of prostitutes in the mid-1850s. Indeed, given the difficulties of tracing prostitutes, especially the street and part-time practitioners, Sanger's figures more likely may be underestimates. The most conservative estimates of the 1830s and 1840s indicated that prostitutes represented from 1.3 percent to 1.4 percent of the female population, while Sanger estimated that they represented 2.1 percent (see table 1). If we accept the Sanger percentage as roughly accurate and calculate that percentage of the female population from 1830 through 1870 in rapidly growing New York, we obtain the following estimate of the number of prostitutes for those years:

1830	2,127
1840	3,283
1850	5,413
1860	8,750
1870	9,894

It is likely, however, that the proportion of prostitutes in the female population was not constant but was in fact increasing, especially after 1850. A recent study of German prostitutes has noted that "prostitution probably reaches its heights in a country during the second wave of industrialization when heavy industry excludes women from participation in the labor force." Only later in the industrialization process, with the growth of a tertiary clerical and service sector, are women able to find opportunities for employment; at this later stage, prostitution declines.[50] Ruth Rosen, in her study of American prostitution, suggests that this same pattern prevailed in the United States in the nineteenth century, with the peak of women's engagement in prostitution taking place between 1850 and 1900 and beginning to decline in the early twentieth century.[51] As applied to New York City, this rather mechanical correlation of prostitution to other job possibilities suggests that Sanger's 2.1 percent rate might well be taken as a rather conservative basis for estimating the number of prostitutes in the years after 1850.

The discussion above has compared the number of prostitutes to the number of females of all ages in New York; intuitively, of course, we would suspect that—and in fact, as will be seen below, we are able to confirm that—the vast majority of prostitutes were women in their teenage and young adult years, roughly between the ages of 15 and 30. If we consider that approximately 2 percent of all women in New York were probably prostitutes in the mid-nineteenth century, we might assume that the rate was considerably higher, perhaps 5 to 6 percent, in the age groups most active in the prostitution trade.[52] In the next chapter, we examine statistical data that will help us develop a composite demographic portrait of prostitutes in New York, but first it is important to focus on the women involved as individuals—working women with motivations, relationships, aspirations, and experiences that help us understand their story in its many human dimensions.

2

"A Lady . . . Whom I Should Never Have Suspected"

Personal and Collective Portraits of Prostitutes

When sixteen-year-old George Templeton Strong drove by a brothel where he hoped to catch a glimpse of some of the prostitutes then involved in the notorious Jewett murder trial, he was rewarded by a sighting of thirty-nine-year-old madam Rosina Townsend. To the boy, Townsend seemed an "old lady, dressed in black with a very good-natured, mild countenance whom I should never have suspected of being such a character as she is."[1] In his comment, the youthful Strong noted a significant point about nineteenth-century New York prostitutes. Both because these women had some incentive not to appear conspicuous and because their lives in this era were closely interwoven with that of the respectable community, they were not always readily identifiable, then or now. Yet we can piece together the life stories of a number of these women—some who were obscure, as well as some who gained notoriety. These brief personal histories give us a sense of the variety and scope of these women's experiences within the context of a broader community life, a helpful perspective for later isolating the statistical components of the prostitutes' collective profile.

Personal Profiles

As keeper of a notorious Thomas Street brothel, Rosina Townsend was a key witness at the June 1836 trial of Richard Robinson for murdering Helen Jewett and attempting to burn down her establishment. Townsend and nine other prostitutes were among the dozens of witnesses who testified at the trial.[2] Observers described Madam Townsend as "one of the most dashing of her infamous line of work."[3] She was said to be a woman of beauty and accomplishments, with "bright eyes, ripe form," and "graceful figure." According to the press, she appeared before the court well-dressed, wearing a gold watch and splendid earrings, and her pretty ankles were "adorned with exquisitely embroidered white silk stockings."[4] Only the New York *Herald*, taking issue with the rival New York *Sun* for giving Townsend's testimony equal credence with that of decent, respectable New Yorkers, disparagingly portrayed Townsend as a "weather beaten courtesan" and "one of the oldest, ugliest, and wickedest of the harridans from that [Thomas Street] sink of corruption."[5]

On the witness stand Townsend was described as "cool and collected."[6] She testified about the murder but also described her own background and her reasons for entering prostitution. Her real name, she said, was Rebecca Rosana Brown, and she was originally from Castleton, New York, seven miles from Albany, where her parents still lived. She was married in Castleton, and afterward she and her husband moved to Cincinnati, where he left her for another woman. Following her abandonment, Townsend returned to her parents' home in Castleton for a few weeks and then moved to New York City in September 1825, hoping to find employment. For three months she boarded with her husband's aunt and took in sewing. By Christmas of that year, her "head was so afflicted" she said she "could not see the light of day."[7] Although treated by a physician, she was forced to give up sewing and became a chambermaid in the home of Henry Beekman, a position she held for just a short time before pain in her arm began troubling her so much she could not do the necessary domestic work. From Beekman's, Townsend, now twenty-nine, moved to Maria Pierce's assignation house, which she left after a few months. In 1828 she took over her own prostitution establishment at 28 Anthony Street. By then she was using several names: Rosina or Rosannah Thompson or Townsend. A year later she moved into 41 Thomas Street, a house she managed for the six years preceding the trial. Townsend stated that in the eleven years since her abandonment, she had not seen her husband and did not know if he were alive or dead.[8]

Rumors abounded concerning Townsend's accumulated wealth. It was alleged she owned property valued at approximately $20,000, and she was said to have lent $10,000 to a Broadway tradesman, whom she assisted with his business by balancing his books and keeping his affairs in order. She also was said to have made a loan of $1,000 to another business firm.[9] Tax records from 1835 indicate that she was assessed on $5,000 in personal property (with no real estate holdings listed), and the press reported she held $3,500 in insurance on the furnishings of her house. A $5,000 property assessment suggests her actual worth was approximately $17,000, which in current dollars would be worth approximately $250,000.[10]

Despite her seemingly secure financial situation, the many threatening letters she received following the murder and trial prompted her to sell her furnishings at auction and relocate. Her whereabouts became a matter of considerable speculation. One local paper reported she was moving to a residence on Prince Street, to quarters provided by a group of New York merchants who were attempting to persuade her not to reveal their names as customers.[11] Another newspaper reported she moved to Philadelphia and established a brothel there. It is also possible that in response to her trial-related notoriety she may have continued to live in New York under an assumed name; in any event, her name disappears from New York directories and tax rolls after 1836.[12]

Townsend's career shows the financial possibilities of prostitution for practitioners with business acumen. Coming late to the profession, impoverished, seriously ill, and marginally employed, she became in just ten years a well-off, comfortable, and successful operator. The Jewett tragedy disrupted her career on Thomas Street, but it did not appear to interfere with her wealth or the comfort and composure that wealth brought her.

A second madam brought to the fore by Jewett's murder ran a house where the victim had worked earlier. Mary Berry, Mrs. Francis or Frank Berry, who sometimes also went by the grand title of "Duchesse de Berri," was born Mary Cisco and was said to have "graduated into the profession under the tutelage of one of the most accomplished harpies on record—her mother."[13] Berry's husband, who was listed in city directories as a tailor, was better known to the public and police as a "con man" and comanager with his wife of the 128 Duane Street brothel. Their house offered guests liquor, women, dice, and cards, and Mr.

Berry was said to specialize in getting the guests drunk and then robbing them. It was said he did not fear the law because hé knew its loopholes and limitations and could always walk away from a court charge for robbery with a profit in his pocket.[14] The brothel was mentioned in the press on a few occasions as the site of riots and assaults, which may well have been caused by his shady dealings with clients.[15] Although Mary and Frank were ostensibly co-owners of the brothel, Mary appears to have been the real manager. The property tax records for 1835 list the house under her name, not his, with assets of $2,000.[16] She was described in the press as a "buxom, bold, resolute landlady of abundant means."[17] Apparently, Frank enjoyed a carefree lifestyle and let Mary worry about finances. A letter from Mrs. Berry to Helen Jewett, who was on vacation in Philadelphia in December 1835, complained that Mr. Berry had written from Washington requesting $50. "He spends money faster than I can make it whenever he gets loose," she wrote; if he came to Philadelphia, Jewett should "talk to him about this extravagance."[18]

Frank either died or disappeared sometime after 1836, because he is not mentioned subsequently, and beginning in 1838 city directories list Mary as "Widow Mary Berry." Along with the loss of Frank, Mary seems to have lost press notoriety, but was evidently still running a brothel at 128 Duane Street ten years later.[19] Like Townsend, she appears to have been able and successful, quietly accumulating a comfortable property, assessed at $5,000 in the 1840s. After the Jewett notoriety, and freed from an extravagant and trouble-making husband, she continued a long, stable career.

Another madam whose career spanned many years of New York history was Adeline (or Adelia or Adelaide) Miller, also known as Adeline Furman, who survived and flourished despite some notable personal and legal attacks. Born in the New York area, Miller became a resident of New York City about 1818. Both the 1850 and 1855 censuses list her age as 70, so by that time in her life she may have quit counting the years. In the early part of her prostitution career in New York (the 1820s), she used the name Furman, and she was known by both Furman and Miller in the 1830s. During this decade she ran several prostitution houses simultaneously, under the name of Furman at one address and Miller at others. From the 1840s to 1860 she is usually listed in sources as Miller. The 1830 city directory said she was the widow of a Henry Miller, and an 1839 source reported she had "buried three husbands" and had had children by two of her spouses. She is known to have had a son, Nelson, who in the 1840s was married and living with his family not far from Miller's brothel. An 1830s source reported that Miller also had two daughters, one who allegedly became a prominent actress and another who was reported to have died "mysteriously." Both daughters were said to have been reared respectably by their mother and given "elegant and classic educations" to keep them free from the "lazaar house of crime."[20]

Like other prostitutes, Miller changed addresses several times in her career. From her first appearance in city directories in 1821 through to the mid-1830s, she was listed at six different residences. In 1835–1836, sources note she was in charge of at least three houses, which she rented; using female managers, she apparently ran several prostitution operations simultaneously. In 1836 Catherine Cochran was managing Miller's house on Orange Street, a Mrs. Brown was managing a second house for Miller, on Mott Street, and Miller herself was overseeing the third house, on Reade Street.[21]

In the 1830s Miller's establishments came under attack from both officials and private citizens. In 1831 she called for help from the city watch in controlling rowdies who were causing trouble in her Elm Street brothel, but a few years later, after the arrest of a sixteen-year-old girl who was being kept by a man at Miller's "most noted and horrible sink of iniquity and prostitution, 44 Orange," legal measures were taken to break up her establishment.[22] Shortly thereafter, six men entered the "recently abandoned brothel at 44 Orange," destroyed approximately $100 worth of furniture, and then proceeded to 133 Reade Street, where most of Miller's belongings had been moved for an upcoming auction. Miller and a servant were alone at the Reade Street house when the men broke through a window, assaulted Miller with an iron bar, destroyed furniture and other items worth more than $400, and took $140 in cash. Miller pressed charges against the men and was awarded $700 in damages. The incident apparently failed to deter her trade, however, and a few months later officials renewed their own anti-prostitution campaign against her establishments, raiding and arresting the inhabitants of her "branch brothel" on Mott Street.[23]

Throughout the remainder of the 1830s, Miller kept a "quiet" house at 133 Reade Street, and by this time she had accumulated $5,000 in personal property, a tenfold increase in her personal wealth from the time she began as a prostitute in the early 1820s. One 1830s source claimed that the combined worth of her real-estate properties throughout the city was as high as $100,000.[24]

In the early 1840s Miller operated a brothel at 134 Duane Street for about three years and then moved to 130 Church Street. During this period, she apparently supplemented her brothel income by offering an extra item for the "sex trade," a "flash publication." In 1842 the printer of the publication sued her to collect $750 she owed him for printing costs. Miller claimed the plaintiff had gone back on a promise to let her pay off the debt in weekly installments, but the plaintiff said she instead had tried to settle the debt by giving him an old printing press of hers. Miller was ordered to pay her debt. A couple of years later, however, her finances seemed stable enough for her to lend $500 to a fellow prostitute, Eliza Clark. When Clark tried to "skip town" without paying, Miller had her arrested.[25]

By the mid-1840s, Miller appeared to have improved her relationship with the police. Police investigator Robert Taylor mentioned in his diary at least five visits to her brothel seeking information about various cases on which he was working. For a while it seemed she also had improved her image in the press. In March 1849, the *Police Gazette* made her the heroine of a story about a sixteen-year-old virgin/orphan who came to Miller's brothel to begin a career in prostitution. After Miller was unable to dissuade the girl, she locked her up overnight and took her to the police the following morning, and the girl was saved from ruin by being sent to the Home for the Friendless. Miller's good press did not last long, however. A few weeks later the *Police Gazette* reported she was in court on charges that she was forcing young women to stay in her brothel. It was said that Miller would threaten her boarders when they did not pay what they owed her for board and clothing, and that she was "bad enough to do anything." Miller was able to get the more serious "conspiracy" charges dropped, but on the charge of "operating a disorderly house" she posted bail and was released on good behavior.[26]

By 1855 Miller owned the property she had rented at 130 Church Street, which was valued at $5,000, and *Boyd's New York City Tax Book* of 1856 listed Miller's total tax assessment as $16,500, a significant net worth for that time and about $825,000 in current dollars.[27] Miller's name disappears from city directories after 1860, presumably because she either retired with a new identity, moved to another location, or died. Her nearly four decades in the profession had illustrated prostitution's possibilities for financial rewards, but her experience also demonstrated some of the occupation's ever-present hazards, notably vulnerability to violence and legal harassment. Miller seemed able to withstand the difficulties, however, and assuming that she reported her true age to census takers in 1850, she would have been eighty when she disappeared from the public scene, ending a very long, and on the whole successful, career in prostitution.

To what extent were Townsend, Berry, and Miller representative of the thousands of New York women who worked as prostitutes? As will be demonstrated later in this chapter when we turn to data that suggests the general contours of a collective profile of prostitutes, Townsend, Berry, and Miller stayed much longer in the profession than was typical and perhaps were exceptionally career-oriented, adopting a businesslike commitment to the trade. Most prostitutes never achieved as much success financially or developed as much stability and security in their social situations. Of course, the same might be said of most non-prostitutes of the time: in the mid-nineteenth century, working women rarely enjoyed opportunities to work their way out of poverty, much less develop economically rewarding careers. In important respects, however, the life stories of Townsend, Berry, and Miller reflect challenges and limitations they shared with many other prostitutes and with working women generally. By also reviewing the personal experiences of several prostitutes who did not rise to management positions in the trade, we can begin to appreciate the options these women perceived in life and the variety of approaches they took to shaping their lives.

Two young women who practiced prostitution for only a few years were the Utter sisters, Mary Ann and Ann Jeanette. Two years apart in age, the sisters were born in Connecticut and New York respectively. Both parents were alcoholic; their father, a basketmaker, had abandoned the family, and their mother had been sent to the penitentiary.[28] By the time the sisters were sixteen and fourteen they had already worked at a number of different jobs before being hired together to pick peas in Williamsburgh. Their free time (Saturday nights and Sundays) was spent in New York City, and during one of these weekend jaunts they and a friend were arrested for using abusive language and throwing stones at a woman who hit them with a broom for taunting her child. All three girls were placed in the House of Refuge. According to Refuge records, the youngest, Ann Jeanette, was already a "deep, knowing and brazen girl" who came into the House with an "unfeeling brazen manner." The older sister, Mary Ann, had stayed with boys, and the Refuge officials were fearful they could not do much for her because "she knows too much." After a year, Mary Ann was of age (eighteen), and so was sent to friends in Connecticut. Shortly after her release she was reported to be "on the town," living in a bad house, being kept by a man.

Younger sister Ann Jeanette, after a few months in the Refuge, was believed to have improved enough to be indentured to a family in New Jersey. She remained at her place of work only three months before running away to "go on the town" and perhaps join her sister. Both sisters were known to be practicing prostitution for the next year and a half. Nevertheless, Refuge officials decided to reclaim Ann Jeanette, and in the early hours of one morning they went to New York's "Hook" and entered a brothel "filled with families." They arrived before the women were dressed, and Ann Jeanette asked them to leave the room while she clothed herself. She then used this opportunity to leave and "ran half-dressed through the streets and escaped." Afterward, she changed addresses, evading officials for a time. The Refuge recorded that Ann Jeanette was "a real old bawd," but interestingly noted that "If we didn't need her help she would by no means be a desirable inmate." They located her again, sent a police officer with two men from the Refuge, and brought her back. Six months later Ann was seventeen, and officials thought her conduct was "pretty fair," but, since she was "cunning and prudent," they felt they "could not with confidence rely on her stability if [they] parted with her." A few months afterward, however, she had improved sufficiently to be indentured successfully to a farmer in Dutchess County.

By the time Ann Jeanette was twenty-one, she had married and was thought to be doing well. She later had a child and visited the Refuge chapel. Officials recorded on the occasion of that visit that she was "considered to be, looked on, as a respected and worthy woman." Sixteen years later, in her late thirties, Ann Jeanette, or Mrs. Sarles, again visited the Refuge and according to the daybook, "gave a good account of herself."

The Refuge kept notes on sister Mary Ann's post-Refuge life and progress for only a few years after she left. She had entered prostitution shortly after her departure, and the last recorded entry about her indicated she was still practicing that occupation. Perhaps the Refuge lost track of Mary Ann, though they could have solicited information about her during one of her sister's visits, or perhaps they did not spend time doing follow-up studies on women they considered their "failures."[29]

House of Refuge records detail many stories similar to that of Ann Jeanette Utter, involving young women from straitened families who practiced prostitution for a few years before returning to "respectable" society.[30] Two such young women who went on to other trades were Sarah Van Norden and Mary Jane Box. Van Norden's father was a boat builder, and her mother was a tailoress; when Van Norden was in her mid-teens, she was learning tailoring from her mother, who was described as "a very pious woman." Sarah did not get along well with her mother, whom she believed was too critical of her. She left home and went to board in a brothel on Walnut Street. Her parents then had her sent to the Refuge, and six months after being admitted she was indentured to a farmer in Westport, Connecticut, where she worked for over a year, receiving good reports. Several years later she visited the Refuge, and officials there were pleased to learn she was then working as a milliner.[31]

Mary Jane Box lived with her widowed mother until she was seven, when she was put in service. Although her mother worked as a tailoress and had three grown children who were employed, they were all so poor that Box had to be put to work also. In her first two years as a servant she lived at eight different locations. Her Refuge case history, written when she was sixteen, said, "It would be too tedious to mention all the places she has been at. She has been wandering about in this way for several years, has been she thinks at more than 50 different places. At none of which she stayed more than 7 or 8 months."[32]

When Box was thirteen her mother died of cholera, and Box began going out with boys and men to houses of assignation. For the next three years she practiced prostitution and/or worked as a servant. Box was unhappy at the Refuge and after several months' residence tried to escape. She was indentured to a family in Norwalk, Connecticut, but after only nine months they sent her back, saying her conduct was far past endurance. About a year later she was indentured to a farmer in Fishkill, was happy with her position there, and stayed on for several years. Five years later, in her mid-twenties, she was described as "respectable" and was living at her sister's in New York, planning to return to Fishkill to work at her old job there.[33]

Hannah Rice's career as a prostitute was also briefly documented by the House of Refuge. Rice was almost seventeen when she was brought to the Refuge. Her father, a cooper, had died a couple of years before, and her mother was supporting the family by taking in washing. Rice was described as "lazy," a girl who "would rather do evil to gratify her pride than work," and it was noted she had a "wrestless [sic], uneasy turned mind."[34]

Rice had been a prostitute for more than a year when she was admitted to the Refuge. She entered prostitution by soliciting on the street—"going with young men to private places for night walkers"—and then boarded with Abby Meade (Myers), who kept a brothel at the corner of Grand and Wooster streets.[35] Following her stay at Abby Meade's, Rice was kept by a Colonel Lee, and afterwards by a Captain Myers, who worked for a steamboat company.

Rice contracted the "bad disorder" (venereal disease), and her mother had her admitted to the Female Magdalen Society home on Bowery Hill. She was not happy there, tried unsuccessfully to escape, and finally agreed to try the House of Refuge to see if she liked it any better. Shortly after her admission, the matron's report noted the "girl is greatly disappointed in the change because she feels she has to work too hard." In over a year at the Refuge, Rice was never indentured, and when she turned eighteen she was released "at the strong solicitation of her mother." For several months after her departure, Rice made return visits to the Refuge. Within a year of her release, however, she was "back on the town" in prostitution.[36]

When Mary Anthony entered the Refuge at age fourteen or fifteen, the admitting matron noted that "there is a mistery [sic] . . . hanging about her parentage. She never saw her mother but says she saw her father about two years ago."[37] Anthony told Refuge authorities she had been born somewhere in Kentucky. Before she could remember, however, she had been left in the care of Patience Berger, who brought her up in her house of assignation at 202 Church Street. The Refuge suspected that Anthony may in fact have been Berger's daughter.

Berger sent Anthony away to school for four years, beginning when she was about ten years old, but following her return to New York,

Anthony became a prostitute. An acquaintance, a mantuamaker who had also formerly been a prostitute, gave her the name of a local gentleman who would help her find a position in some other profession. Anthony did not tell the gentleman, a Mr. Green, that she had practiced prostitution, but rather that she wished to avoid the fate that staying in the Berger household would surely cause. Green placed her with a family in Oneida County, urging them to watch over her and not let men seduce her. She was shortly returned to Green because it was reported that she was not honest and stole money, and that her "propensity" was such that "she would be the one to seduce young men first." Still wishing to "save" Anthony, Green had her admitted to the Refuge.

After six months there, Anthony was evaluated as "an artful deceptive creature in whom we have no confidence." After a year and a half, however, she must have improved, because she was indentured to a man in Geneva, New York. She stayed on in Geneva after her indenture ended, and at age twenty-three, while on a trip to New York City, she paid a visit to the Refuge. The Refuge authorities appeared to have some doubt whether Anthony had completely abandoned her old way of life, because the entry describing her visit stated, "She looks rather gay for a girl who does housework." Five years later, however, when Anthony was in her late twenties, the Refuge recorded that the man to whom she had been indentured informed them that she was married to a respectable mechanic and was living happily in Geneva.[38]

Less is known about Patience Berger than about her ward, or perhaps daughter, but information suggests the general pattern of the Townsend-Berry careers. From the 1820s to the 1860s Berger ran either an assignation house or a brothel in lower Manhattan. In the 1830s her house at 202 Church Street was described as "a quiet house," and, except for the *Advocate of Moral Reform* calling her "a wretch of a woman," she appears to have continued to operate quietly with little notoriety or publicity throughout her career. By 1840, Berger had accumulated enough money to own a house at 132 Church, assessed at $8,000, and she also had $3,000 in personal property. Her personal-property assets appear to have fluctuated between 1840 and 1860; the $3,000 declined to $400 by 1845, then rose to $6,500 by 1848 and stayed there until 1856, when it again dropped to $500. Although her financial situation reflects some degree of change, on the whole, prostitution provided

Patience Berger with a long career of relative security and financial success.[39]

Although black New Yorkers suffered discriminations greater than most other groups in the population, their life stories illustrate the same kinds of circumstances that prompted so many other young women to become prostitutes. Julia Ann Smith was born in Baltimore and moved to New York with her family. Her father died in the cholera epidemic of 1833, when Smith was twelve. Her mother attempted to support the family by doing day work, but young Julia also had to go into service at a gentleman's boardinghouse on Beekman Street. While working in the boardinghouse, she met a white man, a Captain Armstrong from Liverpool, who started taking her to an assignation house on Catherine Lane that was managed by a black woman. Captain Armstrong paid Smith $4 to $5 a night for several weeks, a large sum to be earned by a girl just reaching her teens and considerably more money than she was making as a domestic. Smith left her domestic service position and, according to the Refuge, began "strolling about from pillar to post for two or three years . . . staying in this private way with white men." Refuge officials recorded that Smith said she would "have nothing to do with colored men." At one point Smith worked out of the U.S. Hotel at West Point for several months and then accompanied a friend to Pennsylvania for a few weeks. Afterward, she returned to New York and became a servant to a black prostitute at the Franklin House on Broadway, earning $1 per week. When her family learned of her return to New York, her mother became alarmed by her daughter's lifestyle and "the character of the place" where she worked; Mrs. Smith asked the police to arrest her daughter and send her to the Refuge. Entering the Refuge at age fourteen, Smith was described as "one of the closed mouthed knowing ones," whose conduct was described as "pretty fair, but if out of humor she [would] swear." At the end of a year the Refuge indentured Smith in Otsego County, New York, and after that kept no more records on her. Since biracial marriages were infrequent in the mid-nineteenth century, if Smith continued to "have nothing to do with colored men" she probably eliminated marriage from her available options, leaving menial trades, service, or prostitution as her most likely opportunities.[40]

Like many other Irish females, Eliza Brakey came to America in 1846 to escape difficult conditions in Europe. Immigration was perhaps particularly compelling for Brakey's family because her father had died in Ireland. Arriving in America, mother and daughters went to live in separate places—the mother in New York City and the daughters in service positions on Long Island. Brakey worked for two-and-a-half years for one family but apparently became unhappy with the post and left Long Island for Mrs. Smith's Elizabeth Street brothel in the city. She worked as a prostitute for half a year, until friends discovered her and had her committed to Blackwell's Island. As soon as she had served her six-month sentence, Brakey returned to prostitution at Adeline Miller's brothel on Church Street, where she was satisfactorily residing until her friends again found her and had her sent to the penitentiary for six more months. After her second jail term, Brakey went to live with her sisters on Long Island, but after a short while she again escaped to the city and Mrs. Smith's brothel. This time her mother had her arrested for vagrancy and committed to the Refuge. Brakey's persistence in pursuing prostitution caused Refuge officials to write: "This is a hard case! & we fear beyond the hope of Reform." After fifteen months at the Refuge, Brakey was indentured in rural New Jersey. Six months later Refuge officials recorded that Brakey had "left her place," possibly returning for the fourth time to the "unreformed" life she seemed to prefer in the city.[41]

The preceding cases suggest some tentative observations. The young women who entered New York City prostitution generally came from poor families or from families torn by conflict. Many teenagers seemed to prefer prostitution to the work and protection of the House of Refuge or other reform institutions. Some women provided well for themselves in the trade and thus made a long-term career of prostitution; others found it an easy occupation to pursue if they temporarily fell on hard times. Most of those who can be followed go back into respectable marriage or career situations, but some of them simply disappear from historical sight, possibly returning to prostitution. Of those mentioned, only Jewett, so far as is known, died young.

Although there are dozens of other personal profiles that give insight into the lives of prostitutes and could demonstrate further the diversity of the individuals who worked in the profession, the tentative observations above do help delineate some of the common characteristics of the New York women who practiced prostitution. To gain a clearer focus on these women, we turn to a statistical generalization, or collective profile, of New York prostitutes as a group.

6. HOOKING A VICTIM.   In the 1830s prostitution became much more visible in New York City. This mid-century print, depicting respectable-looking women "hooking victims" on a public thoroughfare, illustrates a situation New Yorkers felt had become a public problem. (Lithograph & Publisher, Serrell & Perkins; gift of Karl Schmidt. Courtesy Museum of the City of New York)

The Collective Profile

William Sanger's 1858 study offered a general profile of the New York City prostitute: she was young, foreign-born, unmarried, had borne a child, came from a poor working-class family, and had experienced economic and/or other problems at home before entering prostitution. Furthermore, Sanger believed the average prostitute spent only four years in the profession before the hard life caused her to die prematurely. This profile did not differ on the whole from what the majority of New Yorkers believed about the prostitutes in their midst, and it also resembled the conclusions of other nineteenth-century social investigators who were concerned with prostitution.[42]

New Yorker Charles Smith, writing a decade before Sanger, also had offered a general portrait, noting that though prostitutes came from every age group and "every rank in life," the majority were poor, had been raised in rural areas, and suffered social disadvantages. Many had worked previously as domestics or in a trade, and almost all were uneducated and because of ignorance had experienced their "downfall."[43] Though Smith and Sanger agreed on issues of age, socioeconomic background, and previous employment, Smith, like several European social investigators, noted that prostitution was usually a temporary occupation, not the final stage of a woman's life.[44]

The nineteenth-century data—particularly Sanger's study, which was by far the most extensive and detailed—can be reevaluated today in light of other evidence. Information from censuses, arrest records, and contemporary newspapers permits us to test the accuracy of Sanger's portrait of the young, foreign-born, desperately poor social outcast who died a few years after becoming a prostitute, thus allowing us to clarify or redefine his profile of the mid-nineteenth-century prostitute.[45]

Most characteristic of the average mid-nineteenth-century New York prostitute was her youth. Youth was a definite asset in the profession, but the late teens or early twenties also represented a stage in life when a young woman might well be needing a job, gaining independence from her family, and making new acquaintances on her own before marrying and having a family. The overwhelming majority of mid-nineteenth-century prostitutes were twenty-five years of age or under. Sanger found 74 percent in this age group, and of the prostitutes identified in the 1850 and 1855 censuses, 74 and 72 percent, respectively, were under twenty-five. Very few prostitutes were over the age of thirty—only 12 percent in Sanger's group, and 10 and 16 percent in the two censuses (table 4).[46]

These figures include both brothel-keepers and common prostitutes, but the two groups can be distinguished on the basis of age. In the 1850 and 1855 censuses, the average age of the brothel-keepers was eight to twelve years higher and their median age eight to eleven years greater. Brothel-keepers were typically in their early to mid-thirties, though the youngest manager was nineteen and the oldest seventy (table 5). Although the madams or brothel managers were generally veteran prostitutes, they were not necessarily older women nor the oldest in the profession; twenty-six of the eighty madams identified (32.5 percent) were not the oldest prostitutes in their respective houses.[47]

If one excludes brothel-keepers from the two censuses studied, the average age of prostitutes was approximately twenty-three.[48] The young-

Table 4 *Age Profile of Prostitutes*

	% in Age Group		
Age Group	Sanger N = 2,000	1850 Census N = 310	1855 Census N = 264
20 & Under	37.5	33.5	35.2
21–25	36.4	40.3	36.4
26–30	14.0	16.5	12.9
31–35	4.9	3.5	7.6
36–40	3.8	3.2	4.2
41–45	1.4	1.6	1.9
46–50	0.8	0.3	0.4
51–55	0.6	0.6	0.8
56–60	0.5	0	0
61 & Over	0.3	0.3	0.8
25 & Under	73.9	73.8	71.6
30 & Under	87.9	90.3	84.5
35 & Under	92.7	93.8	92.1
40 & Under	96.5	97.0	96.3
Median Age	22.0	22.0	22.0
Average Age	23.9	23.9	24.6

SOURCES: William Sanger, *History of Prostitution*, 452; United States Census, 1850, Wards 5 and 8; New York State Census, 1855, Wards 5 and 8.

est prostitutes listed in both the Sanger study and in official censuses were fourteen and fifteen, the approximate age at which most girls physically matured in the mid-nineteenth century. There were, however, many cases of children below this age who practiced prostitution.[49] House of Refuge records list several girls as young as eight who were admitted for suspected or undoubted prostitution; in fact, more than one-third of the Refuge's prostitution-related cases in four selected years involved girls between the ages of eight and fourteen.[50] Police records and newspapers also report instances of very young girls being taken from brothels. Police in the sixth ward found an eleven-year-old girl working as a prostitute in the brothel of Bridget Mangren near the Five Points. Joe Farryall, a notorious recruiter of prostitutes, was arrested with his wife for keeping a disorderly house, and one of the inmates arrested with him was ten years

Table 5 *Age Profile of Brothel Keepers*

| | % in Age Group | |
| | 1850 Census | 1855 Census |
Age Group	N = 38	N = 42
25 & Under	18.4	11.9
26–30	36.8	26.2
31–35	18.4	19.0
36–40	13.2	19.0
41–45	7.9	11.9
46–50	0	2.4
51–55	2.6	4.8
56–60	0	0
61 & Over	2.6	4.8
30 & Under	55.2	38.1
35 & Under	73.6	57.1
40 & Under	86.8	76.2
45 & Under	94.7	88.1
Median Age	30.0	33.0
Average Age	32.5	36.3

SOURCES: United States Census, 1850, Wards 5 and 8; New York State Census, 1855, Wards 5 and 8.

old. In court Farryall was accused of having nine young girls in his house, two of whom were under twelve.[51]

Charles Smith, in his book on prostitution, also noted that police arrested prostitutes who were as young as ten to fourteen, who had been led astray, he believed, by men well advanced in age.[52] In 1835, for example, three young girls were taken from Eliza Webber's assignation house on Church Street, where they had been found "going to bed with grey-haired men."[53] A neighbor testified in court that she had seen the girls enter the house on eight to ten occasions and once had seen a very small girl, accompanied by a middle-aged man, come to her own house before the man realized they were at the wrong place. The Webber arrest led to an investigation of the extent to which young daughters of the poor were being recruited for prostitution. According to the *Sun*, clandestine meetings were arranged by omnibus ticket boys, who were paid by men seeking assignations.[54]

Some professional child prostitutes continued working in the business into their adult years. One twenty-three-year-old veteran stated that she had been a prostitute "ever since it took a yard of cloth to make me a petticoat."[55] The majority of young girls involved, however, like most of their adult counterparts, were not fully professional prostitutes but practiced casual prostitution at intervals, or on occasion, to supplement other earnings. Many were street hucksters whose activities presented opportunities for sexual contacts; the money they earned from one encounter with a man was far more then they might earn peddling fruit or flowers. This type of juvenile street prostitution was described in an 1849 report by New York Chief of Police Matsell, who stated that more than two thousand young girls between eight and sixteen years of age were "addicted to immoralities of the most loathsome description."[56]

Their ostensible business is the sale of fruits, socks, tooth-picks, etc., and with this ruse they gain ready access to counting-rooms, offices and other places, where, in the secrecy and seclusion of a turned key, they submit their persons for the miserable bribe of a few shillings, to the most loathsome and degrading familiarities.[57]

In this way a young girl might earn two to three dollars a day, sometimes given to her parents, sometimes used to purchase some small luxury for herself.

In the middle decades of the nineteenth century, observers noted a substantial increase in childhood prostitution. This growth of juvenile prostitution and pedophilia, in both the United States and Europe, is an aspect of Victorian life that has not yet been fully explored, particularly with respect to the various social and psychological influences on the men involved. We can readily understand, however, why many young girls were easy prey during this period: the compelling social realities of working-family and tenement life made their labor a necessary part of a family's economy, and their unchaperoned huckstering in the streets made them "available" to men seeking young partners. Statistics from child molestation and rape cases support the police chief's observation that sex with female children was very much a part of urban street life in the mid-nineteenth century. Given the security gained from class as much as gender, well-off men with a "taste" for children had substantial protection in pursuing street-exposed girls of the poor. Furthermore, the low age of consent (ten years) implied a legal sanction of sexual relations with children, providing, of course, that the young girl was said to be a willing participant. Many young girls, and sometimes their families, may have been led by ignorance, desperate want, or an experience of forced sex into accepting sexual encounters where they could earn a little extra money.[58]

Contemporary claims that most prostitutes were foreign-born cannot be confirmed as readily as generalizations about their youth. Sanger wrote that it was "frequently remarked and as generally believed . . . that a very large majority of the prostitutes in New York are of foreign birth."[59] The association of prostitution with immigrants was part of an overall linking of foreigners with crime and corruption. Immigrants were thought to be the castoffs of other nations, a "constant flood of immigration" that Sanger noted "leaves a mass of debris behind it."[60] New York's mid-century mayor, Fernando Wood, stated: "An examination of the criminal and pauper records, shows conclusively, that it is but a small proportion of these unfortunate who are natives of this country."[61] The increase in New York crime in the mid-1850s, he believed, could be traced directly to the influx of immigrants.

New Yorkers' tendency to blame evils on foreigners can be explained in part by population changes in the city in the first half of the nineteenth century. Between 1830 and 1860 New York's population more than quadrupled, largely as a result of immigration from Europe. Foreign-born residents constituted 34.5 percent of New York City's inhabitants in 1845, 46.8 percent in 1850, and over half the population, or 52.3 percent, by 1855. Many other foreigners did not settle permanently in New York but landed at the New York port in these years and stayed in the city for a while before moving on. Over a million immigrants arrived in the decade after 1840, and almost two million between 1850 and 1860. In the single month of May 1849, 32,700 aliens landed in New York City, the next month 33,000 came, and, in the peak year of 1851, 289,601 immigrants arrived.[62] The presence of a majority of the population with strange customs, often different faiths and languages, and a need to work cheaply threatened many native-born New Yorkers, who sometimes responded by discriminating against the immigrants in jobs, wages, and housing. Some law-enforcement officials also may have demonstrated discriminatory biases. A study of police docket and arrest records in the 1850s indicates that a woman was most likely to be arrested as a prostitute if she was in an ethnic neighborhood and was foreign, especially Irish.[63] Because immigrant women were usually poor and were not as highly esteemed as native-born women, they may have had more difficulty in finding well-paying jobs and thus possibly turned to prostitution in greater numbers than did their American-born sisters.[64] It is also possible, however, that the high percentage of prostitution arrests of women with foreign names reflects a bias against foreigners, a disregard for their legal rights, or simply their tendency to solicit more often in the streets.[65]

Sanger found that 61.9 percent of the prostitutes he interviewed were of foreign birth. He was impressed by the lowness of this figure—"that five-eighths *only* [italics mine] were born abroad."[66] This was, however, almost 10 percent higher than the proportion of foreign-born in the general population. In contrast, prostitutes identified in wards five and eight using census data include many fewer foreign-born women: 23.9 percent of these identified in the 1850 census and 25.4 percent in 1855. The discrepancy may represent a difference in the types of prostitutes located: almost all of the women identified in the two censuses were from brothels or prostitution boardinghouses, while Sanger's interviewees were not necessarily from establishments. It is possible that immigrants were not considered as desirable as native-born women when hiring for brothels, so that their numbers in prostitution houses would be lower than they would be in the overall prostitute population. Also, though wards did not differ greatly from one another in terms of immigrant population, wards five and eight were in the lowest third of wards in housing foreign-born inhabitants. The overall foreign population of these two wards was 45.2 percent, as compared to 52.3 percent for the city as a whole.[67]

Irish women accounted for the largest immigrant group in both the prostitute population and the general population. In 1855, Irish immigrants represented 28.2 percent of New York City's inhabitants, and 21.7 percent of the residents in wards five and eight. Yet Irish prostitutes, as the largest foreign-born group, comprised only 12 percent of all the prostitutes in these two wards, while they accounted for 35 percent of Sanger's city-wide study done at approximately the same time (table 6).

Table 6 *Percentages of All Foreign-Born and Irish-Born New York City Residents and Prostitutes, 1855*

		Total Population		Prostitute Population	
	N	% All Foreign	% Irish	% All Foreign	% Irish
All N.Y.C.	629,904	52.3	28.2	61.9	35.3
Wards 5 and 8	55,669	45.2	21.7	25.4	12.1

SOURCES: New York State Census, 1855; William Sanger, *History of Prostitution*, 460. Percentages of foreign-born prostitutes in the total New York City population are from Sanger's study, and those for Wards 5 and 8 are from the author's survey of the New York State census manuscripts for New York City.

Interestingly, in 1860 New York's Irish community was the city's only national group in which females outnumbered males. Irish women outnumbered Irish men in New York City at that time by about one-third, or more than 30,000, a number greater than the combined total of all other foreign-born females except German. Within her own ethnic neighborhood, an Irish woman was more likely to remain single than were women of other nationalities.[68]

The relatively low proportion of Irish women among prostitutes in wards five and eight partly reflects those wards' relatively low overall population of foreigners, including Irish immigrants. But it also probably indicated a preference on the part of the ward's brothel-managers for hiring native-born prostitutes. This assumption was supported by the observations of a German visitor to New York in 1858 that Irish and German women generally were excluded from the finer brothels in the Mercer Street area, where Americans and a few Frenchwomen predominated.[69] If we could obtain data on streetwalkers and independent prostitutes that is as complete as the census data on the brothel-based population, it is possible that the foreign-born percentage of prostitutes would appear much higher. The periodic sweeping arrests of streetwalkers may have included many innocent women, but those arrested were mostly Irish and other foreign-born females (table 7). Nevertheless, because the information on nativity from wards five and eight challenges Sanger's and others' assumption that most prostitutes were immigrants, no straightforward conclusion is possible concerning whether the typical New York prostitute was foreign- or native-born.

Table 7 *Nativity of Arrested Streetwalkers*

Date[a]	Total Arrested	Foreign-Born		
		Irish	*Other*	*Total*
28 March 1855	35	20 (57.1%)	5 (14.3%)	25 (71.4%)
23 May 1855	60	34 (56.7%)	10 (16.7%)	44 (73.3%)
24 May 1855	39	25 (64.1%)	7 (17.9%)	32 (82.1%)

[a]Three sample evenings during two months of Mayor Wood's anti-prostitution campaign. The "sweep" of streetwalkers occurred on streets to either side of Broadway, an area that included an ethnically diverse group of prostitutes working independently and out of brothels.

SOURCE: *New York Daily Times.*

Uncertainty concerning the nativity of the majority of New York prostitutes does not extend to race: most prostitutes were white. Although black New Yorkers were even lower on the socioeconomic scale than immigrants and were excluded from most occupations except menial labor, black women still comprised a small part of New York's prostitution community.[70] The small number of black prostitutes may be explained partly by the small proportion of black residents in the city in general: black New Yorkers accounted for no more than 5.5 percent of the city's population at any time during the period 1835 to 1870 and had declined to only 1.5 percent by 1860. Also, prejudice played some role in limiting the chances that black women could improve their economic situations through prostitution.[71]

Certainly there were black prostitutes and black brothels, some of which were successful and mentioned in brothel guidebooks.[72] The 1853 *Fast Man's Directory and Lover's Guide to the Ladies of Fashion* highly recommended the brothel at 196-1/2 Church Street run by Sarah Sweet:

This lady is a Southern Creole and her lady boarders are the same; they are very beautiful. It is the only decent Creole house in the city. . . . Southern gentlemen will find this a very fine resort, and will feel quite at home.[73]

Much of the success of a brothel depended on the mystique surrounding the establishment, and Sarah Sweet cleverly played to the fantasies held about illicit sex in the South. According to the 1850 census, the "Southern Creole lady" was actually a mulatto from Rhode Island and her four Southern creole boarders were mulattos from Massachusetts and New York.[74] Miss Sweet's house and "pretty brunette boarders" were described again in an 1859 brothel directory along with two other "creole" houses.[75] One of these, Virginia Henriques' house at 103 Mercer, was said to be "one of the best conducted houses of its kind in New York," with "six pretty brunette boarders who . . . adhere strictly to the rules of good breeding."[76]

Of the eighty brothels identified in wards five and eight in the 1850 and 1855 censuses, only two were black houses. Sarah Sweet's house with five black prostitutes was listed in 1850, and Jane Hill's brothel with ten black women was recorded in the 1855 census.[77] Nineteenth-century newspapers mention a few black prostitutes and black assignation and prostitution houses in columns on arrests and court proceedings, but even in wards five and six, where many blacks lived, the daily police docket records few arrests of black women for prostitution/ vagrancy or streetwalking. One 1849 ledger, which included 117 arrests for common prostitution/vagrancy, recorded only 3 arraignments of black women, and the 1850 books listed only 20 black suspects among 482 charged with the same offense. Black women were 3 percent of the overall population at the time, and black men and women represented 7 percent of the total population of wards five and six, where most of the arrests were made. Arrests of black women in the ledgers of wards 5 and 6 represented 4 percent or less of total arrests for prostitution/ vagrancy. Because police regularly brought in many more black residents on charges of drunken and disorderly conduct, the low percentage of arrests for prostitution is a further indication of blacks' scarcity in this profession.[78]

Black women may have avoided prostitution more than white women because they were discriminated against by clients, or because they feared racially motivated abuse by customers as well as legal harassment and reprisals by the police and courts. The same 1853 brothel directory that recommended Sarah Sweet's establishment made racial slurs against other houses. Mrs. Bennet's house was described as "a very low place, formerly filled with niggers," and Jane Frances's brothel was said to be "a quiet place but too many niggers are around here."[79] Another establishment was described as a "vile crib. It is a resort for niggers and pea-nut girls."[80] Newspapers were often even cruder in their descriptions than were the directories, such as in a *Herald* account of a raid on a brothel:

A Black "Crib" Broken Up
At the watch returns yesterday morning, the Police Office presented a rich group of niggers, of all sizes and colors—black, white, and grey—but the odor was not quite as agreeable as the sight was amusing, to observe the different countenances, with their big lips. It was really laughable.[81]

It is possible there were more black prostitutes and brothels than public records indicate because white officials may have ignored sexual commerce between black males and females unless it created a public disturbance in the community. Because white New Yorkers commonly assumed an innate "loose morality" among black people, black prostitutes serving black clients may have been disregarded. Nineteenth-century racism also assured that black males usually had access only to black brothels and streetwalkers, or to those integrated houses that were part of the lowest echelons of the trade.[82]

In spite of blatant public racism, officers sometimes protected the interests of black prostitutes. In the Court of Special Sessions, James Woodruff was charged with "taking advantage" of a Negro at a house of ill-fame and was remanded for a week.[83] An article in the *Sun* related that Ebenezer Barney, who visited Eliza Fisher's black brothel to enjoy the company of two of the prostitutes, went to the police to file a complaint that his pocket book with $40 had been stolen in her establishment. According to the *Sun*, Justice Wyman, apparently more offended by the mixing of races than by the commission of the alleged crime, gave Barney "an appropriate lecture on the white gentleman's perversity of taste and his penchant for 'woolly headed quails.'" According to the newspaper, Barney was "compelled to pocket his loss and lose the contents of his pocket for his folly."[84] It seems telling that even black prostitutes, despite doubly deep prejudices, were able to face the law with some hope of protection.

Many black women, too, played significant roles in the daily operations of New York's brothels. Most of the brothels located in wards five and eight had servants, largely black. There were 89 brothel residents in addition to the 310 prostitutes in the 1850 census, and 77 of these were black. Sixty-four were female servants, 7 were male servants, and 6 were black children. In the 1855 census, there were 69 residents in addition to the 264 prostitutes, 44 of whom were black.[85] There were probably many other black household workers who did not live in. Moreover, it was sometimes possible for black women to improve their positions and earnings by increasing their responsibilities and authority as servants. An 1870 directory, describing Kate Austin's brothel, said it was:

A second class house of six boarders . . . [which] seems to be managed by the colored servants. One can never see the proprietor who is concealed somewhere behind these sable breast works.[86]

Of a first-class house, it was said:

The landlady is never seen. It is impossible to say who is head of the house. The door is guarded by a grouty old dame from the south of Africa, whose assumed dignity is so over powering that most people suppose that she runs the establishment.[87]

These black women appear to have been servants, but they evidently assumed some of the management responsibilities of madams, maximizing their roles in a business where black authority commonly had to be oblique.

The statistical profile of the New York prostitute indicates that she was single as well as young and white. Sanger found 61 percent of his interviewees had never married, and 79 percent of the prostitutes working in brothels in wards five and eight in 1855 were unmarried. Of the large group of streetwalkers arrested on one evening that same year, 59 percent said they were single. Some single women probably claimed to be widowed or married, especially if they had children, and brothel madams sometimes went by the title "widow" or "Mrs." even if they had not been married. A widow might have become a prostitute, though, if she experienced an abrupt change in her family's economy on the death of her husband. Both the Sanger study and the 1855 census identified 14.7 percent of the prostitutes as widows. Sanger was surprised by the fact that 25 percent of the prostitutes he interviewed said they were married, and he was appalled to learn that 14.5 percent of these women were still living with their husbands while they practiced prostitution.[88]

Almost half of the Sanger interviewees had had children—about three-fourths of the widows and married women, and about 30 percent of the single women. A little over 40 percent of the widows' and married women's children were illegitimate, however.[89] The children of these prostitutes appear to have had a very high rate of mortality—62 percent overall and an even higher rate among children of single mothers. Sanger assumed that most of these deaths must have occurred before the children were five years old, so he compared his figures to death rates of New York children in the same age category. Because he was certain the women had not admitted to having many abortions, he inflated his figures to account for this omission and concluded that the mortality rate for prostitutes' children was four times as great as that for the average New York child. This conclusion is a statistical invention, though the mortality rate for prostitutes' children probably was somewhat higher than that of the city as a whole. His decrial of the "sacrifice of *infant life*" as "one of the most deplorable *results* of prostitution" (italics added) also flies in the face of his own observation that 43 percent of the prostitutes' children were born before their mothers became prostitutes.[90]

Most New York prostitutes had worked in low-paying trades before entering the profession, and many were still so employed while practicing prostitution to supplement their incomes. Not surprisingly, the practice of part-time prostitution was more typical of streetwalkers than of brothel workers.[91] Of the thirty-nine women arrested for streetwalking on May 24, 1855 (see table 7), a majority listed occupations other than prostitution, perhaps because they indeed practiced prostitution as a second profession but perhaps too because they may have claimed other occupations in hopes charges against them would be dropped.[92] Seventeen of those arrested (44 percent) said they worked in households, or as domestics, and six were from the sewing trades (15 percent). In contrast, only 15 percent of the 2,000 prostitutes in Sanger's study said they were supporting themselves by means other than (or in addition to) prostitution. In listing their prior professions, however, almost half of Sanger's interviewees said they had worked as domestic/household laborers, and another 21 percent had been in the sewing trades.[93]

Although the responses to occupational questions in official censuses depended very much on the census-takers' thoroughness and the questions they asked, some prostitutes indicated they were continuing to work in other professions. In the census of 1855, most of the ward five prostitutes identified themselves as such. In ward eight, however, only 39 of the 158 women responded to the question on employment. Thirteen gave prostitution as their profession, and 26 listed other trades, mostly in sewing.[94]

The occupation of a woman's father seems to have been only vaguely related to whether the woman became a prostitute. Sanger found that most prostitutes' fathers held working-class occupations—as laborers, masons, blacksmiths, farmers, and sailors—but some were clergymen, lawyers, physicians, school teachers, policemen, and men of property. More important than the father's occupation was paternal economic setback, death, or familial alienation.[95] Some women clearly became prostitutes in response to familial need, and others joined the profession because of a break with family, which was sometimes precipitated by perceived or actual sexual indiscretion. Economic stresses that might require wives and children to go to work to help support the family were more likely to occur in working-class families than in families at higher socioeconomic levels, but sexual indiscretions might be committed by a female from any family. The effect of the double standard and social pressure on a young woman who had been sexually promiscuous and thus alienated from her family meant that she, regardless of class, had few options for supporting herself besides prostitution.

The length of time most women stayed in prostitution was an issue debated by nineteenth-century observers of the profession. Sanger believed that most New York prostitutes died after approximately four years, in other words, that one-fourth of all New York prostitutes died every year. McDowall had stated a similar conclusion twenty-five years earlier, and William Tait, writing on Edinburgh prostitutes in 1840, interpreted their short careers (no more than four years) as an indication of their early demise. Another observer, Samuel Prime, in *Life in New York* (1847), agreed that prostitution led to death but stated that the average life expectancy after commencing prostitution might be as long as ten to fifteen years.[96] In contrast, physician Charles Smith, writing the same year as Prime, while agreeing that there was a turnover in the profession every few years (approximately five to seven), argued that this was not attributable to death. Although some died of disease and dissipation, he believed that at least two-thirds of the women left the profession to marry, take a lover, set up a business, start another trade, or migrate to the South or West. Smith's analysis closely resembles Parent-Duchatelet's 1836 study of French prostitutes, which found that the profession was usually a temporary occupation practiced for one to four years before returning to old trades or choosing new professions or lifestyles. Physician William Acton's study of London prostitution also supported the idea that prostitutes had short careers not because of untimely deaths but because they reintegrated themselves into respectable society. Some married; others had accumulated enough savings to be able to go into a trade, establish a shop, or open a boardinghouse. In fact, many of the prostitutes he had treated continued visiting him as patients after leaving the profession.[97]

Although drawing different conclusions, all the commentators agreed that, on the whole, prostitutes practiced their profession for only a few years. Data taken from New York City public records, although selective, reveals little repetition in names of the 310 prostitutes identified in the 1850 census when compared to the 264 in the 1855 census. Most of the women who are found in both censuses appear to have moved "up," or into managerial posts. This finding does not preclude the possibility that other women may have stayed in prostitution for a longer period, perhaps by moving "down" into less desirable situations than those of the brothels in wards five and eight; certainly, however, the data does not confirm their deaths. In fact, a review of the records from 1850 to 1855 produces few names of prostitutes who have been identified from that period. To support Sanger's assumption about prostitution causing early death, prostitutes' deaths would have had to account for approximately one-sixth of all female deaths in the city each year, which is not at all the case; in New York, deaths for females between ages ten and thirty (the age category including approximately 88 percent of all prostitutes) amounted to only one-sixth of all female deaths. It is impossible that almost all women who died each year in this age group, which comprised the earliest and heaviest childbearing years, were prostitutes.[98]

Unfortunately, there is little information about the lives of prostitutes after leaving the profession. House of Refuge records reveal that a few of the prostitutes who were admitted there did die young, usually of disease, and a few returned to prostitution. Others, however, left the Refuge to work as chambermaids, milliners, seamstresses, or industrial workers, and some married and had children. If the stint in prostitution had not afforded the security of marriage or an improved economic position, then most of these women found that their life options had not really changed much: menial labor, the hope of a future marriage, or a return to prostitution. Having learned the economic advantages of prostitution, however, some probably did move in and out of the profession over the years until age or illness diminished their marketability in that occupation, just as it did in other trades.

Attempts to profile the nineteenth-century New York City prostitute can never be definitive, but they can enable us to draw a limited portrait of these women as a group. Although most women entered the occupation when they were very young and practiced it only a few years before moving back into respectability, some women did grow old in prostitution. Contrary to Sanger's profile, most New York prostitutes did not die after only a few years in the trade, but moved on to other jobs or married. For many, prostitution was not far removed from viable "respectable" alternatives, and thus it was taken up by a relatively broad group of women. Prostitution was not an occupation for only the most desperately poor and outcast but was an easy one to pursue if a young woman fell on hard times or wanted to establish her financial independence. Neither personal stories nor the available statistical data permit us to determine the percentage of foreign-born and black women, those New Yorkers lowest on the socioeconomic scale, who worked as prostitutes, but the ethnic spectrum of women in the occupation was probably broader among streetwalkers than among brothel-based women, because streetwalking did not usually involve so major a lifestyle change or so definite an occupational commitment. Nevertheless, those who worked in houses, a higher percentage of whom were native-born, probably were better off than streetwalkers: less desperately poor, better protected legally and medically, and better paid.[99]

It is important to know the similarities of women who chose prostitution—the statistical significance of certain personal and background traits or characteristics—but it is equally important to know something about these women's motivations. Because there was a social stigma associated with prostitution, some set of circumstances, some combination of experiences and needs, had to motivate a woman to practice prostitution instead of a more respectable occupation. The reasons why a woman chose prostitution and why she remained in the profession add another dimension to our understanding of the nineteenth-century New York prostitute.

3

"No Work, No Money, No Home"

Choosing Prostitution

In April 1839, Catherine Paris and one of her two children attended chapel at the House of Refuge. The entry in the Refuge's journal noted that Paris was respectably married to a confectioner and living at the corner of Broadway and Duane. Nothing in the notation indicated how different Paris's life had been three years prior to that month. In April 1836, Paris, known then as Elizabeth Salters, was one of Helen Jewett's colleagues in Rosina Townsend's brothel. On the day of the famous murder, Paris and Jewett had spent the afternoon together on an outing in lower Manhattan, and Paris was one of the prostitutes who testified at the trial.

For the two years preceding the murder, from age seventeen to nineteen, Paris was a prostitute, living most of the time at Townsend's establishment. Before coming to New York, she lived in Albany with her mother, a tailoress and domestic who was twice widowed before Paris was nine.

Paris's life history and the circumstances surrounding her decision to become a prostitute are similar to those of many other women. As a thirteen-year-old, living alone with a mother who was employed full-time, Paris began to run around at night with companions whom the Refuge called "bad girls." Because of her behavior, she was sent to the Refuge. The matrons described her as good-looking and said she appeared older than her age. The only problem mentioned in her records was that she and a group of girls tried to escape from the Refuge the year after she arrived. At age fifteen Paris was indentured by the Refuge to a man in Susquehanna County, who wrote favorably of her work and behavior and said he was recommending her as a candidate in the Presbyterian church. The next year, however, she returned to her mother in Albany and not long afterward came to New York. There she boarded for a short time at Mrs. Berger's prostitution house on Church Street, and then at Mrs. Townsend's on Thomas Street.[1]

Although prostitution was not a lifetime career for Paris, neither was marriage. In 1849, in a story about the Jewett murder, the *Police Gazette* reported that Catherine Paris, alias Elizabeth Salters, had lived with her confectioner husband for only a few years and had then "eloped" from him.[2]

Why did Paris become a prostitute? Her background suggests no single motivating factor. It is possible that she became familiar with the life of prostitution during her years in Albany, and she could compare the lifestyle with that of women like her widowed mother who worked in menial trades. Furthermore, as an indentured worker from the Refuge, she learned the demands and rewards of "honest" hard work. Thus, by the age of seventeen, when released from the Refuge, Paris chose to be independent of her mother in Albany and moved to New York City, where she began working full time as a prostitute. Though it appears that she practiced the trade for only a couple of years, she may have returned to prostitution after leaving her husband in the 1840s.

Paris's story shares several elements with many other accounts of nineteenth-century prostitutes: economic need, a desire to be independent of familial constraint, and lack of comparatively well-paying and comfortable alternatives. Another young prostitute summed up such a combination of factors as prompting her to choose prostitution: "No work, no money, no home."[3] The central point that Paris's and other prostitutes' life stories illustrate about nineteenth-century prostitution is that most women do not appear to have entered the profession for a single reason, but, rather, because of a complex combination of factors. And although contemporaries tended to enshroud motivation in a mantle of moralism that often obscured real causes, it is important to view nineteenth-century prostitutes' choices and responses within the context of the time, considering fully the variety of influences brought to bear on their decisions. We should consider not only the conditions of these women's lives but also society's attitudes about women, sex, morality, family, and work that made prostitution a reasonable occupational option for so many.[4]

In the early years of the nineteenth century prostitutes were believed to practice their profession not because they were attempting to cope with difficult situations but because they were depraved women who suffered from character defects—they were victimizers who corrupted others in society. Although some observers noted that prostitutes were very poor, their poverty was regarded less as a cause of prostitution than as related to bad character and moral weakness. In 1818 the New York Society for the Prevention of Paupers issued a report citing ten causes of poverty and pauperism in New York City, among which was the influence of "houses of ill fame," which corrupted the habits and morals of "a numerous class of young men, especially sailors and apprentices."[5] In this formulation, prostitution was a cause of poverty, not one of its results. Prostitutes were morally depraved women who, in turn, corrupted morally weak men.

The Reverend J. R. McDowall's work among prostitutes in the early 1830s also reflected a belief that women who became prostitutes were morally ignorant and corrupt, and "cause the seduction of heedless youth. . . . A few courtesans corrupt whole cities."[6] Prostitutes were women of "the worst character . . . malevolent, cruel and revengeful," and their lives were the necessary result of voluntary vice.[7] Hence, McDowall and his early followers believed that the way to abolish prostitution and effect the reform of the women who practiced it was to hold prayer meetings with prostitutes in brothels, jails, and almshouses; to distribute bibles and tracts; and to instruct the women in religious and moral teachings. Reclaiming "the crown jewels from the sewers," as another nineteenth-century reform group articulated its mission among the lost, might be accomplished only through moral conversion and proper training.[8] But McDowall's report, though it centrally enshrined the established moralistic victimizer thesis, also acknowledged an idea that would gain support with time: that "sheer necessity" drove many women to prostitution.

Although McDowall's society disbanded, both church-affiliated and secular groups of middle- and upper-class women and men continued his work in other reform societies in New York and throughout the country. Through their efforts to convert and reform prostitutes, reformers came to realize they were working with only part of the problem, and they expanded their objectives to stress the need for moral purity in all members of society. Women's moral-reform societies in particular were quickly persuaded that reform would only be accomplished by revolutionizing the relationship between the sexes and by eliminating the double standard of sexual morality. This new thrust reflected an important change in the public's perception of the role of the prostitute. In 1835, women of the Moral Reform Society unanimously adopted a resolution that articulated the new attitude: "Let the condemnation of the guilty of our sex remain entire; but let not the *most guilty of the two*—the deliberate destroyer of female innocence—be afforded even an 'apron of fig leaves,' to conceal the blackness of his crimes."[9] No longer was the prostitute viewed as the victimizer, but rather as the victim—the person seduced or raped and then scorned by a society that tolerated the debauchers in its midst. Such moralistic reinterpretation led to a change in the focus of moral reformers' efforts from reform to prevention. To eradicate prostitution by prevention, however, reformers had to clarify social causes and educate the public about them. It was through efforts to identify the causes of prostitution that many reformers began to look beyond the lives of individual sinners, female and male, and beyond the issues of morality and purity to larger contemporary social problems, such as poverty, of which prostitution was only one manifestation. This notion that prostitution had socioeconomic roots became a basic tenet of the "scientific" school of reformers, even though the assumption that poor character was often related to poverty never totally disappeared from nineteenth-century thinking.[10]

After the 1830s, however, those who studied prostitution as a social problem, those who worked to reform prostitutes, and the general public began to see prostitution's causes first in more sympathetic and then in more environmental terms. Depraved men and socioeconomic structures became the two favorite explanations. That women could easily become the victims of unscrupulous men was widely accepted because of commonly held assumptions about the fundamental natures of men and women. Nineteenth-century moral reformers, like the general public, came to believe that women were by nature pure, trusting, affectionate, and open-hearted, and that they responded to men only out of romantic love, not carnal desire. Men, on the other hand, were thought to be lechers, controlled by base sexual drives that they often either could not or would not control. The will of a determined male, once sexually aroused, was believed to be far stronger than that of a female. Furthermore, women, especially young rural and immigrant women, were believed to be naive and susceptible to trickery and deception. Prostitutes, in this scheme, were victims taken advantage of or destroyed by the "awful deception of a brute in the shape of a man."[11]

Though not wholly rejecting a moralistic framework, other social reformers put greater emphasis on socioeconomic causes, especially the lack of economic alternatives. Scientific investigators in Europe and the United States differed from one another slightly in their evaluations of the various causes of prostitution, but all stressed the role of poverty and lack of employment. In his study on the prostitutes of New York City, Sanger found that slightly more than one-fourth of his interviewees gave "destitution" as the reason they entered prostitution, making it the most often-cited cause. "It is unquestionably true," Sanger stated, "that positive, actual want, the apparent and dreaded approach of starvation, was the real cause of degradation."[12] Women became destitute, he observed, because they did not have "sufficient means of employment" and because their employment was "inadequately remunerated."[13] "Unhesitatingly and without fear of contradiction," he reported, "were there more avenues of employment open to females there would be a corresponding decrease in prostitution."[14]

Though widely accepted, the economic explanation never went unquestioned. Indeed for some analysts it remained unrecognized. A doctor in the late nineteenth century claimed that his thirty-city survey, which showed that most prostitutes were former factory, shop, or servant girls, proved that "public occupations are dangerous. A woman who works outside the home commits a biological crime against herself and her community."[15] Even for more serious thinkers, the economic argument had troublesome implications. Those who portrayed prostitutes as moral victims could and did see solutions in control of male passions and in discrediting a double standard. Those who stressed economic victimization could and did urge better wages for women, but none envisioned the kind of broad economic changes that would have made prostitution anything but a rational marketplace choice for millions of females. In fact, strong elements of social conservatism contributed to the victimization thesis. If these women were hapless victims who were not responsible for their lives in the profession, they posed no real challenge to the idealized view of women portrayed in the cult of true womanhood, for so long as prostitution was seen as a forced rather than chosen option, the notion of woman as pure and in her proper place as mother and mistress of the hearth was unshaken. Also, victimization denied all positive appeal of the career—the financial and familial independence, the social life, the short-term comforts, and the long-term economic benefits. Such attractions were, in fact, the nasty secrets of prostitution; women became prostitutes not out of inevitable necessity, but because the profession was a comparatively attractive option from among the constricted choices society offered. Given the limits of nineteenth-century women's occupational opportunities, for some women in some circumstances, prostitution seemed and perhaps was the best alternative. As has been noted by historian Barbara Hobson, prostitution was a reasonable choice in an irrational social universe:

one in which social and economic conditions forced some women to earn a livelihood but fostered an ideology that denied them decent wages; one that censured only women in illicit sexuality but insisted that they were the weaker parties unable to protect themselves against male sexual advances; and one that idealized motherhood but did not provide social services for single women who had to raise children.[16]

Without perhaps fully understanding the social, economic, and psychological complexities that underlay the choice of prostitution as a profession, nineteenth-century prostitutes and their observers offered many reasons why women entered prostitution, reasons that reflected the shift in emphasis from causes stressing moralistic factors to those stressing socioeconomic forces.[17] If one were to skim the early- and mid-nineteenth-century popular literature and newspapers, one might believe that seduction and abandonment ranked first as a cause of prostitution, followed by entrapment and trickery, and then, less often, unfortunate or unhappy home lives, the influence of others in the profession, a woman's self-image, poverty and the need for income, and a desire for economic enhancement.

The Causes

Early nineteenth-century reformers, popular literature, and even some of the more scientific studies stressed seduction and abandonment as a major cause of prostitution, a reason that accorded with some prostitutes' explanations. In the typical scenario, women were portrayed as pure, trusting, and affectionate, while men were characterized as unprincipled lechers. An example of this sentimental approach to seduction is found in Sanger's mid-century study:

A woman's heart longs for a reciprocal affection, and, to insure this, she will occasionally yield her honor to her lover's importunities, but only when her attachment has become so concentrated upon its object as to invest him with every attribute of perfection, to find in every word he utters and every action he performs but some token of his devotion to her.

Love then became a "passion" and an "idolatry" that developed gradually in the woman "until the woman owns to herself and admits to her lover that she regards him with affection." Although such an acknowledgment should have inspired the lover with high resolve to protect her, it frequently became instead

the medium for dishonorable exactions . . . fatal in consequences to her, [as he] tramples on the priceless jewel of her honor.

It should be remembered that, in order to accomplish this base end, he must have resorted to base means. . . . Pure and sincere attachment would effectively prevent the lover from performing any act which could possibly compromise the woman he adores.[18]

There were usually two possible endings to the typical story of deception: the young girl was immediately forsaken after the illicit sex, or she was induced to elope with the young man and shortly afterward abandoned and left to fend for herself in a new city. It was said that most of these young women then turned to lives of prostitution, either because they had lost all self-respect or because their families and friends, on learning of their sins and indiscretions, disowned them and turned them out. In April 1834, the New York *Sun* carried a story about a baby left on the steps of a respectable home on Grand Street. A note from "Maria," the baby's mother, said she had run away from home with a man who proved to be a villain, and she could not return home because she had been so disgraced. Because she must resort to an "abode of infamy to get bread," she was leaving the child to the respectable family in hopes that "the blessings of Providence [will] attend the guardian of my child."[19]

7. A MORALITY TALE. In the typical nineteenth-century tale of seduction, an innocent, unsuspecting young woman was persuaded or tricked by flattery and false promises of love and marriage into having pre-marital intercourse. She then was abandoned, usually in poverty, to care for herself and her offspring. (Courtesy of the New-York Historical Society, New York City)

ITS BEGINNING.

Many stories of seduction reinforced the popular notion that men, even apparently trustworthy men, were really lechers. The *New Era* in October 1837 told of Mary Burke, a victim of a variety of men across the professional spectrum, who was arrested in a Walnut Street brothel. Burke told the judge that she had been born in Ireland, where her schoolmaster had seduced her when she was fourteen. Because of her sin, she was thrown out by her father. She bore a child and moved to Quebec, where she became intimate with her confessor, a Catholic priest, which resulted in another child. She then moved to Montreal, was seduced by a constable, had a third child, and eventually went to the Grey Nunnery with her children. Later, she came to the United States with another man who abandoned her in New York, and there, because of economic need, she began a "business of her own." Burke provided the names of all of her seducers, but her tale of "multiple seduction" did not move the judge to dismiss her case.[20] Nevertheless, few explanations of a woman's fall could elicit as much sympathy as that of seduction and abandonment. Seduction certainly played a decisive

ITS END.

role in causing some women to enter prostitution, but its frequency was probably overstated by reformers and possibly by the women themselves, who may have wanted to justify their situation to reformers who favored such explanations. In Sanger's study of 2,000 prostitutes, approximately 13 percent gave "seduced and abandoned" as their reason for entering prostitution. A few more said they were "seduced on board emigrant ships" or were "seduced in emigrant boarding houses," but the total number reporting seduction as a reason still represented only 14.5 percent of the cases (table 8).[21]

Entrapment and trickery, followed by rape, was another scenario said to lure women into prostitution, one believed especially effective with immigrants and young women from rural areas. Joe Farryall was a typical "professional" recruiter whose guile was said to have caused the ruin of many innocent young women. Farryall and his wife, Phebe, operated a house of prostitution on Franklin Street and kept it supplied with inmates from as far north as Vermont. Periodically, Farryall trav-

Table 8 *Sanger Survey: Causes of Prostitution*

	Prostitutes	
	No.	%[a]
Direct Causes		
Seduced and abandoned	258	13.0
Seduced on emigrant ship	16	1.0
Seduced in emigrant boarding house	8	.5
Violated	27	1.5
Ill-treated by family, husband	164	8.0
Persuaded by prostitutes	71	3.5
Bad company	84	4.0
Drink and desire to drink	181	9.0
Wanted easy life	124	6.0
Too idle to work	29	1.5
Inclination	513	26.0
Destitution	525	26.0
Total	2,000	100.0
Additional Contributing Factors		
Death of father	1,349	67.0
Death of mother	1,234	62.0
Intemperance of father	596	30.0
Intemperance of mother	347	17.0

[a]Percentages are rounded to the nearest half.

SOURCE: William Sanger, *History of Prostitution*, 488, 539, 544.

eled through the countryside and, either through his charms or by promises of a better and more exciting life, persuaded young women to follow him to New York, where they were raped or intimidated into sexual compliance. Men like Farryall were rumored to be getting from $50 to $500 per recruit.[22] Another method of tricking young country girls and newly arrived immigrants was by promising training and work in millinery or other trades. Only after arriving at the designated employment address in the city would a woman discover the true nature of the establishment.[23]

It was said that agents and madams seeking new recruits also operated in conjunction with employment businesses, known as intelligence

offices, where women would be told they were being hired as seamstresses, milliners, or domestics. The *Advocate of Moral Reform* reported
that many houses of infamy were connected with millinery establishments, partly to conceal the true character of the houses from the young
women hired and from the public. Reformers also claimed that unsuspecting young women were lured into brothels in response to ad-
vertisements for rooms "to let"; once inside, the new boarders were
allegedly drugged and then seduced or raped so that they agreed to
become prostitutes because of their shame. Employers' sexual use of
women, especially servants, was also said to contribute to prostitution;
many females learned through force or ultimatums that sexual favors
were an expected part of employment, and failure to cooperate might
result in their dismissal. [24]

In the Sanger study, the twenty-seven interviewees who said they
were "violated," or who were immigrants seduced en route to America
or in "emigrant boarding houses," possibly were victims of such methods
of trickery or entrapment rather than of emotional attachment to a
"heartless seducer." But only a tiny fraction of the women Sanger
interviewed—2.5 percent—reported experiences that might be interpreted as entrapment, despite the emphasis on such cases in the writings
of reformers and the popular press. [25]

A few stories of seduction by trickery or entrapment also appeared in
House of Refuge records. Elizabeth McNeal said she had been in service
for eight years, but was forced to seek new places on many occasions.
One place of employment she had obtained through an intelligence
office turned out to be a brothel. Although McNeal said she left this
employment after learning the nature of the place and claimed she did
not have "criminal connection" while there, her record noted that she
frequently had been in the "company of bad girls" and had stayed at two
other prostitution houses. [26] Angela Hadden stated that at age sixteen she
had left her Westchester home for a nearby community to learn the
tailoring trade and get away from her father, who drank too much and
was "ugly." One of the customers of the tailoring establishment, a
druggist, said he knew of a woman in New York City who wanted help
and would hire Hadden. Learning that her father planned to come get
her, Hadden went into the city and sought out the druggist to pursue
the job opportunity. He took her to a house on Mott Street and there,
according to her Refuge case history, Hadden and the druggist "were

locked up, and he succeeded after many threats and much struggle in seducing her, he left her in this bad house and never saw her again. She attempted to escape, but was watched and kept very closely, until she became broadly on the town, where she has been in practice for two years."[27] Joe Farryall, on one of his tours through New England, was reported to have persuaded his orphaned and impoverished fifteen-year-old second cousin, Mariah Hubbard, that she was working too hard and ought to come to New York, live with his family, and become a "lady." Delighted to leave her place of service for such wonderful prospects, Hubbard accompanied Farryall to New York, was seduced en route, and was taken to his Franklin Street brothel, where she said she was forced to begin prostituting herself.[28] Two other young girls, Sarah Buchanan and Frances Day, told of being first seduced by their employers at places of service when each was but twelve years old. Day continued working for her employer, the deputy sheriff, until she was fifteen, but Buchanan reported the incident to her mistress, which ended the employer's marriage and cost Buchanan her position. Employees at the House of Refuge were suspicious that Buchanan's and Day's unfortunate initial sexual encounters had led to further ones, since each girl had had later associations with brothels. Buchanan eventually returned to her mother, who ran a prostitution house, and there, in company with the prostitutes, she began "walking" and going to the theater in the evenings. Her grandmother intervened and had her sent to the Refuge. Frances Day later went to work in a brothel, where she said she was employed as a chambermaid, but she told Refuge officials she only stayed there a short while because of the "bad" nature of the house. Police said they found her wandering the streets with "no friends and no clothes" and therefore committed her to the Refuge.[29]

In the cases of entrapment, as in those of seduction and abandonment, women were usually portrayed as naive victims who, because they were "tarnished," were left with few options in life but prostitution. The women were doubly victims, first of seducers or rapists who took advantage of them and second of the upstanding, respectable members of the community who shunned them. Many nineteenth-century commentators emphasized the role played by respectable society in causing prostitution by not forgiving sexual transgressions or not offering a helping hand when needed. One former prostitute, Susan Striker, was indentured by the House of Refuge to a family in Ithaca, New York. Her behavior was reported to be exemplary, and the family found no fault with her, but a year after her indenture the mistress of the house returned her to the Refuge upon learning that Striker had once been a prostitute. Another young girl, fifteen-year-old Susan Badger, reported that she lived in service with a family in the country for eight months until they learned her mother was a prostitute, and she was sent home.[30]

Perhaps even worse than the seduced woman's rejection, critics argued, was a double standard under which an offending male, recognized as a seducer, would be accepted by society while his hapless victim would be allowed no option but prostitution.[31] One writer reflected on the pernicious effect of this double standard in 1869:

Vice gives a woman's nature a more terrible wrench than a man's. It is harder for her to draw a veil over the past; it seems constantly to come back to her to rebuke her and to overwhelm her with disgrace. Her opportunities to rise are not comparable with the boy's, who finds a hundred doors opening before him, while she finds nearly every honorable door closed. Most ladies are less patient with the frailties of their sex than men.[32]

Although nineteenth-century society may not have been as harsh on "dishonored" women as sources or "ideals" seem to imply, rigid attitudes about female chastity and the acceptance of a double standard probably had a role in causing some seduced women to enter prostitution. Many of these women may have believed prostitution to be the most "appropriate" occupation available to them because they internalized the feelings of guilt and shame expressed by society in comments or actions that indicated they had been "ruined" or "dishonored." Current research indicates that sexual experience, even a terribly traumatic experience, might also indicate to a young woman that "regardless of her other attributes, she can serve as a sexual partner should she wish to," thus establishing prostitution as a possible option for an occupation.[33] Therefore, though seduction and entrapment most likely did not directly create as many prostitutes as contemporary literature would suggest, the seduction experience and the response of others to that experience may have led some women to reevaluate their opportunities and limitations in life, thereby influencing decisions to become prostitutes.

Another way in which women, as victims of circumstances, were said to be led into prostitution was through unfortunate home lives. Although the home as a secure respite from the harsh world was idealized in the nineteenth century, and reformers' reports often described in detail longings they were certain prostitutes felt for the lost warmth and love of their families and homes, most reformers also realized that many prostitutes came from domestic situations that were unhappy, strife-ridden, and oppressive to the degree that prostitution seemed a favorable alternative. Often such homes had a single parent or perhaps no parent at all. Among Sanger's interviewees, more than 67 percent had lost their fathers, and almost 62 percent had lost their mothers.[34] Among New York City girls admitted to the Refuge for suspected prostitution, at least 50 percent had lost one or both parents, usually the father, and for the year 1830, the figure was 69 percent. Parental death obviously forced a change in the family structure, and it commonly entailed the loss of the major economic provider, with frequent family impoverishment and a need for girls to go to work at a very young age, often in service, where they were sent away from family and home. As a result, many suffered from loneliness and a lack of love and affection. Mary Jane Box, profiled in Chapter 2, was sent out to service at age seven and spent the next few years at approximately fifty different places of employment, never staying more than a few months at any one. Box was "led astray" at age thirteen, about the time her widowed mother died. Not surprisingly, the young orphaned teenager stated that "it was her passion for company that led her to do as she did, and not the love of money."[35]

Many prostitutes told of abusive and cruel treatment by parents or spouses. Over 8 percent, or 164, of Sanger's interviewees said they became prostitutes because of "ill-treatment of parents, relatives, or husbands." In response to a question about marital status, 103 said they had separated from their husbands because of "ill-usage"; it is not known if these 103 considered the abuse to be *the* reason they entered prosti-tution and are included in the 164 who gave ill-treatment as the major cause. Several Refuge girls also told of physical abuse by parents. Mary Power, whose family ran a boarding house, said her parents repeatedly accused her of sleeping with young male boarders and would beat her for it, until she finally decided she could take it no longer and ran away from home. Her plan was to go to New Orleans to earn high wages through what Refuge officials described as a "bad life."[36]

Other prostitutes said they had suffered unhappy home lives because their parents were alcoholic. In Sanger's study, 30 percent said their fathers drank intemperately, and 17 percent said their mothers did.

Refuge records also show alcoholism in many of the young prostitutes' families, with the father's intemperance mentioned twice as often as the mother's.[37]

Another abuse influencing some young women to enter prostitution was described by a Refuge officer as "what the thickest darkness ought always to cover," incest.[38] Mary Ann Ray, who was brought to the House of Refuge because she had been "broadly on the town," was first seduced by her father's brother, and even her father had tried to seduce her. Phebe Huson said her first sexual experience was with her brother when she was between twelve and thirteen.[39]

"Respectable" upbringings also appeared to drive some women to prostitution because their home lives seemed too restrictive. As a general rule, young girls in the nineteenth century were not allowed much independence. Many thought it was dangerous for a young female to travel alone on omnibuses, steamships, or other public transportation, or to be without supervision at public amusements, picnics, or on the streets at night since these were the places it was believed women would be "led astray" or even molested. Although this protectiveness may have reflected a middle-class apprehension, the general acceptance or tolerance of this attitude can be seen in the fact that, under the law, any woman alone on New York City streets at night could be arrested as a prostitute.[40] There were legitimate reasons for parental curbs on personal freedom, but many adolescent girls and single women resented the restrictions. Refuge records indicate generational problems also existed over issues such as parental discipline, strict moral values, and requirements that young working women contribute all or most of their income to the family coffers. Such domestic conflict led some to leave home and support themselves by becoming prostitutes.[41]

A final incentive to leave home and enter prostitution was that the life of a prostitute offered the opportunity to meet new people outside one's family or neighborhood. Some may have hoped that a brief period in prostitution would increase their chances of attracting a husband, either through contacts or savings, which could mean economic security or even upward social mobility.

Although nineteenth-century reformers believed that men were largely responsible for the recruitment or "downfall" of most prostitutes, they recognized that women often had some responsibility also. For the most part this was said to be the work of women who were already in the profession who had lost all decency and morality. William Sanger believed prostitutes persuaded others to enter the profession because of "a fiendish desire to reduce the virtuous of their own sex to a similar degradation with themselves."[42] Although there is a lack of evidence to support this theory of devious motivation, there is evidence that prostitutes did recruit others. Much to the dismay of reformers, prostitutes usually did not seek out strangers, but rather recruited those closest to them—their daughters, sisters, or friends. Such women appear to have been motivated not by desire for vengeance, as Sanger would have it, but by their sense of the advantages of their trade.

House of Refuge records list several cases of mothers practicing prostitution with their daughters. One such case was that of Charlotte Willis, who was reported to have become a common bawd after leaving the Refuge. Charlotte's father, who ran a boarding house, tried to have her readmitted to the Refuge but was refused. Later the Refuge recorded that Charlotte's "mother has left her husband, took up with another man, keeps a bad house, and the above daughter is one of her sluts." Susan Brown employed two of her daughters in her establishment at Corlears Hook, and Bridget Mangren's two daughters were prostitutes in her brothel on Worth Street. House of Refuge records also document many cases of sisters working together in prostitution. Julia Decker and her older married sister were arrested by the New York police for being common prostitutes. According to the Refuge journal, the sister had left her "lazy" husband and returned to her former prostitution profession in partnership with Julia. After their arrest, the police released the sister, but Julia, a minor, was committed to the Refuge. In another example of sibling recruitment, the *Advocate of Moral Reform* reported that a prostitute enticed her sister to join her in New York by sending her a silk dress with a note telling her of the good wages she could make there through prostitution.[43]

Friends, probably more than relatives, were responsible for introducing young girls to "the sporting life." Mary O'Grady was sent to the Refuge by her father for staying a week in a brothel. O'Grady said she had gone there to stay with a friend who had once boarded in her home. She claimed she "did not stay with men" while at the house, but several years later, after being released from the Refuge, she was reported to be a "girl of the town doing as bad as she knows how."[44] Frances Sage and

Delilah Harvey were also friends who entered prostitution together. According to a rambling account in Refuge records, Frances's

> first difficulties arose from being induced to attend the chatham Theatre by other girls, by that means she got acquainted with the play actors, who gave her and other young things a general pass, and the actors would stay with them. therefore she increased in ludeness. took board in church st. and also in white st and 3 avenue. was taken up as a girl of the town, and sent here accordingly, I learn from Delilah Harvey . . . that Frances was the first one that caused her to stay with a man.[45]

Another young woman, Sarah Denny, was brought to the police station by the madam of a Church Street brothel who had tried unsuccessfully to persuade young Denny to return home. Denny told police she had been well-treated and happy at home but had received a letter from a friend who described in glowing colors the pleasures and enjoyment of her life of prostitution, so she had come to New York to join her friend in her exciting life.[46]

Sanger's study indicated that seventy-one women, or 3.5 percent, had entered prostitution because they were "persuaded by prostitutes," and an additional eighty-four, over 4 percent, were influenced by "bad company," which probably meant companions who were prostitutes, who frequented places prostitutes might be found, or who observed a more relaxed moral code of conduct. The designation of "bad" companions most likely reflects a value judgment by the interviewers, not the interviewees, and probably represented a woman's close associates or those she considered her friends. Still, a combined total of 7.5 percent in Sanger's study who attributed the cause of their prostitution to the influence of companions or others in the profession does not represent a large percentage of prostitutes. As a secondary cause of entering prostitution, however, the influence of friends and companions probably played a much larger role than Sanger's statistics indicate. If a woman had left home, was abandoned, or was economically destitute and was deciding what to do with her life, the example or encouragement of a prostitute friend or acquaintance might help make prostitution appear to be the best or easiest option. House of Refuge records support this assumption. Intake officers at the Refuge do not appear to have asked directly what caused a girl to begin prostitution, but the "influence" of friends and associates said to be of questionable character was listed as a contributing factor in the prostitution or suspected prostitution of a majority of the cases of New York City girls who entered the Refuge.[47] Current sociological research also supports these findings. Studies indicate that when a woman is under economic stress and has experienced a change in her life (death of a key family member, divorce, a move, leaving home, a new job), and when this change results in her isolation, the disruption of old relationships, and the loss of her network of social support, then contact with persons in the prostitution business may take on a special significance. If the woman is in a position to observe the life of prostitution, she may see "that prostitutes earn large sums of money, that the occupation is not as dismal and degrading as she may have thought, and that the work provides opportunities for excitement, status, friendship, and perhaps even love."[48]

In cases where seduction, entrapment, unhappy home life, or associates were given as causes of a woman's prostitution, nineteenth-century records usually portray the woman as a victim whose "fall from virtue" was the result of the actions or influence of others. Reformers and investigators preferred and doubtless to a degree encouraged such a portrayal because then the woman's role in the decision to become a prostitute, or the fact that she exercised some element of choice, was obscured. More notable, however, are those cases in which women implied or expressed that their decisions were the result of a willingness to become prostitutes or of their enjoyment of the lifestyle of prostitution, remarks that reformers and commentators tended to neglect. Since such a woman was supposedly a victim, and since a female's sexuality was usually denied, commentators provide no analysis of the fact that a woman may have viewed her decision as a positive one. Some women in the Sanger study expressed their choice positively as a wish to be free from limitations. Nine percent of the women said they entered the profession because of "drink and the desire to drink," 6 percent wanted an "easy life," and 1.5 percent said they were "too idle to work." Prostitution obviously appeared to offer the hours, resources, and opportunities for one better to enjoy life as one wished, and it did not require as much hard work as conventional professions. It was not work at all in the usual sense.[49]

A much larger number, slightly under 26 percent, listed "inclination" as their reason for choosing prostitution. These women may have given this answer because they thought the interviewers believed them to be "depraved," or the comment may have reflected a prostitute's self image, her notion that she chose an occupation appropriate to her character or nature. It also may have reflected her belief that the profession was one in which she could do well, or that it was one she preferred to the others available. Sanger observed that the response also might mean "a voluntary resort to prostitution in order to gratify the sexual passions" but dismissed this interpretation as implying an "innate depravity, a want of true womanly feeling, which is actually incredible."[50]

The single cause of prostitution that probably influenced more nineteenth-century women than any other was economics. For most commentators, economic influences were interpreted in negative terms—women were forced into prostitution because of destitution and economic need. Sanger's study reinforced this point in its conclusion that over 26 percent of New York's prostitutes at mid-century were in the profession because of "destitution." Yet Sanger's and others' descriptions of many prostitutes' lives as well as information in prostitutes' tax records indicate that there was another side to economic causation. Prostitution had very positive rewards for some women. Many chose the occupation because it offered a better life—a more comfortable lifestyle and the means to accumulate savings. Though not all of the women who sought these benefits in prostitution gained them, the possibility of significant economic rewards served as a strong incentive in pulling women into the profession.

Both the positive and negative economic reasons for choosing prostitution become clearer when one considers the limited occupational opportunities and wages available to nineteenth-century women. Nineteenth-century writer Virginia Penny, in *How Women Can Make Money*, described wages and conditions in traditional female occupations in New York City in the period 1859 to 1861. Penny noted that most of the jobs open to women were over-filled. She argued this was partly because 100,000 New York men were in pursuits well-adapted to women, jobs such as printing and manufacturing. She also noted that, as a rule, a man earned two to three times the salary a woman might earn for the same job. Although Penny described wages and conditions in over five hundred occupations, most women were employed in a small number of skilled and unskilled trades, notably domestic service and sewing, that had been practiced by working females for several decades. These same limited women's occupations and their inadequate pay had been described by Matthew Carey in the 1830s in *Plea for the Poor*, and little had changed for working women in the three decades between Carey's and Penny's publications. In some trades, such as shirt-making, women's wages had actually declined in this period.[51]

The two mid-nineteenth-century occupations engaging most New York City laboring women were the sewing trades and domestic service, occupations from which women frequently moved into prostitution. Approximately 49 percent of the prostitutes interviewed by Sanger had been employed as domestic laborers before becoming prostitutes, and another 21 percent had been in the sewing trades. Leaving aside the 25 percent of the interviewees who either had lived at home or had not been employed at all prior to becoming prostitutes, 70 percent of all prostitutes with previous labor-force experience had worked in these two trades.[52] The conditions and wages in needlework and domestic service in the period 1830 through 1870 make clear why women found it so difficult to support themselves in both trades, and why prostitution offered comparatively a good livelihood.

A chronically depressed trade, needlework was oversupplied with semi-skilled women and girls who were forced to accept subsistence or less than subsistence wages. Increasing immigration after 1840, and the transition from hand to machine work after the patent of the sewing machine in 1846, exacerbated the problem of labor oversupply in the sewing trades. Furthermore, women in needlework, like other laborers, had to contend with cycles of depression and periodic unemployment, while inflation reduced the value of their already inadequate wages.[53]

In the 1830s, for example, Carey reported that seamstresses were paid from 6 cents to 12-1/2 cents per shirt; depending on her skill, a shirt-maker could produce about six to nine shirts per week, thus earning 36 cents to $1.12 per week. Writers for the next two decades continued to quote the payment for shirts at 6 cents to 10 cents each, with the best seamstresses making two, or perhaps three shirts per day if they worked from sunrise to midnight. Some women working in overcrowded slum tenements were said to be earning as little as 4 cents a shirt.[54] By the time Penny wrote in the 1860s, women were still earning approximately 6 cents per shirt and, on the average, were making from 75 cents to $1.08 per week. After the Civil War wages dropped even lower. If a woman had the opportunity to make linen pleated shirts, she might work fifteen to eighteen hours a day for two days in order to make one shirt, but she would get 50 cents for the finer product and consequently could earn as much as $1.50 per week.[55]

Poor wages were not the only source of hardship for shirtmakers. Their long hours left them with little or no free time, and they frequently suffered from poor health and distorted posture as a result of sewing for hour after hour with neck and arms bent forward. Some seamstresses, such as Rosina Townsend, suffered from eyesight problems probably caused by sewing all day and into the night with poor lighting. Fraud and abuse were common; for example, employers might ask two hundred women to make free shirts to demonstrate their skills and then hire only twelve women from the group. Some employers would require a deposit for materials taken home, from which they would then deduct a sum when the shirt was returned, claiming some fault in the work.[56] And sometimes seamstresses were required to give sexual favors in order to keep their jobs.

Shirtmaking was among the worst paid of the needle trades, but the slightly higher wages available for other kinds of sewing were often offset by long periods of seasonal unemployment. Living conditions for all types of seamstresses were usually miserable. Wages did not keep up with rising food prices and rents, forcing many sewing women into confined and depressing quarters, as noted by the *New York Tribune* in 1845:

These women generally "keep house"—that is, they rent a single room, or perhaps two small rooms, in the upper story of some poor, ill-constructed, unventilated house in a filthy street, constantly kept so by the absence of back yards and the neglect of the street inspector. . . . In these rooms all the processes of cooking, eating, sleeping, washing, working, and living are indiscriminately performed.[57]

Although reportedly many laboring women felt needlework was more respectable than domestic service, household service did not require as much training and thus was a type of employment open to more women. In the 1850s, in one of the poorest areas of New York, the sixth ward, 45 percent of the women under thirty were employed in domestic and personal services. They were usually required to work as much as fifteen hours a day, seven days a week, sleeping in cramped quarters and eating leftover food from the family table. Domestic wages generally were from

$1 to $2 a week, with room and board provided. Many servants complained of long hours, lack of free time, and insulting attitudes on the part of employers' families.[58] A woman with dependent children or others to care for could not live out in domestic service, though she might do housework by the day, earning $3 to $6 a week, virtually all of which went for lodging and food.[59]

Jobs in domestic service were not always easy to get. Because of the oversupply of women laborers, especially after the heavy Irish and German immigration began in the 1840s, there were always more women seeking domestic positions than there were jobs available, and replacement servants were readily available if a woman displeased her employer in any way. As early as 1846, before the influx of the largest groups of immigrants, the *New York Tribune* reported that at least one thousand women were looking unsuccessfully for employment in household service. By the 1850s, it was estimated that approximately one-fourth of the domestic servants in New York City were constantly out of work.[60]

Even at their best, positions in the sewing trade and domestic service did not provide much financial support or security for a woman. For the average worker, these employments probably did not pay enough for a woman to maintain herself, much less children or dependent adults. Sanger found that 65 percent of the women who had worked before becoming prostitutes had earned between $1 and $2 per week, and 75 percent of those employed had received less than $3 per week.[61]

Such wages were inadequate to support a family. Matthew Carey calculated the annual expenses faced by a woman with two children:[62]

Rent (50¢ per week)	$26.00
Clothing/shoes for self and children	20.00
Fire, candles, soap (6¢ per day)	21.90
Food, drink (6¢ per day per person)	65.70
Total	$133.60

Working five days a week, for 18-3/4 cents per day, such a woman would earn $48.94 for the year, resulting in a yearly deficit of $84.66, which had to come from some other source. If the woman had a working husband, Carey calculated, and if expenses were increased only slightly to support a family of four, the husband would need to be earning approximately twice what his wife was earning, if she continued to be employed, and three times the amount of her salary if she was not.[63]

Carey apparently was calculating expenses for a very poor family living at a minimum subsistence level. The amount he estimated necessary for a person's daily food supply in the late 1830s was 6 cents, and by the 1850s the New York Association for Improving the Condition of the Poor was estimating a necessary minimum of 10 cents a day. Carey also calculated rent at a low 50 cents per week. Other sources from 1830 to 1870 indicate rents were usually higher. Two poor women in 1834 were quoted in the New York *Sun* as saying they would do almost anything to earn enough to pay their weekly board of $3. (In contrast, Carey estimated an individual needed 92 cents a week for room and board—42 cents for food and 50 cents for rent.) The *New York Tribune* reported in 1845 that working women usually had to pay at least $1.50 a week for poor accommodations they shared with others, but that some of the filthiest and worst boarding houses charged as little as $1 per week. In the late 1850s a general survey of New York showed that working women paid $1.50 to $3.50 for room and board with washing occasionally provided, but fuel was never included for that sum. Furthermore, the poor often had to pay more for expenses such as fuel because they purchased such necessities by the item instead of in bulk.[64]

Because most laboring women could not hope to command as high a salary as that needed for a family to live "moderately," a woman could only hope she would continue to be completely or partially supported by a parent, spouse, or relative. Otherwise, she would have to seek supplementary income elsewhere. Reformers and charities stressed that they offered assistance and refuge to prevent women from feeling they had no choice but prostitution, but there were limits on this type of help. Rescue homes often would not take a woman if she was pregnant, had a child, was diseased, or seemed "unsuitable," regardless of her great need. Even if a woman met the specifications for admission to the home, strict requirements, daily regimen, and religious training may have made the asylum appear to be more of a punishment than temporary prostitution would be. Furthermore, available public and private charities were not abundant. In 1837, after much publicity concerning the economic plight of the estimated 20,000 poor seamstresses and tailoresses in New York, a benefit evening was held at Hannington's Diorama to raise funds to assist poor needlewomen to keep them from starving or turning to prostitution. The benefit received much publicity in the daily press, yet the total amount raised for the cause was only $70.65, a sum a single seamstress easily could have earned by prostitution in a few weeks. More established forms of temporary aid were available to the needy through societies such as the New York Association for Improving the Condition of the Poor. In the 1850s, the Association estimated that it gave temporary aid to 30 percent of the sewing women of the city. Nevertheless, the AICP's officers calculated there were 195,000 men, women, and children in absolute want in New York City and stated that it would take at least 10 cents a day to supply each with the necessary food. In its role as the disbursing agent of city relief funds appropriated by the Common Council, the AICP expended a total sum of $95,018.47 for the year November 1, 1854, through November 1, 1855, but this amount was $41,500 less than they estimated was required to feed those in absolute need for only one week.[65] Certainly women had reason for doubting that public benevolence could alleviate their destitution.

Thus, when most jobs meant long, hard hours at little pay, when no jobs were available for a woman to fill, or when no friends, relatives, or benevolent groups supplemented inadequate funds, prostitution may have seemed both the easiest and most promising option available. There was always a market for prostitution, and the profession seemed to be convenient because a woman did not have to leave her home and children for long periods of time. It also meant less time on the job than did working in a factory, as a seamstress, or as a domestic. Prostitution especially may have appeared to be an easy alternative or solution for a woman who was being sexually exploited in her job. Those who were expected to extend sexual favors to their employers simply to keep their employment with its meager wage may have decided they might as well be paid for something they were being forced to give away under abusive circumstances.[66]

Some of the women who entered prostitution for economic reasons found that their life situations did not improve—in fact, they sometimes became worse. Though nineteenth-century observers stressing socio-economic factors pointed to destitution as a *cause* of prostitution—the only economic alternative left for some women—observers stressing moralistic causes reversed the argument and claimed that destitution and utter debasement often were the *results* of a woman's choice of a life of prostitution—the dream of a better life gone afoul. Nineteenth-century sources contain vivid descriptions of extreme cases of prostitutes whose lives were in decline. In the dens and thoroughfares of the Water Street area, these prostitutes were said to have "rot[ted] to death . . . [f]oul, bloated with gin and disease, distorted with suffering and despair, the poor creatures do what they can to hasten their sure doom."[67] For women like these whose lives were tangled in a web of alcoholism, poverty, illness, and despair, or who were at the margin of existence, destitution and degradation may have been the results of prostitution— inevitable results according to moralists. Nonetheless, for women who, for whatever reason, found themselves in society's lowest stratum—both those already working as prostitutes and those contemplating the prac- tice—prostitution served as an opportunity, possibly the only way to earn enough for a daily living.

For a broader group of women with limited economic resources but a narrow range of occupational choices, however, the most compelling reason for choosing prostitution was that it was the most lucrative of the available alternatives. As one prostitute said her aunt once told her, "Every young girl is sitting on her fortune if she only knew it."[68] Little education was necessary for a woman to make comparisons between the income offered by the daily wage in any of the trades open to females and the price being paid for "going to bed" with a man a single time. True, lucrative was a relative term. For some women in low brothels or at the bottom levels of streetwalking, prostitution's wage may have been only a little more than they might earn in another trade. For others, however, it offered not only the opportunity for earning more on a daily or weekly basis but also the possibility of accumulating some money for the future. Either way, a woman's choice of the occupation was often an economically sound decision.

Prostitutes were, of course, paid variously for their services, from those who worked in the finest parlor houses in better neighborhoods to streetwalkers in the poorer wards of the city. Payment of less than $1, however, appears to have been considered low for a New York prosti- tute's services. Even reformers who worked at the House of Refuge seem to have had some idea of what was a "disgracefully" low price to be paid in the trade. Giving the case history of one of the eighteen-year-old inmates at the Refuge, the intake officer commented that the young woman had been working as a strumpet "and I judge as low a thing of the kind as we ever had—for she would sell herself for a shilling if she could get no more."[69]

Other sources indicate that a woman could generally count on earning quite a bit more than a "shilling" per customer. In calculating the weekly income in a first-class brothel, Sanger estimated that each prostitute probably entertained at least two customers an evening and seldom took in less than $50 a week, suggesting a charge of several dollars per customer. In calculating the average weekly income of all the New York public prostitutes of all classes, Sanger used a figure of $10 per week.[70] In 1847, another source reported that a man could expect his purse to be $5 to $10 lighter if he spent the night in a brothel, and a decade earlier, Mariah Hubbard told Refuge officers that, while practicing prostitution in a Franklin Street brothel, she had earned from $3 to $10 per customer. One of Helen Jewett's patrons once chastised her that she "might be anyone's for $5," an indication that this was probably less than the going rate at her establishment.[71] By the 1870s, sources reported that prostitutes could earn $20 a week in the less fashionable houses, $30 to $40 in middle-class houses, and $150 a week in the finest houses.[72]

A woman who used prostitution to supplement her income from another profession, who practiced it occasionally when other work was not available, or who did not wish to have to share income with a brothel's management, might operate her business out of her own room or might utilize an assignation house. In 1835 Rachael Near said she was being "kept" by a doctor who visited her two times a week and paid her $5 to $7 a night; with additional customers on alternate nights, she sometimes was able to earn $40 to $45 per week.[73] Other women who used assignation houses and private rooms said they earned from $1 to $5 each time they entertained a customer. Sarah Williams, a black prostitute, said she charged all customers a flat fee of $2 and always had plenty of money.[74]

Although these wages indicate that prostitutes could earn more per week than could other laboring women, and dramatically more than unskilled laborers, a prostitute's expenses were higher. Rents in both brothels and assignation boarding houses were more than in regular boarding establishments, though a part-time or independent prostitute might operate out of quarters no different from, or more expensive than, those used by laboring women. Information in newspapers and reformers' records indicates that most prostitutes in the 1830s were paying between $3 and $10 a week for board. The New York Magdalen Society reported that prostitutes in what they ranked as fourth-class houses paid $3 weekly in rent, third-class houses charged $7, second-class houses, $10, and first-class houses, $15 a week.[75] In the 1860s the more established of the lower-class houses were said to be charging $10 a week, middle-class houses $20 to $25 per week, and the higher-class houses $40 to $50 weekly. In addition to these rental costs, prostitutes living in brothels usually had to pay the madam or management a fee for each visitor they entertained.[76]

Because personal attractiveness was an asset in the business, most prostitutes spent more on clothing than did the average woman. Many newspaper accounts of professional prostitutes describe them as "attractively dressed in the latest fashion," although other prostitutes, especially in the cheaper brothels and rougher neighborhoods, were said to look tawdry and cheap. Expenditures for one's appearance included not only clothing but jewelry, perfumes, and hair dressing. Sanger reported that prostitutes in the higher-class brothels were visited daily by hair dressers, a service that cost them $2 to $3 per week.[77] Although a prostitute might have to be prudent in her expenditures on clothing and personal adornment in order to be able to put money aside, her chances of earning more than expenses were greater in prostitution than in alternate work.

Prostitution's high level of business expenses attests to both ample income and a reasonably comfortable standard of living for many women. Even though in most cases those who achieved significant economic and material comfort were either managers or residents of established houses, their lifestyle was visible to surrounding community residents, and their working conditions must have appealed to other women. Many prostitutes began their day at noon and worked from approximately six o'clock until an hour or two after midnight. In brothels, meals and housecleaning were provided, and women often had assistance with dressing and hair arranging. Although laboring women had little leisure time, prostitutes considered being seen at the theater or strolling in the afternoon on Broadway as public exposure helpful in their business as well as enjoyable entertainment. A prostitute's clothing, whether flashy or fashionable, was better than that of other laboring women, and brothels, attractively or ostentatiously furnished, were more comfortable than the crowded attic rooms and damp cellars that housed the city's poorest workers, male and female.[78] Even the less established prostitutes who worked independently or occasionally may have been able to earn just enough to have some extra necessities and a modicum of free time not available to those females who were trapped in the seemingly unceasing, low-paying labors practiced by most working women.

It is true there were dangers in prostitution for all its practitioners: possible arrest, violence, undesirable company, and disease. Those women who sank to the bottom levels of prostitution usually had these dangers compounded by economic insecurity, additional health problems, discrimination because they were poor, and, thus, limited prospects for improving their lives. But poor women not in prostitution also faced dangers, problems, and limited possibilities in their jobs that may have seemed equal to, or even worse than, those of the least fortunate prostitutes. Laboring women who worked long hours under poor conditions seldom could afford a nutritious diet or medical care, and hence suffered from poor health. Job security was at the whim of an employer, and young working girls had little recourse in the face of employer abuse or cruelty but to run away. In the event of theft at one's place of employment, the burden of proof usually lay on the employee. Consequently, when a poor woman compared the relative wages, hours, conditions, and dangers, prostitution compared very favorably with other professions available to women. More importantly, prostitution offered prospects for improving or enhancing one's economic situation in several ways, including discretionary income above necessary expenses, a long-term higher level of economic comfort, and an opportunity to accumulate savings for the future.

Nineteenth-century reformers often claimed that women went into prostitution in order to have extra funds, or "pin money," to indulge their "love of dress," "love of finery," or "desire to go to immoral places such as the theater." Even though critics may have viewed such desires as moral weaknesses, working women, like the rest of society, commonly wanted to be able to have more goods, better living conditions, and more money to spend on entertainment and themselves. By practicing occasional prostitution in addition to another job, a daughter could make extra cash that could be spent on herself, while her regular wages would continue to help support her parental family.[79]

Prostitution also offered some hope for economic and social mobility and a long-term higher level of economic comfort. Some women hoped to achieve this by meeting better "prospects" for a husband. Whatever the marital disadvantages of prostitution, its practitioners, unlike most other working women, did meet men on the job, and often prostitutes married. Also, some prostitutes raised their standard of living in the trade or even achieved notable economic mobility. If a woman were successful in the profession, her income could rise sharply, and she might accumulate enough capital to set herself up in business, either where she had lived or in a different location with a new identity. Most prostitutes, of course, did not fare so well, but it was one of the few jobs that offered women some possibility of sharing in a "rags to riches" story, or its more reasonable "impoverished to comfortable" variant.

Prostitution also offered some hope for future savings. Insurance against old age or provision for future security was beyond the means of most working people in the nineteenth century. A factory worker or a domestic servant might worry just as much as a prostitute about her physical decline as she aged. In each case, aging could mean a woman would become less "efficient" at what she was doing, leading to a loss of income. But compared to other working women, prostitutes had a greater opportunity to accumulate capital and assets against these threats, and at an earlier age.

Certainly, not all prostitutes achieved one or more of these benefits. Those who made a long-term career of prostitution were most likely to reap its greatest rewards. Nevertheless, the achievement of a small temporary benefit as well as the hope for improved long-term prospects were both encompassed in the positive pull or "dream" that brought women into prostitution on an occasional or a lifetime basis.

Achieving the Dream

Some women grew gray in prostitution. Usually those who chose the profession as a lifelong career became madams of brothels or worked as managers of assignation houses or prostitution boarding-houses. Although successful career prostitutes constituted a small pro-

8. SCENE IN A BROTHEL.   Although life in a brothel was publicly portrayed in terms of debauchery and sin, many women perceived it as promising greater independence, escape from poverty, and the possibility of marriage and upward mobility. (Courtesy of the New-York Historical Society, New York City)

portion of the number of women who practiced prostitution at some period in their lives, the achievements of these successful prostitutes pointed out the possibilities that inspired others to work in the field.

Most often, a woman became a madam or prostitution boarding-house keeper after working as a prostitute, but there were some who entered the profession by discovering that renting a room to a woman

or couple for sex might be more profitable than other rental arrangements. Whether a woman operated discreetly as an assignation-house
keeper, or notoriously as a brothel madam, her primary goal was to run
a profitable business and earn a good living. In spite of certain impediments, this was a realizable goal.

It is difficult to determine what proportion of prostitutes stayed in the
profession on a long-term basis. Contemporaries mistook many prostitutes and managers of brothels for ordinary boarders or boardinghouse
keepers. J. R. McDowall complained that brothels were able to exist in
respectable neighborhoods "under the mask of boardinghouses."[80] Another source, describing nineteenth-century New York boardinghouses,
stated:

It may be safely asserted that the boarding-houses into which improper characters do not sometimes find their way are very few. . . . If the adventuress
wishes to maintain the guise of respectability, she must have a respectable
home, and this the boarding-house affords her. One is struck with the great
number of handsome young widows who are to be found in these establishments. Sometimes they do not assume the character of a widow, but claim to
be the wives of men absent in the distant Territories, or in Europe. . . . The
majority of these women are adventuresses, and they make their living in a way
they do not care to have known. They conduct themselves with utmost outward
propriety in the house, and disarm even the suspicious landlady by their ladylike
deportment. They are ripe for an intrigue with any man in the house, . . . their
object is simply to make money.[81]

A prostitute might carry out her charade of widow or forsaken wife in
a female boardinghouse as well as in a mixed boardinghouse. Furthermore, not only might a respectable boardinghouse keeper rent one or
several rooms to prostitutes, but a prostitute, looking for a means to
support herself on a long-term basis, might decide that renting rooms
to other prostitutes was an easy and profitable way to retire from active
prostitution. Unless an establishment became notorious or earned the
reputation of being an undesirable place, the position of boardinghouse
keeper allowed a woman to appear reputable and merge with respectable
society. In mid-century New York City directories, known prostitutes
often are listed simply as boardinghouse keepers, though other sources
make it possible to identify a sample of prostitutes large enough to
provide some indication of how they managed their economic lives.[82]

In contrast to later periods, management of the prostitution business in the early and mid-nineteenth century was very much dominated by women. Women owned or managed the businesses as madams or prostitution boardinghouse keepers, and the prostitute employees generally worked directly for these female managers without the interference or exploitation of third parties or middlemen. Nineteenth-century real estate records indicate that most madams did not own their own brothel properties but rented the buildings from landlords, both male and female. These landlords were able to exact high rentals from the madams, and, even though periodically there was a public outcry that the landlords were a part of the system, as guilty of immorality and illegality as the prostitutes themselves, there is no evidence that landlords commonly had any direct share in the actual profits of the businesses.

Records show that some men owned or managed brothels, often in husband-wife operations or as part of male-owned saloons or bars.[83] The pimp system, however, did not become a major part of New York City's prostitution business until the late nineteenth century. References are made in early nineteenth-century sources to prostitutes' "lovers," who were lavished with affection and gifts and were even supported by prostitutes, but these lovers do not appear to have played a brokering role or to have controlled prostitutes' incomes the way pimps later did.[84] On the contrary, mid-nineteenth-century prostitutes appear to have been brokers of their own sexual goods in an open marketplace, whether they operated in a casual manner, soliciting on their own while working out of private rooms, or worked in a more structured arrangement as brothel employees. Even when employed in the organized brothel arrangement, prostitutes appear to have had some control over their employment and were able to move from one brothel to another with much freedom.

In spite of this overall freedom of operation, a madam could exercise a large amount of control over her brothel inmates through financial indebtedness while increasing her own profits. A madam, like a mistress of an assignation house, usually charged high rents for rooms, and madams often would provide clothing or other in-house services to prostitutes at prices far above going rates. The madam also levied a fee for each customer a prostitute entertained. Beyond what the prostitutes paid, a madam was able to further increase her income by selling liquor to guests at two or three times its cost to her. Moreover, some women owned or managed more than one brothel at a time, and at least one, as a side business, operated a printing press for publishing pornographic literature.[85]

Clearly, one reason many women spent most of their working lives in the prostitution business was that it was profitable. Evidence of its potential for profitability is found in nineteenth-century New York City tax records, which make it possible to compare the assets of many prostitutes with those of other women living in similar neighborhoods. Such comparison confirms that women could improve their overall economic situations by being in prostitution.

Until 1859, residents of New York City were taxed on their personal property as well as their real estate, though ward ledger books indicate that a very small percentage of New York's population owned taxable personal property—less than 3 percent in most of the residential/small business wards, and approximately two to three times that number in commercial or wealthier wards. Although women comprised approximately fifty per cent of New York City's population between 1830 and 1860, married women's assets and wages were legally the property of their husbands, and thus the great majority of property holders at the time were men. Even though this legal discrimination distorts the actual economic contribution and position of nineteenth-century women, it remains possible to identify from tax records the property of single and widowed females, thereby evaluating the amount of assets that could be accumulated by non-married women who were providing for themselves or their families.[86]

During the first half of the nineteenth century, New York City's prostitutes lived and practiced their trade in all wards of the city. There were no segregated prostitution areas, or red-light districts, but the fifth, sixth, and eighth wards, all predominantly residential, were described by contemporaries as neighborhoods marked by the city's most visible prostitution activity. All three were situated along Broadway, New York's major commercial thoroughfare, with small businesses fanning out from this artery to streets on either side. Much of the prostitution reputation of the sixth ward rested on the fact that it was the location of the Five Points, a small area well known for its streetwalkers, gamblers, drunkards, and criminal element. The activities of these groups around the Five Points seemed to overshadow the fact that the sixth ward was also the home of many lower-middle-class and laboring persons, especially immigrants, who were family oriented, hard-working, and respectable.[87] The sixth, like other lower Manhattan wards, had suffered a socioeconomic decline in the first few decades of the century as the location of the more fashionable neighborhoods followed the population growth in newer wards to the north. In line with this trend, many sixth-ward brothel owners also began moving northward in the late 1830s into wards five and eight, leaving prostitution in the sixth ward to the streetwalkers and the rougher element of the Five Points. Although not as notorious as the sixth ward's Five Points, wards five and eight became known as the main centers of organized brothel activity from the 1830s to 1860.[88]

City tax records illustrate the economic significance of prostitution when women's property ownership in these districts is compared with that in wards fourteen and seventeen, which were also residential-commercial districts where women might have owned small businesses, but not districts that were noted for prostitution establishments (see map).[89] Women comprised only a small proportion of personal-property owners in all these wards (less than 10 percent), but wards with the highest percentage of women on the personal-property rolls were also the wards with the highest concentrations of brothel-based prostitution businesses—wards five and eight (table 9). Some of the female personal-property owners in these wards must have been non-prostitutes, but at least 26 percent of women on the personal-property rolls, and in some years as much as 60 percent, resided on the particular streets notorious as brothel locations (table 10). Based on tax, census, and brothel directory data from the early 1850s, it is possible to identify 40 percent of the female property-owners in ward five and 58 percent of those in ward eight as known prostitutes. Some of these prostitutes held real estate as well as personal property, and their holdings demonstrate the opportunities presented by their profession—and recognized by the general public at the time—for significant accumulation of wealth.[90]

It seems to have been generally believed among contemporaries that many nineteenth-century New York prostitutes had become very prosperous through their profession. Sanger stated that one prostitute was "positively affirmed to be worth over one hundred thousand dollars, . . . and many more are reputed to be rich."[91] Another former madam was said to be living in one of the Italian cities enjoying a large income from the lease of her New York brothel property. House and furniture were being rented to a new proprietor for $9,100 annually.

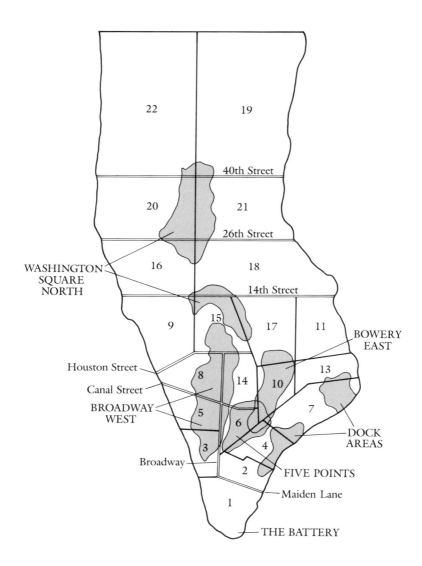

New York City wards and areas where prostitutes lived or congregated between 1830 and 1870.

Table 9 *Personal Property Profile of Women in Selected Wards, 1835–1855*

	Ward[a]	Women Who Owned Personal Property		Amount of Personal Property Owned by Women	
		No.	As % of all owners[b]	$	As % of total $
1835:	5	43	6	347,000	7.5
	8	13	4	89,000	4
	6	15	3.5	109,200	2.5
	14	17	6.5	102,500	4
1840:	5	29	6.5	183,800	11
	8	25	7.5	105,800	4.5
	6	19	4.5	48,000	2
	14	7	6	30,200	1.5
	17	6	3.5	68,500	6.5
1845:	5	30	6.5	101,500	6.5
	8	22	8	176,600	11
	6	31	4.5	41,400	4
	14	6	3	18,300	1
	17	11	6	22,200	1
1850:	5	43	7.5	166,500	6
	8	25	6.5	88,300	5
	6	18	5.5	37,100	3.5
	14	8	4	16,500	1
	17	23	4.5	131,000	5
1855:	5	26	6.5	146,600	6
	8	14	5.5	33,500	1.5
	6	4	2.5	105,000	6.5
	14	4	3.5	37,000	1.5
	17	26[c]	3.5	218,000	3

[a]Wards 5 and 8 were the areas with the best-known brothels. Wards 14 and 17 (the latter was created in 1837) had populations that were comparable to 5 and 8 socioeconomically, and they also had both small commercial and residential establishments. Ward 6 had a combination of brothels and shops.

[b]Percentages have been rounded to the nearest half.

[c]By 1855, Ward 17's population was two to two-and-a-half times that of the other wards studied.

SOURCES: Record of Assessments, 1835–1855; U.S. Census, 1830, 1840, 1850; New York, Census, 1835, 1845, 1855.

Table 10 *Female Personal Property Owners on Key Prostitution Streets,*
1830–1855

	1830	1835	1840	1845	1850	1855
Ward 5						
Church	9	0	3	9	7	6
Duane	4	2	3	4	4	4
Leonard	7	3	2	3	3	3
Chapel[a]	13	4	1	0	1	1
Thomas	4	2	0	0	—	—
Total	37	11	9	16	15	14
(as % of ward's female owners)	(57)	(26)	(31)	(53)	(35)	(54)
Ward 8						
Mercer	—	2	2	2	6	3
Greene	—	2	6	3	2	1
Broome	—	2	4	3	3	4
Wooster	—	0	0	1	4	—
Total		6	12	9	15	8
(as % of ward's female owners)		(46)	(48)	(41)	(60)	(56)

[a]Becomes West Broadway.

SOURCE: Record of Assessments, 1835–1855.

An 1860s source reported that one popular belle was earning $30,000 per annum, which, it was noted, was a "sum exceeding considerably the salary of the President of the United States."[92] Contemporaries may or may not have exaggerated prostitutes' incomes and their overall wealth, but they did not exaggerate the fact that prostitution was a means of accumulating property.

Patience Berger, who previously was mentioned as the guardian of Mary Anthony and madam of a house where Catherine Paris lived, spent over thirty years of her working life in the prostitution business. Before 1830 she ran a small prostitution establishment in ward five, but by 1840 she was able to purchase her own establishment at 132 Church, a property which initially was assessed at $8,000 and later at $8,500. She also accumulated personal property, valued at $6,500 by 1855.[93] Using historian Edward Pessen's formula for calculating the true value of nineteenth-century assessments, one can estimate her 1850 worth at approximately $50,000 and her equivalent worth in 1988 dollars at approximately $844,000.[94]

Mary Gallagher, a friend of Rosina Townsend's at the time of the Jewett murder, also worked in the prostitution business for over thirty years. She owned property in ward five at 122 Chapel from 1830 to the mid-1840s, and then at 90 Chapel from the 1840s through the 1860s. Gallagher's house was assessed at $3,000 in 1830 and by 1840 was listed at $6,000. She had personal property of $3,000 in 1830, and in 1843 the tax assessor penciled in by her name that she had "gone to Urope," so apparently she felt prosperous enough to take a continental tour.[95] She returned to her 122 Chapel house by 1846 and in 1848 purchased the 90 Chapel (West Broadway) property, assessed at $4,800. At this point, when Gallagher was fifty-four years old and perhaps no longer eager for the demands of running a house with fifteen prostitutes, she turned the management of her property over to Rebecca Weyman for about a decade, and then to Caroline Hathaway. During the time others were managing her brothel, Gallagher lived at establishments in both ward six and ward eight, possibly assignation houses or respectable boardinghouses. By 1863, however, the City Directory lists her back at her West Broadway address, which by the 1860s was assessed at $8,000.[96]

Rebecca Weyman, who managed Gallagher's property from 1848 to 1857, had owned 62 Mott Street in ward six from the late 1830s through most of the 1840s. In 1845, her Mott real estate was assessed at $4,700 and her personal property at $2,700. She may have taken over the management of Gallagher's property because it was at a more prestigious address, or she may have felt she would have more opportunity to advance in the new location. Right after the move, her personal property was listed at $5,000, but the next year an assessment challenge reduced it to $2,000, where it remained unchanged for nine years. According to the 1850 census, one of the prostitutes in Weyman's house was a thirty-year-old woman from Vermont, Caroline Hathaway, who followed Weyman in 1857 as manager of Gallagher's property. Her first year in charge (and the last year the city assessed personal property), Hathaway was assessed for $1,000 in personal property. She continued to manage 90 West Broadway for several years (table 11).[97]

Gallagher's tax history illustrates not only how women were able to accumulate property but also how their careers might progress in the

Table 11 *Gallagher Property*

	122 Chapel	90 Chapel	62 Mott	54 Duane	Ward 8
1830	Gallagher, **o**				
1835	Gallagher, **o**				
1840	Gallagher, **o**		Weyman, **o**		
1845	Gallagher, **o**	Gallagher, **o** Weyman, **m** Hathaway, **p**	Weyman, **o**		
1850				Gallagher, **r**	
1855		Gallagher, **o** Hathaway, **m**			Gallagher, **r**
1860		Gallagher, **o**			

o = owner; **m** = manager; **p** = prostitute; **r** = resident business over a period of years. It appears one could work up from prostitute to manager of an establishment, and eventually might take over ownership of the property. One's female friends and associates also appear to have been important in helping one move up, or laterally, in the profession.[98]

Another example of friendship networking, advancement, and property accumulation by prostitutes is found in the complicated relationships of Sarah Tuttle, Fanny White, Kate Hastings, Jenney Englis, and Clara Gordon. Throughout the 1820s and 1830s Sarah Tuttle is listed in city directories as a manager of various boarding houses. In 1843, while she was living at 136 Duane, her personal property was assessed at $3,000. By 1845 Tuttle was able to purchase a brothel at 50 Leonard, valued at $12,000, and was managing at that address. In 1848 Tuttle turned over the management of her house to Kate Hastings, a young prostitute who had been with her off and on for three years. Hastings had $5,000 in assessed personal property in 1848 and by 1850 was able to purchase Tuttle's house. About this same time, in the mid-1840s, Fanny White was living in a brothel across the street from Hastings. In 1851, White purchased brothel property at 119 Mercer and for the next two years managed the property, which was large and very well known. In 1853, a year in which White was assessed for $11,000 in real estate and $5,000 in personal property, she left for Europe with her lover, a married man named Dan Sickles, who had been appointed secretary to James Buchanan, minister to England. During White's absence, Kate Hastings moved to 119 Mercer and ran White's brothel. Management of her own brothel at 50 Leonard (which was assessed at $13,000 in 1853, $14,000 in 1855, and $15,000 in 1859) was turned over to Jenney Englis, who ran the establishment for a couple of years. (Englis had $1,000 in personal property during that time.) In 1855 Englis was followed as madam of 50 Leonard by Ellen Hamilton, who had been managing a brothel at 45 Mercer for several years, and when she took over Hastings' Leonard Street property, Hastings moved into Hamilton's old boardinghouse at 45 Mercer. (Each had personal property—Hamilton, $3,000, and Hastings, $2,000 assessed on Mercer in addition to her real estate on Leonard.) Fanny White, meanwhile, returned to New York from Europe in 1854, and resumed management of her own brothel. In 1856 she again turned it over to new management, and moved with two "lady boarders" to a residence on Twelfth Street. By this time it was said she owned several houses in the city, which were allegedly gifts from suitors, as well as a $5,000 annuity and a real-estate lot reportedly given to her by a male friend. Shortly after her move uptown, White married a lawyer, Edmon Blankman, and she gave up her life as a prostitute. When she died in 1860, she was said to own "three fine city mansions, besides other property. The value of her property was variously estimated from $50,000 to $100,000."[99] At the time of her death her Mercer street property was being managed by Clara Gordon, who had been a prostitute in Kate Hastings' house on Leonard Street in 1850 (table 12).[100]

Many other women in the prostitution business who could be cited from nineteenth-century tax records as possessing much property illustrate the fact that women in the profession for many years were able to accumulate assets. At least twenty-four known prostitutes were assessed for $5,000 or more of real and personal property during these years (table 13), amounts which, especially in light of the practice of assessing property at only a fraction of its actual value, were certainly large enough to establish them as wealthy citizens. When converted to 1988 dollars, their holdings amounted in many cases to one-half million dollars or more. And when their incomes and assets are compared with those of women working in other trades or occupations, prostitution appears to have been an economically sound choice of a profession, financially the best of the limited occupational alternatives available to nineteenth-century women.

The profits of prostitution did not, of course, make the choice of the profession a pleasant one for many. Some tolerated the opprobrium and unpleasant aspects of prostitution because they believed the profession was temporary, and indeed for the great majority it was apparently practiced for only a few years, chosen for the income it could provide or for the economic, social, or sexual freedom it seemed to offer. Also, contrary to what most nineteenth-century literature says, prostitution did not always mean a woman became a social outcast. There is evidence that in some working-class neighborhoods, the temporary or occasional practice of prostitution was viewed as an acceptable means of supplementing one's income when necessary.[101] Furthermore, some women probably felt as much pride in practicing prostitution as others did in working as menial laborers; it was not so different, after all, from most other women's trades in the sense that like them it was concerned

Table 12 *Tuttle, Hastings, and White Property*

	149 Anthony 94 Cross 136 Duane	50 Leonard	120 Church 55 Leonard 74 Greene	119 Mercer	45 Mercer	12th St.
1820	Tuttle, **m**					
1830						
1840	Tuttle, **m**					
1845		Tuttle, **o** Hastings, **p**				
		Tuttle, **o** Hastings, **m**	White, **m**	White, **o**		
1850		Hastings, **o** Gordon, **p**		White, **o** Hastings, **m**		
		Hastings, **o** Englis, **m**		White, **o**	Hamilton, **m**	
1855		Hastings, **o** Hamilton, **m**		White, **o** Gordon, **m**	Hastings, **m**	White, **o**
1860		Hastings, **o**				

o = owner; **m** = manager; **p** = prostitute

Table 13 *Selected Prostitutes with Known Real and Personal Property Assessed at $5,000 or More, 1830–1860*

Name	Sources	Highest Real Estate Property Assessment		Highest Personal Property Assessment	
		$	1988 equivalent[a]	$	1988 equivalent[a]
Elizabeth Pratt	1840s–60s	33,500	2,275,000	2,000	99,700
Jane McCord	1840s–70s	20,000	1,300,000	—	—
Adeline Miller	1820s–60	16,500	1,072,500	5,000	249,200
Kate Hastings	1840s–60	15,000	975,000	5,000	249,200
Francis O'Kille	1840s–50s	13,000	845,000	—	—
Nelle Thompson	1840s–60	12,500	812,500	4,000	199,300
Sarah Tuttle	1820s–40s	12,000	780,000	—	—
Julia Brown	1830s–70s	11,500	750,000	5,000	249,200
Elizabeth Lewis	1840s–60s	11,500	750,000	3,000	149,500
Fanny White	1840s–60	11,000	715,000	5,000	249,200
Jane Weston	1830s–50s	9,500	618,000	—	—
Patience Berger	1820s–50s	8,500	552,500	6,500	323,900
Mary Gallagher	1830s–60s	8,000	520,000	3,000	149,500
Margaret Brown	1840–60	7,500	487,500	—	—
Ann Leslie	1840s–70s	6,300	409,500	3,000	149,500
Rebecca Willis	1840s–50s	5,500	357,500	2,000	99,700
Kate Ridgley	1840s–50s	—	—	8,000	398,700
Abby Meade (Myers)	1820s–50s	—	—	5,000	249,200
Caroline Ingersoll	1840s–50s	—	—	5,000	249,200
Maria Adams	1840s–60	—	—	5,000	249,200
Rosina Townsend	1820s–30s	—	—	5,000	249,200
Mary Berry	1830–40s	—	—	5,000	249,200
Rebecca Weyman	1830s–50s	—	—	5,000	249,200
Rachel Porter	1830s–50s	—	—	5,000	249,200

[a]For method of calculation, see notes to Chapter 2.

SOURCES: Record of Assessments, 1820–1859; William H. Boyd, *Boyd's New York City Tax Book*, 1856 and 1857.

primarily with providing for the needs, or for the service and care, of others, especially men.

The reasons nineteenth-century New York women gave for becoming prostitutes were many and diverse. Clearly, economic motivations were often crucial and were, perhaps, particularly acute in the nineteenth century, when few or no well-paying jobs were available to women. In addition, some social or psychological motivation had economic roots. A woman might say she became a prostitute because she was seduced and abandoned, but, in effect, that meant she had to provide economically for herself and dependents through one of the limited occupational options available, of which prostitution appeared to be the best option. Economic causes or motivations should not be overemphasized, however. Many women comparable to prostitutes in their needs, problems, stresses, or desires did not become prostitutes, and some prostitutes came from comfortable or middle-class backgrounds, choosing the profession despite adequate resources to care for themselves. Cases differ. Economic motivation may well have been the predisposing factor in a majority of nineteenth-century cases, but it cannot be isolated from social influences or from the personal assessments a woman made of herself, her situation, and her goals.

PART TWO

The Public World
of the Prostitute

4

"Notorious Offenders"

Prostitutes and the Law

Around eight o'clock on the evening of Tuesday, March 27, 1855, Matilda Wade left her home at 107 Clark Street to walk a few blocks to her husband's place of business in Spring Street. As usual, the early evening's street activity livened as she approached the vicinity of Broadway. Mrs. Wade walked "quietly and peaceably" until she was stopped by a patrolman and told she was under arrest for being a vagrant and common prostitute. She then was taken along with nineteen other women to the eighth-ward station house, where she was booked. Mrs. Wade objected that she was not a prostitute and for years had lived at home and been supported by her husband. In spite of her protestations, she was not allowed to send for her husband, nor was she one of the fortunate five women who managed to obtain a release. Instead, she and fourteen other alleged prostitutes were locked in cells overnight.

The next morning the fifteen women, along with twenty-six others from ward fourteen, were paraded through the streets to the mayor's office, where "an expectant crowd awaited their arrival."[1] Led single file by police captains Turnbull and Kissner into the mayor's office, the forty-one women, whose ages ranged from sixteen to forty, were taken before Mayor Fernando Wood and Justice B. W. Osborne. Mayor Wood had initiated a full-fledged campaign against the city's streetwalkers, and Justice Osborne had been charged with enforcing the mayor's reform program.[2] With the mayor's office serving as a court of law, the arresting officers presented their charges against the women.[3] Of the eighth-ward

9. CORNER OF BROADWAY AND DUANE.   This busy intersection, as it
appeared at mid-century, was well known for its many streetwalkers. As noted
by Elizabeth Blackwell, first woman doctor in the United States, all women
walking streets alone might be subject to annoyances from "unprincipled men."
In describing her life in New York City in the 1850s, Blackwell stated that "some
well-dressed man" would walk by her side on Broadway, saying in a low voice,
"Turn down Duane Street." (Courtesy of the New-York Historical Society,
New York City. Quotation from Wilson, *Lone Woman*, 296.)

women, one was discharged because her mother convinced Justice Osborne she would leave the city and take her daughter home. The other
fourteen were convicted—ten had admitted working as prostitutes anywhere from two months to two years, and the remaining four, including
Matilda Wade, were said to have "refused to tell" how long they had
worked in the profession. From the fourteenth ward, nine were dismissed

10. THE "BLACK MARIA." This etching of New York City's infamous prison van illustrates the variety of women who rode the van daily from police stations to prison after being arrested for vagancy/prostitution. (Courtesy of the New-York Historical Society, New York City)

because the arresting officers were "unable to substantiate any charge against them," including one woman who had been forcibly taken into custody as she stepped from the streetcar, even though she had protested she was innocent and a married woman. The thirty-one women found guilty of being "notorious offenders" were convicted without trial, testimony, witnesses, examination, cross-examination, or the opportunity to employ counsel. All of the women arrested also apparently had been subjected to medical exams to determine if they had venereal disease.[4] Each woman found guilty was sentenced to from one to six months in the penitentiary, with Matilda Wade one of the thirteen given the maximum sentence. The women were then taken to "the Tombs," or prison of detention, until they were transported in the Black Maria, the city's well-known large red caravan wagon, up Third Avenue to Sixty-first Street, where they were conveyed by ferry to Blackwell's Island. Mrs. Wade was then transferred from the penitentiary to the workhouse.

The next morning, Henry Wade, Matilda's husband, petitioned for a writ of habeas corpus. Mrs. Wade was brought before the court the following day, Friday, where her case and one other were argued on behalf of thirty women, with the court's decision to be applicable to all.

Mrs. Wade was represented in court by a Mr. Tomlinson who had been hired by an anonymous citizen concerned over the abuse of civil liberties. Tomlinson argued on eight counts against the arbitrary manner in which the case had been handled from the initial arrest to final detention. He also requested that Mrs. Wade be released to her husband's custody until the judge made his pronouncement in the case. The custody request was denied, however, and Mrs. Wade was again locked overnight in the city prison.

Finally, after five days in prison, the arrests of Mrs. Wade and of twenty-nine other women incarcerated with her were found illegal, and she was released. The following week, the remaining jailed women were freed.

Even though the legality of the prostitution arrests was being challenged in widely publicized court proceedings, the police continued their nightly raids on alleged streetwalkers throughout that week. Furthermore, the press continued printing editorials supporting Mayor Wood's reform program and calling for new laws to make possible the ongoing arrest and incarceration of the many streetwalkers who were using "Broadway and other quiet thoroughfares . . . to advertise shameless immorality, [a practice] discreditable to our sense of propriety, and disgraceful to our age."[5]

The Wade case and the public response to it bring into focus a number of issues surrounding the legal status and treatment of prostitutes in the nineteenth century, as well as practices regarding the legal treatment of non-prostitute women, especially the poor. Though prostitutes and non-prostitutes theoretically had different social and legal statuses, restrictions governing the behavior of both could blur the distinction. "Woman's sphere," albeit a middle-class construct, expressed a widely shared belief that woman's proper realm was the home; this belief found its way into the socio-legal system in the form of limitations on the jobs available to women, the places they could go, and the influence they had. Gender discrimination was both a cause and result of the devaluation of females, assuring women a secondary status in society. Moreover, a double standard in social and sexual mores served to buttress this secondary status and provided the basis for the social control of women as an "inferior group."

The nineteenth-century legal system, like the economic, political, and social systems, was founded on male dominance and control. Legislators, police officers, judges, prosecutors, and jurors all were exclusively male, and male-only suffrage withheld from women the possibility of contributing to the legal process on even the most basic level. Women's legal status was a result of what males decided it would be. Most nineteenth-century statutes affecting women reflected the ideal of woman as homemaker/wife/mother, setting forth a descending continuum of female behavior from the woman-ideal norm through various levels of deviance to the dissipated, diseased, poor, inebriated, whoring hag whose existence not only offended society but also violated a host of laws. The nineteenth-century mother, wife, or daughter, even if she dealt with the legal system from a position somewhat above that of the ultimately debased female, still could experience the impact of her secondary status in a paternalistic society when seeking legal recourse for domestic violence, seduction, or rape; or when practicing social independence, promiscuity, or prostitution.[6]

Many nineteenth-century women compounded their legal difficulties by being poor. Unless in the care of a husband, father, or other male relative, most women had such limited income and such limited opportunities for economic betterment that they were part of the impoverished classes who were perceived to be degraded and unrespectable, not worthy of the legal consideration given the "better classes."

Thus, as women (often poor women), and as females who deviated from "proper" gender roles, prostitutes were the recipients of questionable legal treatment that was supported by anti-prostitution laws such as the vagrancy law and the disorderly-persons law, which were designed to codify prevailing social and moral values and control social disorganization and chaos. As the *Times* noted in editorials condemning public prostitution, at issue were matters both of "immorality" and "propriety."[7] There was no question of competing social values—no one publicly argued the virtue of prostitution or proposed that there should be *no* laws controlling the practice. Prostitution, it was agreed, was immoral even if economically understandable, and its increasingly visible practice was a threat to the respectable community. Thus, prostitutes—especially streetwalkers—served both as symbols of and as scapegoats for the social uncertainty that accompanied the changing urban community in the mid-nineteenth century. Laws on prostitution codified these attitudes, but such laws were never enforced, or even designed, systematically and effectively.

The Wade case pointed out some of the problems and shortcomings of nineteenth-century prostitution statutes. First was the generality and questionable legality of such laws. For example, the vagrancy act was so inclusive that it covered most of society's "dispossessed." A slight deviance or momentary misfortune—or, indeed, as Matilda Wade learned, wholly arbitrary political or police whim—could cause a woman to be ranked with the community's criminals. [8] George Templeton Strong clearly anticipated the possible abuses of the law in a diary entry from March of 1855:

It enables any scoundrel of a policeman to lay hands on any woman whom he finds unattended in the street after dark, against whose husband or brother he may have a grudge, who may be hurrying home from church or from a day's work, or may have been separated by some accident from her escort, and to consign her for a night to a station house. Till morning no interference can liberate her; and if the policeman did make a mistake, the morning would find her disgraced for life, maddened perhaps by shame and mortification. [9]

A second problem was the frequent and random arrests made of suspected prostitutes. As was illustrated in the spring of 1855, a political administrator such as Mayor Wood could devise and initiate a "reform" program and then for weeks, almost nightly, send law enforcement officials to round up hundreds of women, both prostitutes and non-prostitutes, whose only visible offense was walking alone on the streets. Such laws clearly made crimes of actions that no one in fact labelled criminal. One's "crime" commonly was poverty, the temporary lack of a job or a home, or being an unescorted woman on the street, though an unescorted male was free to walk the thoroughfares any time he chose. Furthermore, prostitution laws were applied inconsistently. "In the Sixth Ward," observed the *Times*, "the officers arrest every female vagrant found in the street, whether acting in a disorderly manner, or walking quietly alone; while in the Eighth, Fifth, and Third wards but such of them as speak to persons in the street, or act otherwise unbecomingly, are taken in custody."[10] The *Times* also described a few individual cases:

The girl Harrington had neither the dress or air of a prostitute, but resembled more what she represented herself to be—a sewing girl. Alice Gray declared herself to be a cap-maker; and Ellen Johnson asserted most strenuously that she

11. WOMAN ALONE ON BROADWAY.   Nineteenth-century women found it "unsafe" to walk the streets unescorted, especially in the evening. Not only were they the objects of leering glances and immoral propositions, but under the law, any woman unaccompanied by a male was subject to arrest for vagrancy/ prostitution. (Courtesy of the New-York Historical Society, New York City)

resided with her parents at No. 33 Watt street, and was on her way home when arrested.

But neither tears or entreaties were of avail—they were all locked up, the officer in command being compelled to detain all persons committed to his charge. He is allowed no discretion in the matter, and cannot rectify the blunders of the ambitious patrolmen, if any such should be made.[11]

Despite the recognized inconsistency, generality, questionable legality, randomness, and unfairness of the laws used to attempt to control prostitution, and despite repeated "blunders" associated with their enforcement and challenged by numerous lawsuits, there appears to have been an unwillingness by society to repeal or substantially change these laws. On the other hand, prostitution was not eliminated by statute, nor does it appear the practice was significantly circumscribed by legal codes. Although many prostitutes and other women who were arrested, if poor or uninformed, found themselves helpless in responding to the legal system, there were many others, including many prostitutes, who effectively manipulated the system—through legal means, economic resources, connections, or sympathy. Thus, to fully understand the effects of the legal system on prostitution and the women who practiced the profession, we will first look at the codes—why they were passed, what values retained them, what conditions altered them, and how they were enforced. Then, in the following chapter, we will explore how the prostitutes responded to the laws, to the legal system, and to the law enforcers.[12]

The Laws and Prostitution

Throughout the eighteenth century and the early nineteenth century, prostitutes were arrested and incarcerated under laws that defined them as vagrants. Under laws enacted in the 1770s when New York became a state, they also could be arrested as "disorderly persons." In 1822, however, the year New York adopted a new constitution, the legal designation of prostitutes as common-law vagrants was abrogated, and under the general law of the state they were given the sole designation of disorderly persons. This designation remained the primary statutory grounds for arresting prostitutes in New York state for several decades. Disorderly persons included "all common prostitutes, all keepers of bawdy houses or houses for resort of prostitution, drunkards, tipplers, gamesters or other disorderly persons . . . on complaint made on oath [by anyone] that one is disorderly."[13] The inclusion here of keepers of taverns with those who keep bawdy houses or gambling dens suggests how central was the law's emphasis on disorder rather than prostitution or gambling per se.

In the case of a disorderly person, the general law of the state authorized a judge to demand bail for good behavior for one year or to commit the accused to jail for a period not exceeding sixty days or until the next meeting of the General Sessions Court. If there were a question of a violation of the bail, the disorderly person would be tried by a jury. Two justices could discharge an offender before the sitting of the General Sessions. The court was to investigate the charges and either dismiss or punish the offender. If found guilty of being a prostitute, the woman could be committed to prison for up to six months.[14]

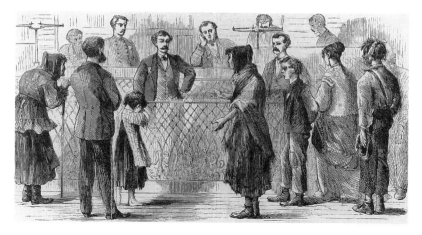

12. WOMAN BEING CHARGED AS A VAGRANT.   Prostitutes and unemployed women frequently were arrested on charges of vagrancy. If unable to persuade officers of the court of their ability to be cared for or to care for themselves, they were sentenced to up to six months in the penitentiary or workhouse. (Courtesy of the New-York Historical Society, New York City)

In 1830 the state legislature passed a new vagrancy law that continued to exclude prostitutes from its purview. Then, three years later, in 1833, the state legislature passed a special law relating to the vagrancy act that applied to New York City only. This law stated that "all common prostitutes who have no lawful employment whereby to maintain themselves" shall be considered vagrants and may be committed to either the almshouse or the penitentiary for six months.[15] This wording ensured vagueness by suggesting "no lawful employment" as the only definition of prostitution, a description that would fit most women and was perhaps intended to fit most unemployed poor women. On the other hand, prostitutes who had other "lawful employment," who owned or worked in taverns or boarding houses or had jobs such as millinering, were exempted from the law's provisions if its wording had any meaning at all.

Interestingly, the 1833 law singled out New York City, while in other parts of the state, prostitutes continued to be designated "disorderly persons." The New York City prostitute, as vagrant, could be brought before the court on complaint of any person, including a police officer on the street, with no preliminary proof or warrant of arrest being required. It was not necessary to provide a prostitute with the names or testimony of witnesses against her, and the presiding court officer alone had the power to try, convict, and punish the prostitute. In one case, the prostitutes from a raided brothel summoned their legal counsel to the police station, and when he argued that the magistrate's refusal to say why the women had been arrested was a denial of their rights, the judge replied that the clients had no rights because they were vagrants. The reporter covering the story noted that "this attitude is current among members of the bar in criminal practice as one of the jokes of the profession."[16] Accused prostitutes and other so-called vagrants "had no rights" and thus no legal protections.

With so little proof and legal proceeding necessary for conviction and commitment to prison, officials found the vagrancy law an expedient tool for temporarily removing from New York City streets prostitutes and others identified as social problems. But that nineteenth-century public officials were willing to employ such extraordinary means, which mocked generally accepted civil and judicial protection, indicates that they must have believed they were facing extraordinary problems.

One such "problem" may have been the great influx of new people into New York at this time, especially foreigners and the poor. Between 1820 and 1830 the city's population had grown by over 73,000, a more than 60 percent increase. Between 1830 and 1835, the population increased by another 71,000, a growth rate of 35 percent in only five years.[17] By 1833 this population trend caused civic leaders to worry about new threats they associated with foreigners and the poor. The special New York City vagrancy act offered one means of dealing with these problems.

New York City's vagrancy law applied to five classes of people— prostitutes, habitual drunkards, beggars, "loafers," and the diseased—all groups that it was believed threatened the social order, suffered from immoral tendencies, and were often foreign born. Although the state-wide vagrancy law passed in 1830 would have included most of these groups, the key problem that provoked passage of the special city-only statute three years later was the perceived increase in prostitution in New York City at that time. New Yorkers had been made very aware of the prostitutes' presence in the city as a result of the controversy surrounding the publication of McDowall's 1831 report on prostitution, and, though McDowall's figures had been challenged, many accepted the fact that, whether 10,000 or 1,000 in number, prostitution had become a major problem—and one that was no longer hidden from public view. Yet even in this atmosphere, the law stressed prostitution not as a distinct sexual crime, but as a departure from expected street decorum, similar to begging, being drunk, or just loafing.

The daily newspapers between 1830 and 1870 are filled with stories of prostitute arrests, most of which, if they mention a specific charge, list the offense as vagrancy/common prostitution. A tally of a sample of the cases reported in this period in the newspapers shows that the great majority were from the sixth ward, a ward known for the notorious Five Points, where drinking, gambling, and prostitution establishments abounded, but also a ward characterized by varied ethnic neighborhoods and extreme poverty.[18]

By the 1850s, when cumulative records for arrests by wards are available in published police reports, the sixth ward still led in the number of arrests for vagrancy.[19] The vagrancy totals in the police chief's semi-annual and quarterly reports do not distinguish male vagrants from female, but by checking the daily entries in the police blotters for lower Manhattan for one year from January 7, 1850, through December 30, 1850, in nearly 500 cases of females arrested for vagrancy/common prostitution, only 7 had other wards listed, 82 had no ward listed, and the remaining approximately 400 were from the sixth ward.[20] Daily police records for the first three months of 1855 noted a slightly different pattern: among 192 arrests for vagrancy/common prostitution, 36 percent were from ward four, a ward with a predominantly immigrant population, and 34 percent were from ward six; these two wards accounted for 70 percent of the vagrancy/prostitution arrests.[21] Thus, it appears a woman was most likely to be assumed to be a prostitute or be arrested for vagrancy/prostitution if she was in an ethnically diverse neighborhood, especially if she was foreign and/or poor (table 14).

Several vagrancy cases during the period from 1830 to 1870 illustrate both the vulnerability of the prostitute under the vagrancy law and the legal problems that resulted from using a statute that was so general in scope that its constitutionality and justness were always open to question. The cases also demonstrate why the vagrancy law was ineffective in curbing prostitution.

One of the first cases challenging the 1833 vagrancy law was *Emma Sands v. the People* in 1838. The young Emma Sands had been arrested

Table 14 *Vagrancy Arrests: Wards Ranked by Number of Both Men and Women Arrested*

	First Ranking		Second Ranking		Third Ranking		Fourth Ranking	
Reporting Period	Ward	No. Arrests	Ward	No. Arrests	Ward	No. Arrests	Ward	No. arrests
1 May–31 Oct. 1849	6	311	3	86	4	66	5	48
1 Apr.–30 Sept. 1850	6	1,234	3	127	5	99	4	84
1 Jan.–30 June 1851	6	670	4	194	5	114	3	104
1 July–31 Dec. 1851	6	735	4	152	3	148	17	121
1 July–31 Dec. 1854	6	673	22	258	3	224	4	217
1 Jan.–30 June 1855	6	554	4	205	1	121	3	112
1 July–31 Dec. 1855	6	372	9	134	7	87	18	86
1 Jan.–30 June 1856	6	323	18	82	7	66	1	61

SOURCE: New York City Chief of Police, *Semi-Annual* and *Quarterly Reports.*

as a common prostitute, convicted as a vagrant, and committed to six months in the penitentiary. She was brought before Recorder Robert H. Morris on a writ of habeas corpus to have the legality of her detention reviewed. Morris had been a member of the state assembly in 1833 when the vagrancy law was adopted for New York City and had voted in favor of the act. He also would be the judge to preside over the case of Matilda Wade in 1855.[22]

In his review of the Sands case, Judge Morris pointed out "that the prisoner is not without resources for her support, that she is respectably connected, and that her father, a respectable citizen, is desirous if he can procure her release, to take her into his house, and provide for her."[23] Morris found the vagrancy law unconstitutional and Sands's commitment void, and he ordered that she be discharged from the penitentiary. In challenging the vagrancy law, the main issue in the case for Morris was the improper use of the judicial process after the prostitute was arrested and incarcerated, not the method by which it was determined she was a prostitute who should be arrested. Morris stated that the vagrancy act, by delegating excessive powers to the justice court, denied the accused a trial by jury and, in effect, created a new kind of court which was not provided for by the state constitution. Morris also noted that justices frequently, but without proper authority, gave early discharges to prisoners they had unjustly convicted and sentenced. Prisoners were released because the justices subsequently discovered that in the hasty proceedings at the police office or penitentiary, incorrect decisions had been made regarding the accused persons' guilt and/or sentencing. And he remarked that the New York state law that designated prostitutes as disorderly persons had proved adequate for the rest of the state, had sufficed for New York City until 1833, and would still be sufficient if used in the city henceforth.

The Sands case received extensive coverage in the press, and though Morris's decision brought some public criticism, the majority of the bar concurred with Morris in his position. Nevertheless, the controversy brought no changes in the vagrancy law or in its arbitrary enforcement.[24]

In 1841, public attention again was focused on a vagrancy case, that of Melinda Hoag. While the Sands case, like that of Matilda Wade later, suggested how a woman might be convicted of prostitution with no shred of evidence that she practiced it, Hoag's legal history made clear how ineffective the law was against even a notorious prostitute and thief who could afford to employ legal counsel. According to the court, Hoag had been convicted "on competent testimony" and was committed to the penitentiary for six months for being a vagrant, "an idle person and a common prostitute, who having no visible means to maintain herself, lives without lawful employment."[25] Hoag's case was brought before the court on a writ of habeas corpus, and her counsel challenged the vagrancy charges and sentence on several grounds. First, he argued that the offense had not been defined with sufficient precision under the terms of any statute setting forth what constituted a vagrant. A second challenge was that it was not clear if the evidence against Hoag had been her own confession or the competent testimony of witnesses. If the latter, the names and testimony of these witnesses had not been given her. A third complaint was that there was no statement of adjudication declaring that the prisoner was either a notorious offender who should be sent to the penitentiary or a proper object of relief who should be sent to the almshouse.

Presiding Judge Lynch stated that it was not necessary in this type of case for the names and testimony of witnesses to be given, but that such testimony must only be in the record, with the offense sufficiently described by a witness with authority. He added, however, that because of technicalities in the statute, the charge of vagrancy had been improperly made. The prisoner, therefore, was to be discharged on the basis of improper procedures. He further cautioned that, when there is a commitment to prison without a jury, the court must be careful not to appear to be acting on prejudice or personal dislike. In his opinion, the police court had been concerned only with the substantive end of justice and therefore had neglected proper legal procedures.

The *Tribune* supported the judge's actions, noting that it "must be obvious to all that such a process is liable to the grossest abuses and ought to be carefully guarded. . . . As a prop to public morals it seems to us to be an exceedingly imperfect and unsafe one."[26] Again, however, even though the vagrancy law had been challenged in the courts and had been termed "exceedingly imperfect and unsafe" by the press, the law remained unchanged.

Melinda Hoag, perhaps encouraged by her experience with the judicial system, saw no need to change her ways and was back in court two years later, again challenging the vagrancy law. Strong evidence indicated that she was involved not only in a life of prostitution but also in theft in association with persons well known to police authorities. She lived with a man named Alexander Hoag but was not his wife. They had been together several years, and he characterized their relationship as one where she "kept house for him by the month."[27] The Hoags were known to the police, and indeed soon to the public, as "panel thieves." In the panel game, a female lured her customers into a bedroom that had a secret panel or curtain where her accomplice could hide until the opportune time to steal money from the pants or coat pocket of the victim's clothes that had been left on a nearby chair or stand.

It was in fact theft, not prostitution, that led to the Hoags' legal downfall. In August 1843, Melinda Hoag was arrested on complaint of Isaac Smith, a Westchester County man, who claimed he had met her on the street, had gone home with her to her house on Greenwich Street, and had gone to bed with her. He said he heard a noise and looked up to find a man trying to steal his pantaloons. Smith dressed and left but shortly thereafter discovered his wallet was missing. He located a watchman, who went with him to the Greenwich Street house, where they found, according to the report in the *Tribune*, "the notorious Melinda Hoag, the robber of a thousand strangers, . . . the little less notorious Alexander Hoag, her paramour," and a man called Charles Watson.[28]

All three were arrested and locked in the watchhouse. Smith's complaint against Melinda Hoag pointed out that she had told him she only "wanted to get acquainted with folks," but that she also had agreed "to allow him the use of her person for any amount that he had a mind to give her."[29] On this basis he charged her with being a common prostitute. On examination by Hoag's lawyer, Smith admitted he had not had intercourse with her, nor did he know anyone who had, but that she had agreed to "give up her person for pay or hire," and had gone to bed with him for that purpose.[30]

The day following the arrest of the three parties, Smith discovered his wallet was not missing but was in his coat pocket. He reported this discovery to the police, who released the two men but detained Melinda Hoag. Hoag was sent to the penitentiary for six months for being a vagrant and a prostitute.[31] Her lawyers filed to have the case reviewed on a writ of certiorari before the New York Supreme Court, and Alexander Hoag posted her $500 bail.[32] The court found the charges and convictions were improperly made under the law and Mrs. Hoag could not be legally detained. She was released, but within the month Melinda and Alexander Hoag were again arrested. This time Mrs. Hoag had taken an Ohio visitor to a house in Robinson Street and gone to bed with him. Shortly thereafter, they heard a loud knocking at the door. Mrs. Hoag said she feared it was her husband and begged the gentleman to leave quickly, which he did. When he returned to his hotel he discovered he was missing $54; he reported the incident to the authorities, and the Hoags were arrested. According to press reports, not only did Alexander Hoag try unsuccessfully to escape, but several bank notes that the Ohioan identified were found in the possession of both Hoags, who were committed for trial on charges of grand larceny.[33]

Melinda Hoag's jury found her guilty without ever retiring to private chambers. This time she was committed to prison on charges of larceny, not vagrancy/common prostitution, and therefore her conviction held. Alexander Hoag, also found guilty, was sentenced to four years in the state prison, a decision he challenged in Supreme Court but a sentence he later served.[34]

That the authorities finally chose to avoid vagrancy/common prostitution charges in their efforts to remove Melinda Hoag from the streets acknowledged that the statute was so general, and its application such an abridgement of due process, that it was unlikely to be upheld under appeal, even when applied to as blatant a prostitute as Melinda Hoag. While useful in arbitrarily attacking or harassing poor females, prostitute or not, the vagrancy law, New Yorkers knew, in fact did nothing to curb prostitution. An 1844 report of a Board of Aldermen committee evaluating the New York police department acknowledged as much, in part using documents from the 1843 Hoag trials as case studies. The report of the committee stated that it was an "established, though melancholy fact" that prostitution and houses of prostitution exist in all large cities and cannot be prevented by law. The report went on to note, however, that several New York jurists and legislators favored laws that would license and regulate the practice, but that the general community would find such laws unacceptable, and thus, they would not be recommended. The vagrancy law would remain in force, requiring "emphatically, the efficient attention of the Police"—which meant that the law would continue to be most effective as harassment of those too poor or too uneducated to provide themselves with legal protection.[35]

Another example of the abuses inherent in the vagrancy law was the case of Harriet Charles in August 1846. Again, as in the Sands case, the plaintiff's counsel questioned the legality of the single magistrate's summary power in such cases. The judge's finding was that the prisoner had been illegally convicted by a magistrate whose power was conferred by a statute not in conformity with the common law. Furthermore, Harriet Charles's denial of both a trial by jury and a hearing where she could know and defend herself against the charges of prostitution—a denial the judge noted was most often practiced against people whose "poverty and destitution makes them wanting in all other forms of protection"—was ruled a withholding of due process.[36] Although Harriet Charles was able to avoid punishment under the vagrancy act in 1846, she could not escape the threat the law continued to pose to prostitutes, or to women unaccompanied on New York streets. The police blotter for November 7, 1850, notes Charles again was arrested as a vagrant/common prostitute, and she was sentenced to three months' imprisonment.[37]

Even though eight years had transpired between the Sands and the Charles cases, their similarities pointed out that, in spite of repeated publicity about the inability of the vagrancy law to withstand judicial review, the law itself had not been modified nor had there been any change in its enforcement in that period. Some New Yorkers, however,

had become increasingly concerned with the vagrancy law's ineffectiveness in curbing prostitution as well as its abuses of justice. A grand
jury was called by the Common Council in 1848 to review vagrancy
convictions, and the inquiry found that of 511 records of vagrancy
conviction, only 3 were valid, and of 746 persons detained in the
penitentiary on vagrancy, only 3 were lawfully held.[38] In spite of this
indictment of the law and the judicial procedures used in its enforcement, legislators were unwilling to change the law substantially. Minor
changes were made in 1849, 1853, and 1854, but only in an effort to
assure that arrests and convictions would more easily stand up in court.
Matilda Wade's case in 1855 clearly illustrated that abuses were not
eliminated by the revisions.[39] As a result of the Wade case and the large
number of prisoners released after the trial, the mayor's and district
attorney's offices drew up a series of guidelines to be followed in making
future arrests: police should arrest only if specific acts or words at the time
of arrest indicated grounds for such action, and they should arrest by
warrant after an affidavit had been sworn before a magistrate noting past
acts of prostitution and lack of lawful employment, and after verification
of evidence by, for example, accompanying a suspected prostitute to her
alleged residence where inquiries could be made as to the truth of her
story. In addition, police were to inform the prisoner immediately of
her right to counsel, give her the opportunity for an on-the-spot cross-
examination of witnesses, and then submit a full record of all signed and
certified proceedings for filing with the appropriate authorities.[40]

That the guidelines were designed more to uphold convictions than
to ensure justice became clear within a couple of months. Under
pressure from constituents to stop the throngs of women continuing to
fill the streets at night, Mayor Wood renewed his campaign against
prostitutes and directed his officers to make arrests. Over sixty women
were brought before the police court on the first day of arrests, forty the
next, and orders were given to continue apprehending streetwalkers until
the nuisance abated.[41] Clearly such numbers could not have been
rounded up had the police paid any heed to the "protective" guidelines
drawn up the previous month. In an article about the initial arrests the
Times noted that the women apprehended were "exceedingly shy and
with but few exceptions behaved themselves with propriety."[42]

One of the women in the first group incarcerated was a twenty-
one-year-old immigrant named Margaret McDermott. The *Times* spoke

with outrage about the fact that Michael Connelly, a police justice, had committed McDermott to prison on vagrancy charges and then over a week later had requested her release because he had learned she was a "virtuous girl only a few months in the country." The paper asked, "If Justice Connelly may do this in the case of Margaret McDermott, why may he not do it in the case of any and of every woman in the city? Is this the tenure on which we hold the security of our persons and our personal rights?"[43] Connelly defended his act by stating there was sufficient evidence against her: "She was friendless, a pauper and unknown, and had not the power to rebut but by her own assertion the charge made against her. Was I to believe the prisoner and doubt the evidence?" The *Times* censured the justice for committing her to prison before he had proved her guilt, stating: "The fact that she was poor and friendless should have made him doubly careful not to augment her misfortune by reckless injustice."[44]

Yet Connelly had acted in precise accord with the intention of the law in convicting McDermott. Under the vagrancy law, being friendless and poor was, in fact, all the "evidence" needed to prove prostitution. A few individuals, such as the *Times* editor writing about the Wade case and the judge in the Harriet Charles case, had pointed out that the vagrancy law was a form of "reckless injustice" practiced on the poor and destitute, but the overwhelming majority of legal enforcers and society in general demonstrated a gross and almost absolute indifference to guaranteeing even a semblance of justice for the underclasses. Even though the vagrancy law left cases open to judicial challenge, New York newspapers and police blotters indicate it was utilized far more widely in nineteenth-century New York than were other statutes for controlling prostitution. A vagrancy conviction offered officials an easier, quicker, and harsher way of handling conspicuous prostitutes, especially those too poor to contest the charges, than did alternative laws.

The other major prostitution law, the law for disorderly persons, covered both prostitutes and keepers of "bawdy houses or houses for resort of prostitution." Arrest as a disorderly person was usually made in conjunction with a disorderly-house arrest and unlike a vagrancy charge had to be proved in court. A disorderly-person case before the Court of General Sessions required police time, court time, and witnesses open to examination. In addition, witnesses called to testify in a disorderly-persons case either had to post bond or be held in jail until the case was heard, a definite drawback for the potential witness as well as a deterrent for anyone wanting to bring charges against an alleged prostitute.[45]

Police blotters show most of those women arrested for vagrancy received sentences of two to six months, with the six-month sentence being frequently given, while those charged as disorderly persons were much less often incarcerated. Notations in the police blotters indicate that disorderly persons were either dismissed or charged bail and set free on good behavior. In many of the cases, the police record mentions no disposition. Some of these cases were heard at a later date before the General Sessions Court, or the police released the women rather than force the police, the prostitutes' clientele, or other witnesses to testify.[46]

Available statistics illustrate the great discrepancy between arrests for vagrancy and those in connection with a disorderly house (table 15). There were a mere 22 disorderly-house arrests for the year 1847 when police records began to be published, and these gradually increased to 167 by the next decade. Ten years later there were 367 arrests under the statute, but only 152 of these were female, and there is no indication how many of the proprietors were operating prostitution establishments rather than groggeries, dram shops, dance halls, or gaming establishments, all of which were also considered disorderly houses. The legal freedom enjoyed by operators of disorderly houses is even more evident when one notes cases where an indictment was actually found. For almost an entire decade, 1860 to 1869, only 85 indictments were issued against houses of prostitution, an average of less than nine a year in a city where disorderly houses were plentiful. The arrest and indictment records illustrate clearly that disorderly-house laws were difficult to wield against prostitution, and they suggest that officials and the public were more tolerant of brothels than of street prostitution.[47]

If the police wished to arrest prostitutes who were inhabitants or managers of houses of prostitution, however, the disorderly person/ disorderly house law did provide a statutory basis. The maximum sentence for operating a disorderly house was one year's imprisonment at hard labor, with one month's solitary confinement and a fine of $250. The maximum sentence for other inhabitants was the same as for any disorderly person—up to six months in jail. Critics seeking strong action against disorderly houses were concerned that police had no power to enter such establishments unless some situation, such as a brawl or a request for help, necessitated their services on the premises.[48] The

Table 15 *Vagrancy and Disorderly House Arrests for New York City (female and male combined, with breakdown for 1866–1869)*

Year	Vagrancy Arrests			Disorderly House Arrests[a]		
	Total	*Female*	*Male*	*Total*	*Female*	*Male*
1844	—			24		
1845	725[b]			9[b]		
1846	2,288			22		
1847	1,229[c]			22		
1848	2,044			34		
1849	1,661			54		
1850	3,450			87		
1851	3,462			141		
1852	3,014			102		
1853	3,342			121		
1854	4,358			176		
1855	3,169			167		
1856	1,071[c]			89[c]		
. . . . . .						
1866	3,873	1,581	2,292	205	82	123
1867	3,518	1,730	1,788	367	152	215
1868	2,449	1,073	1,376	—		
1869	1,766	701	1,065	—		

[a]Includes gambling and drinking, as well as prostitution houses.
[b]For a three-month period only.
[c]For a six-month period only.

SOURCES: Official police reports were not published until the reorganization of the police force, in 1845. Totals for 1844 are from the *National Police Gazette;* 1854–1856, from the Board of Aldermen, *Semi-Annual Reports of the Chief of Police;* and 1866–1869, from the *Annual Reports of the Metropolitan Police.*

Advocate of Moral Reform complained there were no penal enactments that could eliminate such "houses of death" provided they observed external order and quiet.[49] To get around this restriction, police might induce a neighbor to make a complaint, in order to permit the authorities to take out a warrant, enter the house, and arrest everyone found on the premises.[50] This ability to arrest "on complaint" provided police with a method of controlling, or harassing, brothels if they wished to use it. In one case, the son of a highly respectable family had been frequenting Eliza Smith's brothel in Centre Street. His father contacted the police and went with them to the brothel to have the son removed. The police threatened Smith that, if she admitted the son again, they would see that complaints were made against her house and her establishment would be broken up. Inhabitants then would be charged and sent to jail, or the brothel keeper and inmates might be set free on promise they would immediately vacate the house and the neighborhood.[51]

Although disorderly houses could be quickly dealt with by obtaining a complaint, and most arrests probably were not disputed, testimony could be difficult to prove if challenged by the defendant or her counsel. Usually, neighbors testified about external events at a house or the appearance of visitors. The standardized forms filed in the district attorney's office noted that a house was a "resort of tipplers, gamblers, prostitutes, and other disorderly persons who disturbed the peace of the neighbors at all hours of the night." A complaint might also state that prostitutes and persons of "bad character" met there nightly to dance, and "the vilest was allowed and encouraged," or that "men and women, both black and white, were seen entering and leaving the house."[52] Some citizens' complaints contained more specific objections, especially during the summer months, when windows were kept open for ventilation. In 1830 neighbors of Rosina Townsend, Ann Perkins, and Mary Wall filed a complaint against the three women for operating disorderly houses at numbers 41, 39-1/2, and 39 Thomas Street. A letter to the police from one of the complainants, George Chapman, stated that the women operated "noted houses of prostitution" and that on the previous Sunday afternoon either Ann Perkins or a female resident of her house was seen with a male "in a State of Nature with the front window open to the street." This scene proceeded "to drive from their windows every respectable female in view and collected a mob of boys."[53] Chapman said that he hoped the magistrates would

remove the nuisance not by sending a wretched prostitute to the penitentiary for sixty days, whose vacancy in the brothel may be filled in twenty minutes, but by clearing out the houses, indicting their keepers and Livingston, the agent who lets those houses with a knowledge of the infamous purpose to which they will be applied.[54]

It is not certain what immediate action was taken, but a few years later both Townsend and Wall were still living at the same addresses.[55]

In an 1834 charge against Julia Brown, who was said to operate a disorderly house at 133 Reade Street, a neighbor complained that the night before Brown's common bawdy house had been the scene of "a great noise and quarreling to the great annoyance and disturbance of neighbors." A second neighbor complained that men and women regularly met at the house and that "the females expose themselves in the yard and at the windows in an indecent state and the males use indecent language." Brown pled guilty to the charge and vacated the Reade Street address, but she continued to manage brothels at various other New York locations for years afterward.[56]

Another 1834 case against three women in White Street charged that their houses were the common resorts of prostitutes who "sit by the windows and lie on the Beds of the House[s] with windows hoisted and their naked persons greatly exposed."[57] The neighbors were especially annoyed because they had brought disorderly-house charges against the three previous owners of the same establishments in May of that year. These three women had been ordered out and had moved. A month later, however, the houses were reoccupied by the three new prostitutes. After complaints again were made to the police, one of the new owners moved out, but the two others defied the law by staying—and, to the great dismay of the neighbors, the empty house was taken over by the prostitute who had first occupied it in May! Finally, after several months of delay in the courts, two of the occupants were found guilty.[58]

Sometimes neighbors were overly zealous in pursuing exact information to use against suspected prostitutes. One such case was that of Rebecca Davis, a widow with five children, who was said to earn her living selling baby clothing. Mrs. Davis was described as a "wellbuilt little Jewess, with dark eyes and hair, and good expression of face of the Israelite mould."[59] A neighbor, Mr. Roper, testified that he eavesdropped in order to determine the character of Mrs. Davis and her friends. He said the conversations in the house between men and women were "the obscene kind such as women of ill fame use." Roper did not explain how he had become an authority on such conversations. Another neighbor testified that, as he was peeping through the keyhole, he saw a man getting out of her bed. A female neighbor, who lived above Mrs. Davis, said she "heard the bed going." In her testimony she declared: "I am not speculating as to the noise of the bed. I know the difference between the movement of a bed and a chair. . . . I saw nothing but speculate upon the result."[60] Twelve other witnesses were then called who testified on behalf of Mrs. Davis. One, a grocer who lived across the street, said he had never seen or overheard anything improper, but added in response to Davis's accusers: "I never looked through the keyhole." The local watchman, also testifying on her behalf, made a similar statement, saying he "never looked through the keyhole or the back shutters." After an hour's deliberation the jury found Mrs. Davis not guilty. Mrs. Davis then brought charges against one of the neighbors for defamation of character.[61]

Another disorderly-house arrest that did not stand up in court involved Elizabeth Rice. Mrs. Rice retained counsel for her defense, and the court found that "she did not keep such a disorderly house as the law prohibits with its penalties."[62] The prosecutor was able to prove, however, that she sold liquor on the Sabbath, so Mrs. Rice was compelled to pay a fine before she was discharged. The *Advocate of Moral Reform* made note of the fact that her counsel fees and fine together amounted to only $20.[63]

As with the vagrancy law, there were major problems with the justice of the disorderly persons law, which worked better to intimidate than to convict. Judges became more concerned over the years to evaluate charges under the statute and lessen inconsistencies, but this could not be done without undercutting what small effectiveness the law had. The case of Mary Fowler, the keeper of a house on Church Street, suggests well the legal fog, abetted by society's ambiguous attitude to prostitution, that fell over most court procedures in such cases. Familiar to the New York community, the "notorious" Mary Fowler had lived on Church Street for over a decade and was listed in the 1838 City Directory as the widow of Joseph M. Fowler. The 1840 census registered her as the head of a household that included two other women and four young boys. Mary Fowler was one of several prostitutes the well-known editor, E. Z. C. Judson (alias Ned Buntline), attempted to blackmail. Judson also was responsible for reporting Fowler's establishment to the police.[64]

At her trial Mrs. Fowler said she was indignant at the report her house was of bad character. She threatened to sue one of the prosecution witnesses for slander. Mrs. Fowler's lawyer also objected to the "spy system" that had "hunted up" testimony against her, stating that it left everyone unsafe even in her own house.[65]

Judge C. P. Daley's jury instructions wonderfully suggested the general social and legal confusion surrounding prostitution cases. He pointed out that an establishment could be deemed a disorderly house even if it did not disturb the neighborhood; if what was going on in a house had a tendency to injure public morals, and if the place was frequented by individuals of both sexes for the purpose of facilitating illicit connection between them, then it mattered not how privately or correctly such behavior was conducted. Daley's charge clarified what he believed to be the intent of prostitution laws: preventing a "moral" offense to the community. Past de facto implementation of both disorderly-house and vagrancy laws had emphasized enforcement of public decorum and control of undesirable elements of the population, not upholding a moral or sexual code of behavior in the community. In past cases, defense attorneys for prostitutes had even gone so far as to argue in court that if a woman lived alone and did not disturb her neighbors, it made "no difference how many men visit[ed] her and [had] sexual intercourse with her."[66]

Judge Daley challenged this interpretation by pointing to a larger issue present in such cases. He noted that prostitution establishments were great evils and that isolated prosecutions against them were of doubtful utility. Houses of ill-repute were either necessary evils, or they were not. If necessary, then they should be regulated by the police and if not necessary, then the municipal authorities should suppress them by a general systematic effort. The indirect countenance of them by police in New York City he believed to be scandalous, and isolated prosecutions served only to bring the evil to the attention of those of prurient interests, or the young and unsuspecting, the curious, or the salacious.

Nevertheless, the judge said it was the duty of the jury and court to administer the law as they found it, without inquiry into the wisdom of the law. The evidence indicating that women of ill-fame were seen visiting the house and were said to live there was not in itself sufficient to establish that the house was disorderly—even women of ill-fame must have a residence and shelter somewhere, he observed, as had been argued in a case in England. In addition, the jury should presume nothing against the character of the defendant, because the law presumes her character to be good unless shown to be otherwise. Also, if the evidence did not prove beyond a doubt that prostitution took place in the house, and that it was for Mrs. Fowler's "lucre and gain," then the defendant should be found not guilty. After cautioning the jury on all of these issues, however, the judge pointed out that if wine were sold in the house, then Mrs. Fowler could be convicted of keeping a disorderly house under that charge![67]

Despite such clear indication of problems with the disorderly-persons/disorderly-house law, no basic amendment was undertaken. One addition to the law was made that suggested concern about respectable exploiters of prostitutes; as prostitutes came to be viewed more as victims than victimizers, it began to seem appropriate that those who "assisted" in their degradation should not go unpunished. Therefore, in 1849 a law was passed including owners of disorderly houses with the persons who managed them.[68] Absentee brothel property owners were believed to be guilty because their participation for financial gain made them an integral part of the prostitution business, "respectable" people who in fact financially exploited prostitutes' poverty and vulnerability. Reformers argued that property owners earned such money not by a fair business arrangement with the prostitutes but by exploiting the many women who were forced to practice the occupation. The sense of class injustice tied to this reform is suggested by one proposal which recommended that not only should those who own the property be punished by imprisonment and fine, but income from the fine and from the property's rent for five years should go to the Overseers of the Poor.[69]

A sample case under the new law was that of Fanny Howard, who was arrested in April 1849 for keeping a house of prostitution on Church Street. Upon her arrest she signed an affidavit stating that she rented the house from John F. Delaplaine, a well-known property owner who was said to lease several houses as brothels. After Howard stated that Delaplaine knew she intended to keep the residence as a house of ill fame, a warrant also was issued for Delaplaine's arrest. The police blotter for April 20 shows both Howard and Delaplaine were arrested but does not record what happened to them. Since the blotter for July 9, 1849 indicates that Howard was again arrested for keeping a disorderly house, she probably was released with a warning or given a fine. There is no indication what happened to Delaplaine except for a notice six months later in the *Herald* that he was "indicted" for owning a residence operated as a disorderly house by Fanny Howard. Either the court was finally hearing his April case or he had been charged again with the same offense. No disposition of the case was mentioned.[70]

In another case against a landlord, John Devins was indicted for leasing a disorderly house at 24 Elizabeth Street. Even though Devins lived in the basement, he protested the suit and had his young children and an employee testify to his sober character. The judge pointed out that the Supreme Court had been clear on the issue, and that the jury must judge on the facts, which were that he had knowingly leased the residence as a disorderly house. The jury found Devins guilty but recommended mercy, and the sentence was suspended by his "abating the nuisance."[71]

Other laws also included provisions designed to prevent the development of prostitution. For example, immigration laws forbade entry into the United States of women of immoral character, as well as other "undesirables," such as the diseased, maimed, and criminal. Tenement house laws and public health laws included restrictions on prostitutes and the practice of their trade.[72] At mid-century, two further attempts to legislate specific controls on New York City prostitutes were made; although they failed, they merit special attention.

The earlier of these proposals was a campaign for laws to prevent prostitutes from attending public theaters and other public places of amusement. This law was similar to other prostitution statutes in its attempt to control the behavior of the women who practiced the profession by removing them from the public arena. In nineteenth-century American theaters, the gallery, or upper row above the dress and family circles, was customarily reserved for prostitutes. This section, known as the third tier, was periodically the subject of controversy. Moralists believed the presence of prostitutes there was a disgusting custom, offensive to respectable patrons of the theater. For those who questioned the morality of theaters in general, the existence of the third tier was a confirmation of its impurity. Theater managers were constantly under pressure from clergy and reformers who wished to see the third tier eliminated. If any theater went out of business, these reformers were quick to point out that the theater had been unable to attract a respectable clientele.[73]

In 1842, attempting to meet the objections of some of his critics, Edmund Simpson, manager of New York's Park Theatre, scheduled a religious play, *The Israelites in Egypt,* and closed the third tier. In describing opening night, the *Herald* said the house was "well and respectably filled" but "the third tier empty, the manager having for the first time in New York, put forth a moral courage unheard of." The play was scheduled to run for eighteen days, but by the fourth night the prostitutes were readmitted. The *Herald* ran a letter from "Hamilton," a concerned citizen, stating that Simpson should take new courage and reinstitute the reform. The writer ominously warned: "Whether or not you abolish it [the third tier], the time is not far distant when this will be done with or without your consent. . . . There are influences, powerful and strong, at work to abate this nuisance."[74]

It appeared Hamilton's prophecy would be fulfilled a year later when a group of New York City aldermen presented a study of the defects and deficiencies in the existing laws of the city. One of the deficiencies they mentioned was the failure to restrain theaters and others places of public amusement from admitting prostitutes. The aldermen followed this criticism with a suggested statute which said: "The keeper of any public theatre, circus, or other place of public amusement, who shall hereafter wilfully receive or allow any common prostitute to be placed anywhere among or in open view of the audience, shall, for each offence, forfeit the sum of $100 dollars."[75] Although this proposed law was not as restrictive as some had hoped, it still failed to pass. Prostitutes continued to enjoy their own special section of theaters for many more years, but by the mid-1850s the practice had begun to decline, and by the 1880s the custom of the third tier was no longer commonly found in American theaters.[76]

A second and more significant unsuccessful legislative proposal concerning New York City prostitutes was the attempt to license and regulate the profession. This bold initiative reflected a general agreement that the laws to eradicate prostitution were ineffective, despite widespread disagreement as to the cause of this failure. Many felt that inadequate enforcement of existing laws had allowed prostitution to flourish in the community, while others felt it was useless to try to eradicate prostitution by compulsory legislation because, even if officials enforced prohibitory statutes, they only succeeded in driving prostitution into seclusion, or in removing the nuisance from the community temporarily. As one observer said: "No amount of imprisonment as a punishment ever yet reformed a prostitute, and it never will."[77] Other critics pointed to the harmful effects of the prohibitory laws. Innumerable court cases had shown the potential of the laws to abuse the rights not only of prostitutes but of other women as well. Some even questioned whether prostitution was an offense against society serious enough to warrant arrest at all. Furthermore, laws which sentenced vagrants, whether prostitutes or indigents, to the penitentiary were detrimental because the so-called vagrants were returned to the penitentiary time and again for the same or more serious offenses "to keep company with thieves and felons and murderers, and, if there is a vice she is unskilled in, to learn its art and come back again, when the time of the commitment has expired, to practice it . . . proficient in crimes at which society trembles."[78] Finally, some argued against prohibitory statutes because they believed prostitution was inevitable, and thus potentially controllable only through regulation or licensing.[79]

One of the first official suggestions for licensing was made by the Reorganization Report of the Board of Aldermen in 1844. As the report stated, it was a fact that houses of prostitution "exist in every large and commercial city, and cannot by any system of penal laws, be prevented." The report also pointed out that many of esteemed reputation "favor the idea of licensing and regulating these establishments by law, and in some European Cities, this is practiced with success."[80] The aldermen's report approved licensing prostitution on the grounds that it was inevitable, but to sanction prostitution also might imply it was socially and morally non-destructive, an idea which New Yorkers could not accept. The report acknowledged that licensing prostitution would be "repugnant" to the social and moral principles of most of the community.

Three years after the aldermen's report, the New York physician Charles Smith suggested an additional reason for regulating prostitution. Reiterating the opinion that prohibitory laws would not make society virtuous, he pointed out that some laws were necessary to protect society, especially from infectious diseases such as syphilis. This was one area where police could exert some control, he wrote, and he suggested the law should make having syphilis a misdemeanor—despite obvious political problems with defining, say, the wife of a philanderer as a criminal subject to punishment for having the disease. Dr. Smith noted that official regulation of prostitution had been successfully tried by European governments and should be considered by New Yorkers.[81]

The European system of regulation referred to by the aldermen and Smith was best known in France, which had a long history of attempts at controlling prostitution. Police supervision, official bordellos, periodic medical examinations of prostitutes, and the enforced internment of the diseased in separate venereal hospitals were the basic elements of the French system of regulation, a system that had been adopted during the Napoleonic period. The results of this regulatory system were described by Parent-Duchatelet, the French demographer and sanitary investigator, in *De la prostitution dans la ville de Paris* (1836). Parent's ideas had an impact on several public figures concerned with prostitution in New York City. William Sanger and City Inspector John Griscom both made references to Parent's work in their studies of New York's prostitution and poverty.[82] Viewing venereal disease as a major health problem, Sanger advocated regulation as the most effective means of controlling the spread of the disease. Sanger's plan called for the establishment of a medical bureau within the police department. This bureau would be a partnership composed of medical men of "skill and integrity" whose work would be backed up by the authority of the police. There were three major features of Sanger's proposal: the regular medical examination of prostitutes at known houses of prostitution with the immediate removal of those found to be diseased, the establishment of a special hospital for persons infected with venereal disease, and the granting of power to hospital officials to detain infected persons in the institution until such time as they were found to be cured. Sanger also suggested that houses of prostitution eventually might be confined to particular locations and speculated that the regulation system might be expanded to include specifications on the management of houses and the licensing of official brothels.

Sanger conceded there would be opposition to such a system by those who feared it would encourage lewdness through lessening the danger of infection, those who believed venereal disease was a special punishment of Providence, those who daily offered cures for the disease in the popular press, and those who objected to raising public revenues by licensing vice. Sanger countered these arguments by pointing out that, in addition to preserving public decency, regulation would help protect innocent wives and children who were often unsuspectingly diseased and deformed through no fault of their own. Sanger did not elaborate on how the regulation system would be able to include all women who engaged in prostitution but were not found in brothels or assignation houses, nor was he concerned with the fact that male clients of diseased prostitutes were not included in the plan.[83]

Although a system of regulation continued to be discussed by some New Yorkers, the idea was not advocated by lawmakers until a decade after Sanger made his plea. In 1867 the Assembly of the New York Legislature adopted a resolution requiring the metropolitan boards of police and health to furnish an opinion on the possible impact of prostitution regulation in New York City. The report of the boards' research committee proposed that all keepers of houses of prostitution and assignation be registered with the police, that any women admitted to such houses be reported to the authorities, that both the houses and the prostitutes themselves be regularly inspected, that a special hospital be established for prostitutes, and that any medical facility receiving aid from the state be required to treat venereal disease. In 1868, the year following the committee's report, a bill was introduced in the state legislature which embodied the main features of the report. This legislation was unsuccessful, but in 1871 another bill received strong lobbying support from members of the medical and public health fields. Its opponents included individuals who objected on grounds that the law would be licensing sin, and feminists, such as Elizabeth Cady Stanton, Susan B. Anthony, and Lucretia Mott, who opposed the bill because they believed the law would discriminate against and violate the civil rights not only of prostitutes but of other women as well. They argued that any woman alone on the streets could be arrested and subjected to a medical examination under charges she was a prostitute. Even without such a regulation, New York women in the past had been forced to endure similar violations of their personal and civil rights, as Sanger had revealed concerning the women arrested under Mayor Wood's "reform" program. Opponents believed that a legal empowerment to continue the practice would only exacerbate the problem. Although the 1871 bill passed both houses of the legislature, it was allowed to die by the governor's failure to sign it.[84]

Again in 1875 a regulation bill was proposed as a means of reducing the increase of both crime and disease in New York City. This bill also was defeated because women's rights groups continued to argue against the licensing system on the grounds that experience had shown that its inclusion of only a relatively small group of prostitutes would doom it to failure and because it unfairly exempted men from inspection and restraint. As in the past, groups such as the Moral Education Society of New York joined in opposing the measure because they believed it unacceptable to license immorality.[85]

Though regulatory measures were again advocated by official or public bodies in both 1876 and 1877, no legislation was adopted. By this time, the failure of the system of regulation in Europe and in one American city, St. Louis, was being publicized. Furthermore, opposition groups had become well organized in their attempts to prevent any further legislative efforts and had sensitized the public to the dubious aspects of the system. Gradually, the movement for legalizing prostitution in New York City died.[86]

That New Yorkers would neither license or regulate prostitution nor "decriminalize" the profession by repealing ineffective anti-prostitution laws that were blatantly discriminatory is indicative of the general public ambivalence about prostitution. Prostitutes continued to be harassed and abused by being shuttled in and out of court and jails throughout the period from 1830 to 1870, but without any significant impact on the overall practice of the profession. This revolving-door approach to prostitution appeared to satisfy nineteenth-century New Yorkers' need to feel that public morality was being preserved and that the unrespectable classes of society were being kept under control. The gender and class biases of the justice system received few challenges. Certainly nowhere in the laws governing prostitution was there recognition of the fact that the prostitute had an equally culpable partner in her "crime." As one observer has said, "prostitution is really the only crime in the penal law where two people are doing a thing mutually agreed upon and yet only one, the female partner, is subject to arrest."[87] That some could have argued that prostitution was a "victimless crime," or more properly a "complainantless crime," was irrelevant. Prostitution statutes remained firmly based on a sexual double standard that punished the female only. Moreover, the sexual bias of the legal system was equally evident in New Yorkers' approach to juvenile justice. An overwhelming number of the delinquent females arrested and sent to the House of Refuge in the mid-nineteenth century were committed for immoral conduct offenses. Case histories repeatedly note that juvenile female offenders were arrested because they "stayed out all night with boys," yet there are no cases of juvenile boys being arrested and committed to the Refuge for "staying out all night with girls." As one commentator has observed,

The actual situation in the city is that prostitution is accepted by everyone—police, judges, [court] clerks, and lawyers. Arrest and prosecution are purely gestures that have to be made to keep up the facade of public morality. The method of dealing with it is simply a form of harassment, not a form of prevention, abolition, or punishment. There is no conviction at any level that prostitution is a crime on anyone's part, only a total and satisfied acceptance of the double standard, excusing the male, accusing the female.[88]

This assessment was made in the 1970s, not the 1800s, but it is equally descriptive of circumstances a century earlier—making a significant statement about the ineffectiveness of the justice system in confronting the legal abuses surrounding prostitution.[89]

Although the double standard inherent in the anti-prostitution laws was never directly challenged in any major way in the nineteenth century, the concept did receive an indirect challenge through the campaign for laws to punish the offenses of seduction and adultery. Seduction was a civil offense in the early decades of the century, but to make a successful seduction case the plaintiff had to be someone other than the seduced. If the case was won, the plaintiff, usually a parent or guardian, was awarded a financial settlement for "loss of services." The seduced was not allowed to seek justice or restitution for a wrong done to her but was "objectified," technically becoming another's chattel or plaything. Critics of the law felt it was an outrage because it required that a "woman must acknowledge herself the *servant* of somebody, who may claim *wages* for her lost time!"[90] Furthermore, charges could be difficult to prove if a defendant challenged the character of the woman who allegedly was seduced; the burden of proof then lay with the woman, who had to counter any suspicions that she might be unchaste.[91]

Women could be charged with seducing men during the early decades of the century, when prostitutes were viewed as "victimizers of morally upright men." The aforementioned Eliza Smith, who had been warned by police that complaints would be made against her brothel if she again admitted the son of a certain respectable family, was charged under the seduction statute in the mid-1830s. Although there is no evidence Smith readmitted the young man, she later did stand as a witness when he and a prostitute were married at a minister's house. The angry father instituted a suit against Smith for recovery of damages for harboring and aiding in the seduction of his son.[92]

By the late 1830s, some male biases of the socio-legal system were being challenged by supporters of the moral reform movement, whose anger over the unfairness of the sexual double standard led to a campaign for laws that would impose criminal penalties on male seducers. Citizens were encouraged to write letters and organize petitions to send to the state capital. By 1840, 20,000 petitions had been sent to the New York legislature, 5,000 from New York City alone. A seduction and adultery bill was reported in the legislature that year but was not acted upon.[93] Throughout the 1840s debate continued over tougher laws against seduction and adultery, and the issue became a topic in the popular press. Major newspapers such as the *Tribune*, the *Herald*, and the *Sun* supported the drive for stricter legislation and helped coalesce public opinion into a sympathetic stance for women who had been seduced, even those who were prostitutes. A focal point in the debate was the trial of Amelia Norman, alias Lydia Brown, who was charged with stabbing her seducer, Henry S. Ballard, on the steps of the Astor House Hotel.

Norman described herself as twenty-five years old, a native of New Jersey, and "a dressmaker by profession which I follow for a living."[94] According to the *Herald*, Norman had been courted by Ballard and then seduced. She had given birth to one of his children and aborted another with the help of Madame Restelle, the famous abortionist. Ballard had then left her without means for thirteen months while he was on a trip to London and on his return had refused to see her. The editor of the *Herald* called Norman's story the "most heart rending history that ever was read or conceived" and described Ballard as "one of those worthy, honorable, moral men who are continually prowling about our large cities in pursuit of such friendless, unprotected girls as this unfortunate Amelia Norman."[95]

Court testimony verified that Norman had unsuccessfully attempted to speak to Ballard on several occasions. Ballard's brother Francis testified that several months before the stabbing, Norman had come to their home and, when told she could not see Ballard, had threatened that she "was determined to ruin him, and if she could not do it in one way she would do it in another, and that she would either send him to the Devil or to Hell." Francis Ballard responded that if she tried to see his brother again "he would send her to the Tombs or Halls of Justice."[96] Henry Ballard testified that Norman had threatened to take his life on several previous occasions. He said that on the evening of the assault Norman had followed him down the street, unsuccessfully attempting to talk to him before she "assaulted him with intent to kill" as he was entering the Astor Hotel.

The prosecutor described Norman as a prostitute and denied that Ballard had seduced her, though he argued that even if he had, seduction was no justification for her act. He remarked that if the accused were acquitted, "12,000 women living by prostitution in the city . . . would be licensed to commit murder."[97] Several witnesses testified to seeing the wounded Ballard fall on the hotel steps, and one witness said that he had taken the knife from the hand of Norman. After eight minutes of deliberation, the jury found Norman not guilty and acquitted her of the crime. The speed with which the jury made its decision and the decision itself were indicative of much public sympathy for Norman's case, even though she was believed to be a prostitute, and of a desire to see women as victims given greater protection.

Throughout the trial the press took strong stands in support of seduction legislation. "Let seduction be at once made a state prison offense," argued the *Herald*. "Talk of a civil prosecution for damages! It is an insulting mockery—mockery of justice—of morality—of right."[98] However, after such a short jury deliberation and the acquittal of Norman the *Herald* questioned whether or not law had been perfectly satisfied, and said it was an "evil day if claims of justice are decided by feelings."[99] Nevertheless, the *Herald* continued to advocate making seduction a penal offense so that men such as Ballard would not be made "the occasional victim to satisfy public indignation."[100] The *Herald* supported its stand by printing letters from the public such as the one that stated: "Seduction, of all crimes, is the greatest. . . . Murder, I consider far inferior in point of criminality. Murder kills but the body— but seduction kills both body and soul forever."[101]

Several bills on seduction and adultery were unsuccessfully brought before the legislature, including one that mandated three years' imprisonment for seduction, and twelve months' imprisonment for each offense of adultery.[102] Groups of women from New York City as well as other cities traveled to Albany to lobby for the legislation, exerting relentless pressure on the lawmakers. A few lone voices questioned whether the laws on licentiousness ought not to provide for the equal punishment of females, but there was no following for this point of view. Finally, in 1848 the Act to Punish Seduction as a Crime passed the legislature. It stipulated that "any man who shall under promise of marriage seduce and have illicit connection with any unmarried female of previous chaste character shall be guilty of a misdemeanor, and upon conviction shall be punished by imprisonment."[103] Though the law had been reformed, and a seducer now could be sent to jail, the protection of the law had not really been extended, especially not for a woman believed to be a prostitute. A line had been drawn between the chaste and the unchaste, thus eliminating the prostitute from claims under the law unless she could prove that the act of seduction was the cause of her "downhill course." Like the old law, the new statute excluded the prostitute from the purview of legal protection because she was perceived to be outside the "circle"—which was basically the family circle—of those the law intended to protect. Nineteenth-century patriarchal attitudes were so antithetical to women protecting themselves that even the reformed law made any successful prosecution rely on the actions and testimony of the woman's "protectors." Prostitutes were not considered under the law, less because of the illegality of their profession than because they composed a female subgroup which was not familial and thus was outside the protection of the law.

Nevertheless, to a few males the seduction debate and the Norman trial appeared to be enough of a threat to encourage precautions in consorting with prostitutes. A Brooklyn lawyer was arrested and brought to court for seducing a young woman in New York City. He won his case by producing affidavits that had been signed earlier by the woman, Mary Ann Coyle, admitting she was a common prostitute. Whether or not Coyle had been a prostitute prior to the court hearing is unknown, but records show that a year and a half later a Mary Ann Cole was arrested with a group of five prostitutes during a raid on a neighboring house. Regardless of her background, the lawyer had been shrewd enough to protect himself from seduction charges.[104]

Although seduction became a criminal offense, it does not seem to have been used much as grounds for legal action. Six months after the bill was passed the *Police Gazette* pointed out that no convictions had been made under the law, and the community wanted its repeal. According to the paper, the law was encouraging perjuries and conspiracies to extort money, and the public was disgusted with the kind of revelations it caused. In the two years following the law's adoption there were a total of four arrests for seduction and four for attempted seduction.[105] There is no indication that any prostitutes pressed charges under the statute, no doubt because most were realistic enough to know they had little chance of a successful prosecution and would only jeopardize future business by attempting to use the protection of the law. In spite of the extensive public debate and much publicity on the seduction issue, it appears attitudes did not change much, if at all. In 1858 William Sanger was still echoing the same lament voiced in the 1830s and 1840s. Under the existing state of public sentiment, he complained, "the seducer is allowed to go unpunished, and the full measure of retribution is directed against his victim. . . . Legal enactments can scarcely ever reach them, although sometimes a poor man without friends or money is indicted and convicted."[106]

In terms of statutory law, prostitutes were victims of a system whose patriarchal assumptions left them, as a female subgroup, almost wholly unprotected, subject to the random whims and power of males in general and legal officers in particular. The vagrancy act especially, which was used so readily against prostitutes and subjected them to punishment virtually without regard for procedural protections, defined the "crime" at issue not as illicit sex trade but as being female, poor, and without a male protector. What allowed prostitutes to function reasonably effectively in this period was that while New York City moved into a more urbanized and impersonalized era, the common customs and values of the community retained enough strength to avert the full intent of legalized male domination. As will be illustrated more fully in the next chapter, arbitrary as the system was, it was a great benefit in general to prostitutes because the customs of the community were more flexible and more respectful of women as individuals (as well as of men as sexual animals) than the high moralism of the period, which always retreated toward its patriarchal roots and prejudices when pushed toward law.

5

Notorious Defenders

Prostitutes Using the Law

While walking down Broadway, Catherine Wilson, who said she had a good memory for faces, recognized a man she had met five or six months earlier in a prostitution establishment in Orange Street. The man had stolen her watch, beaded bag, handkerchief, pocket book, and ivory rule. Wilson approached the man, made a citizen's arrest, and escorted him to the police station. At the station, Wilson filed a charge of theft, and the man was tried, convicted, and sent to prison for six months.[1] Although Wilson's assertiveness may have been notable, her confidence as a citizen, working with legal authorities, was not unusual for a nineteenth-century prostitute. Because they worked their trade outside the law, prostitutes were always vulnerable to arrest and to abuse and harassment from officials, patrons, rowdies, and the public. Many of them suffered repeated legal indignities, difficulties they accepted as part of the profession, but many, like Wilson, also found ways to deal with the legal system and even to work the system effectively to their own advantage.

Prostitutes and Law Enforcers

The biggest factor in determining the impact of laws on the prostitute was her relationship with law enforcers, especially with the police officers on the street, who represented law-enforcement authority at the level with which the prostitute had the most day-to-day contact. In most cases it was the local police who determined whether a prostitute was to be recognized as such, was breaking the law and should be arrested, or was inoffensive and could operate free of legal interference.

New York was not a well-policed city in the nineteenth century, and twentieth-century notions of police professionalism are distant from the police organization that prostitutes of the time encountered in New York City. For the first few decades of the century, New Yorkers were still close enough to the period of British rule to be suspicious of any form of "military" authority or control in their communities, so they rejected the idea of a well-organized permanent police force. Citizens preferred to depend on police supervision that was casual and sporadic and that was supplied by fellow members of the local community. The result was an inefficient but very personalized form of law enforcement, where many decisions involving conflicts between prescribed law and local customs and communal attitudes were left to the discretion of the neighborhood police. Police discretion defined who was deviant and how deviants should be controlled, and this discretion involved discrimination in the form of selective law enforcement. Thus, nineteenth-century New Yorkers' desire for a limited formal institutional police power resulted in an unchecked informal discretionary police power.[2]

Although by 1830 New York's population and urban problems had increased to the point that many New Yorkers felt that the social controls of a stable society had broken down in many areas of the city, police organization remained much as it had been in the late eighteenth century. Officials such as the mayor, high constable, constables, marshals, and night watch all bore some responsibility for the police protection of the community, as did members of the Common Council and police justices. The mayor was the chief police officer, taking charge at fires, riots, and other breaches of the peace. Constables were elected from each ward annually. It was not always easy to find people who were willing to undertake the arduous duties of the constable's job, but any citizen who refused to accept his election as constable was fined. Occasionally, someone could be found who was eager to serve because of the fees that could be earned or the power conferred by the office. Marshals were appointed by the mayor and held office at his pleasure. Both constables and marshals had the common law duties and powers of peace or police officers, but they did not wear uniforms or carry identifying badges or emblems. They did not receive regular salaries but were compensated by fees for services performed according to a schedule established by the state legislature. Critics of this form of job compensation argued that police officers devoted their time to what was likely to earn the largest fees, not to what was most important, that they made unnecessary arrests of the poor and powerless to collect fees, and that honest officers often earned very little money under the system.[3]

Night watchmen, who patrolled the city at night, did not have police powers and could arrest free from reprisal only if a crime were committed before their eyes or if they were acting under the direction of a police officer. By 1830 there were 512 watchmen in New York, who were paid on a per diem basis; shifts were arranged so that watchmen could also hold daytime jobs, with the result that only 128 of them, one-fourth of the force, were on the streets at any one time. The pay for watchmen ranged from 75 cents to 87-1/2 cents per night. Watchmen owed their appointment and tenure in office to the mayor, aldermen, and assistant aldermen, who competed over the years for power in controlling this valuable patronage. The watch was an ancient institution, as its long history (and the age of its members) attested, but it did not have much prestige since many thought it inadequate and its members incompetent. Watchmen wore leather helmets while on duty and were thus derisively known as leatherheads. If a watchman's helmet was taken from his head twice while asleep on duty, he was to be dismissed. Citizens often joked, "While the city sleeps, the watchmen do too," a jibe borne out by statistics. Men chosen for the watch were often of a low caliber, people who had few other means of earning a living.[4]

Between 1830 and 1845, a marked upsurge in crime, vice, and disorder plus the model of the recently restructured more "professional" London police force spurred efforts to provide a similar police organization for New York City. The number of complaints entered at the police courts in 1835 was 10,168, more than five times the number that had been recorded three decades before. All citizens worried about the growth in violent crimes, and moralists complained about the great increase in the crimes of prostitution, gambling, and intoxication. In 1835 there were almost 3,000 licensed drinking places in New York City, a ratio of one for every fifty persons in the city over the age of fifteen. Riots also greatly increased in the 1830s; there were so many in

1834 alone that it was long remembered in New York City history as the year of riots. At riots in both 1834 and 1835, local law enforcement officials were unable to suppress rioters, a failure that led the mayor to call in the militia. These outbreaks dramatically highlighted the weakness of the city police force.[5]

In the decade and a half after 1830 citizens also worried about the potential for corruption by police. Police appointments were regarded as patronage plums, and thus any changes in the party in power meant an influx of inexperienced men. Policemen were considered entrepreneurs more than public servants, in a system with many openings for bribery and not many rewards for diligence. Reliance on fees rather than salaries was an evil that had grown over the years; in cases involving stolen property, for example, officers were not overly concerned about apprehending offenders, since recovering the property for rewards was far more lucrative. Some New Yorkers believed that police officers made deals with criminals in which the thieves turned over stolen property in exchange for being set free. The competitiveness of the fee system also discouraged cooperation among police officers in the apprehension of offenders. A policeman received 50 cents for each unlawful citizen committed to jail, a seemingly small sum but one that was equal to two-thirds of a watchman's nightly pay.[6]

Between 1830 and 1845 there were a number of formal proposals for reforming the police, but political parties' competition for control of the police as patronage prevented innumerable plans from being adopted. Finally, a reorganization and reform of the New York City police was accomplished in May 1845 by a bill passed in the state legislature and endorsed by the Common Council. Two of the major reforms were the abolishment of most of the existing police offices, with all police functions to be performed by a new "Day and Night Police," and the elimination of the fee payment system by the establishment of set salaries. Although the new plan provided for a better organized and unified police structure, the force retained its "political" orientation because policemen of all ranks were appointed by elected officials. The reform established the basic structure of the New York police for the rest of the century, though some changes were made over the years. In 1857 the city police force was put under the auspices of the state legislature, remaining in the state's control until home rule was once again established in 1870.[7]

New York City's personalized and localized form of law enforcement gave the prostitute the opportunity to establish a working relationship with local law enforcers and reduced the likelihood of a large, citywide vice structure that might victimize the prostitute. As vagrancy and disorderly persons cases make clear, the police arrested and jailed prostitutes under the law, but their toughest enforcement seemed directed more at the poor and less "established" streetwalkers than at prostitutes living in neighborhood brothels. Distressed citizens charged that prostitution was allowed to exist because police received monetary payoffs from brothel operators. In the spring of 1844, when pressure was strong for a police reform, the *Tribune* ran an expose by a writer called "L" on the corruption of the police. The article claimed that thieves, harlots, and other depredators paid off public officials to avoid prosecution.[8] It is likely that some prostitutes were permitted to work in a neighborhood because of payoffs or bribes to police, but, other than public complaints about suspected bribes, there is no evidence that an extensive system of prostitution payoffs existed in the early and middle part of the century. Theoretically, if a policeman collected a bribe for leaving a prostitute alone in the years before police reform, he would then have few other opportunities to collect scheduled fees for legal proceedings against that prostitute. It is more likely that individual prostitutes paid to be kept out of jail after being arrested so that an officer who arrested a prostitute might get a bribe for dropping the charges. If there were a time when brothels paid for protection, it was probably after 1845 when police salaries replaced the fee system—even though salaries were supposed to eliminate police corruption which many believed was caused by the fee system.

Historians have often mentioned payoff practices in the antebellum period but have not clearly documented them. Some have cited as evidence for payoffs the legal system of fees and fines that existed before the police department was restructured. Aside from misconstruing the fee system, however, sufficient documentation has not been presented and examples typically are cited from the post–Civil War era. One contemporary with firsthand knowledge, former police chief George Walling, wrote in the 1880s that police blackmailed poor prostitutes, and he argued that a policy of segregating prostitutes in specified sections of the city would help prevent this practice. Walling did not state if his claims of blackmail applied to the earlier period as well as the 1870s and

1880s, nor did he state how widespread the practice was.[9] Available evidence suggests that the systematic and organized control of commercialized sex through payoffs was not characteristic of New York City until the last quarter of the nineteenth century.[10]

Most sources indicate that prostitutes and prostitution houses were allowed to operate in local neighborhoods because law officers did not perceive them to be "criminal" or a major problem in the community. The women managing and living in these houses were treated as neighborhood citizens operating local businesses, unless their establishments became too disorderly.[11] In 1849 Samuel Prime noted that "nice" houses were protected by the police and even were allowed to exist "next door to police stations," a reference to the brothel of Kate Hastings at 50 Leonard Street, next door to the fifth ward station house.[12] Thus, prostitutes associated with police officials as members of a local neighborhood, and they established a working relationship with law enforcers because their professions interfaced in several ways. Prostitutes were a source of official fees for legal actions taken on their behalf, such as arresting rowdy guests or serving processes, and prostitutes also gave police payments or "tips" for other types of services performed, such as recovering stolen property or helping in various private matters. Whereas prostitutes might have resented a payoff system as harassment, they could regard fees and tips for services as positive rewards for assisting them. Furthermore, prostitutes often furnished information to officials about investigations or other police business, and in some cases the association of prostitutes and police even reached a "friendship" level.[13]

The working relationship between prostitutes and law enforcement officials was brought to the public's attention during the Jewett murder trial in 1836. Officer Dennis Brink, who had arrested the suspect the morning after the murder, testified in court about the nature of his relationship with Rosina Townsend, the madam for whom Jewett had worked. Brink pointed out that he had known Townsend for three years, had been in her brothel about six times, but had not been there as a client or as a participant in a card game. He had served processes against Townsend's boarders and against her servants on different occasions, and he had received the regular fees for these services. One of the processes he served had been against a boarder for assault and battery. Brink also had been summoned on several occasions when there were disturbances in the house, but the rioters had always dispersed before he arrived. He stated he had never paid Townsend money, but she "may" have paid him for legal fees or costs or for serving processes for her. Brink and several other officers had been paid $5 each for helping with Townsend's household sale a month before, but he denied that he had received two vases free from Townsend at the sale. Defense counsel Ogden Hoffman quizzed Brink on whether he had ever received money from Townsend for speaking on her behalf to the district attorney, or if he had ever gone to the district attorney to intercede on Townsend's behalf in regard to an indictment pending against her. When Brink said he could not remember, Hoffman asked him to name the district attorney at the time of the case in question. Brink answered that it had been Hoffman.

Hoffman then questioned Brink's involvement with other prostitutes. Brink acknowledged that on several occasions he had received money from Mrs. Berry for services rendered in suppressing troubles at her brothel, and he estimated the payments to have been approximately $1 each time. He also acknowledged receiving money from a gentleman for settling a case that was pending in the Court of General Sessions against two prostitutes who had torn the clothing of a third prostitute.[14]

Although Brink appears to have had frequent involvement with prostitutes, his actions were not always on their behalf. In several cases brought before the Court of General Sessions, Brink had been the officer on duty who brought charges against a house of prostitution, and on one occasion Brink brought charges of assault and battery against a prostitute, Margaret Ryerson, for "violently seizing hold of him and tearing his shirt while in the execution of his duty" at her disorderly house.[15]

Police often testified alongside prostitutes in court trials, especially in cases of divorce, since adultery was the major grounds for divorce. A policeman usually was asked to verify that a female witness was a prostitute because of his knowledge of her or her house, and this testimony almost always indicated that the police had had amicable relationships with the prostitute. In the 1852 divorce trial of Edwin and Catherine Forrest, eleven active or former policemen were called to testify about Caroline Ingersoll, who had operated several assignation or prostitution boarding houses in the city. Policeman Lorenzo Savage testified he had been to Ingersoll's house before with two other policemen, and he said that he "did not stay but they did." Officer Jacob Carlock noted that he knew Ingersoll because he lived up the street as a neighbor, and he gave descriptions of the types of men and women

who entered and left her residence. Another officer, Augustus Goodrich, said he had only been to Ingersoll's once as a policeman, but since
he was a cabinetmaker by trade, he had done a few carpentry jobs for
her there.[16]

In the case of Mary Fowler, who was charged with operating a
disorderly house, one ward captain and four other policemen testified
indirectly on Fowler's behalf. All of the officers were acquainted with
her and admitted to seeing men and women going in and out of her
house as late as 3 A.M., but none of them "knew" if it was a disorderly
house, and none had ever "seen anything improper there." In sum-
marizing the case, the presiding judge pointed out the obvious by noting
that disorderly houses "exist in all parts of the city, . . . even the most
respectable neighborhoods, and are indirectly countenanced by the
police."[17]

Evidence of the close association of legal officials and prostitutes in
the day-to-day investigations of the police is found in the diary of Robert
Taylor, a police justice for eight years who had earlier served as a captain
of the watch. In the early 1840s, Taylor had played an active role in
pushing for police reform, and after the adoption of the reorganization
plan in 1845 he had prepared the manual for the new force.[18] In his
advice to police, Taylor, advocating an active, investigative force over
a responsive one, wrote: "The prevention of crime being the most
important object in view, your exertions must be constantly used to that
end."[19]

The year and a half of entries in Taylor's diary indicate that he viewed
himself as an investigator as well as a judge, actively pursuing wrong-
doers and seeking their punishment. The diary catalogues his dealings
with thieves, gamblers, drunks, liquor dealers, and prostitutes. The
prostitutes with whom he worked, however, were regarded not as law
violators but rather as neighborhood resources for his investigations. Nor
did Taylor consider himself corrupt in any way for not interfering with
the prostitution operations. He mentioned having seen a daybook and
register that "gave proof that corruption exists to an alarming extent with
many officials connected with the administration of criminal law in the
city," but he obviously did not regard his own relations with prostitutes
in this category.

Taylor recorded over fifty routine visits to brothels. His references
include names of twenty-five different prostitutes, six of whom are

mentioned from three to six times each. Taylor always took one or more companions on his brothel visits—as co-investigators, as voyeurs, or possibly as witnesses to protect his reputation.[20] Taylor went to the brothels seeking information on cases involving divorce, death, abortion, counterfeiting, or theft, but he also noted that on one occasion he took Justice Ketchum for a tour because Ketchum had never visited a brothel before. After seeing what went on in eleven different brothels, Ketchum apparently was fascinated enough to return with Taylor on another evening that included visits to nine brothels.

In most cases the prostitutes appear to have been very cooperative in helping Taylor or in giving him information. Taylor made return visits to those houses where the women were most cooperative, such as the brothel of Adeline Miller on Church Street. In one instance, however, Miller refused to help get information for Taylor because he was investigating her son, Nelson, who had taken a shawl from his own wife. Apparently, Miller felt comfortable enough with her relationship with Taylor to refuse to help him instead of claiming she had no knowledge of the affair. When Miller would not help, Taylor persuaded another woman in the house to assist in locating the shawl, and she later notified Taylor where it had been pawned.

While Taylor was at church one day, a woman called at his home, a visitor he assumed to be prostitute Fanny White, who had promised the night before to get some information for him. That White would make a Sunday morning visit to his house did not appear to surprise or embarrass Taylor.[21]

Establishing a working relationship with a law officer was obviously to the advantage of a prostitute: it allowed her to operate freely in a neighborhood and gave her a contact on the police force in case customers, boarders, or rowdies caused problems in her brothel. Adeline Furman, alias Adeline Miller, summoned the watch to her Elm Street brothel because four men were being disorderly and refused to leave. Officer Harvey forcibly evicted them and ordered them to "be peaceable and go away." The men still lingered outside the house, threatened to prosecute Harvey, and told him it was "a damned shame a watchman should receive pay for protecting whore houses." Harvey then arrested and brought charges against the four men.[22]

Even if a police officer or watchman acted against a prostitute's interests and arrested her, the New York City legal and court system provided her with ways to avoid further legal restraints. Police justices, or magistrates, presided over police court, the first level of administration of the criminal justice system. Before 1848 justices were appointed to office, and after that date they were elected, thus involving them even more in the partisan politics of the city. Few, if any, of the police justices had legal training, and they conducted their courts with little regard for the niceties of legal procedure.

Aldermen and assistant aldermen were elected representatives from each ward to the city council, or Common Council, and they, with the mayor, had the power to make appointments to the police force. Aldermen also possessed magistrates' powers, and many used this power to hold court in the station houses. Thus, a policeman might arrest a prostitute, and an alderman or magistrate could release the prisoner without any sort of hearing. An 1853 law modified this practice by no longer allowing aldermen to bail or discharge persons committed by other magistrates, but aldermen retained the right of releasing a prisoner before a magistrate had committed her or him, and they could also release a prisoner between the time of arrest and an appearance before a magistrate. Although the concurrent jurisdiction of the legal system lowered the morale of court officials, since they could countermand each other's authority, it offered prostitutes alternatives for escaping the heavy hand of the law—alternatives they apparently used to their advantage. [23]

The *Advocate of Moral Reform* frequently voiced complaints about the close relationships between prostitutes and officials. The paper reported that an attractive prostitute from ward five, mother of two children, had sneered at the reformers' threat that the law would root out her vice, and she informed them that "men of the first distinction in the city are the ones who pour from $50 to $400 a week into her treasury." The prostitute told reformers that a judge had offered his name and money if she ever needed it. The reformers further confirmed their suspicions of collusion between prostitutes and officials when two prostitutes and two men were seen walking from the noted brothel of Patience Berger to the home of a judge not far away. In the period before restrictions were put on aldermen's judicial powers, the *Police Gazette* reported an incident in which a sixth ward alderman came with two friends to the station house to order the release of two prostitutes. Because he was drunk, the police locked him up, a response to his disorderly behavior as well as a possible indication of their resentment of the alderman's power to countermand their orders. The press also reported the case of Mary Berry's husband, Francis, who was charged with robbing a man in their Duane Street brothel. Berry offered to return one-third of the "booty" knowing, according to the *Advocate*, that the law usually required the return of much less. The judge refused the offer, but Berry's bail was immediately provided by an ex-alderman.[24]

Samuel Prime also noted the tolerance of legal officials for prostitutes and their close association with the women in neighborhoods: "Hundreds of [disorderly] houses close by the houses of our magistrates spread their allurements before the eyes of our youth and tempt them into the vortex of hell, and the shield of law protects the portal, though all that enter, enter to be damned."[25] At times, however, the close association or neighborhood proximity of prostitutes and officials could cause strain. One of the houses owned by Adeline Miller and managed by a Mrs. Brown backed up to the house of Alderman Erben. As disturbances at the brothel became more frequent, the Erbens became more annoyed because, whenever watchmen were called to Brown's house, the riotous parties "effected their escape by taking the liberty of scaling the Alderman's fence, rushing through his hall, and making their exit at his front door." Finally after one of these late-night "unannounced visits," the *Sun* reported that Erben "had the inmates of the house all removed to the watch house," in the hope of breaking up the "nest of prostitution and iniquity, which he has so long tolerated directly under his own magisterial nose."[26]

The result of New York City's localized and personalized law enforcement was that it was selective, supporting both discretion and discrimination on the part of officials. Prostitutes understood this and hoped that either a lack of true concern or leniency by officials would allow them to escape harassment, arrest, or punishment. Sometimes prostitutes found that policemen's actions crossed the boundary between law enforcement and abuse. Elizabeth Dairey, sent to the Tombs for stealing, reported she had been kicked by an officer. Others noted incidents of sexual harassment and abuse. Emeline Frisby, a black woman who worked in a "house of polluted reputation" in Reed Street, was arrested and put in prison for taking $164 from her "sister." The *Sun* reported that officers had "compelled" Frisby to strip and submit to a "considerable search." Mary Moore, from a brothel in Broome Street, filed charges against watchman John Ostrander for entering her room and attacking her while she was asleep. He was tried but discharged by the jury. Another prostitute from the late 1860s reported she had been taken to an oyster house by an officer who then raped her and threatened to send her to prison if she told.[27] Though some policemen may have believed that a woman in the "unlawful sex trade" was fair game for whatever treatment they meted out, their abuse also may have reflected a disdain toward those prostitutes and other women who were poor and at the bottom of the ethnic hierarchy.

The police were not completely insensitive to prostitutes in the lowest echelons of the trade, however. Many "down and out" prostitutes who felt they could no longer support themselves in prostitution turned to policemen for shelter, food, and medical assistance. There are a number of cases where prostitutes came to police asking to be sent to the penitentiary because they had been turned out of their brothels, had nowhere to go, or were sick and needed medical help. One twenty-three-year-old woman, who said she had been in the profession since she was a child, was committed to prison after having been out of the penitentiary only three days. When given a six-month sentence, she expressed her gratitude and said she would gladly take another six months at the end of her term. In 1850 the *Herald* reported the death of seventy-year-old "English Nance," who had been mentioned in the press for decades and who, at a much earlier age, was said to have had the extraordinary strength to be able to "beat off half a dozen officers attempting to arrest her." After reaching middle age, or for the last thirty years, the *Herald* noted that she had been a constant visitor in prison, "averaging more than half her time there."[28] "Jail as home" was not an unusual choice for these women. There were few public agencies at the time, other than the police, who would have assisted these women in any meaningful way because, on the whole, public assistance was sparingly supplied to anyone in need, prostitute or not. Furthermore, while some might interpret their seeking out law enforcers and imprisoners as a perverse form of psychological dependency, it is also possible that previous interaction with police had established that they could respond to the necessities and limited options of unfortunate prostitutes as well as, if not better than, anyone else in the community. Both familiarity with the police station and personal interaction with legal officials may have made the police the community agency with which many prostitutes interacted most comfortably.

In spite of some examples of police discrimination and abuse, New York's law enforcement system based on officers' personal discretion enabled prostitutes and other law violators to manipulate the system to their benefit. In a letter to Governor Fish in November 1849, New York City Judge J. W. Edmonds complained that "police magistrates and aldermen discharge at pleasure even after conviction anyone with influence enough to procure discharge."[29] This influence occurred in many forms. Usually it was helpful if a prostitute came from one of the "better" brothels. Emma Place, alias Allen, was arrested for robbing a man of $40 while he was at Jenny Sweet's well-known brothel on Church Street, but the justice at her arraignment dismissed the case after she claimed that the complainant was drunk when the alleged robbery occurred. Prostitutes also resorted to the use of monetary rewards to create influence. An example of such a case involved a prostitute who was arrested and sent to jail for assaulting a gentleman while he was with his family at the theater. According to the *Tribune*, the woman was freed after only a few days' confinement because she distributed $25 among the police officers.[30] The *Herald* reported influence of a different kind in a case involving two third ward prostitutes who were arrested for soliciting. One, Kitty Bracket, was described as very ugly, while the other, Emma Howard, was said to be very attractive and well built. Howard's good looks elicited much comment among policemen at the stationhouse but did not prevent the captain from locking her up in the cell next to Bracket. During the night Howard requested a drink of water and was said to be safely in her cell, but by morning she had managed to escape while friend Kitty was sent on to Blackwell's Island. The *Herald* commented that those "who knew more of human nature and the power of a pretty woman" were not astonished by the miraculous escape.[31]

Kate Ridgley was another woman who understood that the power of a pretty woman and friendly relations could be factors in a court case. Ridgley, "a dashing looking woman," managed a house at 78 Duane called the "palace of mirrors," which was said to have sixty superbly furnished rooms. Ridgley filed a complaint against two "sporting men" who visited her house and "alarmed her boarders" by threatening to damage her furniture. She took her case before the mayor to have a decision rendered, bringing along with her six "very fine looking young witnesses" who were "decked out in the tip of the fashion with silks, satin and jewelry." These witnesses "were seated near the mayor, to be called upon in order to substantiate the accusations." The defendants shrewdly hired a well-known political figure to protest their innocence, and even though the mayor found the two men guilty, he demanded only that they each post $100 bail to keep the peace. Ridgley seemed satisfied with the decision, and she and her boarders, "after chatting a little while with some of their old friends, left the office for the quiet of home."[32]

If a prostitute failed to be shown leniency by police, aldermen, or justices, she had one final recourse if her case went to trial: the jury. In describing prostitution and disorderly house cases in the 1850s, Chief of Police George Walling wrote that "as a general rule, juries have something almost amounting to an aversion to convict in such cases, and especially is this so when the jury is made up largely of elderly men; they seem to sympathize, strangely enough, with the elegantly accoutred and apparently repentant Delilah, who sometimes sheds 'crocodile' tears, or else looks as prim and demure as a Puritan maiden fresh from the Mayflower."[33]

Given the informal and personal nature of New York City's law enforcement in the mid-nineteenth century, it is understandable that prostitutes would view law enforcement officials as more important than the law itself in the functioning of their daily lives. Officials decided whether the prostitute faced restrictions or freedom, punishment or accommodation, censure or camaraderie. The discretion allowed legal officials in the execution of their duties could mean a prostitute would be sent to the penitentiary for six months with little or no regard for legal due process or her individual rights, or it might mean she could operate her business in a neighborhood with little interference because she used working relationships, sympathy, personal and sexual favors, or monetary rewards to accomplish this end. Prostitutes understood that their well-being often depended on tenuous and unequal relationships with law enforcement officials. Nevertheless, many nineteenth-century prostitutes effectively avoided the punishments of the legal system and openly and smoothly practiced their profession by a tactful manipulation of the personalism of the system.

Prostitutes as Legal Citizens

No aspect of a prostitute's life indicated more clearly her integration into the mainstream of New York City life and her confidence in that position than did her participation as a citizen in the municipal and judicial processes of the city. Prostitutes accepted the fact that they had to work around the legal strictures of their society, but they also believed they were entitled to certain rights and privileges as members of the community. Prostitutes expected the municipal government to defend their interests and protect their persons and property. When they, their possessions, or their brothels were threatened, prostitutes called the watch, pressed charges, and gave court testimony against their aggressors. In defending their interests, prostitutes were not afraid of being highly visible or of taking public action against another party because they viewed themselves as a part of the public citizenry, not as legal deviants who must function outside the established system.

Besides bringing their own suits against individuals in the courts, prostitutes also were called upon to participate in legal hearings or public inquiries. Sometimes prostitutes were required to give information at inquests into the death of a friend, coworker, or patron, and at other times they were subpoenaed to testify as witnesses in divorce hearings. Although a husband's association with a prostitute proved he had violated a legally endorsed trust and must suffer the consequences, no questions were raised nor prosecutions made over the prostitute's participation in an activity that was supposedly prohibited by law.

Finally, just as serving as a public witness at an inquest or trial was a civic obligation assumed by prostitutes, so too was the payment of taxes on their real and personal property. Prostitutes were assessed on their assets like other citizens, and like others, they readily challenged their tax assessments when they believed they were too high.

A year in the life of Kate Hastings suggests the variety of ways a prostitute might interact with the court system and public officials. A native of New Hampshire, Hastings began her New York career in prostitution in 1845 when she went to work in Sarah Tuttle's Leonard Street brothel next door to the fifth ward station house. This brothel was familiar not only to the neighboring law enforcers but also to Justice

Robert Taylor, who in his diary mentions visiting it several times. Hastings took over management of Tuttle's brothel in 1848 and purchased the property from Tuttle two years later. Following the purchase of the brothel, Hastings went before the tax assessor to have her personal property holdings "sworn off" the tax roll, since she apparently had used her personal assets in purchasing the real estate property.[34] Hastings's appeal before the tax assessor was at least the fifth time over the period of a year that she made an appearance before some legal tribunal, including the police court, the criminal courts of Special Sessions and General Sessions, and the Superior Court.

Like other brothel managers, Hastings periodically had to contend with rowdy guests in her establishment. On one occasion she filed charges in police court against William Dowell for malicious mischief, and another time she gave testimony in the Court of General Sessions against James Berdell for assault and battery. Berdell had gotten into an argument with several of the women in Hastings's brothel and had raised such a disturbance that police were summoned. The officials immediately recognized Berdell as a fugitive from justice who was wanted for violently assaulting a police officer a year before.[35]

Hastings also made an appearance before the Superior Court of Connecticut in the divorce trial of John C. Holland, president of the Norwich and Worcester Railroad Company. Holland's wife, Frances, had subpoenaed Hastings and two other New York City prostitutes to verify her husband's infidelity. Hastings was a cooperative witness and gave a brief account of her years in prostitution, including a description of her involvement with "Marquis," the name by which all three prostitutes knew Holland. Not only did she describe Holland's intimacies with several of the fifteen women in the brothel, but she also stated: "He has never been in bed with me [but] he has had carnal knowledge of me in my parlor adjoining my bedroom."[36]

Hastings's confidence that publicity or notoriety would not jeopardize her freedom to practice her profession was even more evident in a case in which Hastings aggressively defended her "name and reputation" both on the streets and in the courtroom in response to an unflattering article in a local newspaper.

Several of New York City's mid-nineteenth-century newspaper editors were controversial figures. After the 1830s there was an increase in the number of inexpensive New York dailies, the penny press, whose common fare was topics that would have been considered improper or indecent to discuss in print a decade earlier. Many of the stories encouraged a popular taste for vicarious vice and crime, while others appear both to have offended sensibilities and wounded reputations. Editors such as James W. Webb of the *Courier and Enquirer*, James G. Bennett of the *Herald*, George Wilkes of the *Police Gazette*, Moses Y. Beach of the *Sun*, and E. Z. C. Judson of *Ned Buntline's Own* not only squabbled with each other as editors of competing papers but also became embroiled in a number of controversies with members of the reading public.[37] Both editors and citizens were brought to physical blows over the anger and animosities created by news articles. In light of this, editor J. G. Bennett's biographer has stated that nineteenth-century "editorial impact could almost be measured by the number of welts and bruises a newspaper proprietor displayed. Assaulting an editor, generally with a whip, was rarely out of season on the streets of New York."[38]

In April 1849, E. Z. C. Judson, editor of *Ned Buntline's Own*, printed an article in his paper mentioning Kate Hastings. The first half of the small article called "Description of Gamblers" portrayed a local figure, Samuel A. Suydam, as a very unattractive person. The last half of the column said that

if . . . any of my readers feel particularly anxious to see this notorious blackleg, his den is at No. 14 Barclay-Street, and his *chere amie* is the infamous cast-off mistress of a deceased gambler, known as gallows Kate Hastings, the keeper of a low house of prostitution in Leonard-Street. Sam dances attendance to this strumpet when called on.[39]

According to a letter from Hastings printed in the *Herald*, Hastings learned about the article the day after its publication while she was shopping in a store on Ann Street. Hastings stated that the article was "derogatory to my own character and the character of my house. . . . I immediately said I would cowhide Ned Buntline the first time I caught him in a public street." Just as Hastings declared this to her acquaintances, Judson passed the store, and Hastings followed and caught him by the arm. She told him she would cowhide him for the insult the next time she met him, and she would wait on Broadway until the opportunity arose. Five days later, after waiting an hour on the corner near Judson's office, Hastings found her opportunity. As Judson walked down the street with friends, she gave him two blows on the head. Hastings said she "didn't stop to see if he was much hurt and didn't care."[40]

The assault attracted much attention and comment both in the press and from New York citizens. J. G. Bennett appeared to take special delight in reporting an embellished version of the story in the *Herald*. The paper said it was alleged Judson had drawn a pistol and threatened the life of his fair assailant. Infuriated by the reporting of the affair, Judson wrote the paper pointing out that he had not drawn a pistol nor had a word been said. He stated he felt the *Herald*'s reporting was so particularly malignant that he had directed his lawyer "to enter a suit for libel against the paper's proprietor unless he gives a full and immediate retraction."[41]

Judson filed charges of assault and battery against Hastings, and her case went before a grand jury. The grand jury could not find a bill against her, so the case was "laid over." Hastings waived her right to a trial by jury and accepted a bench trial in the Court of Special Sessions. The press gave a detailed description of Hastings's appearance before the court:

She had on a splendid fawn-colored silk dress, and wore a rich broche shawl, with a pearl colored straw hat. She had about her person a profusion of jewelry, charms, watch, bracelets, buckles, pencil head, watch-key, and other like articles of adornment. She came in with a smart business-like air, and seemed to court dispatch.[42]

According to the *Herald*, the trial attracted a large group of spectators who were so eager to view Hastings they "stood to see her, put on eyeglasses, and ran to the balcony."[43]

Hastings's court deposition defended her actions on the basis of the derogatory attack that had been made on her by Judson in his paper. She stated that Judson had for a considerable period published similar gross attacks upon her which had been calculated to arouse her anger, and thus they had succeeded in causing her to "chastise" him. Even though the grand jury did not find a bill against her, Hastings said she wished to save the county the expense of a jury trial so had waived that right. She stated she readily accepted guilt for inflicting the chastisement upon Judson but believed that his "scurrilous attack" on her left him fully meriting the severe punishment she had meted out. Hastings reinforced charges that her adversary had a venomous nature and an unsavory character by submitting as evidence two letters that had been sent to her the day following the confrontation on Broadway. One was signed by Judson and said:

You are an infernal dirty bitch and if you ever attempt to do to me a similar act you may consider yourself shot. Take warning by this you dirty whore. My paper is mine and I am able to be responsible for any articles contained therein.

E. Z. C. Judson[44]

The second letter, which also appeared to be in Judson's handwriting, was signed, "One Who Knows Something." It justified the actions of Judson and accused Hastings of being a destroyer of youthful morals and lives, a "damd [sic] whore . . . [who is] fucked every night by sporting men." The letter ended with the warning: "Woe be to you cursed whore. Look out!"[45]

The judges accepted Hastings's plea of guilty, said they trusted she would not attack the man again, and imposed a fine of 6 cents. The *Herald* reported that when her sentence was pronounced, "Kate very deliberately opened an elegant purse she held in her hand, and was about to pay the sixpence down at once, but her counsel interposed saying to her that the amount was merely nominal, and that she might leave it to him to arrange." According to the press, when the trial ended voices were heard all around expressing approbation at the decision of the court, and as Hastings left the room she audibly remarked that if Judson did not leave her alone in the future he would not be able to come to court the next time.[46]

In spite of the animosities expressed for each other, Judson and Hastings appear to have eventually reached a truce in their relationship. A police officer testified to seeing Judson and some companions leaving Hastings's brothel only a month and a half after the trial for her assault on him.[47]

Many prostitutes were just as active as Hastings in their roles as citizens of the community—or in their interactions with municipal agencies, such as tax assessors. A review of tax records in wards five and eight in eight different years during the 1840s and 1850s reveals twenty-four instances of known prostitutes appealing their assessments. Some prostitutes, such as Eliza Pratt, Adeline Miller, Sarah Tuttle, Fanny White, and Ann Thomas challenged their appraisals on more than one occasion. The fact that prostitutes took advantage of the appeals process

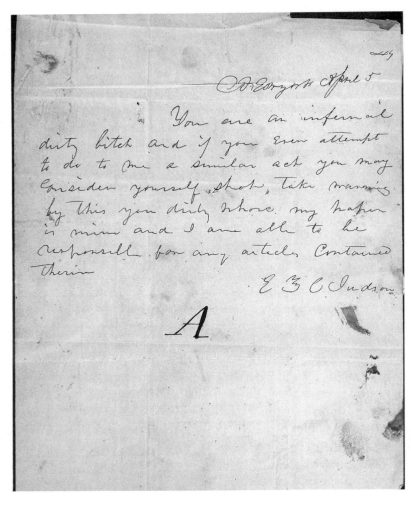

13. LETTER FROM EDITOR JUDSON TO PROSTITUTE KATE HASTINGS.
This letter, written by an angry E. Z. C. Judson after being horsewhipped by
Hastings, was submitted as evidence at the court hearing on the incident.
(NYDA Indictments, *People v. Hastings*, 17 April 1849, Municipal Archives,
Department of Records and Information Services, City of New York)

indicates that they were not afraid of challenging municipal officials and were not concerned about keeping a low profile for fear that public attention might jeopardize their ability to work in the community.[48]

Court records and newspapers also indicate that prostitutes repeatedly were called upon to serve as witnesses at public trials or hearings, especially to supply testimony verifying infidelity in divorce proceedings. When the parties involved were prominent, such as John Holland, the trials became news events, and the prostitutes became well known to the community. Six months after Judson's altercation with Hastings, his wife sued for divorce, and Fanny White and the occupants of her house testified to repeated instances of adultery on Judson's part. Testimony of prostitutes also was used in the 1852 divorce trial of the famous actor Edwin Forrest. Caroline Ingersoll, manager of assignation and prostitution boarding houses, gave guarded but important testimony that was crucial in bringing about a decision favorable to Mrs. Forrest.[49]

Prostitutes also testified at inquests or trials involving the deaths of prostitutes or their patrons and at investigative hearings into suspected crimes, such as the fire that destroyed the National Theatre and Julia Brown's brothel next door. In the case of the fire, officials were investigating both a suspected arson and the death of a young prostitute. In the 1836 Jewett murder trial, ten prostitutes testified about events at the brothel and gave information concerning the parties involved. In the 1843 murder of Charles Corlis, five prostitutes were called to give information about circumstances surrounding the death. In the 1870 murder of Benjamin Nathan, Clara Dale, a prostitute from Irene Mc-Cready's brothel, was a key witness because she provided the alibi for the prosecution's major suspect, Nathan's son.[50]

Prostitutes frequently appeared as plaintiffs in court cases. Some of the complaints filed in court by prostitutes were against their employees or servants, most often in cases involving the theft of clothing, items of adornment, or money. Servants appear to have been named as culprits far more often than were prostitute coworkers, and courts seem to have been tougher about, and less forgiving of, a charge of theft than a charge of practicing prostitution. Two servants in the house of Antoinette Goldstreng stole $97.40 from a stocking where Goldstreng kept the weekly rental fees. Even though police officers recovered part of the money, the two servants were sent to prison for two years. Eliza Fisher's servant Mary Ann Furman also was sent to prison for stealing two frocks, two shirts, two lace collars, and a velvet hat. Fisher made another complaint in court a couple of years later, when a second servant was arrested for stealing four petticoats, two dresses, a veil, a shawl, and $9 cash. Abby Meyers's servant Amelia Thompson was jailed for twenty days for stealing material worth a mere $1.50, and another servant of Meyers was arrested and committed for taking a writing desk and silver valued at $200. Prostitute Matilda Edmonds, a resident in Isabella Stewart's brothel, was arrested and sent to prison for stealing a gold watch, gold pencil, silk dress, hat, and other articles valued at $100.[51]

Theft also was an issue between prostitutes and their clients. Clients often claimed they had been robbed while in a brothel, but prostitutes also brought charges against customers who used their entry into the establishment as an easy opportunity to take unguarded valuables. Prostitute Jane Smith screamed for the watch when she realized a roll of bills had been taken from her pocket while a patron was with her in her room. The man was immediately arrested and taken to the police. Rachel Porter complained to police that a man had taken a safety chain worth $15 from her neck while they were together in her brothel. The customer denied the charges, and the necklace was not found, but Porter said he had given it to another man. Law officials believed Porter's story over that of the customer, and he was committed to jail. The newspaper reporter covering the story commented that the customer's "appearance warranted the expectation of better things from him."[52]

Some prostitutes may have used charges of theft as a means of getting assistance in removing an unwanted customer from a brothel. Abby Meyers called officers to arrest a patron she claimed had robbed her while in her house. Meyers did not appear at the police station the next morning to press charges, so the newspaper assumed Meyers had not been robbed at all.[53]

Prostitutes appeared in court as plaintiffs most often when pressing charges against patrons and other males who created disturbances in their brothels. Sometimes clients got drunk or rowdy and refused to leave, so the watch was called to assist with their eviction. A guest at 24 Anthony who became angry and would not leave when ordered out at 1:30 A.M. got into a scuffle with one of the women in the house. The watch was summoned, and he was put in jail. Mary Jewell refused to let a lawyer into her brothel after midnight, so he kicked in the door. She called the watch and pressed charges in court.

Often customers were destructive of a prostitute's property, and in most cases prostitutes immediately prosecuted the assaulters. Two so-called "Texas patriots" who raised a ruckus in Catherine Cochran's brothel by bragging about their war exploits were thrown out by the other male customers. The two men returned and started smashing glasses and assaulting the women and were sent to jail. Mary Wall admitted five customers who had arrived at her brothel in a hack. Once seated in the parlor, they requested drinks, and then one proceeded to use a fire shovel to destroy decanters and almost all the other glassware on the sideboard. Wall took them to court for their assault.[54]

Much of the property destruction and physical violence that occurred in brothels, especially in the 1830s and early 1840s, was the result of groups of rowdy males who roamed the streets and took great pleasure in wanton attacks upon prostitution houses. Whether these attacks were the result of excessive alcohol, male resentment over the independence of working and sexually active women, or entertainment for men who saw violence as an assertion of their rising social and political power in an increasingly egalitarian society, the victims of the attacks often tended to be those persons perceived to be "oppressed, unpopular, or unprotected."[55] Prostitutes were viewed as vulnerable because they were women and possibly because they operated as "illegals" in the community, but ruffians were often surprised at the persistence and force of both the legal and physical responses of these women to their attacks.

George Gale and some of his friends spent two weeks in the spring of 1831 harassing several brothels, including those of Phoebe Doty and Elizabeth Baker. Both Doty and Baker were attacked three times each during this period. At Baker's brothel, the men threw stones at the house, breaking and destroying windows, and then demolished her stoop and forced themselves inside, where they were "crass and offensive." At Doty's house, Gale and Enoch Carter kicked furniture, took lamps down, spilled oil, and threatened to knock Doty to the floor. Angered rather than intimidated, the women filed charges against the men.[56]

Bullies did not single out prostitutes alone for their vicious rampages. In late April of 1835, the house of Elizabeth Jeffreys at 63 Church was forcibly entered by John Chichester, John Boyd, and several other members of their notorious gang. The men assaulted Jeffreys, moved on to the home of Abel Welles and repeated the same violence, and then attacked three men in a neighborhood store. The next week, the gang went to the brothel of Jane Ann Jackson and threw brickbats and stones against the door and windows, breaking the window shutters and sash. They then entered the brothel, assaulted Jackson with a large gilt ball, and threatened to set fire to her house. From Jackson's they went to Eliza Ludlow's brothel and forced her to serve them brandy. Afterward, Chichester and friends threw the glasses into the fire, burned a rug, broke a bench by hurling it at a prostitute, and threatened to toss a woman out the window. After leaving the brothel, the bullies assaulted three more men in the street and broke several street lamps. The prostitutes, joined by the other neighbors who had been attacked, pressed charges against the Chichester gang, and the men were convicted. [57]

Prostitutes made especially easy targets for the bullies. Brothels were managed by women and were open at very late hours. Also, prostitutes angered some men by denying them entry to their brothels, by refusing to let them act as they wished when admitted, or by refusing sexual service to some. Violence was a response to rejection and frustration, but it was also a form of sport. As the activities of the Chichester gang illustrate, however, many neighborhood citizens besides prostitutes suffered from the increased street violence of the period, indicating that attacks on prostitutes were because they were vulnerable citizens rather than unacceptable social outcasts. Certainly, they felt secure enough as members of the community to prosecute the bullies instead of being cowed by their aggressiveness. [58]

Prostitutes pressed criminal charges against rowdy males to get them incarcerated, but they also pursued damages in court for the property the men destroyed. A gang of six men broke into the vacated brothel of Adeline Miller at 44 Orange Street, destroying about $100 worth of furniture. From Orange Street they went to Miller's house at 133 Reed and in spite of her resistance, broke into the window, threw bottles of liquor at Miller and then began destroying her most valuable property, demolishing $400 worth of oil paintings, glassware, mirrors and furnishings. They asked for money, and as she was giving it to them they grabbed her by the throat and struck her on the head with an iron bar. From Miller's the men went to the house of Jane Weston (alias Jenny Graham), where they drank and demolished a basket of champagne before asking for money. Both women swore out complaints against the men, and they were jailed. They also sought remuneration for damages.

Five months after the attack on the brothels, the men were ordered by the court to make restitution of $700 and fees before they were released from jail.[59]

Court prosecutions were not the only way prostitutes responded to assaults, intimidation, and the loss of property. Many prostitutes responded to physical force by defending themselves with aggressive physical actions. On Christmas day in 1847 John Briggs and some friends came to the brothel of Phoebe Doty at 166 Church Street. Briggs and his cronies became very rowdy, bullied the inmates of the brothel, and began to conduct themselves in a "beastly and indecent manner." When the men refused to leave, one of the women in the brothel, Moll Stephens, put a gun to Briggs's head and pulled the trigger. Fortunately for Briggs, the bullet chamber that was shot was the only one of the six that was empty. Briggs grabbed the gun and ran out of the brothel. The next day Doty filed charges against Briggs for assault and battery, but he countered with the same charges against Stephens. The judge put both parties on bail, but the *Police Gazette* pointed out that, when a black boy had done the same thing with a pistol to a black prostitute a few years before, he had been sent to state prison for nine and a half years.[60]

Another instance of self-defense occurred in a Duane Street brothel when one of the patrons became jealous of the attention being shown another customer by an attractive prostitute named Maria. Later the customer took Maria to her room and threatened her with a dagger. Although Maria was short, she was very muscular and, when the jealous customer threatened her, she jumped up, seized his arm, snatched the dagger, threw him on the floor, put her knee on his chest, called him names, slapped his face, and then threw him down the stairs. Prostitute Mary Gamble, when attacked with a sword and stabbed in the nose, scratched her assailant's face so badly that she was certain he would show the marks for weeks. When three men kicked open the door of Susan Shannon's brothel, she cut one with a sword. Jane Williams also acted to protect herself when twelve men tried to forcibly enter her brothel. She confronted the men with a revolver, but one man hit her, took the gun from her, and ran away. Williams then pursued justice by filing charges in criminal court.[61]

Sometimes prostitutes responded physically to attacks or injuries that were non-physical in nature. Kate Hastings horsewhipped Judson for insulting her, and Amelia Norman stabbed Henry Ballard for abandoning her after making her pregnant. Cinderella Marshall, madam of a Leonard Street brothel, horsewhipped and struck on the head a guest who would not pay after enjoying himself in her house. Mary Stewart confronted a man in her brothel with a gun and threatened to blow his brains out. The man had come to persuade his younger brother, who was living with Stewart, to leave the prostitute and go home. Another prostitute assaulted and attempted to stab a man on behalf of her paramour. The man had given testimony against her lover, charging him with stealing a watch.[62]

The self-assurance prostitutes showed concerning their rights as community citizens is especially evident in a few cases one would have thought would be almost impossible for a prostitute to win. Because rape was generally regarded as a sexual act instead of a violent assault, any woman had difficulty proving her case. If challenged, a woman charging rape usually had to establish that she was chaste, which obviously was a difficult burden of proof for a prostitute.[63] Nevertheless, some prostitutes did file charges of rape and attempted rape, and their attackers were convicted. Even if justice officials thought of the act as assault and battery, the prostitute was better off than in cases where the rape was believed to be what she had bargained for as a prostitute.

One case of rape involved a gang of men led by Thomas Hyer. The men entered the brothel of Ellen Holly and gang-raped one of her boarders, Ellen Bellmire. Hyer and his friends were convicted of the assault—but were out of jail by the end of a year. Eliza Logue's house was forcibly entered by five men who destroyed some furnishings, strangled Logue, and then "threw her across the foot of a bed and endeavored by force and violence to have connection with her." Only the arrival of the watch prevented the rape from occurring, but charges were brought against the men, and they were convicted.[64] Prostitute Hannah Fuller also pressed charges for attempted rape. Fuller was seated in the window of her bedroom at 4 A.M. one summer morning when William Ford passed by and saw her. Ford climbed over the gate and broke into the house. After kicking in Fuller's door, Ford removed his boots and pants and carried her to bed and attempted to "ravish and . . . carnally know her." Mary Ann Grovenor came to help Fuller but left when Ford threatened to split open her head. Only through the intervention of the watch was the rape prevented.

Fuller pressed charges against Ford but later withdrew her complaint, saying she "believed he was under an excitement at the time" and was an "old friend and has been for a long time back and still is." She requested that no further action be taken against him because she now believed they were both at fault. "Had I known the consequences to befall him I would never have made the complaint." The court then prosecuted Ford for assault and battery on the watchman.[65]

A second type of case where a prostitute might not expect to receive a sympathetic hearing involved harassment when streetwalking. By the 1850s, because of the large influx of poor immigrants to New York and the great increase in street traffic, authorities became very strict in policing city thoroughfares if the public complained that prostitutes were being a nuisance. As the 1855 case of Matilda Wade showed, any woman on the streets at night had difficulty proving she was not a streetwalker or vagrant. Streetwalkers in the two preceding decades also had been considered a public harassment as well as a symbol of eroding public morality, but several cases illustrate that these women believed they should be guaranteed—and usually received—personal protection even while plying their trade on public thoroughfares.

Prostitute Mary Smith of Leonard Street filed charges against William Nosworthy for assaulting her as she was walking home from the Park Theater. Nosworthy seized her and "raised her clothes so to expose her nakedness to passers by." Nosworthy was fully prosecuted. Another prostitute who was promenading on Broadway was approached and kissed by a drunken man. She objected to his sexual advances and prosecuted him but dropped the charges after he apologized. Prostitute Julia Meadows also was strolling on Broadway at night when a young man approached her from behind and threw oil of vitriol on her clothes, burning both her silk dress and her visette. Meadows screamed for the police, who pursued and caught the man; she filed charges, and he was committed. Prostitute Jane Williams, while on her evening stroll, picked up hack driver Jim Waters and was taking him to her brothel when they passed another man who touched Williams's shoulder. Williams left Waters for the new escort, and Waters seized her by the arm and objected. After Williams hit Waters in the face, he turned her over to the watch, charging her with assault and battery. Williams told the judge she hit him in order to get away, and the judge ruled against Waters, dismissing the case on grounds of self-defense.[66]

Although there are many examples that demonstrate how prostitutes enjoyed the rights and privileges of community citizenship, there are also instances that illustrate that the prostitute was always vulnerable in public disputes because of the illegal status and stigma of her profession. Even though prostitutes frequently used the legal and judicial system for their own interests, there was the possibility their credibility would be challenged because of their way of life. In the case of a theft or other conflict, it was the prostitute's word against the client's, and the reports of these cases indicate that the lack of an "irreproachable character" sometimes worked against prostitutes. In the well-publicized Jewett murder trial in 1836, for example, the major thrust of the defense counsel's argument was that the testimony of prostitutes could not be received in a court of justice, even in a trial for murder. According to the defense counsel, "the connection between chastity and veracity is so vital that the loss of the former is the instant destruction of the latter."[67] The judge in the case concurred with the defense, and in his charge to the jury warned that jurors must

consider well the character of the persons brought forward as witnesses. Testimony principally is drawn from . . . persons of very bad repute . . . [and] their testimony is not to be credited unless corroborated by testimony drawn from more credible sources. In the judgment of the law you are not entitled to conviction upon it; but if it be corroborated and strengthened by other credible testimony then give to it all the credibility which it is in justice entitled.[68]

Since one young man contradicted the testimony of the prostitutes at the trial, the suspected murderer was found not guilty. Most of the editorial opinion was against the decision of the court. The *Sun* noted that the defense counsel's argument was based on a "specious and dangerous principle" on the basis of which crimes need only be committed in the presence of prostitutes for the murderers to walk away free. The paper also pointed out that the counsel himself had won many convictions in the past based on "testimony of the same character."[69] The *Advocate of Moral Reform* voiced similar sentiments, adding that it saw

no reason why the testimony of Mrs. Townsend and her inmates is not worth as much as that of the young men, who by their own confession are in the habit of visiting her house constantly . . . thus reducing themselves to her level.[70]

There were a number of sources in the period that reinforced the notion that "prostitutes are known to be notorious liars." The *Advocate of Moral Reform* ran an article in 1841, "The Habit of Lying Among Prostitutes," which was taken from William Tait's study, *Prostitution in Edinburgh*.[71] In the February 1840 trial of a group of men who were charged with assaulting Susan Shannon at her brothel, the jury was unable to reach a verdict because one juror stated that he "did not consider a prostitute a human being, and could in no event find a verdict from her testimony." Two weeks after the Shannon trial, however, Justice Wyman found two men guilty of assault and battery on Julia Brown and her prostitutes, even though the defendants claimed the prostitutes had lied. After hearing the verdict the men expressed indignation that the testimony of the prostitutes had been valued over theirs.[72]

Although prostitutes' credibility in testimony continued to be challenged periodically throughout the middle decades of the nineteenth century, judicial experience confirmed that a prostitute's veracity could be accepted with the same care as that of any other citizen. In the disorderly house trial of Mary Fowler, nine years after the Shannon and Brown cases, Judge C. P. Daley declared that "bad and vicious habits do not necessarily imply a want of veracity, for it is a matter of familiar experience in the courts of justice, that persons otherwise of the most degraded character, not unfrequently manifest a strict regard for truth."[73] A prostitute's testimony would continue to be accepted or rejected based on the plausibility of the evidence given—or the attitudes of the legal officials in charge.

Thus, whether challenging laws that discriminated against them or working with law officials, courts, and municipal agencies to further their own interests, prostitutes of the mid-nineteenth century demonstrated that, in spite of the existence of anti-prostitution laws, they and their profession were very much a part of the social fabric of New York City life. The ambivalence shown by both ordinary citizens and officials toward prostitution underscored this position in the community. Anti-prostitution laws were kept on the statute books in an effort to satisfy a public need to feel that morality was being preserved and that the unrespectable and poor classes would be kept in control when necessary, but the actual casual and discretionary enforcement of the laws illustrates that many citizens did not find the existence of prostitutes in their neighborhoods so offensive. Prostitutes did not, however, achieve the status of coworkers and fellow citizens in the urban community merely because New Yorkers showed a tolerance or lack of concern about them. Prostitutes actively worked to create a positive customary and legal environment for themselves in ways that helped integrate them into New York City life. In theory, they were faced with laws vastly indiscriminate and procedurally unrestrained, but in practice, the more successful prostitutes particularly were able to use their money and their working legal knowledge and connections to make vigorous use of the law to protect themselves.

6

"Thronged Thoroughfares" and "Quiet, Home-like Streets"

The Urban Geography and Architecture of Prostitution

[Prostitution] no longer confines itself to secrecy and darkness, but boldly strides through our most thronged and elegant thoroughfares, and there, in the broad light of the sun, it jostles the pure, the virtuous, and the good. It is in your gay streets and in your quiet, home-like streets; it is in your squares . . . and summer resorts; it is in your theatres, your opera, your hotels; nay, it is even intruding itself into the private circles.[1]

William Sanger's description of the pervasiveness of prostitution gives a clear indication of how integrated prostitution had become in the geographic and social structure of New York City by the mid-nineteenth century. New York was different in this respect from large European cities, where prostitution was confined to specific areas of the community. In New York, no neighborhoods were exempt from the profession. It was found in "quiet, home-like streets" and "private circles" as well as in public places; in the neighborhoods of the rich as well as those of the poor.

New York's prostitution population had not always been so widespread throughout the community. In the eighteenth century and the early decades of the nineteenth century, practitioners of the profession tended to congregate in areas near the taverns and cheap lodging houses of New York City's dock area. More importantly, most prostitution at that time was hidden from public view. By the 1820s, however, the prostitution community began to disperse, spreading into a variety of residential and commercial neighborhoods. Prostitution also became so blatant in its public display that by 1831 the Reverend John McDowall felt compelled to publish his *Magdalen Report* apprising the community that many of the over 10,000 prostitutes he estimated to be in the city were to be found in respectable neighborhoods, operating "under masks of boarding houses . . . [and] shops of various kinds."[2] A few years later, in 1835, the *Advocate of Moral Reform* summarized the contemporary situation by noting that there was "an open and almost legalized existence of houses of prostitution everywhere in the city."[3] The *Advocate's* appraisal was confirmed by other observers, all of whom drew the same conclusion—prostitution had become very much a part of New York City life and was found in all areas of the city.[4] In the decades following the 1830s there would be periodic protests and efforts to control the profession in its most public aspects, but prostitution's pattern of city-wide dispersal would remain basically the same until the last part of the century. Even when prostitution later became more concentrated in specific neighborhoods, it never returned to its eighteenth-century status as a geographically confined and little visible profession.[5]

In placing prostitution within the larger social context of New York City in the mid-nineteenth century, one finds that the demographic and geographic patterns characteristic of the profession at that time are very similar to those of the urban community as a whole. Antebellum New York not only lacked segregated red light districts, but it also was not characterized by other significant segregated population clusters, such as racial and ethnic ghettos. Interestingly, New York City's immigrant segregation lessened in this period as immigrant population increased. An index of the segregation of foreign-born inhabitants of New York City in 1855 was almost half what the index had been three decades earlier. Not until after the Civil War would New York develop the large segregated immigrant areas that were characteristic of some other major cities.[6]

Although black residential patterns were somewhat the reverse of those of foreign-born New Yorkers—racial segregation increased as the black percentage in the population decreased—blacks also continued to be represented in nearly all geographic areas of New York City through mid-century. In 1825 blacks represented 7 ½ percent of the population, while by 1860 they comprised only 1 ½ percent of the city's inhabitants. Although the largest concentration of blacks was found in wards five and eight, no area of New York City in the antebellum period could be designated a black ghetto since black residents never comprised more than 12 percent of any ward's population.[7]

Just as there were always small concentrations of ethnic and black citizens in New York City, so were there pockets of poverty and extreme destitution. But economic segregation, like other forms, did not become prevalent in New York City until after the Civil War; rich and poor lived side-by-side, as did black and white, and native and foreign-born. Certainly, many wealthy citizens chose to live near each other, and some neighborhoods had "notable concentrations of wealth," but wealth was dispersed enough throughout the city that one could say at mid-century that at least half of the wards had a "gold-coast-and-slum" character. Local citizens as well as visitors to the city commented on the strange contrast of "costly luxury and improvident waste" with "squalid misery and hopeless destitution."[8] In spite of the diversity in its population and an increasing economic stratification of rich and poor, however, New York City retained a "social wholeness" unusual for an urban community of such large size.[9]

New York's integration of diverse populations was encouraged by the fact that a concept of restricted land use, or zoning, was not a part of the mid-nineteenth-century New York urban picture. In 1850 the commercial and industrial concentration in lower Manhattan was unmistakable, but every ward still had retail businesses, public markets, and dozens of small manufacturing establishments.[10] Consequently, commercial businesses, "vice" institutions, and private residences of the rich and poor were found next door to each other and continued to be established together as the city expanded north into new areas of Manhattan Island. This intermingling of diverse population sectors and institutions caused one newspaper editor to complain in 1841 that he could not stand "the strange and disreputable anomaly of theatres, churches, and houses of ill-fame all huddled up together in one small block."[11] Thirty years later, in spite of a few efforts toward urban planning, regulation, and reform, another New Yorker noted that the city's development was continuing in a haphazard fashion and that the "strange anomaly" of mixed classes and mixed land use still existed in New York: "Only a stone's throw back of the most sumptuous parts of Broadway and Fifth Avenue, want and suffering, vice and crime, hold their courts. Fine ladies can look down from their high casements upon the squalid dens of their unfortunate sisters."[12]

The designation "unfortunate sisters" also included some women who did not live in squalid dens but who, nevertheless, appear to observers today out of place in their chosen neighborhoods. In the 1830s and early 1840s, one of New York's most elite areas, the fifth ward neighborhood around Park Place, Broadway, Warren, and Leonard streets, was only a block or two from several well-known brothels. Residents such as Philip Hone, former Mayor Walter Bowne, and merchant Cornelius Low had to walk a mere block to stand in front of a neighboring brothel.[13] New York social historian Charles Lockwood has noted that in the 1860s, prostitute Julia Brown operated a stylish prostitution establishment at University Place and Twelfth Street, where her immediate neighbors included James Lenox, a wealthy citizen whose library collection served as the foundation of the New York Public Library; merchant William H. Aspinwall; the socially elite Mrs. Peter A. Schemerhorn; Union Theological Seminary; and the New York Society Library. Julia Brown's close proximity to some of New York's wealthiest citizens and most august institutions reflected a certain tacit acceptance of prostitution as part of the urban landscape, but her presence in the neighborhood also probably went unchallenged because neither Brown's establishment nor her clientele were disruptive.[14]

Prostitute and non-prostitute also lived close together in the many poor tenements of the city. In most of these cases, the "work" of the prostitute was not hidden from view or practiced unobtrusively because "inmates know no such thing as privacy. . . . Within the same walls are gathered the virtuous and the depraved."[15] Describing the living situation in one of the multiple-roomed tenement houses, a mid-century reporter noted that one room, twelve feet by twenty, housed five families totaling twenty persons, but only two beds; a much smaller room nearby was home to a man, woman, and three children who helped pay their rent by allowing prostitutes to bring their customers there for their nightly business.[16] Another contemporary described a large building in ward six that had been subdivided into dozens of small "apartments" rented to the poor and the prostitute alike, where it was "not unusual for a mother and two to three daughters, all prostitutes, to receive men at the same time, in the same room."[17] In such indigent neighborhoods, geographic and social intimacy with prostitutes existed in part because

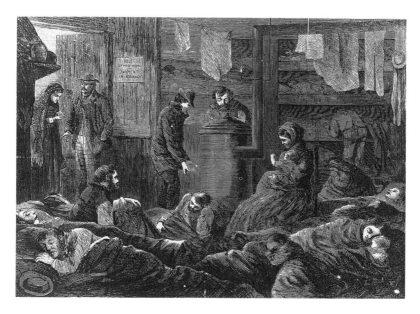

14. LODGING FOR THE POOR.   Nineteenth-century New York City's housing for the poor was crowded and miserable. Reformers were shocked that the city's poorest prostitutes were said to have serviced their customers in public lodging rooms such as this. (Courtesy American Antiquarian Society)

the poor and laboring classes accepted prostitutes as fellow citizens who needed some way to eke out a living in a depressed economic environment, but geographic intimacy also was a function of limited affordable housing options.

The degree of prostitution's integration within the community as a whole becomes even clearer, however, when one looks at residential configurations in mid-century censuses. Many brothels and prostitution boarding houses are interspersed among the homes of middle- and lower-middle-class families. It is most likely these prostitution establishments did not operate surreptitiously, since it would have been very difficult for several brothels on a street to conduct business without drawing the attention of neighbors, especially given that the locations of many were openly advertised in brothel directories. Prostitutes Eleanor Barrett and Caroline Cook lived on a block of Mercer Street with several other brothels, but the block also housed the families of a chemist, druggist, broker, engraver, physician, importer, merchant, grocer, painter, music teacher, and two respectable boarding houses, one of which rented to male laborers. Margaret Brown owned a brothel with thirteen prostitutes, and her neighbors included a widowed Baptist clergyman, a lawyer with his son and a servant, and several merchants and their families. Prostitutes Emma Clifton, Jenny Grey, and Kate Rowe shared their block with a "psychologist" gentleman, several clerks, a blacksmith, a physician, marble cutters, female teachers, a hairdresser and family, and several boarding houses with families, one of which was a German establishment. Even in more intimate or shared housing situations such as renting rooms in one's own house, censuses further indicate that prostitutes were accepted as residents. The 1855 census records that millwright Lawrence Archer, his wife, and their seventeen-year-old son and twelve-year-old daughter had been landlords for more than two years to Ann Swift, whose occupation was listed as prostitute. They also had a servant living with them. Likewise, Kate Cannon and her fifteen-year-old son Leland boarded thirty-five-year-old prostitute Mary Lewis in their home.[18]

Although a general tolerance of prostitution as a part of urban living was one reason women like Ann Swift and Julia Brown lived openly and relatively hassle-free in most nineteenth-century New York neighborhoods, social historian Charles Lockwood has offered other explanations. In referring to Julia Brown's Twelfth Street establishment, he wrote: "The apparent ease with which prostitution could flourish in so select a location reflects the social strains of the time as well as patterns of urban development."[19] Perhaps a gradual process of urbanization might have reduced "social strains" and altered residential patterns, but with the population multiplying monthly during these decades, New Yorkers seemingly had little time for orderly urban development. Population pressures forced the city to expand physically, and New York's geographical limitation as an island necessitated that expansion be to the north. Either because of or in spite of the fact they were suffering from the "social strains" of a rapidly growing population and urban change, New Yorkers appeared to be very flexible about making residential shifts in responding to the city's growth, and they appeared to worry little about who their neighbors were.[20]

Another reason citizens' attitudes about neighborhood diversity seem so flexible is that nineteenth-century New Yorkers appear to have enjoyed, in fact thrived on, mobility—not establishing long-term roots in any household but happily changing residences and neighbors often.[21] New York prostitutes seem to have responded to the same mobility impulses as the general population, changing brothel locations and boarding situations frequently. Even though a stable location may appear to have been desirable for a brothel or an individual prostitute seeking repeat business from customers and a well-known business address, this business factor was not significant enough to keep prostitutes stationary very long. The desire to change locations seems to have outweighed the desire for stability. Several reasons, with both negative and positive implications, help explain this impulse.

Without a doubt, some prostitutes moved because of pressure from community individuals or the law. Some landlords, who unwittingly rented houses or rooms to prostitutes, evicted the women once the true nature of their establishments was discovered. Disorderly house cases illustrate that some neighbors also complained about prostitutes, and some of these women thought it wise to move to avoid a court hearing, fine, or possible incarceration. Pressure from the law, however, usually was in response to complaints, and the small number of disorderly-house cases suggests a relatively small number of neighbors' complaints. Still, in spite of few objections before the law, some prostitutes possibly moved because of other forms of harassment. Even though physical assaults on houses appear to have been as much a factor of prostitutes being females without male protectors as their being socially unacceptable neighbors, and even though many prostitutes responded to attacks by pressing charges in court, violence by street youths may have frightened some prostitutes into relocating.[22] But on the whole, one might conclude that in the absence of either rigorous legal restrictions or profound social pressures, prostitutes often made decisions to relocate for more positive reasons.

One such reason involved personal preference and business calculation: prostitutes were as interested as other New York residents in moving to new and more fashionable, or "better," neighborhoods. They also wanted to remain close to their clientele. Those prostitutes such as Julia Brown who catered to the middle and upper classes would relocate along with their customers as new neighborhoods opened in the "advance guard north." As poorer residents moved to occupy the houses formerly inhabited by the more well-to-do, prostitutes who catered to the working classes also occupied vacant establishments in these areas.

Another reason nineteenth-century prostitutes moved frequently was that many of them, like other New Yorkers, celebrated the "May Day" custom. Although incomprehensible to many observers today, May Day, or moving day, was an "institution" in antebellum New York, practiced and apparently enjoyed by many citizens. Originating in the early Dutch colonial period, the custom continued well into the nineteenth century. According to tradition, February 1 marked the day residences were put on the market "to let and all go snoop in others' [houses]." On May 1 citizens moved to their new dwellings, illustrating, according to the *New Era*, the extreme "restlessness of New Yorkers who have no attachment to their homes."[23] In January 1837, the *New Era* also noted: "The period of the year is fast approaching when persons begin to look out for new residences, according to the custom of New Yorkers, not to remain under the same roof, more than twelve months."[24]

Several nineteenth-century diaries and records, including those of Philip Hone and George T. Strong, contain personal testimonies concerning the May Day practice. William Dunlap, playwright, theater manager, and artist, noted in his diary that he followed the May 1 moving day custom but was not a frequent participant: "Got my family removed to No. 64 Sixth Avenue by noon on this first of May 1832 after living in Leonard St., No. 55 for sixteen years."[25] When Dunlap moved out, prostitutes moved in, and 55 Leonard became a well-known brothel address for several decades afterward. Prostitute Caroline Ingersoll, a much more regular observer of the custom, testified about her moves during a divorce trial before the Superior Court:

I first came back to New York from Philadelphia. I went to reside at 355 Greenwich Street . . . about a year and a half; I moved here in the fall; I left it on the first of May; the second first of May after I went there, I moved from that house to 628 Houston Street, and lived there about two years; I left that house on the first of May last, 1851; I went there the first of May and left it on the first of May [for 4 Murray Street].[26]

Tax records, city directories, censuses, and newspapers indicate that Ingersoll was not unique among prostitutes in being so mobile on May

Table 16 *Residential Changes of Selected Brothel Keepers*

Adeline Miller (Furman)		Phoebe Doty (d. 1850)	
1818	Unknown	1820	123 Anthony
1821	167 Church	1821	129 Anthony
1822	32 Orange	1830	167 Church
1826	85 Cross	1833	44 Orange
1829	53 Crosby	1834	9 Desbrosses
1831	44 Orange	1835	35 Leonard
	39 Elm	1838	29 Leonard
1835	133 Reade	1843	107 Mercer
	44 Orange	1845	12 Elm
	— Mott	1846	166 Church
	39 Duane		
1838	133 Reade		
1842	134 Duane	Jane McCord	
1845	130 Church		
1859	139 Church (last address)	1842	35 Warren
		1845	75 Duane
		1848	80 Reade
J. Ann Malloy		1853	71 Mercer
		1859	633 Houston
1842	112 Canal	1862	6 Staple
1845	112 Church	186–	56 W. Houston
1850	18 Mercer	1870	42 W. 15th
1852	155 W. Broadway		
1853	14 Mercer		
1859	24th Street		

SOURCES: Record of Assessments, City Directories, Brothel Directories, Court of General Sessions Indictment Papers, Newspapers.

Day and other days. Table 16 illustrates the extent to which some madams or prostitution house keepers changed residential locations during their careers.

It is more difficult to trace the mobility of ordinary prostitutes who were inmates of brothels, but they too seem to have changed residences frequently. One 1860s source stated that the residents of brothels changed every two to three months.[27] If an ordinary prostitute continued in the employment of a particular madam, she moved with the household, but apparently many prostitutes were not, or did not feel, obligated to stay with a madam for very long. Many prostitutes left the profession altogether after a couple of years; others, like Helen Jewett, stayed in prostitution but looked for "change" by shifting to new locations. Although Jewett was killed at the young age of twenty-three, she had practiced prostitution in at least three different cities, and in the four to five years she was in New York, she lived in six different houses. All indications suggest that Jewett's changes, like those of many other prostitutes, were at her volition rather than that of madams or officials. [28] The frequent movement of madams and ordinary prostitutes from house to house was not as disruptive to the overall trade, however, as might first seem to be the case. Many addresses of prostitution houses became notorious because brothels remained in operation at the addresses for several decades even though the madams and prostitutes in these residences changed often (table 17).

Despite prostitutes' frequent relocation and their dispersal throughout the city, one can nonetheless pinpoint areas of prostitution activity that gained notoriety in different time periods and follow the geographic shifting of these regions in the decades between 1830 and 1870. Such findings probably overemphasize areas with brothels and prostitution boarding houses, as opposed to neighborhoods frequented by street-walkers, since the visible "temples of Venus" could be identified readily and represented to contemporary observers a localized vision of urban evils. Furthermore, the "brothel bias" is accentuated because addresses of known houses are easier for the historian to locate than the private rooms used by the floating and part-time prostitution population. However, as certain thoroughfares were famous for streetwalking activity, one can assume many of the prostitutes working these streets either used assignation rooms in the area or boarded nearby. A prostitute would not want to risk losing her time or a client's "ardor" by having to walk a couple of miles to her quarters before consummating her proposition. Still, there were many women who practiced prostitution on a part-time or casual basis—servicing the local men in their immediate neighborhoods or trading sex for money with male companions when the opportunity was available or when they were economically pinched. Because these women may have worked very privately in quiet neighborhoods where commercial sex was less prominent, their numbers would not be reflected in a prostitution-activity-area evaluation. And finally, although special

Table 17 *Long-Term Prostitution Establishments*

55 Leonard		28 Anthony	
1835	Mary Blaylock	1824	Abby Meade/Meyer
1836	Ann Welden	1828	Rosina Thompson
1838	Ann Miller	1829	Ann Boyd
1841	Julia Brown	1830	Mrs. Thomas
1845	Rosanna Turner	1831	Mrs. Shott
1846	Mrs. Lyons	1834	Lavina Stafford
1848	Francis O'Kille	1840	Mary Ann Foster
	Cinderella Marshall		
1851	Maria Adams		
1853	Rosina Styles (for Adams)	**39 Thomas**	
1856	Maria Adams		
		1825	Eliza Smith
		1826	Caroline Andrews
100 Church		1830	Mary Wall
		1831	Susan Scott
1828	Rebecca Cooper	1836	Mrs. Price
1835	Jane Ann Jackson	1837	Susan Shannon
1837	Mary Benson	1839	Mary Robinson
1840	Julia Brown	1840	Mrs. Smith/Clark
1841	Harriet Brandley	1846	Matilda Green
1843	Susan Sweet	1859	Mrs. Kelly
1851	Emma Andrews		
1853	Dorothy Myers		
1859	Dorothy Myers	**136 Duane**	
		1833	Mrs. Meyer
		1838	Jane Williams
		1843	Sarah Tuttle
		1845	Jane Wilson
		1850	Jenny Winslow
		1851	Mary Howard
		1856	Mrs. Bushnell

SOURCES: Record of Assessments, City Directories, Brothel Directories, Court of General Sessions Indictment Papers, Newspapers.

time periods and geographic areas of concentration can be delineated, such time-frames and areas appear to be more precise than they actually were, since the expansion or shifting of prostitution activity to a new area was a gradual process.

One can discern the geographical changes in New York's prostitution activity from the 1830s to the 1870s by dividing these years into roughly three periods. The first period, from 1830 to 1850, was the early period of expansion when prostitution "went public" and spread through lower Manhattan. Although prostitution activity moved inland, commercial sex establishments in the dock areas were not abandoned, and they continued to serve seamen, transients, dock laborers, and other poor males for the remainder of the century. The most famous area of prostitution in this early period was the Five Points and the sixth ward neighborhood surrounding it. Less raucous but equally well known to New Yorkers at the time was the area of parlor houses and prostitution boarding establishments in the side streets along Broadway, especially those on the thoroughfare's western side in wards five, eight, and the northern part of ward three.

In the second period, from 1850 to 1865, the Five Points was still considered the scene of much of the city's most debased prostitution activity, and sixth ward arrests for prostitution continued to lead those in other wards. In this decade and a half, prostitution in the Broadway West area showed the greatest expansion, both numerically and geographically, as it moved north toward Washington Square, shifting its locus from ward five to ward eight.

In the final period, from the end of the Civil War into the early 1870s, prostitution's main center of activity again shifted further to the north, to the area beyond Washington Square between Seventh Avenue and Lexington, with a few scattered houses as far north as Fortieth Street. Some prostitution activity continued in the older neighborhoods of the Broadway West district to the south, but prostitution declined and became less fashionable as commercial and industrial establishments and warehouses took over the area. Opposite the Broadway West district in south Manhattan, prostitution fanned out from ward six into adjacent wards to the north and east, into the Bowery East area. The Five Points was more a district of the poor than of vice in this final period, and prostitution no longer drew the great numbers of men to the vicinity that it had in earlier years. Prostitutes in the dock areas, especially along

Water Street, continued to find customers among neighborhood in-habitants and unwary transients, but New York residents considered the district not only a poor slum but also one of its most dangerous neigh-borhoods (see map, p. 97, for areas of concentration).

This overview of prostitution population shifts tracks geographic changes that can be illustrated both chronologically and cartographi-cally. A much clearer understanding of prostitution mobility is gained, however, by focusing in depth on each neighborhood area, so that the social changes that accompanied geographic shifts become more evident.

The Dock Areas

Since New York was a preeminent port and shipping terminal throughout the nineteenth century, the dock areas along the East River and up the west side on the Hudson River continued to be populated with seamen, laborers, and travelers. Ships stopping at the New York port brought approximately 22,000 crewmen to the city in 1835 and approximately 66,000 in 1860.[29] Catering to these seamen, other transients, and dock workers, prostitutes attached themselves to the many drinking and lodging establishments that were crowded into the vicinity of the docks. Two waterfront districts were especially well known for prostitution activity in the period 1830 to 1870—the Water and Cherry streets area, in the fourth and seventh wards, and Corlears Hook, a point of land at the east end of Grand Street, also in the seventh ward. The Battery, the riverfront park at the tip of Manhattan Island, was a favorite promenade of streetwalkers in the colonial period and remained popular until the mid-nineteenth century.

Even though known to be riotous and disorderly, the Water–Cherry streets area in the 1830s and 1840s still housed some of New York's wealthiest families, especially along Cherry Street, where a number of substantial mansions were found. By the mid-1840s, however, most of the well-to-do had moved to other wards, and their once-grand resi-dences were converted to tenements and brothels inhabited by poorer citizens.[30] Dock area streets also were filled with saloons and their attached prostitution quarters, usually second-story rooms above the saloons. In some saloons the basement was used for dancing, and these dance houses became famous for their raucous activity. Prostitution and drinking establishments on one street in this area were so numerous they were said to be "standing almost cheek by jowl—more than forty of them in a single half-mile stretch."[31] After mid-century, all commentators agreed that women practicing prostitution in the Water–Cherry streets area had sunk to the lowest depths of prostitution, becoming "living corpses."[32] Having made the final descent to Water Street, a prostitute "almost immediately . . . falls a victim to the terrible scourge of these places. Disease of the most loathsome kind fastens itself upon her, and she literally rots to death."[33]

Prostitution at Corlears Hook, northeast of Water and Cherry streets, had a similar reputation for degradation. Long known as an area of prostitution, "the Hook" has been proposed as the origin of the slang term *hooker*.[34] The district known as the Hook was located mostly in Walnut Street, a seven-block-long thoroughfare. Like prostitutes of the other dock areas, the women of the Hook were described as "bloated with rum and rotten with disease," and they occupied themselves "chewing snuff, smoking tobacco, and eating opium, . . . exposed to every description of brutality and victims of every kind of excess."[35] Because of the clientele of seamen and dock workers, the area was known to be rough, and it retained a reputation for low prostitution and drinking throughout the century. Yet it is difficult to determine how much of the vice-ridden and "low" reputation earned by the Hook and Water–Cherry streets areas was a function of their poverty and squalor and how much was a function of vice and corruption. There is also some abstraction in contemporary descriptions of such places, as if they were less observed locations than comfortably isolated moral locuses for all the broad evils urban observers both feared and found fascinating. As would be the case in other parts of New York as the century progressed, often those areas that became centrally defined by their poverty also became famous as centers of vice.[36]

The Five Points

Even more vital as a circumscribed symbol of all the new urban dangers was New York's most notorious nineteenth-century pros-

15 and 16. TWO VIEWS OF THE FIVE POINTS. These two nineteenth-century prints of the notorious Five Points illustrate the variety of characters said to congregate in this neighborhood, an area known for both licentiousness and poverty. (Courtesy of the New-York Historical Society, New York City)

titution area, the Five Points, a small commercial vice district in the sixth ward. Located on the site of a former swamp, the neighborhood became known throughout the United States and Europe as America's "most famous slum." To New Yorkers, it also was the symbol of all that was degenerate, debauched, and sinful in the city. The Five Points, which was formed by and got its name from the intersection of five streets, did not exist until the second decade of the century, when the Collect Pond was landfilled, and streets and structures were built over the site.[37] Attracting vice activities of all types, the Points was one of the first places to which prostitutes moved after dispersing beyond the dock areas.

Contemporaries who wrote about the Five Points could find little that was redeeming about the neighborhood. "Mere words can convey but a faint idea of the Five Points," maintained one mid-century writer, though his and others' descriptions seem to give a pretty good indication of the depth of their feelings: "sink of iniquity," "plague spot," "nest of vipers," "hell of horrors," "that infected district," "the great central ulcer of wretchedness," and "the very rotting Skeleton of Civilization, [from] whence emanates an inexhaustible pestilence that spreads its poisonous influence through every vein and artery of the whole social system."[38] Respectable New Yorkers clearly enjoyed believing that the Five Points was the receptacle housing all of the city's human garbage.

At the crossroads of the Five Points was a one-acre triangular plaza with the euphemistic title of Paradise Square. Emanating out from this park, the streets of the Five Points were lined with gambling dens, lottery offices, liquor stores, pawnbrokers, second-hand dealers, and all of the institutional forms of prostitution: brothels, cheap lodging houses, saloons, dance halls, and theaters. The concentration of this type of business establishment in the area prompted one contemporary to say that "nearly every house . . . is a groggery below and a brothel above"— a comment that had some truth in it, since during the decade of the 1830s almost two-thirds of the forty-three blocks surrounding the Five Points housed prostitutes on at least one occasion.[39]

Structures at the Five Points had been crowded into every conceivable open space along the quarter's streets and alleyways, and about one-third of them were constructed of wood and were very ramshackle. Inside the buildings, prostitute and non-prostitute poor residents were crammed into every nook and cranny, giving the Five Points at mid-century the highest density of population in the city, twice as great as in the rest of the sixth ward. Because of the establishments' appearance and activities, many of the Five Points' buildings were given sinister names by which they became well known to contemporary New Yorkers and out-of-town visitors such as Charles Dickens. Cut-Throat Alley, Squeeze Gut Alley, Bagler's Alley, Cow Bay, Diving Bell, Swimming Bath, and Arcade were some of the "hotbeds of debauchery, wretchedness, and poverty" along Orange, Anthony, Little Water, and Cross streets.[40] Philip Hone described the establishments on Orange Street as "abodes of filth, destitution, and intemperance, . . . where water was never used internally or externally, and the pigs were contaminated by the contact of the children." Using his swine analogy more than once in reference to Orange Street, Hone also said that the street's inhabitants suffered "from personal neglect and [were] poisoned by eating garbage which a well-bred hog on a Westchester farm would turn up his snout at."[41]

The descriptions of respectable contemporaries illustrate not only their objections to the immoral and vice-ridden Five Points residents but also their disdain for other large population groups that were housed in the community: the poor, blacks, and immigrants. Given the biases against these groups, it is often difficult to distinguish between situations that indicated blatant depravity and those that were indicative of extreme destitution, unfamiliar customs, and racially integrated social activities. Articles in the *Sun* in May 1834 illustrate this descriptive confusion. Writing about the Points during several days of May and June, an editor of the *Sun* noted it was a "resort of vagrants, vagabonds, and crime," "of indecency, squalid poverty, and intemperance," where people "riot and revel in continued orgies, and sober humanity is shocked and horrified. People are constantly attacked and robbed."[42] This initial appraisal was followed by a visit to the Five Points and a first-hand account of what was seen. According to the journalist, those who live in and near the Five Points "endure literally, a hell of horrors, arising from their poverty and wickedness, such as few others on earth can suffer." Houses known as the locations of prostitution activities were said to be divided and subdivided into numerous small and comfortless apartments, "the inmates sleeping or lying on heaps of filthy rags, straw, and shavings, the stench from which was almost insupportable . . . white women, and black and yellow men, and black and yellow women with white men, all in a state of gross intoxication, and exhibiting indecencies, revolting to virtue and humanity."[43] Prostitution at the Five Points was promiscuous, unrefined, and interracial, and it thus offended respectable citizens. Sixth ward vagrancy/prostitution arrests at mid-century, which were almost totally of immigrants and blacks, also indicate that officials saw little distinction between public immorality and the poor, the immigrant, and the black. Offering an interesting counterpoint to these descriptions is Carol Groneman-Pernicorn's analysis of the 1855 census, which reveals that the resident population of the Five Points was not primarily young, unattached individuals as one might suspect; rather, the area's residents were actually slightly older than in the rest of the city and more likely to be married.[44]

Although the Five Points retained its reputation as a "haunt of vice, debauchery, and misery" for the remainder of the century, by the Civil War many citizens became more aware of the fact that the area's population was most distinguished by its poverty. After 1850, groups such as the Ladies Home Mission Society moved into the Five Points and bought property formerly housing disreputable establishments. Offering job training and wages as well as redemption, they worked to change the Five Points. The northward movement of commercial development also helped alter the area.[45] Whatever the reasons for change, by 1860 many residents no longer viewed the neighborhood as the city's center of sin. After conducting a house-by-house survey of the major streets of the vicinity in 1860, Samuel B. Halliday, a Five Points House of Industry missionary, noted that the Five Points no longer fit its stereotype. Strangers, he said, often assume the district is simply a collection of brothels, but his firsthand observations led him to conclude that "the number of abandoned women is very much smaller than those familiar with the region have supposed."[46] Less than a decade later, James McCabe described the Five Points as "the realm of Poverty. Here want and suffering, and vice hold their courts. . . . Yet, bad as it is, it was worse a few years ago. There was not more suffering, it is true, but crime was more frequent here."[47]

The Bowery East

Although prostitution at the Points declined somewhat, it remained significant in other parts of the sixth ward. Not far away, the Bowery, the favorite promenade of the working-class Bowery b'hoys and g'hals, also was the favorite thoroughfare of many poor streetwalking prostitutes, who looked to working-class males for their customers.[48] After the Civil War, prostitution expanded beyond the region surrounding the southern end of the Bowery, moving into ward ten and the southern part of ward seventeen, or the Bowery East area. Although more significant later in the century, this enclave was characterized mostly by immigrant and working-class prostitutes and clientele. A contemporary described east-side prostitutes by saying:

The principal difference between them and their sisters of the west side is the fact that they are of a lower order, not so good-looking, and attire themselves in a very gaudy and showy manner in order to attract the attention of the passer-by. . . . There are many foreign girls on the east side—the Germans and the Irish predominating.[49]

Prostitutes in the Bowery East were patronized mostly by seamen, mechanics, workingmen, "fourth-rate actors and the Bowery b'hoys."[50] Many New Yorkers considered the Bowery East to be a "closed and insular world, most of whose inhabitants worked, shopped, and played close to where they lived."[51] Since play included commercial sex, local working-class prostitutes met the demands of their neighborhood.

Broadway West

Less famous to out-of-towners than the Five Points, but well known to nineteenth-century New Yorkers, was the Broadway West area of prostitution. Seemingly spilling out of the western sixth ward into the fifth ward and the northern part of the third ward, prostitution then flowed northward into ward eight and the western part of ward fourteen. Prostitution in this district was almost exclusively parlor houses, prostitution boarding houses, and assignation establishments. Catering to local residents, to travelers who lodged in the hotels only a block or two away on Broadway, and to patrons of the theaters and other amusement institutions, this region contained most of New York's finest prostitution establishments from the 1830s until the Civil War.[52] The vicinity also contained many modest prostitution establishments, as well as some very "low" ones, and it attracted prostitutes from a variety of economic situations who, as streetwalkers, strolled up and down Broadway and its side streets looking for customers to take to some nearby room.[53]

During the period when prostitution flourished most in this area, Broadway and the adjacent streets also contained some of New York's most elite residences and most prominent citizens as well as a cross section of the city's blacks, immigrants, and poor. No part of New York better exemplified mixed land use. Churches were across the street from brothels, police stations were next door, and, when the National Theatre was destroyed by fire in 1841, it toppled onto the brothel of Julia Brown, partially destroying that establishment and killing one resident prostitute. Columbia College, New York's oldest institution of higher education, was surrounded by brothels housing black and white prostitutes, and the great commercial establishments of Broadway served as a backdrop for a large proportion of the city's streetwalkers. Interspersed among all these institutions were the homes of respectable New Yorkers.

As prostitution expanded northward between 1830 and 1870, the largest and most fashionable centers of parlor houses gave way gradually to neighborhoods further uptown. Brothel directories and other sources confirm this trend in both their brothel appraisals and numbers of houses listed in each ward. Through the 1840s, the fifth ward section of Broadway West had the greatest concentration of fashionable prostitution houses, but by the 1850s and early 1860s, ward eight and the southern part of ward fifteen below Washington Square surpassed ward five in brothel numbers and clientele status.[54] In the late 1860s, ward eight and the northern part of the Broadway West district experienced decline, as centers of prostitution activity continued to move northward. By 1870, Greene, Mercer, and Wooster streets, which only a few years earlier housed some of New York's finest brothels, were described as "a complete sink of iniquity." Within the area of six square blocks there were said to be forty-one houses of the "third class" or lower. "The scenes enacted here, the filth and turmoil would lead a stranger to suppose that he was in Baden Baden, or that old Sodom and Gomorrah had risen from their ashes to greet the sun once more." By the 1860s, ward eight also became known for concentrations of black prostitution houses.[55]

Washington Square North

The region of prostitution that became most notorious after the Civil War was the Washington Square North area. Following the migration of the general population up the island, some prostitutes had moved into the vicinity of Fifth Avenue and Twelfth Street as early as the late 1850s. By 1870 a few houses of prostitution were found as far north as Fortieth Street, but the greatest concentration was from Twenty-Second to Twenty-Seventh Streets, between Broadway and Fifth Avenue on the east, and Seventh Avenue on the west. This area would become famous as New York's Tenderloin district, home to the seven brothels along West Twenty-Fifth Street that would be known as "the Seven Sisters." Another area of concentration was around Union Square and the vicinity of Fourteenth Street, which was later referred to as the Rialto. This neighborhood had attracted many of the city's wealthiest citizens in the late 1840s and the 1850s, and after the Civil War it remained a location of some of the best places of leisure and amusement for the upper classes.[56]

Most of the prostitution in the Washington Square North area was housed in magnificent brownstone row houses. These structures were decorated even more elaborately and luxuriously than had been their sister institutions in the Broadway West vicinity a decade or two earlier. As one contemporary noted:

The furniture and appointments of the house[s] are of the most elegant description. Everything is there that money can procure which will gratify the eye or charm the senses. . . . The parlors are the same as those of any fashionable mansion on Fifth or Madison avenue, and in furnishing them it is aimed to make them look as nearly like the parlors of the fashionably respectable houses as can be.[57]

Although prostitution would continue to expand northward, moving into many new neighborhoods, the Washington Square North area would remain New York's predominant district of prostitution into the twentieth century.

The Prostitute's Workplace

Nineteenth-century New York neighborhoods contained a variety of institutions from which prostitutes plied their trade. No longer feeling bound by the secrecy that was required of their eighteenth-century sisters, New York's nineteenth-century prostitutes also did not feel restricted to the same institutions primarily used by eighteenth-century prostitutes for marketing their profession: taverns and waterfront lodging houses. This diversification in commercial sex institutions was both a contributor to and result of prostitution's geographic and social expansion throughout the New York community.

Nineteenth-century prostitution institutions can be classified as either primary or secondary. The primary institutions, such as the brothel, the prostitution boarding house, and the assignation house, were established for the express purpose of marketing sex, and a male (or female) sought out one of these residences with that objective in mind. Although buying or selling sex might also be the primary motive of people attending other entertainment institutions, such as saloons, theaters, concert halls, and dance halls, these establishments ostensibly served other commercial functions, and prostitution was available as a secondary activity. Primary sexual institutions were residential in nature and were most often managed by female proprietors, while the secondary institutions featured leisure or entertainment and were predominantly operated by males.

The most common primary institution of prostitution was the brothel, also known as a parlor house, bawdy house, disorderly house, whorehouse, bordello, bagnio, or seraglio. [58] Structurally, the brothel was most often a row house (New York's architectural answer to limited, expensive land space), a narrow, several-storied residence linked to neighboring structures. The brothel usually had a parlor or living room for receiving and entertaining guests, with one to three floors of bedrooms above. In lower-class brothels the parlor or living room was a bar–reception room. Row houses served as brothels, prostitution boarding houses, rooming houses, assignation houses, and tenements, which allowed them to blend in with the houses of ordinary neighborhood citizens.

In its purest form, the parlor-house brothel was inhabited by from two to possibly twenty prostitutes who were managed by a madam in a communal or family-type arrangement. The madam and the prostitutes worked together as a "team," creating the house's ambience and reputation, though individual prostitutes might be well enough known to attract their own customers. Since the parlor house was both a workplace and residence, meals were provided, as was domestic service. The madam functioned as household mistress, chief social hostess, and business manager. As business manager, she was responsible for paying all household bills. In some cases she may have been the recipient of all of the income of the house, granting each prostitute room, board, and a salary for her services. However, sources that elaborate on the financial practices of New York City brothels indicate that the madam seldom had total control over the receipts of the house, and prostitutes were not salaried; instead, they appear to have paid a weekly fee for room and board and then shared customer profits with the madam, or else they paid her a per-guest fee for each customer entertained.[59] This individual payment of room and board was one characteristic that caused many parlor house brothels to be referred to as prostitution boarding houses, a blurring of two institutional types that were popular in this period.[60]

The prostitution boarding house developed at the time that respectable boarding houses became popular in New York City. Just like individuals or families in respectable boarding houses, prostitutes rented separate rooms from the housekeeper but dined in common with the other resident prostitutes. Theoretically, the boarding house had less of a "team approach" than did the parlor house, since each prostitute was responsible for recruiting her own customers, but in practice, boarding prostitutes also serviced customers who knew of the existence of the boarding house but came without being recruited by a particular prostitute. A boarding house keeper, like a brothel madam, most likely charged the boarders a fee per customer and shared in the profits of liquor sales. Although a prostitution boarding house might not rent exclusively to prostitutes, in most cases a respectable woman would not wish to rent at such a house for fear of risking her good name. Many madams referred to their brothels as "boarding houses," and they also established their businesses along the same principles as respectable boarding houses, muddling the terminology but taking advantage of the camouflage of respectability for the illicit operations of the house. Many brothels outwardly appeared as ordinary boarding houses to neighbors and authorities, and they were listed in city directories along with their reputable counterparts. Consequently, the distinctions between reputable and disreputable boarding houses were completely lost to the casual observer, and the operational distinctions between parlor-house brothel and prostitution boarding house ultimately disappeared. The term *parlor house* eventually came to designate an exclusive and finely furnished brothel, as opposed to a lower-class or more commonplace brothel.[61]

The third type of primary prostitution establishment—the assignation house—also eludes precise definition because of the variety of functions it served. Theoretically, an assignation house was not a prostitution house, but a bedroom establishment where illicit and adulterous lovers could meet for a tryst. Rooms could be rented for a short period—a few hours or overnight. The most important characteristic of an assignation house was secrecy, so that couples could be assured that their identities would never be known to others inside or outside the house. Many assignation houses, like upper-class parlor houses, were lavishly decorated, with special attention given to the furnishings in the bedroom quarters. The parlor was not a communal entertaining room but served as a private waiting room until an individual or couple could be taken to a bedroom.[62] It was said that if prostitutes were allowed to patronize assignation houses, then the so-called respectable clientele would shun the establishments. This may have been true of some patrons, but on the whole New York's assignation houses appear to have been well-integrated into the commercial sex structure, and business did not suffer because of it. Streetwalkers frequently used assignation houses for their prostitution activities, and there are numerous examples of assignation houses having a few prostitutes as permanent residents to serve patrons who were seeking prostitution in an establishment less notorious than a regular brothel. Some men found that, when having an extended liaison with a prostitute or non-prostitute, an assignation house offered both private and convenient quarters for lodging the "kept woman," while other men rented assignation rooms on a long-term basis so that a private room would be immediately available for use whenever wanted.[63]

Although assignation houses were in plentiful supply and were increasingly popular during the period from 1830 to 1870, one should note that alternative establishments were also utilized by prostitutes as the century progressed. In effect, an assignation house functioned as a very private hotel and was particularly convenient since the early Broadway hotels resisted prostitutes as patrons. After the Civil War, discreet prostitutes found the large hotels not so reluctant to take their business, and some of New York's more sophisticated prostitutes were able to use even the most fashionable Broadway hotels for servicing clients. James Mc-

Cabe noted in 1872 that "impure women of the 'higher,' that is the more successful class . . . abound at the hotels. The proprietor cannot turn them out unless they are notorious . . . for fear of getting himself into trouble."[64] Bed houses and furnished rooming houses also became popular with some independent prostitutes who were attracted to the privacy gained by avoiding the boarding arrangements of the more common multiple-resident dwellings. The disadvantage of such an arrangement was that prostitutes had to worry about their own meals. At the bottom end of the scale, prostitutes worked out of tenement houses, often sharing crowded quarters with non-prostitute residents.[65]

Although panel houses are sometimes mentioned as an additional form of residential sex institution, in reality they were a form of brothel or assignation house to promote thievery. One or more rooms of a brothel or a bed house might be furnished with a curtain, wall, or movable panel from which another prostitute or a partner-in-crime could gain entry into the locked bedroom. While the customer was occupied in bed, the intruder would steal from the client's pants pocket. The sex-for-money exchange had a new twist, but the institutional structure of the establishment remained the same.[66]

In spite of the fact that New York's primary sex institutions were numerous, and their existence and locations were well known to many citizens, it was the public, undisguised presence of prostitutes in secondary sex institutions and public thoroughfares that made the profession so visible and seemingly pervasive throughout the urban social structure. Here prostitution moved openly in the public arena for all but the most naive or sheltered eye to see. Although some prostitutes remained discreet, for most prostitutes secondary sex institutions were public forums for sexual solicitation. Both male patrons and prostitutes attended the theater, the saloon, concert hall, or dancing hall expecting an evening of good entertainment but also an opportunity to buy or sell sex.

The theater was the most popular of New York's entertainment institutions, and its connection with commercial sex was unmistakable because of the designation of the third tier as the exclusive province of prostitutes and their male suitors or friends. Just as mid-century New York led the nation in other fields, it also led the nation in numbers of theaters, and these establishments catered to all classes of the population. Although theaters like the Bowery had greatest appeal to boisterous masses such as the Bowery B'hoys, while the Park and Broadway theaters attracted a more refined clientele represented by Philip Hone and George Templeton Strong, all theaters had their prostitute population.[67] According to mid-nineteenth-century physician Charles Smith, "a particular set habitually and constantly frequent the third tiers of the theaters. There may be two hundred in all who nearly every night are seen at the Park, Broadway, Bowery, Olympic and Chatham theatres." Smith also noted that the character of the "ladies" in the third tier varied with the house, just as did that of the regular audience. "The Park and Broadway are genteel and formal; the Olympic, bizarre and grotesque; and the Bowery and Chatham, sensual, bold and roystering."[68] According to Smith there were three places a prostitute could appear in the theater—the third tier, the gallery (if thickly veiled), and the stage. The rest of the house was "considered sacred even by the third tier [who] won't allow one of their own to appear elsewhere if they know it."[69] An incident reported by Madam Mary Berry about three prostitutes from her brothel indicates that Smith may have been right about a "common code of theater behavior." As Berry related the tale: "Hannah Blisset and lady Elizabeth stole out last night, and graced the Richmond Hill Theatre with their presence. They went in the first tier of boxes, got gloriously drunk, and were turned out. . . . English Ann was going to whip the pair."[70]

New Yorkers generally understood that the third tier was a meeting place for prostitutes and their clients. Prostitutes made arrangements to join their customers of long standing at the theater, but they also made new client contacts there, both in the third tier and at the nearby bar that serviced their gallery. Some men went up to the third tier without previous arrangements in order to look over the prospects, while others were taken by mutual friends to be introduced to a prostitute.[71] A prostitute hoped to be escorted home by a customer at the end of the performance, or even better, to be taken out to dinner before going home. Sometimes suitors were impatient about waiting until the end of the evening. Prostitute Louisa Wilson met a man in the third tier of the Park who asked her to leave in the middle of the performance and accompany him to a house behind the theater, where he paid her a $2.50 retainer. They returned for the remainder of the performance and then left for her brothel.[72]

17. **THIRD TIER OF THE PARK THEATRE.** This 1822 watercolor of the Park Theatre, which clearly shows the "ladies of the third tier," includes actual portraits of eighty-four well-known New York figures. One of the patrons in the second tier was Jake LeRoy, who shocked New Yorkers by his highly visible relationship with prostitute Fanny White. (Courtesy of the New-York Historical Society, New York City)

Prostitute Mary Steen entertained a customer at her brothel on Chapel Street early one evening, and afterward he suggested they catch the performance at the Park Theatre. Steen said she and her "girls" were in the habit of going to the Bowery because they liked the manager there, so her escort consented and bought two tickets for the third tier of the Bowery. During the performance Steen slipped away to the bar, where her date shortly discovered her drinking with another man. She refused to return to her date, apparently because she was trying to line up a second commission for the evening. Later, the spurned escort spotted her in an adjoining box and was so enraged he attacked her with a pen knife, cutting up the sleeve of her dress.[73] Such disruptive and rowdy behavior was not unusual in the third tiers of theaters and often triggered complaints from the rest of the house. There are several instances of prostitutes having men arrested for tearing their clothes or bonnets, and one third-tier frequenter had a man arrested for trying to kiss her.[74] More often, however, arrests were made for prostitutes fighting with each other or being drunk and disorderly.[75]

Another complaint from theater patrons was that the numerous prostitutes attending the theater "enter by the same door as the chaste."[76] Contemporary George Foster lamented that prostitutes "come up the same steps and stairs as our wives, and into the same lobby."[77] Although a separate stairway for prostitutes was incorporated into the building design of many nineteenth-century theaters in other cities, this feature was late in coming to some of New York's biggest theaters, which sometimes required remodeling to add a staircase on the outside of the building.[78] Even though the third tier and, later, the special stair separated prostitutes from the general public, there was a limit to the isolation of prostitutes. When the manager of one of the city's dramatic establishments erected a partition to shut off the prostitutes from other patrons altogether, "he soon yielded to the dreadful necessity of the stage, and the protest of this class, and removed the partition."[79]

Nineteenth-century newspapers and contemporary accounts note how frequently prostitutes attended the theater, but to credit this popularity primarily to the desire or need to solicit clients is to ignore the full dimensions of the prostitute's working life. With the prostitute's workplace and residence the same, the theater offered a way to "get out of the house." It was also a place where her presence was not legally questioned. Furthermore, the theater was one of the opportunities a prostitute had for escape, for vicariously experiencing the lives of others. For those who were illiterate and did not have the alternative option of reading magazines and popular novels, the theater may have been especially important. Theater attendance was also a social occasion—a way to meet new people or old acquaintances in an environment not necessarily associated with sex. Many theaters opened the third tier one to two hours prior to the performance, which allowed prostitutes a longer time to socialize with fellow prostitutes and male friends—while increasing the bar revenues for the house. The early entry hour also was a way to avoid the complaints of respectable patrons who preferred not to mix with the unchaste.[80]

Documents pertaining to the life of Helen Jewett repeatedly attest to the importance of the theater in the lives of Jewett and her fellow prostitutes. In the Jewett correspondence there are twenty-three letters in which some reference is made to the theater, usually in the context of meeting a client or lover at the Park Theatre, of which Jewett was a devoted patron. (See Appendix 2 for a full explanation of the Jewett correspondence.) One letter discussed a man's failure to get Jewett together with one of his friends at the end of the previous night's performance. The intended acquaintance had hoped to "escort her home," but there was a misunderstanding. The same client/friend wrote two other letters mentioning the theater—one of which asked why Jewett left the playhouse without him the night before, without even saying goodbye. Jewett apparently had gone to the theater with the friend, had become perturbed, and left in a carriage with fellow prostitutes from other brothels.[81]

Most of the letters to and from Jewett's lover discussed the couple's hoping to see, or failing to see, one other on various evenings at the theater. While the letters were solicitations to meet together at the playhouse or at her brothel, the relationship was of long enough duration that attendance at the theater was a social outing for the couple as well as an attempt by Jewett to have the lover's company at the brothel afterward.[82] In one letter Jewett indicated she went to the theater for two nights in a row hoping to see the lover; failing, she wrote with some irony and humor:

You will think I have degenerated sadly to go to the theatre two nights in succession, but to tell you the truth, the sole inducement in going last night was the pleasure I anticipated from seeing you, in which you are aware I was disappointed.[83]

On another occasion, Jewett wrote that she had failed to persuade a male acquaintance, to whom her lover wished to be introduced, to meet her at the theater that evening. Even though she was unable to arrange the introduction for her lover, she stated: "I wish you would drop in there tonight, as I am going quite early." Her reference to her early attendance at the theater is a further indication of the prostitutes' enjoyment of the theater's "third tier social hour."[84]

Jewett also kept up with the Park's performance schedule and made an effort to attend those shows that promised to be special. In June of 1835 she wrote:

Tonight is Chapman's farewell benefit at the Park. I have an engagement to go with Clara, and if you get in town, and my letter in season, you will have arrived most opportunely, for then we may expect the pleasure of your company.[85]

On another occasion she hoped ill health would not keep her away from a promising performance:

I am quite unwell this morning, and unable to go out. Wallack plays tonight in two of his best pieces, and I should very much like to go, and hope by evening to feel well enough. You know it will be Saturday night, and I do not ask you to promise, but may I expect you to bring me home?[86]

Jewett also appeared to have some personal associations among theater personnel. She once wrote to her lover teasingly: "I had a little private chat with the manager of a certain theatre since you have been gone; which, however, I intend to explain and obtain entire absolution for."[87] She also entertained another theatrical personage as a client and received letters from him discussing dramatic and literary affairs. In December 1835 "J.J.A.S." wrote:

I went last evening with my good lady and her daughter, to watch the performance of Reeve, but we were all much disappointed. . . . I hope you will pardon the shortness of this feeble attempt to assure you of my regard for you. It is not the want of friendly sentiment, but of time, as I am now busily engaged with Simpson, the manager, in bringing forward a drama, of which I am the humble author.[88]

Many prostitutes were connected to actors and actresses, and the comment of Chapel Street madam Mary Steen that she liked the Bowery manager because he was a "clever fellow" may have indicated she knew him more than just by reputation.[89]

The open toleration of prostitutes at New York's dramatic establishments left no doubts in the minds of many that theatrical institutions were immoral. Many parents were certain that unchaperoned attendance at the theater meant that a daughter would become a prostitute—or already had become one. Thus, if a girl were found in one of the city's playhouses, parents sometimes had her arrested and sent to the House of Refuge.[90] One young man, who said he "accidentally" had gone into the third tier, discovered his sister there and had her taken to the police station.[91] The *Advocate of Moral Reform* believed that theaters were responsible for corrupting not just young women but also New York's children. They reported that girls as young as ten and eleven were in the habit of attending the third tier of the Franklin Theatre "for purposes of prostitution," and young boys of similar ages were found there with them. The *Advocate* also reported that one officer had said that girls from as young as *three* to thirteen (italics mine) had been found in the third tier. Given such information, it is not surprising that some observers believed that the increasing immorality of the entire city could be traced to its dramatic establishments.[92] As one editor wrote:

To the theatres of this city, above all other places, is the iniquity that abounds to be traced. . . . They are sinks of vice and pollution—houses of assignation and incipient prostitution—in four words, The Vestibules of Hell![93]

Whether it was the fact that prostitutes frequented the theater or a belief that the clientele and productions induced licentiousness in others, many people shunned the theater as an immoral establishment. One nineteenth-century scholar of the theater went so far as to estimate that seven-tenths of the population in mid-century America looked on attendance at the theater as a sin.[94]

Public condemnation of the third tier ultimately led to a movement to have prostitutes banned from New York's theaters, but either the prostitute's presence was not deemed offensive enough or her patronage was found to be too financially important to allow such legislation to pass.[95] Nevertheless, by the end of the 1850s the third tier as a place where prostitutes could solicit clients had begun to disappear. According to William Sanger, "many of the managers of our best theatres have abolished the third tier . . . and if any improper woman visits them she must do so under the assumed garb of respectability and conduct herself accordingly."[96] Even after the demise of the third tier in the period after the Civil War, New Yorkers commented on the continued importance of prostitutes' attendance at the theater. By this time, however, it appears prostitutes had come to prefer matinee performances to evening shows. One 1869 source noted that New York prostitutes "entirely support the theatre matinees," and another 1860s commentator pointed out that the attendance of prostitute patrons was important to theaters throughout the East: "In some instances in Eastern cities, in addition to free admissions, messengers have been sent to the haunts of vile women, to invite their attendance as the necessary attraction of a large and indispensable portion of the patrons of the stage."[97] Whether "under the assumed garb of respectability" or not, the prostitute's attendance at the theater remained important to the American stage in the postwar era.

No other secondary institutions appear to have had as wide an appeal to the prostitution population as did the theater, but various other entertainment establishments were popular with many of these women, whose presence in turn was a draw for male patrons. Taverns, groggeries, and saloons had long served as complementary establishments to the prostitution business. Eighteenth-century prostitutes entertained their customers in small rooms behind or above saloons, or they picked up clients in the vicinity of public taverns and took them to nearby lodging houses for sexual transactions. As prostitution spread throughout the city in the nineteenth century, however, new varieties of public leisure developed just as did new forms of residential prostitution. The traditional saloon continued to thrive along the waterfront and in such areas as the Five Points, but some proprietors added music and dancing to their businesses. German prostitution establishments introduced a variation of the saloon to mid-century New Yorkers. A German couple often ran the business together, the husband working as bartender and the wife as madam, with both overseeing the young women who served as waitresses and dancing partners in the barroom and as prostitutes in the bedrooms behind or above. Mid-century New York also witnessed the development of another form of drinking establishment, the concert saloon. Although a few concert saloons (or concert halls) existed in the 1850s, their great surge in popularity came after the Civil War when more than three hundred such establishments existed in New York City. Furthermore, the concert saloon rose in popularity at the same time the New York theater was restricting prostitutes in its effort to become more respectable, thus filling a "leisure-entertainment recruiting" void for some women in the prostitution business as well as a general cultural void for New Yorkers who wanted cheap but lively entertainment.[98]

Most concert saloons were located on major thoroughfares, in the basement or second floor of a building. The essential ingredients of the business were a bar, music, and "waiter girls." Some establishments also offered keno or billiards. Most concert halls had a stage for performances, and the music of the establishment was provided by one or more musicians who alone or with other entertainers might also provide the stage show. Waiter girls were a major attraction of the establishment and varied from the elegantly clothed, dignified woman with the "sister-like" demeanor employed at the Broadway and Fifth Avenue concert saloon to the "beastly, foul-mouthed, brutal wretch" who worked on Canal, Chatham, or Water streets.[99] Cheap liquor was furnished at inflated prices, and the waitress got a percentage of the drinks she sold. Her prostitution business was a private negotiation, which she arranged at the concert saloon but practiced in quarters elsewhere, unless private alcoves were made available by the establishment. Police records indicate that as many as seventeen hundred women were employed as waiter girls in the post–Civil War years. Although at first considered improper entertainment for respectable women, by the latter part of the nineteenth century concert halls were attracting a non-prostitute clientele, especially young working women.[100]

Another entertainment institution that was sometimes identified with the concert saloon was the dance hall. Dance halls were popular in New York as early as the 1840s, especially in areas like Water Street and the Five Points. According to one contemporary, dance halls differed from concert saloons in that "they are one grade lower both as regards the inmates and the visitors, and . . . dancing as well as drinking is carried on in them."[101]

Another contemporary described one of the dancing houses of the Five Points as "a large dimly-lighted cavern" having an "intolerable stench of brandy, tobacco, and steaming carcasses." A fiddler, sitting on a barrel by the bar, played for a group of dancers while "around the sides of the room in bunks, or sitting upon wooden benches, the remainder

18. JOHN ALLEN'S DANCE HALL.   John Allen's was one of New York's most famous "secondary sex institutions," a place of public entertainment where prostitutes could recruit customers. (Courtesy American Antiquarian Society)

of the company wait[ed] impatiently their turn upon the floor—meanwhile drinking and telling obscene anecdotes, or singing fragments of ribald songs."[102]

The most reputable of the nineteenth-century dance houses was Harry Hill's, which opened in the mid-1850s and was located on Houston Street near the Mulberry Street police station. Men paid twenty-five cents to enter, but women were allowed in free. All patrons were "required" to act with decorum, a house rule that the owner, a former pugilist, enforced for the thirty years his establishment was in business. Soliciting was an accepted part of dance halls, but at Harry Hill's it had to be done unobtrusively, and any illicit activities had to take place off the premises. Hill's had a large barroom as well as a dance hall, and patrons were treated to floor shows, one reason why some referred to his establishment as a concert hall. Harry Hill's closed in the late 1880s, the era when the concert hall was declining in popularity; his establishment had spanned the heyday of this form of entertainment. By the end of the century, former patrons of the concert saloon, including prostitutes, turned to the cabaret as the latest form of public entertainment, which prostitutes regarded as the newest secondary sex institution.[103]

One form of prostitution was centered not in buildings but outside them—the practice of streetwalking. The most well known of the soliciting techniques used by prostitutes, streetwalking was a very significant part of nineteenth-century New York's prostitution culture and, more than any other aspect of this culture, tested the limits of tolerance of New York citizens. Streetwalking became a major political issue.

Many women chose streetwalking as their arena of prostitution because of its ready availability. For the casual prostitute wishing for a quick source of money, streetwalking was a way temporarily to enter the profession without the "commitment" associated with a house of prostitution. Some career prostitutes chose this method of solicitation because they wanted to operate as independents—neither sharing their profits with nor having to adhere to rules set by the madam of an establishment. Other women had no alternative but streetwalking because they had descended the professional ladder of brothel prostitution and were considered too old, sick, or slovenly to be accepted again as brothel inmates.[104] Many very young girls, in fact child prostitutes, gradually eased into streetwalking as an extension of their peddling and huckstering activities and looked on their prostitution less as a new job than as another aspect of the street-world's exchange and barter of whatever commodity one had or could find.[105]

When Sanger wrote that "prostitution no longer confines itself to secrecy and darkness, but boldly strides through our most thronged and elegant thoroughfares," he accurately described the transition of streetwalking from the out-of-the-way streets of the eighteenth-century dock areas to the city's busiest thoroughfares and walkways—the Battery, the Bowery, and Broadway. Although the Battery had long been a resort of New York's streetwalkers, it gained new prominence in the antebellum period. The Battery was said to be "the favorite park of New Yorkers, and was indeed the handsomest."[106] For prostitutes, it was a convenient and pleasant promenade where one could stroll looking for business. In the 1840s a plan was proposed for enlarging Battery Park through landfills, a plan many commercial groups opposed. Preferring to see the enlarged area used for commercial development, the *Journal of Commerce* noted that the city could ill afford to have a park where land was worth $150,000 an acre and there was so little to be had at any price.

"If land is wanted for solitary meditation, or for the concealment of villainy, it would be better to select a site where land is cheaper."[107] By mid-century, however, the "villainy" of prostitution, as well as the respectable New York citizenry, had all but abandoned the area for other favorite walking places. The conversion of Castle Garden to an immigrant depot in the late 1850s, along with the use of poor landfill materials, helped bring on the decline of the Battery, causing it to become a virtual slum until it was reclaimed in 1869.[108]

Next to Broadway, the Bowery was said to be "the most thoroughly characteristic" of New York streets. The street originated in Chatham Square, "the great promenade of the old time denizens of the Bowery." Once a respectable thoroughfare, "the Bowery commenced to lose caste" after the city began to extend up the island. A nineteenth-century citizen noted: "Decent people forsook it, and the poorer and more disreputable classes took possession. Finally, it became notorious, . . . known all over the country for its roughs . . . and its doubtful women."[109] The street was filled with pawnshops, dance houses, lodging houses, concert saloons, and lower-class theaters. Although always a busy thoroughfare, at night and on Sundays the Bowery came especially alive with noise and throngs of people, including the Bowery streetwalkers whom George T. Strong described as "members of the whore-archy in [their] most slatternly *deshabille*."[110]

By far, the most famous New York thoroughfare was Broadway—New York's pride and her shame, celebrated as "the most wonderful street in the universe."[111] Filled with elegant shops, "monster" hotels, and the latest in transportation vehicles, a look at Broadway was a "must" for all visitors to New York. Few contemporary sources discussed the city without mentioning the beautiful, elegantly dressed women who promenaded the famous thoroughfare in the afternoons—and few discussed Broadway without mentioning the "flashily dressed" females found there at night, "walking rapidly, with a peculiar gait, and glancing quickly but searchingly at every man they pass."[112] As the heart of the city moved from the tip of Manhattan in the 1830s to the middle of the island in the postwar years, streetwalking shifted in location and intensity along Broadway just as did the centers of brothel prostitution. First concentrating in the area from Fulton to Prince Street, then from Canal to Bleecker, by the 1870s the prime areas for streetwalkers were from Grand to Fourteenth Street, and from Twenty-third to Thirtieth Street.[113]

Working the streets exposed prostitutes to a number of dangers—mugging, rape, and other abuses, as well as disease and physical decline. Whatever the reality of the streets' deleterious effects on these women, one nineteenth-century observer expressed a common belief when he noted: "A healthy Street Walker is almost a myth."[114] Another risk faced by the streetwalking trade was harassment and possible arrest by police, since streetwalking was the least tolerated of the various forms of soliciting. Streetwalking prostitutes were subject to arrest if they stopped to talk to male pedestrians, and police enforced this rule much more aggressively on a major street like Broadway than on the less traversed side streets.[115] Sometimes a difficulty with the law occurred because of the streetwalker's unfortunate choice of patron; several streetwalkers were arrested for propositioning justices. Justice Hopson said he was on his way to court when Anne Miller stopped him at the corner of Water Street and, as she stated, "made the mistake of soliciting directions." He had her arrested, questioned what she did for a living, and sent her to the penitentiary for six months.[116] Catherine Cochran detained Justice Lowndes on Pearl Street one December evening and "made certain delicate but immoral overtures." Lowndes had Cochran brought in to the station house but released her after she promised to behave herself. Six days later she was arrested again by the watch for annoying a man in the street, and this time Lowndes sent her to Bellevue as a vagrant.[117] A few months later, Justice Bloodgood said he was taking a "sentimental stroll" through the Five Points when a woman stopped him and asked "if it wasn't time to go to bed." He had the watch lock her in jail until the next morning, when she went before Justice Lowndes and complained that she had "accidentally run against a stout gentleman" who was "so ungallant that he wouldn't listen to her apology but roughly and gruffly sent her in." Lowndes reprimanded her severely and let her go.[118] Since "evidence" was seldom necessary to arrest a suspected prostitute, it is unlikely the justices were in questionable neighborhoods for entrapment purposes. These occurrences were probably unfortunate accidents for the prostitutes as well as examples of how prostitutes approached pedestrians, but it is also possible that the justices were out strolling for voyeuristic reasons, observing and experiencing up close the underworld of illicit sex.[119]

By the 1850s pressure from citizens and politicians caused officials to take, on occasion, a more aggressive approach to the problem of streetwalking. The practice had become too obvious and too intrusive, characteristics that challenged the community's usual attitude of quiet toleration of the profession. Articles in the press decried

the shame of our city, . . . the open and indecent parade permitted of miserable women of the lowest sort in Broadway at all hours from nightfall until far past midnight. . . . Has not this abomination been borne about as long as society can safely bear it? Is not this . . . a favorable time to attempt to purge Broadway of this, its greatest disgrace?[120]

The perceived boldness of streetwalkers was partly a function of the sheer numbers of prostitutes who were found on the major thorough-fares, but as distressing as their numbers was the nature of the women walking the streets. The streetwalkers of the 1850s were women who overwhelmingly represented the disinherited and undesirable of New York. The majority of them were drawn from the immigrant and poor classes, those who were hardest hit by the economic stresses of the decade. Also, the practice increasingly included children, or young girls who were described by George Strong as "hideous troop[s] of ragged girls, from twelve years old down, brutalized already almost beyond redemption by premature vice, . . . with whore [written] on their depraved faces."[121] With the increasing presence of children added to the im-migrants and the poor in the ranks of prostitution, the rhetoric of reform shifted away from the immorality of illicit sex to what really bothered respectable citizens most: the specter of social disorder, a threat they believed was created more by unacceptable appearances than by sexual immorality itself. Discussing Mayor Wood's reform program, Strong wrote:

What the Mayor seeks to abolish or abate is not the terrible evil of prostitution (for the great notorious "ladies' boarding houses" of Leonard and Mercer Streets are left in peace), but simply the scandal and offence of the *peripatetic* whore-archy.[122]

Nevertheless, Strong agreed with the Mayor's reform intent—for prostitution's "conspicuousness and publicity are disgraceful and mis-chievous and inexpressibly bad."[123] William Sanger, writing a few years later, confirmed that the general attitude among contemporaries sup-ported Wood: "Being a prostitute is acknowledged by all as a degradation; while a vagrancy commitment . . . is a positive disgrace."[124] As with prostitution establishments, where the distinctions noted by contemporaries between the elegant and the poor establishments seemingly reflected New Yorkers' fear of and fascination with new or strange aspects of urban living as much as they did actual differences in the types of houses, the streetwalker or vagrant also became a moral locus or symbol of urban chaos and social disorder. Not only was the streetwalker often poor and foreign, but she also walked through the streets unchaperoned, an act which further challenged patriarchal notions of proper social order.

The presence at mid-century of so many child prostitutes represented a different kind of threat to society, one that involved a failure of the family, the institutional backbone of American society. In response to this threat, interest groups coalesced to become advocates and protectors of this segment of the population. While Chief of Police Matsell and Mayor Wood attacked prostitution in the streets, organizations like the Children's Aid Society and the Association for the Improvement of the Condition of the Poor attacked its perceived source, the poor man's home. Yet all of the moralistic rhetoric and public statements condemning streetwalkers and the improper homes of child prostitutes obscured the fact that streetwalking was a quick source of income, often the best option a female had for supporting, or helping to support, herself and her family.

The end result of the 1850s legal and reform campaigns against streetwalkers was the issuance of municipal directives providing a more cautious method of arresting and pressing charges against adult prostitutes. Even so, most of the women found their fate still dependent on the whim of the officer on duty. Most of those arrested continued to be sent for a short while to prison, the revolving door of prostitution. For child prostitutes, a different approach was tried. In the past, young girl prostitutes had been sent to the House of Refuge where, through the strict regimen and rigid discipline of the Refuge or indentured positions, the girls, it was hoped, were taught respectable habits—a remedial approach that met with modest success. In contrast, the Children's Aid Society trained working-class girls in the domestic arts, because such skills were believed to offer these girls an alternative to prostitution and to create, in the long run, a new kind of working-class woman. By the 1860s, the large anti-streetwalking campaigns of the 1850s were a thing of the past, but streetwalkers, both adults and children, continued to throng the city's thoroughfares, seeking a readily available source of income.[125]

Although streetwalking was the most common form of soliciting by prostitutes, some found other creative ways to attract clients. In the early decades of the nineteenth century when New York was a "walking city," streetwalking on the city's thoroughfares was an adequate way to be exposed to potential clients. With the rise of each new form of public transportation, however, prostitutes extended their solicitation efforts. They not only congregated at depots of ferries, ships, and omnibuses to seek out disembarking passengers, but they also rode the routes to allow greater time for establishing "rapport." Some observers complained that prostitutes had overrun the night lines of steamers traveling from New York to cities like Albany and Boston and consequently had become a great nuisance to respectable travelers.[126]

New York's prostitutes also utilized literary forms of solicitation. Some corresponded with prospective and established clients, using both mail and messenger services. Helen Jewett wrote to men who had visited her previously, requesting that they return, and she wrote to new acquaintances encouraging them to call sometime.[127] Soliciting through correspondence gave Jewett greater control over her time and her calendar. She scheduled visits for particular nights and hours, thus avoiding the surprise of spontaneous visits and the embarrassment and difficulty of having two or more well-liked clients show up at the same time.[128]

In addition to private correspondence, the personal columns of the daily newspapers became popular in the postwar period for arranging both introductions and assignations between illicit lovers. Even more offensive to some newspaper readers than these printed messages between lovers was prostitutes' use of the personals column to announce to the public their moves from one brothel to another. For example:

Miss Gertie Davis, formerly of Lexington Avenue, will be pleased to see her friends at 106 Clinton Place.[129]

Another form of literary solicitation popular in this period was the brothel directory, several of which were published from the 1830s through the 1870s, each giving locations of the most reputable brothels as well as descriptions of the establishments, their madams, and the house prostitutes.[130] Though the establishments and neighborhoods

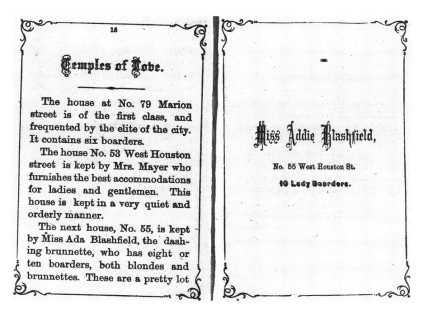

15

Temples of Love.

The house at No. 79 Marion street is of the first class, and frequented by the elite of the city. It contains six boarders.

The house No. 53 West Houston street is kept by Mrs. Mayer who furnishes the best accommodations for ladies and gentlemen. This house is kept in a very quiet and orderly manner.

The next house, No. 55, is kept by Miss Ada Blashfield, the dashing brunnette, who has eight or ten boarders, both blondes and brunnettes. These are a pretty lot

Miss Addie Blashfield,

No. 55 West Houston St.

10 Lady Boarders.

19. GENTLEMAN'S DIRECTORY. This 1870 brothel guidebook assisted patrons in locating and evaluating the city's "temples of love." (Courtesy of the New-York Historical Society, New York City)

described in brothel directories were usually the more appealing and elegant places of prostitution, such as the places George T. Strong called "the great, notorious 'ladies' boarding houses' of Leonard and Mercer Streets," newspapers and reform tracts repeatedly reminded New Yorkers there were also "dens of filth and debauchery" located at the Hook, in Water Street, or at the Five Points. Both sorts of descriptions were of real places, establishments that actually existed within more broadly defined geographic divisions of prostitution. Yet one sees within the descriptions of what actually was, visions of what must be—the moral prototypes of what New Yorkers feared was threatening the social fiber of the city. Both the tempting licentious palaces of sumptuous luxury and the retributive pestilent dens of debauchery were generalizations within a moralistic framework that helped residents deal with what seemed worrisome in their changing society.

In spite of New Yorkers' attempts at a geographic and institutional ordering of prostitution and related evils, the women to whom George

T. Strong referred as the "peripatetic whore-archy" or the "noctivagous strumpetocracy" were not readily "ordered."[131] As Sanger noted, they were boldly striding through the most "thronged and elegant thorough-fares, and there, in the broad light of the sun, . . . jost[ling] the pure, the virtuous, and the good."[132] Some citizens may have been alarmed by the public specter of prostitution, but there was another aspect of prostitutes' existence in the city that reflected a different relationship with New Yorkers. Censuses and tax records demonstrated that prosti-tutes also were quietly living in the next block, down the street, or in an adjacent room—fellow New York citizens and neighbors who were coping with daily living in the nation's largest urban metropolis.

7

"Upon the Foot-stool of God"

Working Conditions of Prostitutes

Many nineteenth-century contemporaries believed that the degrading and dehumanizing conditions of prostitution caused a woman unavoidably to experience a complete character change. The woman who was once pure in nature supposedly became totally depraved, capable of an assortment of crimes and the most disgusting actions. Charles Smith devoted an entire chapter of his 1847 book on prostitution and abortion in New York to a discussion of a phenomenon which he said "astonished all observers": the "extreme and marvelous rapidity with which the purest girls become depraved" once they became prostitutes. According to Smith, a pure girl would become a prostitute, and within a few months she would be bold, brazen, impudent, audacious, foul-mouthed, and vulgar, apparently destitute of all sense of decency and shame. "An angelic woman," he claimed, "becomes the most revolting creature that crawls upon the foot-stool of God."[1] An 1837 commencement speaker at Columbia College argued that "in the female character there is no mid-region; it must exist in spotless innocence, or else in hopeless vice."[2] The "poison" of prostitution, wrote contemporary George Foster, "is active as lightning, and produces a kind of moral insanity, during which the victim is pleased with ruin. . . . The woman is transformed to a devil and there is no hope for her."[3]

These observations helped uphold contemporary notions that women must be either mother-angels or whore-devils and also helped rationalize why women, though initially victims, would stay in the prostitution profession. Part of the attempt by contemporaries to explain the nature of women who would violate accepted norms of womanhood and become prostitutes also involved an attempt to explain and impose some kind of order on the underworld of commercial sex which had expanded so greatly. Most nineteenth-century observers who wrote about prostitutes utilized an elaborate hierarchical cataloguing of prostitution establishments and their inhabitants, partly as a way of imposing order on the institutions of sexual commerce and partly as a distancing technique. As Judith Walkowitz has pointed out, the use of stratification helped to depersonalize the social underworld and establish a demarcation between the respectable and "dangerous" classes of society.[4]

The hierarchical method of describing commercial sex establishments was first used in 1836 by Parent-Duchatelet, whose method was apparently imitated by most of New York's observers of prostitution. Writing in the decade after Parent-Duchatelet and basing his observations on his experiences as a physician among New York's prostitutes, Charles Smith was the first to analyze and classify New York's prostitution businesses. Sex establishments were judged by the luxury and comfort they offered; the refinement, behavior, and attractiveness of the women who worked in and managed them; and the socioeconomic status of clients who patronized them. Establishments also were characterized by the types of "lovers" drawn to the class of prostitutes who resided there. Writing a decade after Smith, William Sanger used the same types of classifications and categories but was more "scientific" and more like Parent in that he incorporated into his study not only his professional observations but also statistical data from actual research among these women. Sex establishments and prostitutes' working conditions also were described in more "popular" antebellum works, the urban sketches in which readers were guided on fictional tours through the dens of vice and poverty of the New York underworld. In the late 1840s and early 1850s several journalists published book-length sketches, such as Solon Robinson, *Hot Corn: Life Scenes in New York Illustrated*; Ned Buntline (E. C. Z. Judson), *Mysteries and Miseries of New York*; and George Foster, *New York in Slices*, *New York by Gas-Light*, and *New York Naked*. Literature published after the Civil War drew from both types of antebellum works, keeping the class stratification of the scientific observers but combining commercial sex classifications with the voyeuristic style used by Foster, Robinson, and Buntline. These postwar authors attempted to educate the reader on the "other," "under," or "nether" world of prostitution. Most of these writers, such as George Ellington, Matthew Hale Smith, James D. McCabe, and Edward Crapsey, not only adopted the format of earlier authors but also closely followed each others' works in content, organization, and style, basically repeating the information given by the most recently published of their group.[5] In spite of the fact that many of these nineteenth-century descriptions were manipulated to create a well-delineated hierarchy, they are valuable as general descriptions of how urban prostitution was organized in the United States from the early decades of the nineteenth century into the twentieth, and they offer examples of the vast range of conditions under which nineteenth-century prostitutes worked.

For most of the laboring population of nineteenth-century urban America, working conditions were less than desirable. A sweatshop; a poorly ventilated, often unsafe factory; or the crowded, dark, unsanitary home-laborer's tenement provided the physical environment most New Yorkers could expect for their daily employment. The majority of New York prostitutes were poor, so they, too, faced a work environment oftentimes as dismal as that experienced by their non-prostitute peers. Yet there was another side to prostitution, visible to all and tempting to many, that offered prospects for improved working conditions—conditions far more comfortable than the ordinary working woman could ever hope to experience. The possibilities for wealth and luxury increased greatly over the century, and well-to-do New Yorkers built residential structures that reflected their economic success, surrounding themselves with material objects of the finest and most luxurious kinds. Those prostitution houses that catered to a prosperous level of client duplicated this opulent atmosphere, appealing to a client's economic aspirations as well as his sexual fantasies. Some brothels were filled with the best furnishings available, while others settled for ostentatious or tawdry imitations. Many women entered prostitution dreaming of working in a more luxurious atmosphere, but most hoped simply to achieve comforts and working conditions better than those they faced in respectable employments. Since clients' expectations and economic resources varied, there was always a demand for houses with different levels of luxury and comfort, as well as for prostitutes who exhibited distinctions in refinement and behavior commensurate with the status of the houses. Responding to market demands, the prostitution business in nineteenth-century New York supplied a diversity of houses and women, establishments that could cater to patrons from every social and economic class—the rich and the poor, the refined and the vulgar.

Observers developed various systems for classifying prostitution establishments. Most distinguished between brothels, assignation houses, and leisure or secondary prostitution institutions, and within each of these categories they noted from four to eight different class levels. In general, however, one could say that establishments and their employees were grouped as upper or first class; middle class, with subcategories related to inmates' ethnicity, methods of solicitation, and other norms of behavior; and lower class. Contemporary descriptions of houses in each of these classes give an indication of how establishments were evaluated and how they differed in terms of physical and social environment.

Extremes often attracting most attention, observers tended to describe either those brothels that were the most lavishly decorated or tenements that were disgusting and filthy. In the 1830s, Rosina Townsend was said to have one of the "most splendid establishments" in the city, a large, four-story, double house that was painted yellow. The interior was "elegantly furnished with mirrors, splendid paintings, sofas, ottomans, and every variety of costly furniture." An elaborate staircase led to the upper rooms. The second-story bedroom that was the scene of the Jewett murder was described as "elegant and extravagant." The room had a large draped bed and a number of other pieces of furniture, including a work table with "pen, papers, and pamphlets," and a "library of light novels, poetry and periodicals." Over the fireplace mantle were hung several theatrical fancy sketches, and on another wall was a print portrait of Lord Byron.[6] Even more elaborate than Townsend's brothel was Kate Ridgley's place at 78 Duane Street, described in an 1853 brothel directory as the palace of mirrors, with sixty superbly furnished rooms, including "two lower parlors lined with mirrors which alone cost $8000. The furnishings of the palace cost upwards of $70,000."[7] Two decades later, the equally posh but smaller brothel of Kate Woods, located further uptown on West Twenty-fifth Street, was popularly known as the Hotel de Wood. Wood's brothel was a "three story, brownstone house furnished through with the most costly and newest improvements. Her gallery of oil paintings alone cost $10,000. Rosewood furniture, immense mirrors, Parisien figures, & c. The house is furnished at a cost of $70,000."[8]

Although the houses of Townsend, Ridgley, and Woods offered the physical working conditions most prostitutes dreamed of having, the majority of them worked in much more modest surroundings. According to one mid-century observer, the difference in the first- and second-class (or middle-class) brothels was that "what is costly luxury in the one is replaced by tawdry finery in the other, and for expensive mirrors and valuable paintings they substitute cheaper ornamentation."[9] Some middle-class establishments were in very old houses, where the inhabitants' plain rooms contrasted sharply with the well-decorated private quarters of Townsend's brothel. Prostitutes of this class might rent an apartment "of middling size, . . . having but little furniture . . . a bed, two or three chairs, some rude toilet conveniences," and perhaps a stove for cooking meals.[10] A different type of middle-class establishment was the German house. Small and often located in a basement, German houses were entered through a reception/barroom in which the windows were decorated with crimson and white curtains, a symbol that the business was a prostitution establishment. "The room is very clean; a common sofa, one or two settees, and a number of chairs are ranged round the walls; there is a small table with some German newspapers upon it; a piano, upon which the proprietor or his bar-keeper at intervals performs a national melody; and a few prints or engravings complete its furniture."[11] Behind the barroom, the remainder of the floor space was partitioned off into very small bedrooms to accommodate the three or four women who worked as prostitutes in the house.

Prostitution establishments of the lower class were often characterized by abhorrent working conditions that a woman found hard to escape. The *Sun* described a prostitution "kennel" in Cross Street as a place where the prostitutes "sleep promiscuously heads and points on a field bed of straw spread over the whole floor like so many pigs, men and women, drunk and sober, and black and white."[12] Places of this sort were "without a table, chair, or any other article of furniture, save a cooking utensil, a few plates, and knives, and bottle, with which to carry on the business of living."[13]

Acknowledging that contemporaries often exaggerated their descriptions, the hierarchy of prostitution made clear that, even if only for a brief time, a woman in prostitution had the opportunity for working conditions that at best could be far superior to those of thousands of her working-class sisters and at worst might not be any more degraded. Thus, if the prostitute herself thought about a hierarchy of prostitution, she thought of it first in economic terms—wishing to create a level of luxury or the ambience necessary to attract the desired clients who would provide the greatest economic profit for her and her house. Second, prostitutes judged or "ranked" their work environments by the personal comforts and pleasures afforded by the house, their coworkers, and their clients. Lastly, prostitutes were concerned with the degree of physical security the workplace provided. Most prostitutes, therefore, considered themselves to be moving up or down within the profession as they increased or decreased their profits, comforts, and security. As far as clients were concerned, most prostitutes did not entertain men who had vastly different socioeconomic backgrounds from their own, though many hoped through personal attractiveness, social skills, and cleverness to have the opportunity to improve their social and financial situations. Some succeeded in this goal, but many others, especially long-term prostitutes who did not go into management, often suffered from the debilitating aspects of the profession and experienced a decline in socioeconomic status, personal comfort, and physical safety. [14]

The person who was key to ensuring the benefits expected of a prostitution establishment was the madam or house keeper. A large portion of her success was determined by her personal traits and individual talents and skills, but the house customs and practices she established also played a role in ensuring profits, security, and comfort.

Like house prostitutes, the madam was a part of the profession's hierarchy, and her refinement, sophistication, cleverness, and skills were directly related to her success in her job. The madam was a major factor in determining the "personality" of the house. The key phrases describing houses of prostitution in brothel directories usually were those concerning the madam's disposition, which appeared to set the tone for the house. The following examples illustrate the importance of the madam's personality:

Miss Ridgley is a lady of high order and conducts her house in a manner that is an honor to herself, while her lady boarders pattern after her.

Mrs. M. Gardner . . . is the most honorable landlady in New York; her word is good for any amount. . . . Gentlemen will receive the best of treatment at her hands; her young lady boarders take after her.

This pug-nosed thing [Mrs. C. C. Cook] . . . pretends to be very nice- . . . [but] gentlemen had better not trouble her crib as there are enough better places where a person can enjoy a little pleasure with perfect safety.

Miss Marshall . . . [is] not much liked by sister landladies; her boarders are apt to be saucy. The landlady is a little too set in her ways and not very benevolent.

Mrs. C. Hathaway [is] experienced, witty, etc. The house is elegant through-out . . . and much frequented. Her young ladies are healthy, amiable, pretty, accomplished, and know how to entertain.

Mrs. Redding—Sweetness of temper being no prominent ingredient in this lady's (if we may so call her,) composition—boarders never stay long with her.[15]

No matter how charming or witty a madam was, if she did not possess certain business skills, the house probably did not prosper as a profitable enterprise. As a business manager, the madam supervised the resident prostitutes and in larger houses also managed the staff that serviced the women and the customers. The better brothels had staffs to cook and serve meals, clean the houses, and keep linens fresh, and some used the services of musicians, hairdressers, seamstresses, porters, bartenders, and maids who helped with dressing. In some cases the number of brothel employees was so large that the madam was, in effect, running a small hotel. In 1850 Ellen Thompson had sixteen resident prostitutes, six female servants, one coachman, and a baby of one of the servants in her house. Jane Winslow also had sixteen prostitutes and one black male waiter in residence; she must have used day help for domestic chores. Kate Hastings also must have had day help because no servants were listed in a parlor house that had twenty prostitute residents. Amanda Parker housed nine prostitutes, four female servants, and one male servant. Maria Adams, noted for her benevolence as the "Queen of the Landladies," had fourteen resident prostitutes and also boarded six female servants and four children. By 1855 several of these madams had slightly reduced the number of inhabitants in their establishments, but others expanded their operations, like Cinderella Marshall, who employed seventeen prostitutes, five female servants, and one male servant. With staffs as large as these, madams needed effective personnel and communication skills as well as business management talents.[16]

Keeping finances in order often meant a madam had to be tough with business associates. Julia Brown was brought to the court because she refused to pay fees she had been assessed for legal services. According to testimony, Brown had engaged a lawyer to transact all of her legal affairs, and, unbeknownst to her, he had subcontracted the legal work to another attorney. Arguing that she had not been consulted and thus was not financially responsible, Brown refused to pay the second attorney. The court supported her action and ordered a "nonsuit."[17]

A major portion of brothel management involved overseeing household purchases and other expenditures. As household mistress, the madam had to see that there were adequate supplies of wine, fuel, and other staples, and she was in charge of ensuring that the building was properly maintained. Just like any other homeowner, a brothel madam made certain that carpenters, plasterers, and painters were available for repairs, and that these were done quickly and properly, especially since rowdy and destructive patrons and bullies were a frequent problem.[18]

Physical stamina was also important for a madam. A household mistress was "on duty" as long as there were customers in the house, which could be until the early hours of the morning. Household chores then had to be taken care of in the pre- and post-noon hours so that the brothel was ready for business by early evening. One of the complaints voiced by several brothel managers was that the job was a twenty-four-hour endeavor and was extremely demanding physically. One nineteenth-century madam noted that as a result of the physical and psychological stresses of running a brothel, she lost weight and was "too tired to care" about the attractive men in her life that she should have been enjoying.[19] Furthermore, in some of the middle- and lower-class brothels, physical strength as well as physical stamina was an asset because madams often had to try to control rowdy patrons.[20]

As friend and "mother" to her prostitutes, a madam frequently had to counsel the women about their problems. She also served as mediator in an effort to keep quarrels, conflicts, and competition among residents to a minimum. Her role as confidante and friend, however, had to be balanced with her role as efficient manager, and this sometimes meant that tough decisions had to be made about dismissing a prostitute who was too diseased to work or who no longer was attracting enough customers to pay her way.[21] In addition, madams often were called upon to have some knowledge of first aid and a little do-it-yourself gynecology. Finally, if a prostitute died, the madam usually saw it as her role to see that the woman had a "decent" funeral and burial.[22]

The internal affairs of a house were only part of a madam's responsibilities. Tact and diplomacy were key skills in dealing with customers and community members. Care had to be taken that neighbors were not offended enough to make complaints to the police, and it was important to keep a congenial working relationship with local officials so they would be as lenient as possible in the event of complaints. Most important of all was being discreet about customers. Prostitutes pretended not to know customers if they met them in public situations.[23] If subpoenaed to testify in court hearings, prostitutes cooperated with legal officials, but the testimony of brothel or assignation house managers was often extremely evasive. Rosina Townsend was willing to have her court testimony discredited rather than reveal the identity of a respectable client, and Caroline Ingersoll's testimony in the Forrest divorce case was a paradigm of evasiveness. The transcript of her testimony ran to four pages characterized by claims that she saw or remembered nothing:

I never saw him in the room or go into it; I never saw him in any place in my house, except my parlor, which is in the front room on the first story; I received him in the parlor and left him there; . . . I retired because of my household duties; I cannot recollect the charge for the room; when he asked for a room, he simply asked for a room; . . . I don't know whether he occupied it or not; . . . I never saw him bring anyone with him; I never heard any one with him; it may appear very strange to you, but nevertheless it is truth. I did not usually endeavor to hear and understand all that I could, or to see what he did with the room; that is not my character; I never saw any one with him, never heard anyone with him, and I could not know what business he had in the room; . . . I kept a boarding-house.[24]

Although a madam's personal skills were key to the success of her establishment, she could use certain "house customs" or practices as a means to further control brothel security or increase profits. A few of the more select houses had requirements or rituals for entry which allowed housekeepers to screen clientele. Rituals also served to make clients think they were being admitted to discriminating houses. Some establishments required a letter of invitation or recommendation from a previous patron-in-good-standing, while others had a special knock and password or counter-sign known to the select few. In others, the door was kept locked, and the madam or doorkeeper looked at the patron through a peephole or glass panel before allowing entry.[25] Townsend had a special door lock that was used after midnight, so that each prostitute letting out a customer after that time had to awaken Townsend to get the key. Another house had a spring chain on the inside of the door, and the only way to enter or leave was to have the chain loosened by a special instrument kept by the madam.[26]

Madams also helped subsidize house income with the custom of "treating." Although many customers bought wines or champagne over the course of an evening, in some houses customers, especially new customers, were expected to treat the house, or buy drinks for everyone in the parlor. Some customers, such as John Kinmon, found that failure to treat caused difficulties for them. Kinmon reported to police that "the old hag" of an Orange Street brothel asked him to treat everyone (at 50 cents a glass), and when he refused, she told him: "It is always customary to treat." When he persisted in refusing, he said the women of the house gathered round him and taunted him by taking off his hat and goading him with a pin. In response, he knocked down several prostitutes, which set off a free-for-all with broomsticks, shovels, tongs, and pokers. The women brought charges of assault and battery against Kinmon, but the judge released him.[27]

Although madams or prostitutes might have tried to increase revenues by servicing as many customers as possible, sources do not indicate that efficiency was even overtly emphasized, at least not in the more established brothels. There are several late-nineteenth-century and early twentieth-century references to an "assembly line" approach to patrons, noting that a prostitute might have sex with as many as thirty customers in an evening and might spend only three minutes with a customer from the time he entered the bedroom until he left. One turn-of-the-century prostitute was said to have had sex with fifty-eight men in less than three hours.[28] This kind of "efficiency" might have been characteristic of lower-class "cribs" rather than high-priced establishments, but references such as these are not readily found for the early half of the nineteenth century, regardless of the class of house. Antebellum prostitutes appear to have been more "task oriented" than "time disciplined," and such pre-industrial rhythms apparently prevailed in brothels through most of the century.[29]

William Sanger gives some indication of the range in numbers of customers that might have been seen by mid-century prostitutes in attempting to illustrate the alarming possibilities for the spread of venereal disease. In estimating the number of New Yorkers exposed to venereal disease each day, Sanger used a factor of one to two clients per prostitute but noted that an estimate of one customer was "ridiculously small, . . . even two visitors is a very low estimate, and four is very far from an unreasonably large one."[30] At one point in his discussion he stated that "each prostitute in New York receives from one to ten visitors every day" and, in a few instances, "sometimes double" that number, a total that would alarm anyone calculating the possibilities for the spread of disease.[31] Even when trying to create a sense of urgency over the need to pass contagious-disease legislation, the closest researcher of prostitution in the age put twenty clients per day as an extreme. When not discussing disease, but rather determining the "most correct" total of fees earned in parlor houses, Sanger recommended calculating on the basis of two visitors per prostitute per day.[32] Apparently, most mid-century patrons expected their sex transactions to be allotted more than a few minutes, and prostitutes also expected to give more time. The nineteenth century's increase in public prostitution may have been indicative of the widespread impersonalization of sex, as historians have noted, but antebellum commercial sex transactions still appear to have retained characteristics of sociability. If prostitutes had but two clients on average a day it seems that the relationship must have been somewhat social as well as sexual—though that of course does not prove the prostitute liked the one any better than the other.

Even though prostitutes and madams tried to ensure that their working conditions were comfortable and secure, they could not avoid all the risks and dangers that went along with the profession. Of all of the prostitute's problems, perhaps the least harmful, but bothersome, was harassment from other members of the community. Neighbors who found prostitutes offensive seldom took direct action but made complaints to the police asking that officials use legal measures to close the houses. The relatively small number of disorderly house cases brought to court, however, is an indication of the general ineffectiveness of this procedure.[33] In one instance, neighbors took direct action by offering to pay a madam more than $1,000 to move her house to another neighborhood. She refused unless they would double the payment. Angry, the residents went to the police but would not file charges because they did not want attention focused on their neighborhood. The police came to the group's aid by posting an officer at the entry to the house. As each customer arrived, the officer flashed a light in his face and told him not to enter because the house was to be "pulled"—a tactic that quickly caused the madam to remove the brothel from the area.[34] Though in this case harassment was successful, the complexity of these offers and transactions, capped by the police engaging in illegal tactics to aid the neighbors, underscores the bargaining position of prostitutes in conflicts with the community.

Other community members who were concerned about prostitution houses were missionaries and moral reformers. Representatives of these groups who visited brothels in their spiritual capacities usually reported that they were treated with courtesy, but the prostitutes who had to listen politely to lectures, Bible verses, and prayers must have become impatient with the visitors at times. Still, the reports suggest rather notable politeness on both sides, much like that between gentler home owners and the Mormon or Jehovah's Witness missionaries who might knock today. Of course, rougher places of prostitution sometimes were the scene of rougher responses. McCabe stated that in the lowest sort of dance houses on Water Street, missionaries might be met with vile abuse and be driven away with curses.[35]

Another form of harassment experienced by prostitutes was the claim by customers that prostitutes had stolen from them. Certainly thefts occurred, as panel houses show, but since theft was commonly touted as one of the dangers of patronizing prostitutes, disgruntled clients believed they would receive a ready ear to such claims. Although cash often was at issue, watches were said to have been stolen almost as frequently. Jane Brown of 136 Duane Street was charged with stealing a watch from a German man. She told the judge it had been given to her for her "services," which the customer did not deny, so she was acquitted and discharged.[36] Jane Robinson was not so fortunate in the court. Her client tried to leave without paying, so she made a fuss, and he, too, gave payment with his watch. The customer then went to the police and charged that Robinson had stolen the timepiece. After hearing her story, the judge released her but forced her to return the watch, leaving her with no remuneration for her night's work.[37] Whether or not claims of theft were true, prostitutes had to take the time to defend themselves before the police, and, if the item in question was found in the prostitute's possession, she had to persuade the authorities it was legitimately hers.

One mid-century case illustrates the confidence (or perhaps naiveté) with which some prostitutes operated in the community. The police had received information that a $500 bank bill had been found in Elizabeth Williams's Greene Street brothel, after being reported missing by a previous client. They went to the house, and Williams turned over the note—but later she read in the paper that a $100 reward had been offered for its return. Feeling she had been cheated out of her rightful reward—not that she might be the prime suspect for theft—Williams went directly to Mayor Havemeyer and argued her case. The mayor promised to review her claim, even though the reward money already had been divided among the police and the person who had provided the tip leading to recovery of the note at Williams's house.[38]

Finally, loss by theft was also a danger for prostitutes themselves, since they daily opened their private quarters to strangers. Prostitutes' possessions were periodically stolen by customers, leading to legal hassles as prostitutes sought to reclaim lost valuables, get restitution, or press charges.[39]

Many times disgruntlement or harassment turned into violence. Prostitutes had a long list of potential adversaries—clients, local bullies, lovers, creditors, madams, and each other. Many examples of violence have been noted in Chapter 5 in relation to cases brought by prostitutes in the courts. (Also see Chapters 8 and 9.) Prostitutes certainly worried about their property being destroyed by violent attacks, but they worried even more about being physically assaulted. Newspapers and court records detail an enormous catalogue of acts of personal violence: prostitutes were beaten, stabbed, stomped, kicked, burned, bludgeoned, stoned, cut, bound, raped, seared with acid, shoved down stairs, and finally, murdered.[40] In one episode described by the *Sun*, two sailors who were visiting a brothel

took bureau drawers and threw them downstairs breaking them to pieces, tore bedding and attempted to set fire to beds, and did set fire to the hair of a girl and burned her severely. They threw two chairs at her as she was going upstairs to prevent further destruction of property, broke and destroyed trunks and threw them downstairs and left the place a scene of destruction.[41]

In most cases the prostitute found legal recourse in the courts, but court action could hardly repair the physical and emotional damage suffered by the women.

Some of the prostitute's legal problems and personal abuse were caused by the criminal element that hung around many brothels and secondary prostitution establishments. Participants in the "panel game" were the most well known of the prostitute's criminal connections, but willingly or unwillingly, prostitutes also found themselves parties to other illegal schemes. A number of sources noted that prostitutes often had close connections with gamblers, a profession from which Sanger, Foster, Ellington, and other contemporary writers believed many prostitutes' lovers were drawn. Some prostitutes' acquaintances were known to use brothels to unload counterfeit money, while others found the houses of their prostitute "molls" convenient places to stash stolen items.[42] One brothel owner's husband was convicted of robbery and election fraud, and another prostitute, "grass widow" Harriett Smith, was said to have five "husbands" in five different prisons. According to the *Police Gazette*, Smith was considered an asset to the state because marriage to her seemed to ensure that a lawbreaker would be brought to justice. The newspaper further noted that Smith "stands with arms open for a new alliance, but thieves are getting shy of her."[43]

Prostitutes easily could become partners in blackmail schemes, sometimes without full knowledge of the implications of what they were doing. One notorious extortion case in the 1850s, which the press believed was representative of many in the city, received daily coverage in the papers for the several months it was being heard in the courts. Prostitute Ellen Williams, who had been "kept" in an assignation house by an older man named Henry Havens, became pregnant and asked attorney George Niles to assist her in getting financial support from Havens during her period of confinement. Niles and his co-conspirator, attorney Nathan Roberts, told Williams they probably could not get much money for her unless she could claim she had a husband, and then they could pursue heavy damages on charges of criminal connection. Williams had been married previously, so the case was brought in the name of her ex-spouse. In the end, the lawyers told Williams they were able to get only a few hundred dollars, which actually was only a portion of the $2,000 they had extorted from Havens. Apparently, Havens learned he had been misled and brought conspiracy charges against Niles and Roberts for obtaining money by false pretenses. The *Herald* seemed to show sympathy for Havens, who was characterized as one of the "many rich old fathers, bachelors and husbands who have paid the penalty" of getting caught in various types of extortion schemes. Such men were both innocent and guilty: "No sensitive old man wishes to be subjected to such an ordeal. . . . Dupes pay thousands to be held harmless of exposure." The judge in the case, recognizing the person really defrauded, pointed out that Williams rightfully should recover the full amount of the money.[44]

A number of prostitutes tried to offset the complications arising from their associations with the criminal world by helping authorities with cases. The *Police Gazette* intimated that Harriett Smith may have "squealed" on her five husbands' illegal activities, and Eliza Fisher actively intervened as an intermediary in several robbery cases in 1839. One of Fisher's acquaintances, a man known as Black Hawk (George Rollough), apparently stole some money which he first hid in a brothel in Mulberry Street and then moved to Fisher's brothel. After Black Hawk was arrested, Fisher visited him in prison and advised him to give up the money. He instructed her to give the officers $36, and he then was released from prison. On another occasion Fisher was asked to keep a hundred-dollar bill for a man known as Green Jacket (James Charles). Green Jacket was arrested on grand larceny charges for taking some "Texian bank bills" from a man at a restaurant. Fisher visited Green Jacket in prison and got his permission to give the bank bill to the police. At first she refused to identify the man who had given her the money, in hopes the issue would be dropped and Green Jacket freed, but the authorities were able to confirm he had been the culprit. Another time, James Smith, alias Mouse, was identified by an eyewitness (a prostitute whose husband also was being sought by the police) as the thief of a fur cap which was taken from a store near the Astor House Hotel. Officer Bowyer then went to Eliza Fisher's and asked her to get word to Mouse that the police wanted to see him as soon as possible. In a short while, Mouse and his accomplice met officer Bowyer, were arrested, and were found guilty of the theft. In spite of her well-publicized connections with criminals, Eliza Fisher appears to have taken exception to publicity that she would allow a lawbreaker to live in her house. In January 1840 the *Sun* printed an article about the arrest of two men on burglary charges, and it noted that one of the men resided at Eliza Fisher's in Leonard Street. Fisher went to the paper and insisted that a correction be printed, noting that the man was not an inmate of her house, had not been arrested there, and had no connection whatsoever with her. [45]

Some of the risks and dangers faced by prostitutes were considered occupational hazards. One of the most widespread dangers was venereal disease, or what William Sanger described as a "frightful physical malady." [46] In his survey of prostitutes, Sanger asked if the women had had "any disease incident to prostitution." According to Sanger, two-fifths of the prostitutes examined "CONFESS that they have suffered from syphilis or gonorrhea." He then noted his belief, based on his professional experience, that "the real number far exceeds this average; that, alarming as is the confession, the actual facts are much worse." [47] Sanger stated that venereal disease was seldom found in the first- and second-class brothels and assignation houses, but was very common among prostitutes of the lower orders, being a major reason for a prostitute's decline to the bottom levels of the profession. He also believed that venereal diseases were much more prevalent among foreigners than the native-born. Aside from his general class bias, Sanger attributed some credit for a better health environment in upper-class brothels to the fact that a few of the brothel keepers paid "a physician a liberal salary to visit their boarders every few days for the express purpose of carrying out [medical examinations and] resorting to treatment whenever he finds it necessary." [48] In *The Gentleman's Directory* of 1870, the entry for Lizzie Goodrich's establishment on West Twenty-seventh Street confirms this practice, noting in the midst of a description of the attributes of the brothel that "there is a regular physician attached to this house." [49] The practice of in-house medical exams was especially popular among house keepers who were from Europe and were accustomed to laws that enforced regular medical examinations of prostitutes, a procedure that William Sanger, Charles Smith, and other members of the medical and public health professions were campaigning to have accepted in American cities. [50]

But whatever medical treatment a prostitute might receive for venereal disease was of questionable effectiveness. Salvarsan was not introduced until 1910, so nineteenth-century medical practitioners largely depended either on mercury cures, which had terrible side effects, or on surgery, the most gruesome of possible cures. Mercury treatment was dreaded because it was known to cause bleeding gums, ulcerated cheeks, gangrene, necrosis of the jaw bones, frothing at the mouth, and occasionally, strangulation.[51] But as ineffective as physicians' treatments might be, the cures advertised through newspapers and journals and in handbills distributed on the streets were even less helpful. Patent medicines such as "Red Drop" and "Unfortunate's Friend" could easily be ordered through the mails. One mid-century brothel guidebook contained an advertisement which read: "Private diseases of both sexes cured without mercury. Seminal pills for Nervous Debility, $1 a box or 6 boxes for $5. Mail or office circulars sent."[52] Drugstores also sold a variety of cures both over the counter and by prescription, and one could even mix one's own remedy without having to purchase ingredients from a druggist. Pine Knot Bitters was a favorite home remedy sold in liquor stores, said to be used most frequently by the "lower classes." Even if poor prostitutes had the resources to purchase Pine Knot Bitters or one of the other ineffective popular remedies, many sooner or later were forced to resort to the only professional treatment available to the diseased poor, the penitentiary hospital. A prostitute wanting "public" treatment could go to the police station, request a commitment to Blackwell's Island Hospital, and be committed to the penitentiary on the grounds she was a vagrant, "having contracted an infectious disease in the practice of debauchery."[53] Police court proceedings in the newspapers record that this was not an uncommon practice. Elizabeth Burgen, like many other poor prostitutes, went before the local magistrate and requested to be sent to the Island so she could be cured of her "chronic syphilitic disease." Justice Wyman committed her for ninety days, a term she never got to serve because, as she was ascending the jail stairs, she became faint, sat down, and instantly died. The inquest held to determine cause of death confirmed that her diseased condition had indeed been desperate.[54]

It is difficult to say what percentage of prostitutes contracted venereal disease since, as Sanger noted, the number "willing to confess" they had been infected may have been much lower than the number who had actually had the disease.[55] Knowledge that a prostitute had been infected surely was a deterrent for customers, so the woman would not want the fact known if the disease's manifestations were in remission. No class of prostitute was exempt from the danger, but some were able to hide it better. The majority of victims may well have ended up as diseased, dissipated "hags" at the bottom of the prostitution hierarchy, but the upper echelons of the profession were equally vulnerable. The coroner's report of the examination of Helen Jewett's body noted that: "The uterus was unimpregnated but labouring under an old disease."[56] No age group was immune to the problem either. As distressing as it was for New Yorkers to think about the number of adult prostitutes who were infected with venereal disease, the large number of juvenile prostitutes who were being treated in public institutions was even more distressing. Mary Kemp became diseased in her young teens while living in a prostitution house in Albany. Though treated by a doctor for five months, the disease got worse, so she moved to New York City hoping to find a cure. In New York she lived with a girlfriend at a prostitution establishment on Greene Street. She was discovered there by a missionary, Mr. Brown, who took her to the Magdalen Asylum, where he paid her board and put her in the care of a physician. Since she did not improve, the Magdalen Asylum asked that she be moved to the Almshouse. After five weeks at the Almshouse, Mr. Brown found her employment, but Kemp was so weak she could not keep her job. She was then fifteen years old and was admitted to the House of Refuge, where it was recorded that her disease was "filthy in the extreme" and was marked by sores that were "disagreeable" to anyone coming near her. After some improvement she was indentured away from the city, but the employer sent her back because she was so badly infected.[57]

Many prostitutes tried to hide their venereal disease, and all of them wished to avoid it, but their multiple sexual contacts made them likely victims as well as carriers of the "frightful physical malady." Few contemporaries, however, recognized the prostitute as the "victim" of venereal disease. Blame was passed in only one direction, and it commenced with the prostitute. Husbands who consorted with prostitutes were condemned for spreading the disease from the brothel to their respectable wives, but no one worried about or condemned the men who gave the disease to prostitutes.[58]

Another occupational hazard of prostitution was pregnancy. Since pregnancy caused a prostitute to be out of work for at least some period of time and created post-delivery concerns as to how or whether to care for a child, many prostitutes took steps to avoid or stop a pregnancy.

Full-time prostitutes were assumed to be well-versed on birth control methods, and part-time prostitutes also were probably familiar with some of the techniques, which were well-publicized in contemporary literature. Although contraception literature was labeled "obscene," it was not until the post–Civil War period that legal restrictions made the dissemination of birth control information difficult.[59]

Almost every birth control method used today existed in some rudimentary form by the middle of the nineteenth century; the notable exception, of course, is the contraceptive hormone pill. None of the nineteenth-century methods was sure, some were totally ineffective, and others were harmful. Also, some of the techniques, such as the then-popular rhythm method, were unsuitable for commercial sex. Even if it had been practical for prostitutes to arrange their business calendar around their fertility cycle, the rhythm method still would have been ineffective for them, as it was for everyone else until 1924, when the ovulation cycle was first identified with precision. Methods requiring the customer's cooperation, such as coitus interruptus and condoms, were obviously risky for the prostitute.[60] Nevertheless, some men used condoms as a protection against venereal disease, and the prostitute benefited by reducing her chances for conception—and infection. One mid-century brothel directory advertised condoms, noting their dual purpose as well as their differences in cost and quality:

French Imported Male Safes—A perfect shield against disease or conception, made of both skin and India rubber. Can be procured at the following prices at office, or by mail. $2, $3, and $4 per dozen; 3 for $1, 4 for $1.[61]

The same source advertised "Ladies Protectors, $3.00 each," which probably referred to vaginal sponges, pessaries, cotton tampons, or suppositories, all of which were used at the time. The most popular form of contraception employed by nineteenth-century women was douching, often with plain water, or with alum, perlash, zinc sulfate, carbolic acid, saline solution, or infusions of white oak bark and red rose leaves.[62] Some of these solutions were ineffective; others were so strong they were harmful, causing damage to tissue, which then led to infections and other complications.

In spite of efforts to prevent conception, some prostitutes became pregnant. If the child was not wanted, abortion was the quickest solution. An abortion was not difficult to get in mid-century New York, and

French Imported Male Safes.

A PERFECT SHIELD AGAINST

DISEASE OR CONCEPTION,

Made of both Skin & India Rubber

Can be procured at the following prices at office, or by mail. $2, $3, and $4 per dozen; three for $1, four for $1. Ladies' Protectors $3 each. Circulars free.

LADIES CURED AT ONE INTERVIEW. with or without medicine $5. Regulating Pills, $6; sure and safe.

PRIVATE DISEASES BOTH SEXES, CURED without mercury. Seminal Pills for Nervous Debility, $1 per box, or six boxes for $5 by mail or at office. Circulars sent.

Call on or address,

DR. CHAS. MANCHES,

651 Broadway, N. Y.

Office Hours from 9 A. M. till 9 P. M.

20. ADVERTISEMENT FOR MALE SAFES, REGULATING PILLS, AND BIRTH CONTROL DEVICES. This advertisement for condoms, abortifacients, and birth control devices was included in an 1870 brothel guidebook. (Courtesy of the New-York Historical Society, New York City)

well-known abortionists advertised widely. Notices were put in news-papers, handbills, and brothel directories, and their messages were only slightly veiled: "Ladies cured at one interview with or without medicine, $5. Regulating Pills, $6." Also advertised were "monthly pills, to remove obstructions and irregularities, however produced."[63]

The abortion business boomed despite laws regulating the practice. In 1828 New York was one of the first states to pass a criminal statute on abortion, which would hold an abortionist criminally liable if he or she performed an abortion on a woman after her pregnancy had reached "quickening," or the first perception of fetal movement around the mid-point of the pregnancy. Because the law was intended not so much to control abortions as to protect women from quacks and unsafe medical practices, it did not penalize the woman on whom the abortion was performed. The abortion rate during the first three decades of the century has been estimated at approximately one abortion for every twenty-five to thirty live births, and initially the anti-abortion law ap-peared to effect little change in abortion practices. In the decade of the 1840s, however, there was a marked shift in the birth rate, perhaps caused by women's greater understanding of birth control and inter-vention methods as well as the increased availability of abortifacients; by the 1850s, the estimated ratio of abortions to live births was one abortion for every five to six live births. This trend continued for two more decades, while abortionists such as Madames Restelle and Costello became famous and prosperous, as did male practitioners such as Jacob Rosenzweig and Dr. Charles Jackson.[64] A number of court cases and sensational news stories involving abortionists in the 1840s were in-strumental in the passage of a new anti-abortion law, which made pre-quickened abortions illegal and imposed penalties on the woman herself for seeking or performing an abortion. But the provisions of this tougher ordinance were never enforced. Law officers looked the other way, and the public and the press appeared fairly quickly to become less concerned.[65] Consequently, women from all walks of life and marital statuses, prostitutes included, took advantage of the tolerant attitude toward abortion that existed until the end of the Civil War.[66]

When William Sanger surveyed prostitutes about their abortion his-tories, he got a very small response—only 1.75 percent of the two thousand women said they had ever had an abortion: one widow, five women who had been married, and twenty-eight single women.[67] Since officials believed that fully 20 percent of all of the city's pregnancies were being aborted, Sanger concluded: "That prostitution largely contributes to this crime can not be doubted, but to what extent must remain unknown, from the secrecy which surrounds it." The actual number of abortions procured by prostitutes, he was sure "would be startling."[68] A quarter of a century earlier, the Reverend McDowall had voiced the same belief, based on what a reformed prostitute had told him: "It is a common practice every three months to use means preventive of progeny." He noted that the "means" used were "balsam copaiba and spirits of turpentine," which, he added, "won't work."[69] These two substances were only a few of the products used by nineteenth-century women as intended abortifacients. Other substances ranged from quinine, iodine, oil of tansy, seneca snakeroot, and black cohosh to patented pills containing hellebore, ergot, iron, aloes, powdered savin, and extracts of tansy and rue. Internal medicines such as these produced abortions only in dosages so large that they caused harsh bodily reaction—treatment so severe that the result was sometimes lethal. Mechanical abortions were considered less dangerous, although they, too, were painful, harmful, and sometimes fatal. Most mechanical abortions were induced with rudimentary catheters, but some were caused by knitting needles, sticks, or wires.[70]

Although the extent of abortion among prostitutes cannot be accurately determined, newspapers confirm that prostitutes were among the many New York women utilizing the services of "professional" abortionists. During an investigative hearing about Madame Restelle, one woman testified that while visiting Restelle's house she had seen a socialite, a Sunday school teacher, and a twenty-three-year-old "kept woman" who pretended to be a milliner and had been to Restelle's nine times before for the same purpose. Some prostitutes, such as Susan Smith, never had the option of making a return visit. In March 1840, Dr. Charles H. Jackson performed "an abortion with an instrument" on Smith, a procedure from which she subsequently died, causing Jackson to be charged with manslaughter. A number of prostitutes' abortions may have been performed in their brothels, and, unless a death occurred, no one was the wiser. Sarah Tuttle, a brothel servant, tried to self-induce an abortion by taking oil of tansy, but instead caused her own death.[71] In 1846, the *Police Gazette* reported that a "so-called doctor" had delivered a five-month-old fetus to a young prostitute named Mary

Arkley, in the attic of Honey Brewster's den at 474 Broome Street. Arkley
later died, and an investigation was conducted. In a notation in his diary
two weeks after Arkley's death, Robert Taylor mentioned that he and
police clerk E. T. Cory had gone to:

Mrs. Brewster's, 474 Broome Street, and Mrs. Pratt's 472 Broome, houses of
the same character . . . to obtain information in relation to an abortion said to
have been caused at Mrs. Brewster's, and the mother of the child died in
consequence.[72]

One prostitution-house keeper knew the legal risks involved in having
an abortion performed in her house, so refused to allow a young woman
to take the prescribed treatment at her residence and warned her that
only a fool would try to get rid of the child at that point in her pregnancy.
This house keeper, Eliza Taylor, was one of many people who testified
in the abortion trial of Dr. Thomas E. Gage, who was charged with
killing the child of prostitute Ellen Gallagher. The proceedings of the
Gage trial give one a glimpse of the milieu surrounding the practice of
abortion as well as the complicated and dangerous procedures often
faced by young women who had unwanted pregnancies.

The Gage trial occurred during the period when reformers were
working to get seduction laws passed in the state legislature, and abortion
was frequently coupled with the seduction issue in the press. Within this
emotionally charged atmosphere, each party in the Gage case tried to
discredit the other on charges that related as much to issues of seduction
as to the abortion for which the trial was being held. Gage and his
co-defendant, William Davis, the man who had made Gallagher pregnant and arranged for her abortion, brought witnesses to court who
claimed that Gallagher was a prostitute and was unsure of the paternity
of the child. Furthermore, Gage argued that the medical procedures he
used on Gallagher were "normal" and could not have produced an
abortion. Gallagher, on the other hand, claimed she had been forcibly
seduced by Davis, her employer, and that he had subsequently abused
her during and after her pregnancy. She also described how he had
arranged for her to have an abortion.[73]

Between the allegations and disclaimers was the story of a young
woman who at age sixteen or seventeen became unhappy with child care
and domestic service and left these positions to become an employee in
Davis's refectory. After being "seduced" in a manner approaching

rape, she lived in several assignation or prostitution boarding houses. In about her fourth or fifth month of pregnancy, she was taken by Davis to visit two separate abortionists, who treated her with a variety of abortion procedures. It was not until her sixth month of pregnancy, however, that these procedures succeeded in causing Gallagher to abort a live fetus, which was "thrown into the vessel under the bed" and then "wrapped in paper and thrown from the dock." In the weeks after the birth of the baby, both Davis and his business partner physically abused Gallagher, causing her finally to file assault and battery charges against them, which led to the abortion investigation and trial.

Davis, the seducer or paramour, seemed far more familiar with the world of illicit sex and abortion than did Gallagher. In fact, it appears that it was Davis who informed her she was pregnant. He first took her to Madame Restelle, who said she was no longer performing abortions because she was in court at the time on an abortion charge. Davis challenged Restelle's refusal by pointing out that she had recently given medication to a woman he was living with at another address! Apparently, Restelle agreed to give Gallagher some pills, but they had been "like sawdust and did no good." Gallagher then went to see Dr. Gage and moved into Eliza Taylor's, where she planned to live while having Gage's treatment. When Taylor would not let her stay, Gallagher moved to Sarah Clarke's house, an establishment that Dr. Gage had used previously for keeping a woman. Apparently the doctor first prescribed several types of abortifacients, one of which was administered by house mistress Clarke in some tea. In all, Gallagher lived at Clarke's for five weeks before the abortion was successful. Presumably she was continuing Gage's various forms of treatment with no results during this period of residency. She testified that during the last week of her stay, she had "daily operations." The final operation, performed with a wire, brought on premature labor. Once in full labor, Gage was sent for, and he "had to use an instrument to get her to deliver."

At the trial, Gage was able to bring several members of the medical profession to testify on his behalf, claiming that he was an excellent doctor and that the procedures described by Gallagher could not produce an abortion and were the normal actions of a doctor. In response, the prosecution presented the testimony of a doctor who had practiced obstetrics for twelve years and who stated that "what Gage did had been calculated to produce an abortion." After twelve and a half hours of deliberation, eight jurors voted for conviction and four for acquittal, so Gage and Davis were discharged, a result that appeared in keeping with usual dispositions of abortion cases.[74]

Since legal practice did not hold a pregnant woman liable for her own abortion (even though technically she should have been under the revised laws of 1845–1846), one New York prostitute openly used the abortion statute to wreak revenge upon her doctor/lover. Ann Lloyd, who was living at the brothel of Mrs. Phillips on Church Street, went to the local druggist, Dr. John Sloat, for medical advice. After an examination, he gave her some pills which made her very sick and caused her to abort. A few days later Sloat persuaded Lloyd to let him keep her as his mistress at Mrs. Balch's, and he also took her savings to ensure that the money would "be properly cared for." Evidently, Sloat soon tired of the arrangement and failed to return, leaving unpaid bills. When Lloyd went to Sloat's office looking for him, he abused her and kicked her out, prompting her to file charges against him for procuring an abortion, false pretenses, and assault and battery.[75] Apparently the opprobrium of having had an abortion was not great enough to offset the satisfaction Lloyd got from bringing three charges against Sloat.

Lloyd's actions also raise the question of whether prostitutes considered abortion so much of a disgrace as Sanger assumed they must have when he received so few affirmative responses to his questions on abortion. Instead of indicating reservations about the propriety and legality of abortion, the prostitutes' lack of responses may have indicated that they did not have as many abortions as contemporaries believed. One of the reasons the public believed prostitutes had numerous abortions (beyond the assumption that prostitutes were characteristically profligate) was that so few pregnancies or offspring were observed among members of the profession relative to the number of sexual encounters they had. Judith Walkowitz has suggested that few children were visible in prostitution residences because many were boarded away from home; because prostitutes successfully used a combination of contraception, abortion, and infanticide; and because prostitutes were sterile as a result of venereal disease.[76] It seems probable that prostitutes controlled their reproduction less by abortion and more by contraception and sterility, as the Sanger responses suggest.

Recent medical research has suggested that immunological factors may also contribute to a lesser role for abortion as a form of birth control among prostitutes. As early as 1871 Charles Darwin suggested that a direct relationship between sexual promiscuity in women and infertility may exist on the basis of exposure to semen. Several studies since have pursued this question, including one at the Department of Obstetrics and Gynecology at the University of Michigan Medical Center which confirmed that prostitutes have "poor reproductive histories and a high incidence of spontaneous abortion." The Michigan study suggests that prostitutes' frequent exposure to sperm causes a high percentage of them to develop an allergic reaction to sperm (or immunization to sperm) that results in infertility. Furthermore, prostitutes were found to have twice as many spontaneous abortions after becoming prostitutes as they had had before joining the profession, though the cause could not be attributed to the same immunologic reaction.[77] Consequently, the combination of venereal disease, contraception, and immunologic reaction may have meant that, while their respectable sisters were using abortion more and more as a means of birth control, nineteenth-century prostitutes resorted to abortion less frequently.

With all other birth control methods failing, the prostitute's final option for avoiding the burden of a child was infant abandonment or infanticide. Many newspaper stories attest to the fact that this was a community-wide problem in the mid-nineteenth century, and some of the unidentified infants must have been the children of prostitutes. In fact, infant death statistics rose so sharply in the middle decades of the century that the issue became a topic of concern to the Common Council, and infant deaths were given special scrutiny by authorities.[78] When prostitute Arabella Martin's one-week-old baby boy died, a coroner's inquest was held to determine the cause of death. The coroner ruled that the baby "came to death by being accidentally suffocated while in bed with his mother," a believable accident under the circumstances, but also a means of infanticide that would be difficult to prove. Although prostitutes, like other women, might resort to infanticide, the more common and acceptable alternative was having and raising the child.[79]

A prostitute may have felt that others were to blame for many of the problems and dangers she faced on the job—harassment, violence, disease, pregnancy—but some potential problems, such as alcohol and drug abuse or an inactive or indolent lifestyle, she "chose" for herself, even though her work environment fostered the development of these

21. BAR AT THE FIVE POINTS.   Illicit sex and alcohol were linked together in the minds of most nineteenth-century New Yorkers. Prostitutes frequented barrooms, such as this one at the Five Points, for entertainment as well as recruiting. (Courtesy of the New-York Historical Society, New York City)

problems and seemed to exacerbate their severity. These "self-inflicted" problems also were those that contemporary observers believed reflected a weak and debased nature and for which they had less sympathy. Consequently, observers' remarks and histories often tended to distort the reality of prostitution by ignoring prostitutes' own accounts and presenting a stereotypical portrait of an inebriated and lazy prostitute.

Alcohol and drugs appear to have been part of many prostitutes' lives, and contemporaries viewed alcohol addiction among members of that profession as a most serious substance abuse. The Reverend McDowall asserted that "intemperance and prostitution are inseparably connected," and Sanger claimed that "not one per cent of the prostitutes in New York practice their calling without partaking of intoxicating drinks." Even though Sanger's survey question asking prostitutes if they drank intoxicating liquors received a five-sixths affirmative reply, he said he was "compelled to believe that this is not the whole truth, for it is almost certain that . . . [those] who claim to be total abstinents indulge themselves in occasional potations."[80]

Alcohol was definitely a part of the prostitution culture, as well as of society generally, because it was a major source of revenue—in the brothel, saloon, concert hall, and dance hall. Most brothels sold high-priced champagnes, wines, or other forms of liquor, but contemporaries generally agreed that, in all but a few brothels of a higher rank, what one bought had "nothing in common with the genuine articles of commerce but the name." The same was true of the liquors sold in many secondary prostitution establishments; they were either watered down or "the cheapest and most poisonous 'raw spirits' that the markets afford."[81]

Contemporary observers noted that it was considered a disgrace among the "more aristocratic prostitutes" to be intoxicated, and alcoholism could cause a woman to be dismissed from an upper-class brothel. Although the lower establishments often did not consider inebriation so disreputable, proprietors knew intoxication could interfere with business, and many would not allow inmates or waiter girls to drink liquor until the end of the evening. To keep customers drinking, prostitutes were supposed to join them with "temperance drinks" or colored water. Still, presumably many prostitutes, like their customers, were under the influence of alcohol some of the time.[82] Streetwalkers were said to be the most intemperate of the profession, and many of them used "liquor stores" (small local bars) as their resting places during their nightly perambulations. With their pocketbooks rather than a brothel keeper governing their drinking habits, some streetwalkers bought the strongest liquors they could afford.[83]

Writing in the 1860s, George Ellington noted that the kinds of alcoholic beverages imbibed by New York's parlor-house prostitutes were greatly influenced by their Parisian sisters. He gave a list of recipes for fashionable drinks popular with prostitutes, which included liqueurs such as curaçao, anisette, Kimmel, Beaumarchais, and absinthe or oil of wormwood, the latter ingredient being considered strong enough to have a deleterious effect on the nervous system of the women. Although "fashionable" drinks may have been popular with some, the vast majority of prostitutes depended on gin, rum, beer, and cheap wine for their daily tippling.[84]

Alcohol was the most widely used drug by prostitutes, but it was only one of several addictive substances resorted to by women in the profession. Sanger did not inquire about the use of drugs other than alcohol

22. SMOKING OPIUM. Opium, a popular drug among men and women of many social classes in the nineteenth century, was believed to be used frequently by prostitutes. (Courtesy of the New-York Historical Society, New York City)

and is surprisingly silent on the subject, since most other observers noted prostitutes' frequent use of other drugs. In the 1840s Smith noted that:

Drinking gin is exceedingly common. Use of opium scarcely as much so, yet among prostitutes is sufficiently common, but the almost universal stimulant is the yellow scotch snuff, with which they fill their mouths several times a day, rubbing it upon teeth and gums, until they induce a complete intoxication.[85]

Two decades later, writer James McCabe also noted that among prostitutes the "use of narcotics is . . . very common." He went on to point out that all the drugstores in the vicinity of prostitution houses were known to sell large quantities of opium, chloroform, and morphia.[86] George Ellington put the problem in its larger context by noting what others had often pointed out:

Women of all classes of society in New York use stimulants and narcotics to a greater or less extent, but the demi-monde in particular, above and beyond all others, are addicted to these unwholesome and life-destroying habits. If the women of fashion are compelled to use various kinds of opiates to induce sleep, how much more are the women of pleasure.[87]

The popular use of opium also had been noted in the 1840s by George Templeton Strong, who wrote in his diary that "opium chewing prevails here extensively, much more so than people think,"[88] an indication of the intentional use of the narcotic over and above the amount many people ingested as one of the ingredients in a variety of popular patented medicines. In fact, one historian has stated that there is considerable evidence now "that a large proportion of middle-class American women in the late nineteenth century stayed stoned for most of their adult lives," an evaluation which also possibly could have been made about a large proportion of prostitutes but which indicates a behavior not at odds with that of other contemporary women.[89]

Ellington concurred with McCabe that morphine and opium were two of the most popular drugs in use, but he stated that laudanum (tincture of opium) was the favorite of the demimonde, being used by these women to a "fearful extent." He noted that hashish and arsenic had been popular a few years before, but their use had declined. Although some prostitutes and other citizens may have become addicted by morphine or opiate-laden medications prescribed by doctors, it was not difficult for them to continue their habits afterward or for a new-comer to begin a habit. Narcotics could be bought cheaply at drugstores, and, as a contemporary pointed out, most New York drugstores were located in the area where prostitution houses were concentrated.[90]

Most contemporaries believed prostitutes used drugs and alcohol because their lives were so degraded and dangerous. Alcohol was said to help prostitutes maintain an "artificial state of excitement, which is indispensably necessary to their calling," and both alcohol and narcotics helped the women escape their problems by reducing inhibitions. Alcohol addiction was also believed to be hereditarily and environmentally induced, since studies like Sanger's showed that three-fourths of the prostitutes' fathers had had intemperate habits, as had over half of their mothers. A prostitute's environment encouraged intemperance because she had to try to get customers to drink in order to raise profits, and joining the clients was always a temptation. George Strong also expressed the novel conclusion that the consumption of opium had increased for the New York populace because "the blessed Temperance

Movement" had made alcohol less acceptable. A final reason given for why prostitutes used drugs and alcohol was the moralistic evaluation that "a love of stimulation seems naturally to follow a life without industry or objective." As with most of the evidence, it is impossible to decide where statements of fact end and moralistic presumptions that all vices were more extreme among prostitutes begin. The tone of most such claims, however, suggests self-righteousness more than observation.[91]

Whatever the causes of alcohol and drug use, the results were injurious to some prostitutes. Alcohol was a precipitator for much of the violence associated with prostitution, and inebriation sent many prostitutes to the penitentiary for drunk and disorderly conduct. Equally important were the effects on the prostitute's health from long-term use of addictive substances. In some cases, one did not have to wait very many years to see harmful physical consequences. Twenty-five-year-old Julia Potter, a girl of the town, went on a "spree" for a couple of days and then "before going to bed drank half a pint of gin at a draught." The next morning she was found dead, and the coroner ruled that intemperance had been the cause of her death.[92]

A final hazard of the prostitute's working situation was emotional and psychological strain—mildly symptomized by boredom, escapism, and lack of incentive, or more severely experienced as despair and depression. One critic stated that the "prostitute's life is as idle as it is dissolute"—a vacuous existence without effort or goal. Supporters of this opinion believed the prostitute was "only intent on killing time," and had no taste for literary amusements or any kind of employment such as sewing or needlework. Card playing was said to be a common pastime, but commentators believed prostitutes seldom "gamed" or gambled with each other because it was assumed they had little to win or to lose. Most often, cards were used for fortune-telling since prostitutes were believed to be "ignorant, superstitious, and living by luck; they place great reliance upon this mode of looking through the curtain of the future." Physician Smith also pointed out one more peculiar characteristic of prostitutes that he said had been noted by many other physicians besides himself: "They eat and sleep much and have a tendency to obesity. Three-fourths of the prostitutes are of more than ordinary fatness." With no recognition of the relationship between eating and sleeping disorders and depression, Smith attributed these characteristics to the fact that "prostitutes are sensual by nature."[93] These descriptions of the prostitute's depraved, idle, dissolute, and wasteful life are often at odds with other information available. Although observers may have disapproved of the prostitute's leisure activities and domestic pursuits, evidence suggests that prostitutes were as active, as literary, as involved with life, and as goal-oriented as other women.

Prostitutes also were not unlike other contemporary women (and men) in expressing "despair" about their lives. Lewis Saum has noted that expressions of despair were commonplace among nineteenth-century Americans, illustrating an essential grimness in the life views of many ordinary citizens.[94] Many observers likely assumed that, if life was grim for respectable Americans, it must be even worse for the prostitute. One contemporary noted that "in the melancholy peculiar to fallen women there is an amount of suffering and disease that few of our readers have any conception of."[95] "Melancholy," "remorse," and "mental anguish," phrases euphemistically used for depression, were often applied to prostitutes and used as explanations by contemporaries for alcoholism and drug abuse and for the prostitute's ultimate act of emotional desperation—suicide. A number of contemporary writers claimed that: "Suicide is quite common among this class of women," or more simply, "[Prostitutes'] suicides are frequent."[96] Another observer took a more fatalistic view: "Once entered upon a life of shame, however brilliant the opening may be, the end is certain, unless she anticipates it by suicide."[97] Newspapers confirmed that suicides were common in mid-century New York, and some of these were of prostitutes, such as nineteen-year-old Mary Bishop, who "ended her miserable existence by a dose of laudanum."[98]

Although suicide reflected the prostitute's ultimate inability or unwillingness to cope with her life situation, there were coping strategies used by prostitutes that made the difficulties inherent in the profession more manageable. Current sociological research indicates that a "socialization process" is necessary for a woman to become fully integrated into the prostitution profession, or what the nineteenth century would have termed the "underworld" of prostitution. Part of the socialization process involves adopting the argot and social mores of the prostitution culture, but it also involves some identity changes. Symbolic of such identity changes for most nineteenth-century prostitutes was taking a new name, a step that, though it may have served to hide one's true identity, or to protect one's family or future options, also seems to have been important in initiating one fully into the prostitution subculture. [99]

Nineteenth-century New York prostitutes always used two names—a given and a surname—and in most cases both of these were new. Prostitutes did not feel bound to the new name, however. After a while, some took a new pseudonym, and some used several aliases simultaneously. Others used variations on their names: Jane Graham Western sometimes went by Jenny Weston or Jenny Graham, and Rosina Townsend was sometimes listed as Rosanna Thompson. A few chose flamboyant nicknames such as Cinderella or Honey, but most used very conventional names with no special significance, at least to those unfamiliar with the woman's private motives. One prostitute stated in a court hearing that the surname she chose for working in New York was that of her last lover in Boston. The pseudonyms of prostitutes suggest an element of shame and subterfuge in the profession, but also an ability to choose an identity rather than being given one by a father or husband. [100]

Many patrons of prostitutes also went by aliases or nicknames. This was done partly to hide their true identities but was also an aspect of the fantasy world of brothels and illicit sex, where one could select a title and persona different from one's socially defined respectable self. Most of the men who frequented Rosina Townsend's parlor house went by aliases—Richard Robinson, for example, called himself Frank Rivers— and the John Holland divorce case brought out that Holland went by the illustrious title of "Marquis" when he visited New York brothels. Testimony in the Gage trial also noted that the co-defendant William Davis had used the name Brown in a Grand Street brothel. [101]

Once a prostitute gave up her real name, she appears to have continued using a prostitution name even though she may have employed several variations or nicknames of the new chosen name. Census, tax, court, and death records all appear with the prostitute's selected name, not her given name. One ingenious prostitute challenged this custom by arguing in court that a disorderly house case against her should be thrown out on the basis that she had been charged under the name Emily Tooker, the name by which she was known to brothel residents, patrons, and officials, but her real name was Emily Tucker. The judge refused to accept her argument, and she had to pay the $100 fine. [102]

Whatever the psychological value of the new nomenclature in helping one adapt to the life of prostitution, it seems to have been significant to the socialization process in the profession. Becoming part of a subculture with its own special customs, language, folklore, and history was important in helping one cope with working conditions and life situations that were often difficult; it also permitted creation of a new world and self freed from some of the difficulties and unhappinesses prostitutes had encountered in the respectable culture. Equally important, however, and perhaps even more critical in determining how one dealt with the day-to-day life of prostitution, were the people a prostitute interacted with and the personal relationships she established with these individuals, relationships that created for her a private as well as public life.

PART THREE

The Private World
of the Prostitute

8

Friends and Lovers

Relationships with Men

An 1853 brothel directory description of Mrs. Cornell's prostitution establishment at Grand and Mercer Streets stated that she "lives at home with her folks but attends to business here evenings." The images created by the use of the words "home" and "folks" at first seem incongruous with the connotations of words such as "prostitution" and "business," but the juxtaposition of multiple identities is precisely the key to understanding the several dimensions of prostitutes' lives. Prostitutes as "public women" can be traced through newspaper accounts, brothel directories, court records, and censuses, but information about their private lives—their personal and family relationships and their feelings about their life situations and themselves—is much more difficult to find. Nonetheless, by exploring the available information on these women's interactions with others, one can learn much about their interpersonal relationships and private lives. [1]

By definition, men were a dominant factor in prostitutes' lives. The majority of a prostitute's male associates were her customers, and as a rule her relationships with these clients were brief and impersonal. Although some men patronized brothels in search of emotional solace, most customers were primarily or entirely interested in sexual contacts only. Many of the men who migrated to New York as permanent or temporary inhabitants found the city to be large and impersonal and sought out prostitutes because they felt lonely and uprooted. For others, the many brothels and prostitutes of the city promised excitement and the opportunity to indulge in forbidden pleasures, activities that would have been frowned upon in their home towns or in more close-knit communities. Although a prostitute's or a brothel's primary function was to minister sexually to customers—both those seeking excitement and those seeking solace—nineteenth-century brothels also served as social gathering places for men, providing a male club atmosphere in much the same way saloons or gambling establishments did. As a rule, a man could patronize a prostitution house for an evening, enjoying female companionship (not necessarily including sex), the fellowship of male peers, wine, and perhaps gambling. In this environment he did not need to fear that social or emotional obligations would be exacted from him.

Since nineteenth-century surveys and studies of prostitutes do not include research on their customers, it is difficult to establish a definitive profile of these men. Records indicate that all sectors of the male population were represented in the clientele, though socioeconomic status and race strongly influenced brothel access. Helen Jewett had some customers who were older family men, but most of her clients were young, unmarried clerks, businessmen, and professionals such as accountants, journalists, and playwrights. An indication that brothel patronage was widespread among young, white-collar, male New Yorkers was provided by diarist Philip Hone in his description of the courtroom crowd at the trial of Richard P. Robinson for the murder of Helen Jewett.

I was surrounded by young men, about his [Robinson's] own age, apparently clerks like him, who appeared to be thoroughly initiated into the arcana of such houses. . . . They knew the wretched female inmates as they were brought up to testify, and joked with each other in a manner illy comporting with the solemnity of the occasion.[2]

Mid-nineteenth-century daily newspapers also printed stories about young working men who patronized brothels, a number of whose wives complained to authorities that their husbands were spending most of the family's income on such escapades. Sources indicate that men tended to frequent brothels where women were of approximately the same, or a lower, social class.[3] Though all classes and races in New York participated in the city's sexual commerce, black males were the most restricted of prostitutes' clients. They patronized poorer prostitutes and the few integrated or black prostitution establishments that existed in the lower wards of the city, especially in the Five Points area, but the strong stand against "mixing of the races" expressed in the newspapers (especially concerning black males with white females) indicates that sexual-racial integration was limited.[4]

Tim Gilfoyle, in his study of nineteenth-century sexual commerce in New York City, also has noted that by mid-century, brothel patronage was extremely common among New York men of all social classes, age groups, and marital statuses. Gilfoyle argues that in the eighteenth century and early nineteenth century American men infrequently consorted with prostitutes, and the majority of those who did were transient mariners and longshoremen. By the mid-nineteenth century, however, "sex with prostitutes was customary for significant numbers, perhaps the majority, of males," increasingly including middle-class residents as well as transients, a pattern that continued to the turn of the century. According to Gilfoyle, increased patronage of prostitutes was caused by the anonymity and freedom offered by the growing city, a dramatic commercialization and impersonalization of sex, an increasing inability of many laborers and journeymen workers to economically afford marriage and family, and a male resentment of the increasing power of women within marriage over sex and reproduction.[5] New York's prostitution clientele may not have been as large a proportion of the population as Gilfoyle indicates, but the large supply of prostitutes was indicative of a high level of demand as well as of a lack of alternative opportunities for female employment.

Since money was less personal than sexuality, the customer gave less than he received in a sexual transaction with a prostitute, but a customer's advantage in the exchange was tempered by the fact he was on the prostitute's turf and was subject to the conventions and practices of her culture. She was more knowledgeable about sexual commerce than he.[6] Furthermore, prostitutes had a certain power over clients if the men feared exposure. Although brothel visits were often forgiven as lapses in morality which were not totally unexpected of the male, a man might fear that consorting with prostitutes could jeopardize his marriage, job, or social position.

Many prostitute-client relationships were characterized by hostility and mistrust. For some prostitutes, hostility probably originated as much in their childhoods or in early sexual experiences as in their more immediate circumstances. Hostility also was a response to violence and verbal abuse from clients and to the fact that many prostitutes had to have daily sexual relations with customers for whom they felt physical in-difference or revulsion. Prostitutes like Jewett who could exercise much control over their choice of clients were fortunate and a minority. In many situations, prostitutes accepted whichever customers they could get, regardless of how repulsive or frightening they were.

Many prostitutes acted out their hostility, or supplemented their fees, by stealing from their clients; some probably considered most men fools and believed a prostitute should take as much as she could get from the exchange. As a rule, however, prostitutes accepted that the customer was their source of income and needed to be kept happy, in hopes of both a smooth, conflict-free business transaction in the present and con-tinuing regular visits in the future.

In some situations hostility may have been assumed rather than demonstrated. A popular notion existed that prostitutes brought to their profession a pre-conditioned hatred of men. The *Herald* printed an editorial digression on the topic in its coverage of the Jewett murder, accepting the assumption that Jewett was "possessed of a very devil, and a species of mortal antipathy to the male race. . . . She seems to have declared war against the sex . . . and would say . . . I despise you all . . . you have ruined me—I'll ruin you—I delight in your ruin."[7] The difference between this picture of Jewett and the complicated and often positive feelings and ties indicated in Jewett's correspondence with her clients suggests that this vision was more the product of the guilty underside of male fantasy than of reality.

Although most men sought and were given exactly what they bar-gained for—impersonal sex—at times the prostitute became an unde-manding friend to the customer, a pleasant companion whose company he enjoyed and in whose presence he felt comfortable. For the pros-titute, this meant she would be guaranteed his patronage and money. Thus, unless a customer was considered undesirable for personal or safety reasons, a prostitute would feign interest or would genuinely enjoy a relationship that created a little more security in the present and possibly offered the opportunity and resources for a better situation in the future, whether within the profession or outside. Although these friendships might seem genuine, they were usually unequal because of the social stigma associated with prostitution, which meant the prostitute did not fully share the respect necessary for a true friendship. When put to a test of public recognition of the relationship, the friendship was flawed. For the prostitute to have expectations usually meant she would have disappointments.

The violence and hostility underlying some relationships between prostitutes and customers has been described in discussions of the legal system (Chapters 4 and 5) and prostitutes' working conditions (Chapter 7). What is missing in these descriptions of violence and overt adversarial confrontations, however, is a sense of the more congenial relationships that existed between prostitutes and clients, including the ways in which prostitutes interacted with, manipulated, or covertly sparred with their customers.

The Jewett correspondence contains letters from nineteen different men whose relationships with Jewett ranged from that of a potential customer who had not yet met her to that of Robinson, or Frank Rivers, who became her lover. Many of the letters are straightforward, explaining why an appointment or liaison had to be canceled, but even these suggest a level of politely affectionate consideration that seems remarkable.

Thursday morning, Oct. 9, 1834

My Dear Helen,

I may not possibly call on you this after-noon, as I have a sick friend, who engrosses nearly every moment of my time. If I can steal away, however, for a time, I will do so, and meet you this afternoon. I hope, my dear girl, you will pardon this apparent neglect, and indeed I know you would, could you fully comprehend the unpleasant situation in which I am so unfortunately placed.

Very affectionately yours,
William[8]

From Charles H., Jewett received a note stating that: "It is with deepest regret, that I inform you, I cannot fulfil my engagement with you this evening. My sister and her husband arrived here this morning from Havana . . . after an absence of nearly two years." Charles promised, however, to call on Jewett at the first available opportunity.[9] From "Pupil," Jewett received a note saying: "I am extremely sorry to say that it will be out of my power to wait on you either Thursday or Friday, as I leave town Thursday morning for Boston." Since his return was planned for the following Monday, Pupil asked that Jewett drop him a note, in care of his office, informing him what night it would be possible to see her.[10] More mysterious about his reasons for canceling was Robert, who wrote:

My Dearest Helen,
Circumstances quite beyond my own control compel me to remain at home this evening, and you would I know, pardon this apparent neglect could you be aware of the *cause* which will deter me from keeping my engagement with you this evening.

Truly yours,
Robert

P.S. I will see you early tomorrow evening.[11]

Although equally mysterious about the reasons for his last-minute absence, Stanhope notified Jewett he would send a substitute, "a proper friend, who *insists* upon usurping, what I would not forego even for friendship under other circumstances, and who [assures me] of his *perfect* gentleness. . . . Tomorrow evening . . . I shall be most happy to perform an attention, which in truth, I do not feel myself capable of this evening."[12] Such complicated consideration and stress on "perfect gentleness" suggest concerns unexpected in prostitute-client relations.

In most instances the customers indicated they would like to reschedule their appointments. In other cases, however, such as that of "J.," who had not yet met Jewett personally, the reason for not coming may have been legitimate but also may have been an excuse for postponing a visit until he was more secure about his proposed action. "J." had fallen for Jewett's flattery, was delighted with the prospect of corresponding with her, and was eager to hear more about himself.

I am highly gratified at the promptitude, with which you have responded to my desire to form your acquaintance, the more so, because if I am to believe you, (and as yet I have no reason to doubt your sincerity) it is a favor which has not been granted to all who have sought it. My gratification, however, is not a little alloyed by my present inability to avail myself of the permission you have given me. Since I wrote you two days since, I have had the misfortune to be thrown from a gig, and though not seriously hurt, I am just enough so to be obliged to keep my room and in the language of my physician to avoid all excitement. This would be sufficiently annoying at any time; but it is particularly vexatious now, because it deprives me of the pleasure of seeing you. You can, however, alleviate in some measure the sufferings of my confinement, by writing to me, which I feel assured, even from the little billet which I have now before me, you can do well. Tell me what impression I have made upon you. Any thing so that you write. Do not disappoint me I pray you.

J.[13]

Several of the letters to Jewett indicate that their client-authors had casual friendships with her, enjoyed doing favors or picking out gifts for her, and wanted to know her better. From one man Jewett received a gift with the following note:

My Dear Helen,
Stopping a few minutes in a book store in Broadway to see a friend, I noticed a new publication called the "Magnolia." Thinking it a pretty thing and knowing your taste for reading, I bought it . . . and the acceptance of it will confer upon the donor more satisfaction than the receiver can possibly derive from it.
    . . . I am going to the theatre where I may possibly meet you, or see you ere this note.
    . . . From one who wishes to be called your friend "frequently, if not oftener."

Cambaceres[14]

Literary interests seem to have been a significant tie between Jewett and several of her customers. J.J.A.S. wrote Jewett: "Being aware that you as well as myself are amateurs of literature, I send you the *Boston Pearl*, for which I have put your name as a subscriber. . . . I shall probably call and see you Saturday, till then, adieu."[15] Another client, Frederick, appealing more to a possible interest in imported finery, wrote to Jewett to tell her that a friend would be leaving for Paris the next day and had said he would bring back any goods requested. Asking Jewett to select "whatever you feel desirous of having" from Paris, he reminded her not to forget "the pretty little shoes."[16]

Some clients, like out-of-towners John P. and Ben, found Gotham enthralling and wished to continue their newly found "friendships" through correspondence:

Friend Helen,
How are you? Have you not received a letter from your friend Ben? If not you must blow up the postoffice. He has written to you twice, and is in a duced pucker to hear from her whom he deems the most fascinating of her sex.
    . . . I wrote Catharine a long nonsensical love letter four week since, and have not yet received an answer.

. . . Now my good girl be so kind as to write Ben or myself immediately, inform us of your health, whether Catharine has gone to Charlestown or not, and all the news. And I assure you that you will contribute to the happiness of two poor unlucky dogs "what" cannot forget Gotham. Do write soon and greatly oblige your friend.

John P. [17]

John's "nonsensical love letter to Catharine" suggests that Jewett was far from alone in getting such affectionate letters.

The correspondence also shows the rebuffs Jewett's writing might trigger. Although N.J. said he "remains her friend," he rejected her overtures for a visit or for public conversation:

Your letter, my dear Helen, has been received. In answer to your inquiry why I don't call to see you, I know 'tis enough to satisfy you to say I have good and substantial reasons, which no doubt you can imagine. Your feelings with regard to speaking to me at the theatre are very proper. You know perfectly well that I am always happy to speak to you, but if I were to do so in such a place, you are aware, what inference would be drawn by those who know us only by name. Wishing you all happiness, I remain your friend.

N.J. [18]

Another customer, Archibald, had made plans to "share" his wealth with Jewett and then lost it all gambling. In a letter of apology and self-flagellation, Archibald said he knew she must think him an "ungrateful villain," so he requested that she make inquiries of a gentleman in South Street to verify his good name and associations—but he asked that she do this "in such manner that he may not be acquainted with our connection." [19]

Demeaning or insulting statements also came from those who professed love and admiration for Jewett. T.C., or Henry, wrote to Jewett in February 1834 apologizing for leaving abruptly for his home, stating he would have found a farewell an impossibility. T.C. wrote that Jewett had "wrongfully abused" him and that she had called him a "snot," but he forgave her and professed great love for her and unhappiness at their being separated. He looked forward to his return in two months for a longer stay and noted that, if she were to find herself short of money, he would send what she needed. T.C. then ended the letter with a postscript saying:

My friend P. will see you and state my feelings towards you. Pray do not make yourself too common, excuse me for so saying, but my reason is, that I was told you were any one's for five dollars, *I* will not believe it. Write me at Montreal speedily.[20]

Another out-of-town customer, Charles C., wrote to Jewett saying he was "one who is happy to call you friend." His letter contained a number of passages from "Lallah Rook," and he reminisced about their previous discussions of the poem. He also complimented Jewett's virtues, especially her "regard for truth" which he found unusual for one in her "circumstances," since most women in her position usually "display more or less deception."[21] Several months later Charles wrote again reiterating that he was one "who wishes to be called your friend," stating that he was looking forward to an upcoming trip to New York and the "great pleasure" of her company. He chastised Jewett, however, for her "lack of judgement" when she was recently before the police court:

I am sorry to see your name in the police reports, and particularly to hear that you should have shown the bad taste to notice in any way the reporter who so coarsely bespattered you with praise.[22]

Charles, like several of Jewett's other customer-correspondents, included in his letters greetings and "compliments to all old friends," mentioning some by name. The letters from these men indicate that the authors were part of a group of males who hung around Jewett and were friendly with each other as well as with her. Charles asked the whereabouts of "your Englishman" (possibly T.C.) and mentioned correspondence from their friend Harvey. Bob of Cincinnati sent his "best respects to Frank" (Rivers) and asked Jewett to tell Frank he would be pleased to have him call if he were ever in Ohio. On his trip west, Wandering Willie had a letter from Jewett to give to Mr. P. of Cincinnati (possibly Bob), and he wrote home to Jewett requesting news of Frank and Bill (Easy). Frank and Bill discussed their activities with each other in letters to Jewett and also mentioned the names of new clients, such as Mr. Cook, Harry, and Cashier, that they and others had introduced to her. Most of these men appear to have been customers simultaneously, and all would have liked to be Jewett's "favorite," but they did not seem to resent greatly the fact that another of the group temporarily held this position. For them, the brothel was a social gathering place as well as a house of prostitution. This social role of the brothel and Jewett's centrality to the group is demonstrated by an incident mentioned in a letter from Mrs. Berry to Jewett when Jewett was visiting in Philadelphia in December 1835.

Last evening about seven o'clock, Bill Easy and Mr. Cook called to the house. I had a fire made in your room so they went up stairs and sat there some time. Bill Easy appears rather melancholy at your absence. He thought he would send you a letter, so he gave it to Hannah to carry to you. . . . Bill Easy is very anxious to see you. . . . Sam and three of his friends were here last night and enquired for you, but as you were not here they went away.[23]

Bill Easy (George P. Marston) was one of Jewett's most frequent companions and correspondents, at least for the year preceding her death. He greatly enjoyed receiving and sending her letters but seems to have been intimidated by the exercise, usually excusing his responses as being composed in haste because of business. Responding to one of her "beautiful letters," he said: "You must not expect my letters to be equal to yours, in any respect whatever, for I am wholly incompetent to answer letters so far superior to any I can write."[24] In another letter he tried to find the right word to finish a compliment to her and finally gave up: "My language fails me, I can't draw any comparison, no how I can fix it. Your own imagination must conclude the sentence, which I was unable to do."[25]

Jewett's friendship with Bill Easy illustrates, however, how friendships formed because of great emotional needs could become personally exploitative. Easy worked as a clerk in a store and lived in a respectable boardinghouse but appears to have spent much of his private time at the brothel, the theater, and with people he knew through these places. His letters to Jewett caused the *Police Gazette* to describe him as "one of those harpies who hang around brothels to receive chance favors from regardless women for services of business."[26] The term *harpy* seems ill-chosen. Easy was one who "wished to please"—he wanted to please Jewett by bringing her his finest friends as clients, and he wanted to ingratiate himself to his friends by introducing them to Jewett. He was a close enough friend of Jewett's for her to make and mend shirts for him.[27] Even though he accepted the fact that his good friend Frank Rivers was Jewett's "favorite," he was so infatuated with her that he seemed blind to Jewett's use of him in a love triangle to get even with Rivers for neglect and disloyalty.

Easy's efforts in bringing Jewett his best friends were not always successful. In an early letter to Jewett, Easy explained that the dislike she felt for his friend Harry should not affect their relationship.

I know you was [sic] not serious when you told me that Thursday night might be the last one which I should pass with you, for I won't believe that you could tell me that, and not manifest any feeling of regret at all on parting. The deprivation of your society would be a serious loss to me and one that could not be repaired.[28]

Eager to offer a more acceptable friend, Easy then inquired, "How do you like my tall friend Mr. Cook? I hope you feel a better disposition toward him than to Harry. He is a very fine man. In fact I never knew a person in my life, whom I like better than Mr. Cook." He informed Jewett that Cook would be with him at the theater that night and would probably want to go home with her, and he hoped she would agree. "I would rather forego the pleasure of your company myself than be the cause of disappointment to him."[29]

Apparently, Cook missed his cue, because Easy wrote the next day to explain:

My friend Cook was disappointed in not seeing you home from the theatre last evening, though I don't see as he can blame you any for going with another person. You certainly waited long enough for him to acquaint you with his intentions, and I thought we gave him hints enough to that effect.

. . . I don't believe he could be angry with you if he tried, he loves you too well. . . . When I introduced him to you, I little expected he would so soon become infatuated. Whether his feelings toward you are reciprocated is no business of mine. I was not jealous of him, but I do hope he will never have your miniature in his bosom.

From your friend, W.E.[30]

Easy must have felt he should give Jewett some remuneration for the "missed opportunity," so he added a note at the bottom of the letter: "Do not be angry that I enclose the piece of paper accompanying this. It is all I have or it should be more."[31]

When Jewett's relationship with Rivers (Richard Robinson) began to crumble, she turned to Easy as both a source of information and an instrument to create jealousy. On learning of Rivers's supposed infidelity, Jewett abruptly ended her visit in Philadelphia and returned to New York, paying an immediate visit to Easy's place of business to get information. Easy's response again pointed out to Jewett the fatal flaw in many of her friendships. The need for public camouflage meant she could not be publicly acknowledged and thus did not really have a friendship of mutual respect.

I have just this moment heard that a young lady was in the store this morning after paper, and that she also enquired after me. From the description I had of her, and from having learned that you was [sic] in town, I think it must have been you. I regret very much that I was out at the time, I can assure you. Our porter has just told me the circumstance of your being in, and says he did not know what to make of you. I hope when you enquired of the clerk for me, that none of the bosses were near. I must confess I was not a little surprised that you should mention my name at all, for instance, if it had been D. Felt himself that you asked, I should have been blown slick as a whistle. . . . I hope you will never ask for me again in that manner, for you must be aware that a discovery would be a serious evil to me.[32]

Easy's later letters indicate that Jewett's conduct toward him vacillated between showers of affection and gifts, and barrages of slights and reprimands as she used him to try to reestablish her old relationship with Rivers. Eager for her affection and attention, Easy consciously or unconsciously allowed himself to be used. Both men were her companions until the time of her death—but the degree of affection she held for each can be seen in the testimony of Rosina Townsend as she recalled the details of Jewett's last evening.

Helen Jewett told Mrs. Townsend at Tea Table that Frank Rivers will be there and stay all night and also Bill Easy would come but requested that B. Easy would not be admitted in the House. . . . Mrs. Townsend had the keys of the place at 8 o'clock and kept watch at the door so as to prevent Bill Easy to come in.[33]

Even when a prostitute and her client mutually enjoyed each other's company, friendships sometimes failed because each had different expectations of the relationship. In Edward, Jewett had a pleasant companion who was refined, interesting, and older. He admired her mind, enjoyed their conversations, sexually desired her, and was fond of her. In the midst of their relationship, however, Jewett's "young" lover returned to town, changing the terms of Edward's and Jewett's association. Neither wished to let go of the relationship entirely, but neither could accept it on the other's terms. Jewett conceded the public limitations of her liaison with Edward—that she could "not see [him], nay, not even recognize [him] at the theatre," but she wanted to continue their correspondence and occasional visits in a non-sexual friendship. Edward wanted everything—intellectual and sexual companionship with emotional commitment, but he granted he "could not be to [her] the friend, which, perhaps, [she] anticipated." Thus, Edward wrote to Jewett:

Had not this correspondence better be discontinued for the present, at least. Start not at the proposal; it is with reluctance that I speak of it, but you are with your young friend, and . . . your attachment for him must increase, while for me, it must lessen for want of that occasional intercourse which is necessary to the very existence of any decided preference. . . . During our last interview your partial refusal on a certain matter, convinced me that I reigned in your bosom with no deep seated preference. It spoke volumes in favor of your feelings for your friend, and your regard for your word, but very little for your partiality for me. Pardon me for alluding to the circumstance even in this remote manner.[34]

In spite of Jewett's "partial refusal" and his pessimistic assessment of their relationship, Edward wrote that he would "still call at the house to enquire of [her] well-being," and in closing the letter he requested time for a visit at the end of the week.[35]

Perhaps the most genuine and long-lasting of Jewett's male friendships was that with Wandering Willie. He was the reporter whose story about Jewett's appearance in police court caused Charles C. to reprimand her. Jewett's and Wandering Willie's friendship began with this police-court incident and continued for two years until her death. In contrast to most of Jewett's other "friends," Willie did not hide his association with Jewett, even though he may have partially camouflaged it as "journalistic interest." Willie went on an extended trip to the West in 1835, and their surviving correspondence is from this period. His letters are long and filled with experiences he wished to share with Jewett. His affection and desire for her are obvious.

God has given me a sufficient share of sincerity to entitle me to full credence, when I state that the receipt of your letter this day, gave me much real and unmingled pleasure. . . .

I wish that you had been with me, my girl, on the glorious river of the Lakes, and on several other occasions. . . . Had I been rich enough, Ellen, I would have requested you to make my journey completely delightful by accompanying me. On my soul, Ellen, I never knew but two women whose society I thought worthy of accepting on a journey. . . . I trust, however, that the day is not far distant when we shall make a tour together through two or three places.[36]

In another letter he added:

God bless you Ellen; I long to see and talk to you, for I have seen such sights—but I have not yet transgressed with an Indian girl, no, nor with any other kind since I left New York, but this is not virtue, for I wish, oh, how I wish I had you with me this very night.[37]

Willie expressed his respect for Jewett's "soul" as well as her mind. He used extensive literary references to convey this message, noting that Jewett, like Ellen in Scott's *Lady of the Lake*, "was cast *pro tem* among a set of rude and rough mortals, yet she preserved her mind's bright purity; her soul was unpolluted; so it is with you my girl." Doing small favors was also a part of the friendship. Willie thanked Jewett "for the numerous acts of kindness which your letter tells me you have conferred upon me . . . relating to the commissions which I gave you to do." A postscript to another letter stated: "See that my *Boy* obeyed my mandate."[38]

Jewett's client associations offer a wide spectrum of different types of customer-prostitute interactions, and they reveal common factors that influenced many prostitute-client relationships or that were impediments to genuine friendships. A more comprehensive view of the full range of customer associations is gained by adding data from sources such as House of Refuge records and police reports. Most of the young women who were committed to the House of Refuge for prostitution had had as their first sex partners young men in their teens who had run around with them on the streets at night. A hair ribbon or a walk in Battery Park for these girls could be equated with a magazine subscription or evening at the Park Theatre for Helen Jewett—added currency in the sexual exchange. From young boys many teenage prostitutes graduated to the local grocer, hackman, or boardinghouse resident, and then to men of a variety of ages and occupations that they picked up on the streets at night. Some women preferred totally impersonal transactions with a transient population, while others hoped to be taken on for a period as a kept mistress.[39]

Prostitutes' interactions with customers covered the full range of possibilities—from impersonal, perhaps hostile, sexual intercourse to genuine friendships. The impersonal associations occurred more frequently than did friendships, but the latter did exist. In the nineteenth century, as now, for prostitutes or non-prostitutes, a "testing" of friendships had the potential to reveal flaws in those relationships. Thus numerous friendships existed without the ideal components of mutual respect, compatibility, loyalty, or lack of exploitation but were nonetheless acceptable and satisfying to the parties involved. Prostitutes accepted less than perfect relationships even though some genuine, sustained male friendships did exist for them. Wandering Willie appeared to have had such a relationship with Helen Jewett—he first was her customer, then also became her friend. "Customer" and "friend," however, were only two categories of relationships that existed between prostitutes and their male associates. On many occasions the mutual affection of friendships blossomed into deeper relationships, and a client or male friend became a prostitute's "lover" or husband.

A man could be called a prostitute's lover when the liaison was of long duration (several months), was intense, and was rooted as much in emotional attachment as in material considerations—even though the lover might continue to pay or to gain through her as a business associate or recipient of gifts and cash. It is difficult to give a precise definition of a lover because relationships differed greatly from case to case and because the roles men played in the lives of prostitutes—customer, friend, lover, protector, spouse, business associate—were not exclusive. An emotionally attached lover might live with a prostitute and at the same time also serve as her protector, work with her as a partner in a panel-thief operation, or operate a bar that catered to her clients; or he might have a social role separate from her prostitution operation, earning some of his income as a gambler, thief, policeman, or employee of another business.[40]

If a man depended on a prostitute for more than temporary support, he might be thought of as a pimp, but the use of the term can be very misleading when referring to the nineteenth century before 1870. Pimps, as they are known today and have been known since the last decades of the nineteenth century, can be defined as men who exploit prostitutes financially, living off their earnings, and who have control over the women's public and private sexual lives. Pimps may or may not be the recipients of a prostitute's affection and gifts. Some men who related to prostitutes as pimps existed in nineteenth-century New York, just as they must have existed in all ages. In New York City, however, it was not until around 1870, when prostitution began to be more segregated in red-light districts, that evidence of the presence of pimps becomes clear. Furthermore, not until the last decades of the century did a full-fledged pimp system develop in New York, as males gained control over the complete range of citywide prostitution operations. The distinction between a lover and pimp basically involved whether the woman or the man was primarily in control of both the personal and professional ties. Clearly, up until the last decades of the nine-teenth century, women were in charge of the operation and profits of prostitution.[41]

The use of the word *pimp* is found in only a few sources in this period. John R. McDowall, in the Magdalen Society report, stated that in some prostitution houses pimps "beat the girls and drug those who want to reform."[42] Most sources in this period that mention males who are associated with brothels (including *McDowall's Journal*) do not refer to them as pimps but as bullies or "bouncers" hired to provide protection, sentinels who kept watch on the street and warned the houses when police or other trouble was approaching, or business associates.[43] The term *pimp* also is found in sources as an epithet for one's adversaries or a disliked member of the community who was associated with a pros-titute. In 1872 the *New York World* referred to Dan Sickles, former Civil War general, state legislator, Congressman, secretary to James Bucha-nan, and Minister to Spain as a "pimp" because he had had a liaison with prostitute Fanny White and allegedly had accepted funds from her for his political campaign.[44]

Romantic "lovers" were important to prostitutes, and most nine-teenth-century social commentaries note the prevalence of lovers among these women. As with their analyses of brothels and prostitutes, which were neatly categorized and placed in a hierarchical order, these authors attempted to impose a structure on the existence of lovers, endeavoring to find distinctions, often based on moralistic fantasy, that would fit them into the prostitution hierarchy. Because romantic attachment is more difficult to categorize than functions within a relationship, func-tional distinctions were usually emphasized. Thus, nineteenth-century commentators indicated that lovers were taken on for romantic reasons and were lavishly treated, but they also usually were expected to protect, to steal, to assist with the brothel operation, to accompany, or to entertain.

According to New York physician Charles Smith in 1847, all classes of prostitutes had lovers—thus satisfying their "natural desire of having one man as a constant friend and companion. . . . The woman who keeps a house of ill fame has her man, the kept mistress has her lover and prostitutes have their 'friends' "—none of whom pay for the affection they receive and many of whom draw some of their support from the women.[45] "The lover is not jealous of her profession because he knows she does not enjoy it."[46] According to Smith, women made great sacrifices for these men and remained devoted even when treated brutally. Smith believed most of these lovers spent their time on billiards, dominoes, races, and elections, and that the liaisons sometimes led to retirement from prostitution and to marriage.

A decade later, in the 1850s, William Sanger noted the existence of lovers among keepers of brothels who

have an exaggerated affection for some man to whom they are passionately attached. Some few of them are professedly living with their husbands, but this is an exception to the ordinary rule. Generally speaking, they are the mistresses of some persons upon whom they lavish all their tenderness, and for whose gratification they willingly incur any amount of expense. Some of these individuals are men upon town, gamblers, or rowdies of the higher class, whose noblest aspirations are satisfied by a liberal supply of money.[47]

Sanger went on to point out that first-class madams did not as a general rule allow prostitutes' lovers to reside with them, "although they allow them to visit; a constant residence is considered as likely to engross too much of the girls' time to the neglect of the interest of the proprietress."[48] Madam Berry handled the problem by granting each of her boarders the "privilege of having one night a week at her own command, in arrears or not, in which to see her 'private friend.' "[49]

Sanger also noted that a lover or "bully" was characteristic of middle- and lower-class prostitutes. The lover, usually indolent, acted as the prostitute's protector if she became involved in any difficulty with rowdies and strangers, but at times he also exercised an arbitrary and brutal control over her. "In many cases, singular as it may appear, an actual love is felt by the woman for 'her man.' "[50]

A similar description of lovers was given by George Ellington in 1869: "Sometimes the girls support the lovers, and sometimes the lovers support the girls—the first custom being the more common, and the latter more honored in the breach than in the observance. The lovers are supposed by the women to be their best friends," who give them advice about business matters and introduce them to men with money. Ellington considered the lovers to be of the lowest sort, frequently thieves and gamblers, or partners with the women in the "panel house game" or "husband game."[51] Ellington conceded, however, that in better houses, the prostitute's lover "gives more than he receives." As often as the house rules would permit, these lovers would take their women to the theater or other resorts of pleasure and appear proud of their company.[52]

Some of the negative intricacies of prostitutes' relationships with their lovers are spelled out in contemporary newspaper accounts of prostitutes' conflicts with these men. The brutality noted by Smith, Ellington, and Sanger is borne out in some of the incidents described in the papers. One of the worst attacks of brutality was perpetrated on prostitute Mary Mansfield by hack driver Dennis Diamond, who had been her lover and for four years had "measurably lived with the girl" at a brothel at 128 Anthony Street. Diamond had quarreled with Mansfield and had knocked her down, kicked her, and jumped on her stomach, breast, and face. Her face was so lacerated that her features were barely discernible, and her internal injuries were so serious that, since the incident, she had been in a "torpid, senseless state with little prospect of surviving."[53]

Prostitute Ann Burk found that the violence she experienced with her lover was not much different from that she had endured as a married woman. Burk's husband was a seaman, and while she lived with him he beat her frequently. As a result of marital violence, Burk left her husband, "turned out upon the town, and opened a house of infamy," even though her husband still visited and beat her whenever he was in port. For over a year Burk had had a "sleeping partnership" with John Rue, who also worked with her as a business partner. During a quarrel about their business establishment, Rue beat, knocked down, kicked, and stomped upon Burk. A "battle royal" ensued in which "glass lamps were hurled at each other's heads, broken andirons were thrown about, shovels and thongs were used as weapons and broken, and the furniture was battered and destroyed." Rue was arrested by the watch, and Burk pressed charges against him. In revenge, Rue made out a complaint against Burk for keeping a disorderly house and had her and all of the inhabitants of the house arrested. The prostitutes and "their bully" were committed to Bridewell until they could find bail to keep the peace.[54]

Sources indicate that prostitutes often forgave and returned to their violent lovers. Mary Reffell and Benjamin Rhinggold came from Washington, D.C., to lodge with Frank and Mary Berry in Duane Street. After two days in the city, they had a "domestic quarrel," and Rhinggold beat Reffell savagely and "threatened her with a huge Bowie knife—nearly one-half as large as she—with which he cut her on the head." Reffell attended court when Rhinggold was arraigned, appearing "to suffer considerably from injuries upon her head, which was bandaged up." As the judge was about to sentence Rhinggold to Bridewell, Reffell intervened and begged he not be punished, saying they would leave the city in a day or two. Because of her intercession, Rhinggold was discharged, but the judge extracted a promise from Reffell that she would leave town for a different destination than her lover—a promise she most likely did not keep.[55]

More philosophical about her lover's temper was Ann Farmer, a friend and correspondent of Helen Jewett. In a letter to Jewett she wrote: "You ask if Mr. W. and myself have become friends; we have made up and fallen out twice since you left. I have become so accustomed to his freaks of temper, that I almost find them a necessary evil."[56]

Violence between prostitutes and their lovers was not perpetrated by the men alone. Prostitutes were strongly attached to their paramours, and their intense feelings were often manifested in jealousy, anger, and rage which resulted in physical conflicts. Police officers were called to Anthony Street where an "old bawd named Delia May, nineteen years on the town," was beating and swearing oaths at W. Purse, "her *particular* friend and keeper," who the night before had gone off with another woman. May, covered in soot and coal dust, was arrested and sent to prison to keep the peace.[57] In another incident, a young prostitute named Mrs. Baker was jilted by her lover, a man called Burke. Not long afterward, while sitting in the third tier of the Bowery Theatre, Baker saw Burke with another woman in the first tier of boxes. Baker went down to Burke and his friend and began hurling insults at him. Burke told Baker she must be mistaken, he had never seen her before, and then shortly afterward he went to Baker's and beat her for "taking such liberties with him when he was in respectable company." Baker filed charges of assault against Burke.[58] The theater also was the scene of another assault by a prostitute on a gentleman who apparently had played with her emotions. In this case, the former paramour was accompanied by his family when he was attacked by the distraught woman.[59]

Although relationships between prostitutes and their lovers were frequently volatile, even brutal, police reports in the press often distort the full range of feelings that existed in these relationships. Clara Hazard, friend of Helen Jewett, left New York for her hometown of Philadelphia in pursuit of her lover, "Conch." The following is part of a letter she wrote to Jewett describing the events that transpired on her arrival in Philadelphia and on a subsequent trip to Baltimore a few days later:

Baltimore, Friday, June 12, 1835

Dear Helen,
Excuse my not writing before to you, my esteemed friend, for my mind was in such a way that I was incapable of writing. I arrived in Philadelphia Tuesday afternoon, and saw a woman who [sic] my Conch had sinned with, though he denied it all. But we had a fight. He struck me and I scratched his face awfully. He threw me down and jumped on me, after which I followed him out of the house for two squares, running down the street after him, almost naked, having nothing on but my night clothes. He ran in the house of my wash-woman and I after him, when he begged me to let him alone. I then made him go back, when it was all right. He was in Baltimore last week, and misbehaved himself all around. One Maria Gartzher is in love with him. He walked Baltimore streets with her, and blame him, he shall pay for the sport.[60]

A month and a half later, Clara wrote again from Philadelphia describing her life with Conch:

Philadelphia, July 26, 1835

Dear Helen,
. . . Conch and myself arrived here safe on Wednesday, at half past 2 o'clock. There is no news in this place, no theatre is open or place of amusement of any kind, the streets look forsaken, you scarcely see fifty persons during the day. The weather is very warm, and yesterday was the warmest day we have had this summer. Conch and myself fight every half hour, and are friends the next. He starts home on Friday next, and I expect to go with him, and if you do not receive any letter from me until I return from Virginia, I beg of you not to think hard

of me, for it would never do to have letters sent there in my name, as the place is small, and the fellows in the Post Office are acquainted with Conch and myself, and then we would be found out.

. . . Conch and myself roll on the floor all day. I really think we have the coolest room in the city. Nothing more at present.

I remain your friend,
C. Hazard[61]

Three months later, Clara's relationship with Conch seemed to have stabilized somewhat. She appeared to be contentedly spending most of her time in domestic pursuits and suggested she was pregnant.

Philadelphia, October 20, 1835

Dear Helen,

I received your letter last Friday, and would have answered it before, but have . . . been very much engaged in darning stockings, making night caps, & c. I have turned very industrious and economical since I have seen you. I spend most of my time at home, and walk out but very seldom, and when I do, it is only to my mother's. I find that there is more real happiness by staying at home and mending up my old clothes, until my dear Conch comes, than in running up and down the streets with the girls. Helen, I never was happier than I am now, C. giving me all that is necessary, and remaining with me altogether. . . . I do not go to the theatre but once a week, and that is Saturday night, it being the only night in the week that Conch can go, he being compelled to read every night until twelve and one o'clock. If you see me in three or four months from now, you will see good signs of the first duty of life. . . . Conch's respects to you. I remain your friend.

Clara Hazard[62]

Prostitutes took many different forms of action in trying to hold on to their men. Prostitute Mary Ann Barnes was living with a seventeen-year-old youth at her brothel in Walnut Street. The boy's mother made repeated trips to see Barnes and beg for her son's "release" and was finally told by Barnes that she would "rather go to Hell" than part with the young man. In order to force the removal of her underage son from the brothel, the mother filed charges of seduction against Barnes, who was then arrested.[63]

More emphatic in her efforts to keep her lover was prostitute Mary Stewart. Stewart also was living with a young man who, on coming of age, left his guardian-aunt and moved into Stewart's brothel. When the young man's brother came to persuade his sibling to leave the brothel,

Stewart became enraged, pointed a loaded pistol at the brother, and threatened to blow his brains out. The issue was settled, at least temporarily, when Stewart was arrested.[64]

Brothel madam Rosina Townsend was more subtle in her actions to maintain her relationship with a lover. The night of Jewett's murder Townsend spent with a man described by the press as her "paramour." When the court refused to give credence to Townsend's testimony incriminating Robinson because it was not corroborated and the testimony of this companion could have offered the necessary corroboration, Townsend refused to give his name because he was a respectable merchant. Conscious of the effect of public disclosure, Townsend opted for companionship over credibility.[65]

A more poignant example of the loyalty and devotion felt by a prostitute for her lover as well as a prostitute's tenacity in trying to hold on to her special relationship is found in a letter written to Helen Jewett by prostitute Agnes J. Thompson, who had once been acquainted with Jewett.

Baltimore, Maryland, Nov. 2, 1835

Dear Friend,

Some three years have transpired since I had the exquisite pleasure of seeing you, and I may have grown entirely out of your recollection; therefore, I must ask your excusal in my assumption of this boldness, but believe me that I am urged to trouble you on account of my man—having been informed by a gentleman of your city that my lover was acquainted with you. His name is Lawson M. [The name was "suppressed" by the *Gazette* in case the man had since redeemed himself.] Should it prove that you are acquainted with him, please, in the name of Heaven, persuade him to return to me, and tell him I am almost dead by the intermission of his absence, and that I will do anything on earth, or give him anything I can, to make him happy. Also tell him I have been true to him. Should he not heed your entreaties, please write me forthwith, and I will proceed to your city. My anguish is so great that indeed I can hardly pen these lines.

The wife whose affection glows in true love for her husband, and in return meets with only cold indifference, can but faintly imagine my anguish.[66]

Thompson then went on to say she would leave the next morning for Philadelphia and requested that Jewett send a response there to Madam Western's on Race Street. She stated that, if she did not receive news of her lover, she would then leave for New York and would "stop at your house if I can be accommodated."

One prostitute who demonstrated a limited tolerance for her lover's transgressions was a Mrs. Howard who ran an assignation house on Elm Street. When she was robbed of a $45 necklace, fifteen or twenty half eagles, and a gold-framed miniature of her daughter, Howard suspected the thief to be her lover, Dr. Benjamin A. Jocelin. Since she was not absolutely sure of his guilt, Howard had Jocelin arrested on an old assault and battery warrant. After he was locked in jail, Jocelin admitted stealing the items and told where they were hidden. The *Sun*, accustomed to the forgiveness of prostitutes, was certain Howard would take back "to her chaste embraces the lover who captured her kisses, and then cabbaged her goods."[67]

The best-documented example of the development of a relationship between a prostitute and her lover is that of Helen Jewett. Jewett met Richard Robinson in 1835, and their correspondence covers the period from June 1835, when their emotional involvement intensified, until shortly before Jewett's death less than a year later. From the beginning of their association, Robinson appears to have used the pseudonym Frank Rivers. At the time they met, Rivers was seventeen and Jewett twenty-two. Jewett's brothel madam, Mrs. Berry, said that she did not at first allow Rivers to visit her house "because he made quarrels—and was under age." She also noted that he and two co-workers "did not spend much money with her."[68] Berry soon relented, perhaps because Rivers reached either his majority or some money; by midsummer he was a regular visitor at the brothel.

The correspondence between Jewett and Rivers reveals that both "fell in love" during the early part of the summer. In late July Jewett wrote to Rivers:

I have often wished I possessed your amiable disposition. . . . You have such a happy faculty of rendering yourself agreeable, witty and engaging that whatever society you may come in contact [with], you cannot fail to please.

. . . I have often told you that I loved you, (which perhaps a woman should blush to do) but it is, not that I have told you so that I would have you believe it, but in all my conduct I would evince the devotion I feel for you.[69]

Although Rivers expressed similar sentiments to Jewett in his letters, he also disclosed an ambivalence which was to lead to future difficulties.

You was [sic] offended Wednesday evening at my language. I do not wonder that you were. It was harsh—very harsh but I could not help it. No one can

23. **PROSTITUTE HELEN JEWETT.** Jewett, one of the best-known prostitutes of the nineteenth century, was brutally murdered in 1836 at the age of twenty-three. The details of her life story and relationships with customers and other prostitutes fascinated New Yorkers for several decades. (Courtesy of the New-York Historical Society, New York City)

SKETCH

OF THE LIFE OF

MISS ELLEN JEWETT,

WHO WAS MURDERED IN THE CITY OF NEW YORK, ON
SATURDAY EVENING, APRIL 9, 1836.

BOSTON:
PRINTED FOR THE PUBLISHER.

24. SKETCH OF MISS ELLEN JEWETT.　Publications describing the life and
death of Helen (Ellen) Jewett began to appear shortly after her murder. This
Sketch was one of the earliest to be published, and its cover illustration portrayed
a more demure young woman than later works. (Courtesy of the New-York
Historical Society, New York City)

love you more than I do, dear Nelly; yet how strange, whenever I meet you I cannot treat you even with respect. You must think it very strange that I profess to love you so much, and yet always treat you so harshly. Yet I have told you over and over again, that loving you as I do and not being able to see you, it makes me most crazy, and I have no control over my feelings, but Nelly you must forgive me.

. . . I know my letters cannot be very interesting to you, Nell; they are full of oh! how I love you, and a piece of other nonsense, exactly what they all write you. They all call you dearest Nelly, so do I.

I suppose you think us all alike. I shall see you again Sunday at one o'clock, until that time I shall count the hours.[70]

Jewett continued to see many other clients during her relationship with Rivers, including some arranged by him. Wishing to please him, she followed his directives in arranging meetings with his associates, in corresponding with them, and in giving to and getting from them certain pieces of information. In one letter she stated: "I wrote you a letter and took the liberty of enclosing one to Mr. G. . . . that you might have the pleasure of reading it first—after which you were to seal and put it in the office for me."[71] In another letter she wrote: "I last night saw the person whom you are desirous of meeting and tried to induce him to go to the play tonight but he refused."[72] On a different occasion Jewett stated: "I cannot imagine why you wish to know so particularly about Mr. G. Your request alarms me, and I beg you may assign some reason for it."[73]

In spite of Jewett's efforts to please Rivers, by late August their relationship began to undergo some strain. Jewett wanted more attention and more visits from Rivers and this became a recurring theme in most of her letters. Some letters contained only a line or two on the topic: "You will recollect I spoke to you relative to visiting me oftener than twice a week,"[74] but more often an entire note was dedicated to the complaint:

Unkind, ungenerous Frank, to remain away from me so long, when you know with what anxiety I expected a visit from you. I do not think I merit such treatment from you, or if I have, an explanation is due me, and if you ever liked me you would put an end to the painful suspense I am enduring by replying immediately.[75]

In addition to complaints, Jewett tried other tactics to get Rivers to visit her. Some letters tried to arouse his sexual interest:

I beg you will wait tonight until half past eight, when I promise you my door shall be kept unlocked for you, and you shall have all the fun you anticipate.[76]

Another letter ended with a more explicit sexual invitation: "I feel amazingly like blowing you up, if I dared—not with powder."[77] Other letters tried to arouse River's curiosity with lines such as: "I have something to tell you which from anyone else you would never give credence to";[78] "I want to see you tomorrow afternoon or evening very much, as I have something urgent to say to you";[79] and, "to-night you must call upon me, for I have something very particular indeed to communicate, which interests you more than you are aware of."[80]

The less attentive Rivers seemed, the more insecure Jewett became about their relationship, fearing he was unfaithful.

You often speak to me relative to my jealousy. but you must, ere this, be aware of my feelings; and it is not strange that I should wish you all my own, and feel vexed when you do not come at the time I expect. Then I fancy that you are engaged by ladies who are fond of you, praising them and giving them smiles . . . and they are kissing you . . . and that would be a sacrilege.[81]

At times Jewett's jealousy and insecurity became self-pity.

You have so much to occupy you which I can never share in. You of course cannot enter into the succession of frivolous pursuits and uninteresting engagements that occupy all my time, and I dare not, nay, have not the inclination to describe them to you, for if I should do so you would really be disgusted with the description.[82]

In another letter she wrote: "I . . . solicit you, if you ever liked me, to pass an hour with me this evening, if you have one that you can spare from your numerous friends."[83] As Jewett's anxieties increased, so did the conflicts with Rivers. Thus, in November 1835, Rivers wrote asking that the relationship be ended and his miniature be returned.[84] In spite of this near-break, a reconciliation was reached, and they remained lovers for a while longer. In mid-December, however, a complete break occurred after Jewett learned that Rivers allegedly had tried to stay with a friend and co-worker in Berry's brothel while Jewett was in Philadelphia. Although the couple began seeing each other again after a few weeks, the relationship never completely mended. Rivers had proved he was not considerate, loyal, or loving. He took the relationship for what it was on the surface—a liaison with a prostitute which required no commitment on his part. Jewett, on the other hand, wanted a deeper relationship, and in her efforts to achieve it became insecure, possessive, and nagging—a very different person from the vivacious, witty, and understanding woman she appeared to be with her female friends and most other clients. Shortly before her death, Rivers asked to have his correspondence returned, and it was rumored he was going to marry someone else. He was, however, the last guest Jewett entertained before she was murdered.

Some prostitute-lover relationships came to the attention of the authorities or public not because of the female's devotion to her lover but because of the male's attachment to the prostitute. Conventional wisdom held that it was the prostitute who was desperate for the lover, not the male who might want the relationship. Only when the involved male was married did his attachment merit comment, and only then because it seemed so incomprehensible. The *Herald* thought it disgraceful that five young married mechanics who were just starting out in business would pay the bail of their special "syrens" who had been arrested during a raid on Leonard Street.[85] The *Sun* hinted its approval of the arrest of Adeline Watson, a young prostitute who had "completely entangled in her toils" a young married clerk. The young man had virtually abandoned his pregnant wife and had spent almost every night for the past several months in the "polluted arms of this lascivious syren." He also was spending most of his money and "much of his employer's, which he had clandestinely taken," to feed and clothe his companion. The merchant employer followed the clerk to the brothel and broke up the relationship by pressing charges against Watson for prostitution/vagrancy; she was sent to prison for six months.[86] In a case recorded in the House of Refuge records, a young married woman walked all the way to the Refuge on a bitter cold day to ask that Refuge officials recommit a former inmate and "girl of the town," Mary E. Graham. According to the distraught mother of two children, Graham had taken her husband—his time, money, and health (he now had the "bad disorder")— and had left her supporting the family on a $2 a week allowance.

Sympathetic to the woman's plight, the Refuge had the police arrest Graham and return her to the Refuge.[87]

Although most prostitute-lover relationships probably were not sustained over a long period of time, some were based on a mutual devotion which appeared to offer a stable association and possibly a way out of the profession. One of New York's most famous madams, Fanny White, is an example of a prostitute who practiced her profession for a number of years, had several liaisons, and finally left the profession to marry a lover. White came to New York in the mid-1840s and by the end of that decade was running her own brothel. Also at this time she began her most famous liaison, one with Dan Sickles, which was to last over five years. The son of a wealthy New York family, Sickles was a lawyer who became involved in Tammany politics and was elected to the state legislature in 1847.[88] He was flamboyant and indiscreet, and his relationship with White was well known to New Yorkers. On one occasion Sickles took White to Albany with him and allegedly scandalized even those who had come to expect the unusual from him by introducing her at the table of the hotel where he regularly boarded. He also shocked observers by taking her on the floor of the assembly, an act for which he received the censure of his colleagues. Sickles's association with White further fueled gossip because it was believed Sickles had helped finance his political campaigns with money White had earned in prostitution.[89]

In 1852 Sickles married a sixteen-year-old named Teresa Bagioli, but this union did not interfere with his liaison with White. Because of his adulterous behavior and his contemptuous attitude toward his wife and her family, Sickles had a difficult relationship with his in-laws. It was rumored, among other things, that Sickles had forged notes in his father-in-law's name. Interestingly, the personal tax record for 1851 for White's brothel at 119 Mercer lists "M. Bagioli" as the payer of taxes for the property along with Fanny White. It is possible that White was involved with Antonio Bagioli, but it is also possible Sickles was using his future father-in-law's name or funds to assist his mistress.[90]

In 1853 Sickles was appointed secretary to James Buchanan who was serving as Minister to England. When Sickles sailed for Britain, he left wife Teresa at home but took Fanny White with him. Not able to avoid controversy for long, Sickles caused an uproar by introducing White at court. White returned to the States in 1854 and again took over management of her brothel. She continued keeping company with wealthy, flamboyant, prominent New Yorkers. George Strong wrote in his diary that his friend Bob LeRoy's father, "semi-millionaire Jake LeRoy," had caused a scandal "for all respectable people by driving Mrs. Fanny White up Broadway in his flashy wagon."[91]

By 1856, having accumulated considerable assets, White moved with two of her boarders from her Mercer brothel to quieter quarters on Twelfth Street. At this time she also met a lawyer, Edmon Blankman, whom she married a year later. White was said to have "reformed and retired" after her marriage, and she lived happily with Blankman until her premature death several years later.[92]

Another marriage between a prostitute and a man of some stature and wealth was that of Eliza Bowen (or Brown) and Stephen Jumel. Bowen, the daughter of a prostitute, was born in Providence, Rhode Island, in 1775. She moved to New York at age nineteen and worked with a theatrical troupe. For six years she was well known to New Yorkers as an actress and prostitute, attracting the attention and affection of French-born wine merchant Stephen Jumel. Bowen and Jumel lived together for several years until 1804, when they married. In 1810 Jumel bought the Roger Morris mansion in the northern part of the city, and the couple lived there until Stephen Jumel's death in 1832. The following year, Aaron Burr, then nearly eighty, married the widow Jumel. This union caused Philip Hone to note in his diary: "It is benevolent in her to keep the old man in his latter days. One good turn deserves another."[93] William Dunlap, dramatist, critic, and artist, was not as complementary of Mrs. Jumel-Burr when he recorded in his diary a meeting with her a year later. His comments also indicated that the marriage to Burr was not as beneficial as her first one had been.

Today in the street a woman accosted me by name who [sic] I immediately recognized as the Madam Jumel Aaron Burr married about a year back. She had been a supernumerary at the Theatre before Jumel married her. 'You don't know me, Mr. Dunlap.' 'Oh, yes, Mrs. Burr, How does Col. Burr do?' 'O, I don't see him any more. He got $13,000 of my property, and spent it all or gave it away and had money to buy him a dinner. I had a new Carriage and pair of horses cost me 1000 dollars he took them and sold them for 500.' . . . I turned off glad to part from her. What confidence can be placed in the words of such

25. MADAM JUMEL (MRS. AARON BURR). Prostitute and actress Eliza Bowen, who married the wealthy Stephen Jumel and later Aaron Burr, represented success in the eyes of women who entered prostitution with hopes of improving their socioeconomic situations. (Courtesy of the New-York Historical Society, New York City)

a woman it is hard to say, but Burr's marrying her makes anything told of him credible.[94]

The intimate details of the Burr marital split received much publicity, thus continuing to keep Burr embroiled in controversy until shortly before he died in 1836. Mme. Jumel-Burr lived another three decades, to the age of ninety, and on the occasion of her death she was remembered somewhat fondly by George Strong in his diary.

July 19 [1865]. . . . *Died*, old Mme. Jumel, or more strictly, Mrs. Aaron Burr. She was very old. When I was a boy she was spoken of mysteriously as a very wonderful, wealthy, wicked old lady, living in great seclusion.[95]

Jumel-Burr was buried in the uptown cemetery of the distinguished Trinity Church.

The marriage of middle-class lawyer Edmon Blankman and well-known, long-term prostitute Fanny White, and that of wealthy merchant Stephen Jumel and prostitute Eliza Bowen were exceptions for men in Blankman's and Jumel's professional and social positions. The correspondence from Jewett's middle-class patrons points out that most often men feared that social and business repercussions would result from public knowledge of their associations with prostitutes, so marriage was not likely to occur. The marriage of wealthy businessman Thomas Smith to a local prostitute appeared to confirm this assumption. Strong noted the marriage in his diary and called it a "case of deliberate infatuation":

Thomas H. Smith is actually married—I did not believe the rumor before—and his blushing bride is a protege of that respected female, Mrs. Miller of Duane Street, a damsel who has been on the town for twenty years. . . . He urged and implored her to marry him for a long time, and she wrote a Southern friend to know whether he'd keep her or not if she didn't. He declined and she thereupon consented. Very pleasant this for [Smith's business partners] Bruen and Waddell. I should be sorely tempted to shoot a brother of mine who should perform such an operation. . . . Poor devil, he's to be pitied.[96]

Shortly after the marriage, partner Bruen sold out his share of the business partnership, and a few weeks later Smith's commercial establishment burned. Smith's misfortunes were further compounded when only six months after their marriage

Smith's amiable bride . . . left him, having cleared out across the Atlantic with a young gentleman of nineteen (we are growing precocious), Goodwin, by name, a clerk . . . who carried off at the same time the snug amount of $6,000 from his employers.[97]

The fear that marriage to a prostitute would result in social and business repercussions seems to have been more operative at the upper levels of prostitution, with full-time prostitutes and women catering to the middle classes, than with part-time and occasional prostitutes and those whose clientele was drawn from the laboring classes. Less well-known and part-time prostitutes found it easier to slip into marriage or other roles with no one being the wiser. In addition, the line separating respectable from disrespectable sexual behavior was much clearer for middle-class women than for those of the poorer classes. The laboring poor understood that public shame was associated with prostitution, but within their milieu a "fallen woman" could return to respectability, and a marriage to one who had practiced prostitution was not necessarily a disreputable union. The temporary or occasional practice of prostitution was viewed as an acceptable means of supplementing one's income when necessary, not a permanent stigma.[98] As Christine Stansell has noted in her study of nineteenth-century New York poor women:

Laboring people saw the connections of prostitution to problems of ordinary life. . . . For the laboring poor, prostitution was part of a complicated and dense web of relationships between men, money and sex; a web in which marriage and courtship were woven as well. . . . [Whereas] urban moral reform groups saw prostitution as a moral choice conditioned by economic necessity, . . . working people perceived prostitution [as] an economic choice with moral implications.[99]

There are numerous examples in nineteenth-century records that illustrate that marriage to a former prostitute was judged acceptable and not unusual. The Water Street Home for Women noted in its second annual report that two marriages had taken place at the Home during the preceding year. The report stated that the two brides, former prostitutes, had "married Christian men who knew of their past life."[100] Although the House of Refuge did not keep complete records on the lives of women after they left the Refuge, there are numerous notations telling about the marriages of former inmates who had been prostitutes. When follow-up information is available, it appears that most of the prostitutes who were wedded went on to live normal married lives and worked to help support their families; many of them had children.[101]

Ann Jeanette Utter, who was introduced in an earlier chapter, was one of the Refuge prostitutes who married after spending a few years in the profession. Refuge records follow the life of Utter over a twenty-year period, noting her placement in a job as a Refuge indenture, her marriage to a Mr. Sarles, the birth of their children, and the progress of what appeared to be a successful married life.[102]

In some cases, although a husband did not care that his wife was a former prostitute, his family did, and this led to marital difficulties for the couple. Felicite Lavoie had been visited frequently by John Waters before their marriage, when she, under the name of Catherine Stone, had lived at the well-known brothel of Mrs. Reed at 46 Laurens Street. John Waters was "barely of age" at the time they met, while Felicite was said to be "on the off side of thirty at least." After a three-month courtship, Felicite and John were married in St. Catherine's Church in Canal Street and then celebrated their marriage with a cake and wine reception at Mrs. Reed's brothel. The couple moved in with John's family and were seemingly happy until "a family member thought she saw some eccentricities in the movements of the lady." On making inquiries, the family discovered that Felicite had been of "vicious reputation" before marriage and had continued the same course of life after marriage. Their accusations were strong enough to raise questions in John Waters' mind over her marital fidelity, and testimony elicited for the subsequent divorce trial confirmed that acts of adultery had been committed. Felicite, who apparently would have liked to continue her double life, protested that the testimony was "a monstrous conspiracy gotten up to rob her of her husband and honor." After listening to the witnesses at the trial, Felicite's lawyer told the court that the testimony had taken him "by shock," and though he believed every word his client said, he had no means at hand to disprove the plaintiff's evidence so would submit the case under the direction of the judge and would not take any more of the court's time. The judge found in favor of the plaintiff, and Felicite's marriage was ended.[103]

In another case, the son of a "respectable" family was spending too many nights away from home, and his parents became suspicious. The father followed the son to a brothel and had a police officer remove him; the brothel inhabitants were threatened with arrest. Evidently, the son was more serious about one of the prostitutes than the parents realized, and he followed his love to Philadelphia, where she had gone to avoid trouble. Again the son was brought home and again he left, this time marrying the prostitute before they departed from the city in order to escape the interference of the family. After their departure, the groom's family discovered that the new bride was already married to but separated from a man who had tried unsuccessfully to get her to leave prostitution. When the case was last reported in the paper, the angry father was trying to get the bride arrested and imprisoned for bigamy and was suing the brothel owner for aiding in the seduction of his son.[104] In both of the above cases where families objected to their sons' marriages, objections appear to have been made mostly because of the wives' occupation but partially because of the sons' young ages.

Some prostitutes were offered marriage and declined, even though matrimony could have offered respectability and a certain degree of security. Keziah Anne Kidd, a streetwalker who had worked as a prostitute for about six months, was "discovered" by her mother and sent to the House of Refuge after she contracted a venereal disease. While she had been working as a streetwalker, "a decent young mechanic was visiting her and proposed marriage," but because of her disease she refused. Even after she was in the Refuge and confined to bed, the mechanic accompanied Kidd's mother on a visit to see her. According to the Refuge matron, "we declined to allow an interview," even though Refuge officials said they believed the mechanic had not "known" her. Kidd's prostitution was not seen as an impediment to marriage, however, because the matron noted: "I suppose if she was well [he] would marry her."[105]

Some prostitutes who accepted marriage became discontented and decided respectability and marriage were not worth the sacrifices of an unhappy union. Consequently, some reversed the process and "chose" or returned to prostitution.[106] Thirty-nine percent of the prostitutes interviewed by Sanger stated that they had been married at some time. Certainly, some of these women lost their husbands because of desertion, but others left their spouses for prostitution because it was preferable to abuse, infidelity, or general unhappiness.[107]

Catherine "Kitty" Seely was "a visitor of all the lowest dens of prostitution" at the Five Points for two years, until she married William

Seely and moved to his home in New Durham, New Jersey. Mrs. Seely was described as

a chunky looking Irishwoman, with a very red face very much freckled, a short, turned-up nose, and fiery red hair cropped short behind. Her dress consisted of a loose dress, open in front, giving her general appearance [that of] a kind of negligee, which is only to be found amongst the beau monde on the Five Points.[108]

After two months of married life in New Durham, Mrs. Seely apparently pined for the "oyster cellars, groggeries, and dance houses" of the city. One day, when given two shillings by her mother-in-law to buy salt, she bought a drink instead and left for New York. Seely found his bride in a Five Points prostitution den, drunk and with "the worst thieves," so he took her before the local magistrate. Seely admitted that his wife had been living with another man at the Five Points at the time he decided to marry her, but said she was a good woman, a hard worker, and very smart, and he wanted to keep her. He told the judge he did not want a better woman. But his bride protested, saying she did not get enough to eat in New Durham and calling her husband a "devilish old fool and an old jackass." She went on to say that he had known what she was when he married her, and that the marriage was not valid because she would not have married him had she not been drunk at the time and unaware of her actions. After hearing both parties, the judge pointed out that he had no power to force her to return to her husband and encouraged the reluctant Seely to get a divorce.[109] Another prostitute, a Miss Decker, married Hamilton Dobbs, a blacksmith, and after six months she decided he was lazy and did not support her well, and she returned to a brothel. Dobbs found her streetwalking one evening and "solicited her strongly to return home with him but she would not—so he had her taken to the watchhouse." Mrs. Dobbs was committed overnight but then discharged the next morning, apparently free to return to her profession instead of her husband.[110]

Even though most nineteenth-century contemporaries assumed that a successful marriage was an avenue out of prostitution because the practice of the profession was incompatible with matrimony, in reality, it was not unusual for practicing prostitutes to be married. Sanger noted that 25 percent of the prostitutes he interviewed said they were married at the time, and more than half of these were still living with their husbands while practicing prostitution.[111] Some women remained in the profession because prostitution was a lucrative means of contributing to the family economy, while others returned to prostitution occasionally when economically necessary or when they were so inclined. Many prostitutes may have married for the same reasons they had entered prostitution—it was a practical and convenient way to cope with the issues of everyday life—but marriage did not necessarily solve all their problems nor meet all their needs, so they continued in prostitution. Susan Striker worked as a streetwalker for six months before meeting and marrying her husband, a barber. He died less than a year later. In telling about her married life, Striker voiced no complaints about her husband but noted that during their year of marriage she had occasionally stayed with other men. After becoming a widow, she continued working as a prostitute.[112] Catherine Cosine and Charles Ray worked together in service positions before getting married. A week after their wedding, Ray left for two months to be a sailor on one of the Charleston packets. Catherine, assuming that she would receive part of her husband's wages, quit her place of service and went home to her mother's. When she learned that no salary arrangements had been made for her, she requested help from her new father-in-law, who said he thought she should work and provide for herself. Consequently, Catherine started going in the company of "careless girls" to earn some income until her husband returned.[113] Prostitute Cecelia Smith, at her mother's urging, married James Hentwish, a printer. They lived together about three months, and during that time Cecelia occasionally went to prostitution houses. According to her case history at the House of Refuge, Cecelia contacted a venereal disease so decided she could not stay with her husband. She did not view her disease as an impediment to prostitution, however, and continued in the profession. A few months later Hentwish saw his wife "and told her if she would return with him he would support her decently—and they might live very comfortably." According to the Refuge record, Cecelia refused because she still had "her bad disorder hanging on . . . she fear'd to accept his offer." For Refuge matrons, fear of contaminating one's husband was a logical explanation for choosing prostitution over marriage, which may have been true in this case, but it is also possible that Cecelia's disease was used as an excuse for leaving her husband and continuing in a profession she had never given up anyway.[114]

Sometimes husbands accepted the fact that their wives were practicing prostitutes at the time of their marriage, but had difficulty living with their involvement in the profession after marriage. In 1848, James Becket married Frances O'Kille, keeper of a well-known brothel at 55 Leonard Street, "considered to be one of the *bon ton* palaces of that class." For several months the couple lived "harmoniously and might have still if the green-eyed monster hadn't appeared to Mr. Becket." Becket "enforced his legal rights" and threw out all "seventeen elegantly attired females." Under legal advice, he then began taking an inventory of stock in the house. This action infuriated O'Kille, who summoned her lawyer. "Maintaining jurisdiction of his own castle," Becket physically forced the lawyer out of the house, an act which caused him to be the recipient of an assault and battery charge.[115]

A direct contrast to the O'Kille-Becket marriage was that of Jacob and Mary Browning in the 1860s. Jacob married Mary expecting she would "go out upon the street and solicit and allow men to have connection with her for money." When she refused, he beat her. Tiring of the beatings, Mary left the marriage and filed for divorce.[116]

Mary Browning ended her marriage by obtaining a legal divorce, but many prostitutes do not appear to have bothered with court procedures when they wished to escape a marriage. "Separation" tended to be the method of divorce used most often by prostitutes, just as it was by the nineteenth-century working class. Many times a woman was abandoned, as was Rosina Townsend, but often it was the prostitute who left, and the lack of legal procedures would become important only if one of the parties wished to remarry rather than cohabit or if a husband were to lay claim to her property later on.[117]

In many cases where prostitutes were married, both parties looked upon the marital union as a business arrangement as well as a marriage. In both the O'Kille-Becket marriage and that of Jacob and Mary Browning, difficulties arose because one of the two partners appeared more interested in the business association than the conjugal union. O'Kille was running a large, successful brothel when she married Becket and took him on as a partner, and she had no intention of giving up her career and commercial enterprise to please her spouse. Jacob Browning, on the other hand, viewed the marriage contract as a business contract, and wife Mary was failing to use her earning capabilities for their mutual benefit. In many other cases, however, prostitutes entered into marriage, common law relationships, or other living arrangements with men because the couples found their associations—which were based on the woman's prostitution business—to be economically beneficial to them both. The relationship was a practical arrangement for dealing with the issues of everyday life, and it might or might not include mutual affection. Melinda Hoag took on Alexander Hoag's name, and they lived together but were not married. He characterized the relationship as one in which she "kept house for him by the month," even though the more important aspect of their relationship was their business association as panel thieves. As a prostitute, she lured customers; as a thief, he robbed them.[118] Mary and Frank Berry ran their brothel together—she managed the arrangements between customers and the prostitutes, and he oversaw gambling, drinking, and, according to some, a little customer theft. When Susan Shannon was charged with keeping a disorderly house, her co-defendant in the case was John Taylor. Shannon described Taylor as the man from whom she hired the house, paying him $25 per week for the house and furniture. She further noted that he lived in the house with her and five other prostitutes and that he did the marketing for the house but did not pay board because he was her friend. One of the other prostitutes in the house referred to Shannon as "Susan Taylor," and another stated that John Taylor "lived with" Shannon, insinuating that Shannon and Taylor probably had a relationship closer than that of co-residents. Both of these women pointed out, however, that Shannon paid rent to Taylor while he did the marketing for the house, a clear division of labor and responsibilities in the partnership. Joseph Farryall and his wife, Phebe West, operated a brothel together; he recruited their inmates on trips to New England, she served as madam of the house, and together they took care of brothel management. Mrs. Jackson and Cyrenus Stevens also ran a similar establishment at 87 Mercer Street. A number of German couples, such as Louisa and Charles Kanth and Catherine and Shay Hoffman, ran prostitution house/saloons "on the German order," which meant that he served as saloon-keeper/bartender, and she oversaw the prostitution business.[119]

With such business arrangements, the economic nature of a prostitute's involvement with a male associate is clear because the prostitute and her husband, lover, or friend were co-workers—they shared responsibilities in a joint economic endeavor. There were numerous other males in the community, however, who were less intimately related to the business operations of prostitution but whose economic well-being depended in some part on the profits made in illicit sex. Some people claimed that the police benefited from prostitution. The *Tribune* noted in 1844 that several police officers had homes in brothels, and, in exchange for lodging, they allowed the establishments to function free of official harassment, a domestically related form of payoff. One former policeman was even said to have left his wife and family for a prostitute, with whom he managed a prostitution establishment on Mercer Street for many years before moving to Long Island. As noted earlier, William Applegate worked with Adeline Miller publishing pornographic material for customers until they got into a legal dispute about the business. [120] And finally, less visible but more frequently found among male business associates, or the profiteers of prostitution, were landlords who leased the brothel properties. Many men, such as John Delaplaine, John Livingston, and James Ridgeway, not only earned a substantial income but became wealthy from the profits earned in real estate that housed illicit sex businesses. [121] A few court cases suggest some landlords may have been ignorant of the nature of their lessees' businesses but, in a community such as New York where prostitution was openly practiced and tolerated, most probably knew what was going on and accepted it, in effect becoming "silent" business associates of the prostitutes. In most cases landlords probably had little personal contact with the women who rented from them, since the relationship was based primarily on an economic exchange, but it is also possible that some were clients or exploited the inhabitants personally by asking for sexual intimacies as well as rents.

Because prostitutes spent most of their working lives surrounded by men, male relationships were an important part of their private as well as public lives. A prostitute's interactions with men spanned the range of possible relationships from casual associations to intimate unions. Some relationships were structured and well-defined, while others were more fluid, with men having overlapping identifications and functions. A lover could be a prostitute's customer or her landlord, and a spouse could be her protector and/or business associate. Often male relationships were exploitative and adversarial, but commonly they were congenial or mutually beneficial.

9

"As a Friend and Sister"

Relationships with Women

When prostitute Clara Hazard began a letter to Helen Jewett by saying she was writing "as a friend and sister," she gave an indication of the warm relationships that often existed between prostitutes. Several of Hazard's letters, as well as information from other prostitutes' records, reveal that close but complex relationships often characterized prostitutes' friendships. This evidence contrasts with the descriptions of prostitutes' associations frequently found in nineteenth-century literature. Contemporaries' superficial appraisals of prostitutes' female peer relationships resulted in the creation of two distinct stereotypes: a "negative" image that characterized such associations as fraught with jealousy, rivalry, and hatred, and a "sympathetic-idealized" image that assumed a scenario in which prostitutes were believed to bond with one another in opposition to men and respectable society.

According to the negative stereotype, prostitutes' need for customers led to cutthroat competition, and their jealousies over their lovers often led to feuds and even violence. Supposedly, female adversarial relationships were especially noticeable between madams and the prostitutes in their brothels, whom the madams tried to exploit. Because of the degradation inherent in their occupation, prostitutes lost the normal womanly feelings of tenderness, compassion, and love and thus seldom were good women who would care for the sick or love children. This lack of womanly feelings also was the reason many sought the downfall and destruction of fellow females by trying to lure them into the profession. [1]

In contrast, the sympathetic-idealized scenario presented the prostitutes' natural adversaries as predatory men. Although non-prostitute women also had to deal with male predation and discrimination, respectable women were unable to have mutual friendships with prostitutes. Thus, prostitutes were bound to each other by their opposition to customers and their social separation from other women. They demonstrated mutual loyalty in several ways, such as offering assistance if another prostitute's customer became abusive and adhering to a common code that governed their conduct in relation to each other's lovers. Because prostitutes understood the extreme devotion one felt for a lover, there was a mutual understanding that one should not get involved with another prostitute's man, and, if one knew a lover was being unfaithful, one should tell her fellow prostitute. Furthermore, since prostitutes understood how difficult "the life" could be, they often displayed "hearts of gold," giving even their last cent to help an unfortunate sister in great need. Finally, a life of exploitation enhanced some womanly feelings, causing prostitutes to become especially compassionate nurses to sick friends and nurturing caretakers of children. [2]

The persistence of both of these images suggests that each stereotype was rooted in an element of truth. Some professional competition existed between prostitutes: clients were money. A prostitute always hoped to attract new customers to become part of her regular clientele, and she carefully guarded those clients she already had. Incidents of violence between prostitutes, reported in the press and in court documents, indicate that some antagonisms and jealousies were very real. The third tier of the theater, where prostitutes congregated in large numbers, was often the scene of such feuds; the *New Era*, for example, reported that Lydia Wilson, an "old, well-known prostitute," and Mary Barton, newly arrived from Philadelphia, were arrested in the third tier of the Park Theatre for "kicking up a rumpus" when they fought over who was the prettiest, who could drink the most champagne and walk a crack, and who had the handsomest and most agreeable male friend. Wilson reportedly called Barton names and "drew a dirk" on her, seriously cutting Barton's cheek. In another incident, a prostitute named Maria Tracey brought vitriol into the Bowery Theatre and threw it on two other prostitutes, allegedly because Tracey was jealous of their good looks and hoped to spoil their faces. Fortunately, she damaged only their clothes. According to the *Sun*, two black prostitutes, Maria Mitchell and Adeliza Coin, got into a fight in the gallery of the Park Theatre over "who had the blackest complexion and who was the boss of the Five Points." Both were arrested; Coin was sent to prison, but Mitchell was given leniency because she was known to the magistrates for having adopted an "unprotected babe." The saloon of the Park Theatre also was the site of an attack by Matilda Phillips on Frances Mills. Phillips became drunk and "split open the head of Mills."[3] Although the precipitator of much disorder and violence among prostitutes was drunkenness, most of their quarrels were rooted in smoldering frustrations, jealousies, and antagonisms.

Another common scene of conflict was the brothel or prostitution boarding house, not only because of problems in living arrangements or the strains of forced intimacy but also because those in closest proximity were vulnerable to displaced anger generated by frustrations a prostitute might feel about her life in general. Prostitute Mary Fowler was arrested for biting off the ear of Sarah Ann Cooper while both were working at the brothel of Mrs. Powell in Elizabeth Street. Cooper was a servant who had angered Fowler by not giving her a "properly cooked breakfast." The *Sun* reported no cause for an attack by Sarah Hall on Mary Ann Foster in their brothel at 28 Anthony. Hall was sent to prison for giving Foster a "considerable gash in the region of the abdomen with a table knife." Ann Wilson was arrested for an assault on Mary Kelly, a coworker in her house. Wilson attacked Kelly, beating her with an iron griddle, tearing her hair, and cutting her hand to the bone. Wilson claimed she was acting in self-defense because Kelly first had hit her several times over the head with a poker and also had pulled her hair. The judge believed Kelly, and Wilson was committed to prison.[4]

One of the most vicious examples of female violence was the killing of prostitute Mary Drake by her madam, Catherine Hoffman. Drake, known as a very intemperate woman, boarded with Hoffman and her husband Shay. On a May evening in 1839, Drake was sitting on the step at the door of the Hoffmans' bar/brothel. A young man stopped and propositioned Drake, who refused his offer, so he went away. Infuriated, Catherine Hoffman seized Drake by the hair, slapped her face, and dragged her into the barroom. Hoffman then threw Drake down, hitting her head against the door, beating and kicking her violently, and desisting only when her husband cried out, "Catherine, you have given that girl enough," and pulled her away from Drake. Drake lay in bed at a neighboring saloon for several days "in a stupid state" before dying. Hoffman was convicted of manslaughter.[5] Although few conflicts between madams and prostitutes reached this degree of violence, the potential for discord was so built into a relationship where one's success depended on the exploitation of another that clashes were bound to occur. Aggressive reactions were not limited to the brothel keepers alone, however. Prostitute Mary Barton, perhaps angry over a perceived mistreatment by Mrs. West, brothel keeper at 3 Franklin Street, went to West's house while West was ill and "fell upon and beat her severely." West lodged a complaint at the police office, obtained a warrant, and was escorted home by two police officers. While West was at the police office, Barton had returned to the brothel with a prostitute-friend, Mary Redstone, and together they had abused and beat other inmates before stoning and throwing mud at the house. Barton and Redstone were arrested and sent to prison.[6]

Since police records, court reports, and newspaper stories tend to emphasize the conflicts and problems that characterized prostitutes' associations with each other, these sources offer a distorted view of the role of female peer relationships in a prostitute's life. Day-to-day events involving compatibility and congeniality are, as a rule, not newsworthy stories, but they present a more complete picture of the prostitute's life and the female friends that were such an important part of her daily existence.

A female support network was as essential to the prostitute's life as it was to other nineteenth-century women's lives, and certain structural aspects of prostitution—living and working together—facilitated close female friendships. Prostitutes shared living quarters and leisure activities, visited each other, exchanged gifts and small favors, corresponded with each other, fought and reconciled, protected and nursed one other, and died together.[7] At a minimum, these interventions in each other's lives created cooperative relationships; at best, they led to intimate friendships built on genuine affection and mutual concern, and often reinforced by the family rejection experienced by many prostitutes. Prostitutes turned to one another for the emotional support and comfort they might otherwise have found at home, and to counteract feelings of isolation from the respectable community or demonstrations of hostility sometimes experienced in customer relationships. Thus, prostitutes assumed an emotional centrality in each other's lives, which often led to deep, mutual friendships characterized by strong female bonding and a special sense of solidarity.

Several letters found in the Jewett correspondence vividly illustrate the important role female friendships played in the lives of prostitutes. Clara Hazard appears to have been one of Jewett's closest friends. Three letters to Jewett from "Friend Clara" were written after Hazard left New York and returned to her home town of Philadelphia; three others are mentioned in the police inventory but were never published. Clara also is mentioned in three letters between Jewett and Frank Rivers.

Hazard wrote in language demonstrating obvious affection for Jewett, whom she called her "esteemed friend" and even, as noted earlier, her "sister." Hazard wrote: "As a friend and sister I embrace this time to write you a few lines."[8] Her letters close with expressions of affection such as, "I remain, yours affectionately until death, Clara." The nostalgia Hazard felt in being separated from her friend was indicated in her description of things that reminded her of Jewett: "I tell my fortune with the cards, when I think of you, and hope you do of me."[9] The intimacy of the friendship is suggested by the personal nature of the details Hazard chose to share with Jewett, including the ups and downs of her love life, the minutia of everyday life, and her innermost feelings about her relationship with her lover.

In Hazard's letters one sees evidence of the many kinds of services and small favors performed by prostitutes for each other, which cemented their friendships. Before moving from New York, Hazard apparently was sick and was nursed back to health by Jewett. On her arrival in Philadelphia, and later in Baltimore, Hazard gladly executed a series of errands for Jewett and other New York friends.

I called on the lady you requested me to [in Baltimore], and left the small package with her sister, as she was not in. . . . I left JoAnn in Philadelphia and she was well. Little Mary called on her landlady and left $40 the day before JoAnn arrived in Philadelphia. . . . Tell Mr. Berry I called on Catherine to-day. She sent the cape by Hannah Blisset.[10]

In another letter she reported, "Tell Josephine as soon as Mrs. Smith gets an opportunity to send the cloak safe, she will do so."[11]

Hazard's letters also give a clear indication of the existence of a close friendship network among prostitutes within a city, such as New York, as well as between one city's prostitutes and those who worked in other major cities of the East Coast, such as Philadelphia, Baltimore, Washington, and Boston. Jewett made her first trip to visit friends in Philadelphia in late June 1835 and apparently returned there in late July or early August. She discussed a third trip to Philadelphia in the fall (which she may or may not have taken) and then made her final trip in mid-December 1835. Jewett wrote home from her first trip that Clara had given her "a warm reception," and she added that "there is much pleasure in going where people are glad to see you."[12] Jewett was not alone in taking trips to visit friends in other cities. Letters mention other prostitutes making short visits to East Coast cities to stay with friends, including some out-of-town prostitutes who traveled to New York to visit Jewett and other prostitute-friends in the network there. During Hazard's short trip to Baltimore, she made a call on Jewett's "lady friend" and also on "Catherine," who was acquainted with a number of New York prostitutes as well as with brothel owners Mr. and Mrs. Berry. Catherine sent a message that "she will be on to see you [Jewett] shortly, and sends her love to you and all other friends."[13] Hazard also mentioned that Catherine had just seen their mutual friend Hannah Blisset, who also was visiting in Baltimore but was on her way back to New York.[14]

The importance prostitutes placed on trips as a means of maintaining close contact is evident in repeated requests to one another for additional visits. Hazard mentions in her first letter: "I want much to see you, and will do so next week," and in her next letter she states: "I want to see you very much, and would be very glad if you would pay me a visit this week."[15] She also is eager that her correspondence be answered: "My dear H., be sure to write me as soon as you receive this, and let me know the news of your city."[16] Clara apologized to Jewett for an anticipated interruption in their correspondence while Clara was on vacation.[17]

Letters from Jewett's other friends confirm the existence of a strong network of friendships among prostitutes. Ann Farmer of Philadelphia, like Clara Hazard, was grateful to Jewett for nursing her through an illness: "I've almost recovered from my indisposition, perhaps I should have been quite well had you have [sic] been here to attend me with your kind nursing, which I shall never forget."[18] She also asked Jewett to extend words of appreciation to Mrs. Gallagher, a New York brothel keeper and friend of madams Mary Berry and Rosina Townsend:

. . . Dear Helen, I wish you to go to Mrs. Gallagher's, and tell her for me, I have not forgot her kindness to me while in New York. I hope she will not prevent my returning the compliment. I hope to see her this summer when I will have more time to devote to her ladyship; for she was truly attentive to me.[19]

Farmer followed this request with a few lines that revealed she felt a financial as well as emotional obligation to Mrs. Gallagher: "I am only sorry that disagreeable occurrence took place—losing her money. Tell her I have not forgot the handsome dress which she fairly won. I shall do myself the honor of paying it soon."[20]

Farmer ends her letter with an evocation of the warm feelings for Jewett held by the inhabitants of Farmer's brothel, suggesting the extent to which a sense of "family" existed in the brothel among the prostitutes, servants, and children.

The ladies are well, the fish are well, the servants are well, and we are all well. Your favorite, little Steve, says you must make haste and come on here and bring him a pair of trousers and some money. The family all join in sending their love to you, and I expect if old John, the hackman, knew I was writing to you, I presume he would send his love also.[21]

Farmer also sent Jewett greetings and messages from some of her male admirers in Philadelphia, indicating that Jewett had spent enough time there to know the circle of men who hung around Farmer's brothel, who were similar to the group that gravitated to Jewett in New York. Farmer further noted she was familiar with some of Jewett's closest male friends in New York, such as "Mr. Crockett," who was traveling in the West at that point.

Some of the most interesting letters received by Jewett were those from her brothel madam, Mary Berry. Although a brothel keeper and one of her prostitutes might be friends or fond of one another, the fact that the madam's economic well-being depended on her ability to exert some control over the prostitute in order to manage a business and earn a profit militated against a completely mutual tie. Thus, a friendship with a madam was complicated—as a "mother" and friend she might demonstrate genuine affection for her prostitutes, but her actions could always be interpreted as having ulterior motives designed to guard her economic interests.

On Jewett's trip to Philadelphia in December 1835, she sent a letter to Berry and received two letters in return. Much of what Berry wrote was about the members of their "brothel family," and it gives evidence of the close relationships that existed within their brothel-home. Mr. Berry was on a trip to Washington, and Mrs. Berry sent a message to him through Jewett because she thought he might visit in Philadelphia for a while.[22] The light-hearted manner in which Berry related the "escapades" and activities of Jewett's brothel friends reflects the congeniality that existed in the relationships of the brothel females:

I want to tell you a good joke. Hannah Blisset and Lady Elizabeth stole out last night and . . . got gloriously drunk. . . . Hannah was somewhat more sober than Lady E. . . . Hannah will be on to Philadelphia on Monday, so you will have some fun in plaguing her on the matter. Saucy Caroline and Elizabeth send their love to you. Elizabeth is going away to-day.[23]

Berry also noted that Jewett's presence was missed by brothel inhabitants and clients as well: "There has not been any of our folks to see us since you have been gone, only the Englishman. . . . You don't know how I long to see you. We are all quite lonesome without our Merry Nell."[24] In her second letter, Berry again illustrates that a warm companionship existed among the female friends of the brothel:

Hannah, Louisa and Caroline send their best love to you, all wish you to come home, particularly Hannah, for she has no one to dig round town with her.[25]

In this second letter, however, the cash nexus of the madam/prostitute relationship is much more evident. Berry was concerned with protecting her business, which apparently was suffering because of the absence of the brothel "favorite." Berry pointed out that some clients were so eager to see Jewett that they left the house on learning of her absence. Berry also asked Jewett for a loan.

. . . Dear Helen if you have got any more money than you know what to do with, I wish you would oblige me by sending me some, and I shall not forget you, for the times are very hard indeed.[26]

Her most important piece of information was the revelation that Jewett's lover, Frank Rivers, had come to the brothel to be with Jewett's friend, Hannah Blisset. Berry reported that Blisset's behavior had been beyond reproach: "She, in a very ladylike and candid manner, told him she would not, and rejected his offer with becoming dignity, so he went away."[27] If Berry's motive was to adhere to the "code" by telling a fellow-prostitute of the infidelity of her lover, she suffered for being the bearer of bad news. If her motive was to get Jewett back home so business would pick up, she made a terrible miscalculation. Jewett did return home immediately and broke off her relationship with Rivers, but she also had conflicts with Berry which strained that relationship and caused her to move to another brothel within a few weeks.

The importance of prostitutes' friendships is also evident in admissions records at the House of Refuge. These records verify that friendships were crucial both initially in bringing a woman into the profession and as companionship after a woman had become a prostitute. Young girls started streetwalking together, shared rooms with each other, entered a brothel together, and were brought to the Refuge together. Maria Williams and Keziah Anne Kidd, both daughters of working-class parents, had another girlfriend who first took them "walking in Broadway for company" to find men who would escort them to assignation houses. Williams and Kidd also accompanied each other to the third tier of the Bowery Theatre. For several months the girls lived at home while practicing prostitution in the evenings but then decided to move in together at Mrs. Langdon's prostitution house on Greene Street. They had been there only a short time before their parents discovered their whereabouts and had them arrested and sent to the Refuge. Another set of friends, Mary Ann Brewer and the Utter sisters, also were sent to the Refuge together. All three had worked and lived with each other for several months in Williamsburgh, often coming into the city together on their nights off and once getting arrested together for harassing a woman and child, the incident which led to their being sent to the Refuge. Brewer and the older Utter sister had both been casual prostitutes before they were admitted, but presumably twelve-year-old Ann Jeanette had not. After a year at the Refuge, each girl was either indentured or sent to the care of friends, positions which lasted only a brief period. At roughly the same time, all three ran away from their new homes and returned to New York, where they again went on the town.[28]

Census records also reinforce the assumption that friendships existed and were important to women who lived in prostitution boarding houses or in brothels. Since censuses contain no narrative histories, information is more speculative, but it is still suggestive of supportive friendships. Carry Belmont and Ellen Stevens were in Emma Clifton's house in 1855, and both had come to the residence from Massachusetts three months before. Of the names recorded in Jane Winslow's house, three besides Winslow were in the house in both the 1850 and 1855 censuses. If these women remained together for at least five years, and maybe more, they probably got along together well enough to consider each other friends. The same was probably true of the women in Maria Adams's house. Adams was listed as the head of household at 55 Leonard in both 1850 and 1855. A Miss Stiles also is listed as a resident in both censuses, and in an 1853 brothel directory, R. Stiles is listed as the "keeper" of Adams's house at 55 Leonard. The house also lists a Miss LeCount from Canada in 1850 and a Miss LeCompt from Canada in 1855, possibly the same person, who may have found the company and living situation pleasant enough to remain a number of years with Adams and Stiles. Another situation indicating possible friendships is that of Margaret Brown, who owned and was a resident of a brothel run by Frances Barton at 35 Mercer. Both Brown and Barton had been residents of New York for twenty years. By 1859, Brown still owned the house, but Mary Clinton, who was a resident in the house in 1850, was listed in a brothel directory as manager of the house.[29]

Other indications of the existence of friendships among prostitutes were the leisure activities enjoyed by these women. Although "walking out" and attending the theater were methods of attracting clients, they also were important leisure events enjoyed by prostitutes together. Prostitutes frequently strolled in company with each other in both the afternoon and evening, and, as Madam Berry wrote, her boarder Hannah was wishing Jewett would return home soon because she had "no one to dig around town with her." The theater also might be attended several times a week and usually was visited with other prostitutes. One contemporary noted that the "demi-monde" were very fond of picnics and balls, and often the profession predominated at these events. He added that occasionally "a number of the cyprians of the city and their friends go on a pic-nic by themselves, . . . the whole company is fallen."[30] He made special note of the fact that male companions were

26. TWO PROSTITUTES ON AN OUTING TO THE PARK.   Prostitutes enjoyed each other's company and friendship. Those with sufficient economic resources accompanied one another on carriage rides in the park, evenings at the theater, and outings to the country. (Courtesy of the New-York Historical Society, New York City)

not necessary for prostitutes to enjoy an excursion from the city—prostitutes had "ways of enjoying themselves alone":

A number of them have formed themselves into a boat club, and every summer enjoy the sport of rowing on a little river in New Jersey, away from the vulgar gaze. They have a tasty uniform, fashioned so as to fully display their graceful and beautiful forms, and are said to be expert oarswomen.[31]

Although it appears that most of a prostitute's friends were within the profession, there is evidence that prostitutes had some female friendships outside the profession as well. Hazard's and Jewett's friend Catherine, who was visiting in Baltimore, possibly was visiting non-prostitute friends because Hazard reports: "She says she is living *virtuously* with her friends" (italics mine). Since Hazard "called on her," however, it does not appear that she was making a special effort to hide her other life.[32]

Helen Jewett also corresponded with a Philadelphia woman named Emily who seemed to be a friend from outside the profession, perhaps from the days before Jewett entered prostitution. In one letter she commented to Jewett: "Helen, I feel for your situation, I regret that you have fallen," and she chastised Jewett: "if you have some bad qualities, I am sensible you have many redeeming ones, and I look forward to the day when you may set more value on them. . . . You [are] unkind to none but yourself."[33]

Emily's two letters to Jewett are filled with intimate feelings of sorrow and grief over the loss of her infant son, feelings she wished to share: "I have lost my dear, dear baby. . . . I thought he was only lent to me, and now I know it, for he was an angel. Helen, his little cherub face is ever before me. I cannot write."[34] In Emily's first letter, she commented on Jewett's having recently sent her money, a gesture which did not seem to surprise her. Emily acknowledged that she was one who had "seen much trouble." From her second letter Jewett learned that their relationship, like some of her male friendships, had its limits: apparently, Jewett needed a character reference or a court alibi, and the friendship stopped short of Emily's "coupling her name" with that of Jewett before a public forum.

. . . Helen, you are aware that I would oblige you at almost any risk, *but that of losing my character,* which I do not estimate lightly, and I trust your sense of honor is not so far lost, that you would couple my name with yours in a court of justice, where my motives for obliging you could not be appreciated. I do not wish to wound your feelings; my Heavenly Father knows I would not do so. . . . You say that you have been in the police office. . . . I believe you to be innocent of any crime that would bring you there, and I'm sure the world would think so too, if they knew you were unkind to none but yourself. . . . If I can honorably assist you in any difficulty, [I] will do so.[35]

In spite of her refusal, Emily ended her letter by encouraging her friend both to confide in her and solicit her aid: "When you write, keep nothing back. Write soon and let me know how I can assist you."

Even though Emily felt she could not be completely supportive of her prostitute friend, there are many examples of prostitutes demonstrating strong loyalty for their colleagues as well as receiving it from them. Samuel Prime commented on an incident that occurred when a watchman was dragging a prostitute to the police station from one of the "dens of vice" in lower Manhattan. Another woman followed close behind, declaring she would go with her, even though a man was holding on to the second woman, trying to pull her back. Prime noted:

There was devotion in the woman who would follow her friend to the prison; and she did follow her, in spite of the force and entreaties of her husband. In this extremity of vice there was such friendship as we rarely meet.[36]

Prostitutes also came to one another's rescue when situations appeared dangerous. Catherine Erriott picked up William Branton while she was streetwalking on Chatham Street. She took him home, and in the middle of the night a scuffle started between them. Branton soon found himself in a "pitched battle with seven to eight female demons," Erriott's prostitute friends.[37]

Mary Louisa Clark, who was probably both a seamstress and a prostitute, received support from her friend, Sarah Edmonds, when Edmonds testified on her behalf as a character witness before a court. Clark was arrested along with two other women for operating houses of prostitution at 3, 5, and 7 White Street, addresses long known as brothel locations. On being ordered out, one woman vacated immediately but the others, Clark and Mary Ann Demarest, "defied the law" and stayed. The neighbors then took the case to court and testified that "persons were passing to and fro from these houses frequently, particularly at night when a free intercourse has been observed." The neighbors went on to say that

it may be attempted to prove that Mrs. Clark, No. 3 White St. keeps an establishment for Ladies Dressmaking—a sign appears on one of the window shutters "French Dress Making." No indications of a respectable establishment of this kind have appeared . . . respectable females do not visit the House and no persons are seen going to or from it with bundles or parcels as is usual at Dress Makers.[38]

The neighbors also pointed out that at each step in the complaint and court process, pictures of fashionable ladies' dresses had been placed in Clark's windows for a couple of days and then removed.

At the court hearing, Demarest admitted her guilt, but Clark denied hers and brought in Sarah Edmonds as a character witness. In her testimony, Edmonds, wife of George Edmonds, said that she met Clark through another acquaintance who had "learned the mantua making trade" with Clark. Edmonds said Clark was the widow of a respectable man and was now maintaining herself by dressmaking, a profession "at which she labors with a great deal of industry." Edmonds stated that she usually walked past the house daily and had visited Clark frequently, both in the day and night, and the house was not a house of ill fame but was perfectly proper.

Despite the testimony of friend Edmonds, the Court believed the neighbors, and Clark was convicted of operating a disorderly house. Clark may have been using the dressmaking alibi as a subterfuge, but it is also possible she considered herself (as did Sarah Edmonds) a dressmaker by trade who worked at sewing and practiced prostitution, if at all, for supplementary income. [39]

At times prostitutes may not have fully appreciated the loyalty and support of their friends. The friends of Eliza Hall, concerned about her future, went to the police and requested that the authorities arrest her and remove her from a house of prostitution. Hall was arrested and committed to jail in hopes she would consider reforming. [40]

Because attitudes hostile to a prostitute's way of life, such as those exhibited by Hall's friends, made friendships with women outside the profession relatively difficult to sustain, most full-time prostitutes probably had few "straight" friends. Current studies show that breaking with straight friends is considered by those in the trade to be a crucial step in the socialization into prostitution. [41] For occasional and part-time prostitutes, however, a woman's friends probably did not change much when she began to practice prostitution, since friends themselves may have experienced the same pressures, i.e., economic, familial, social, that led to occasional prostitution.

Whether nineteenth-century female friendships among prostitutes also included lesbian relationships is not known. Very little is recorded about homosexual relationships at all, male or female, so there were either few relationships of this nature or they were literally unmentionable. The *Sun* printed one story about Jane (alias James) Walker, a "man woman," who was not associated with prostitution. Walker was arrested in the street drunk, in male attire. She told the authorities she was born in Scotland and orphaned before age twelve. While in Scotland, she began wearing male attire, a practice she said was common in that country. She also took the name George Moore Wilson and was hired as a male in a cotton factory. Walker said she had "entered a bonafide courtship" with the factory superintendent's daughter and married her in a Scottish church. The couple soon after left for the United States, and en route to America Walker's wife discovered she had married a woman, "but it didn't appear to upset her and they continued to live and labor together in harmony and love." The wife, described by the paper as "a rather hard visaged woman of thirty or thirty-five years of age . . . [with] a rather fiery temper," corroborated the story. An indication that such relationships were infrequent is the *Sun*'s comment that the couple had "the most singular of all connubial ties with which we were ever acquainted."[42]

Another story covered by the *Sun* which did have some connection to prostitution was that of a black New Yorker, Peter Sewally, alias Mary Jones, alias Eliza Smith. "Miss Jones" was arrested by police for stealing a wallet and money from Robert Haslem. Haslem met Jones walking in Bleeker Street and was taken to a nearby alley, where Jones and Haslem "caressed and conversed." After parting, Haslem discovered the theft and went to the police, and Jones was arrested. While officers were searching the prisoner for the wallet they discovered that "Miss Jones" was really a man, Peter Sewally.

In court, when questioned about why he had dressed as a woman, Sewally replied:

I have been in the practice of waiting upon Girls of ill fame and made up the Beds and received the Company at the door and received the money for the Rooms and etc. and they induced me to dress in women's clothes, saying I looked so much better in them and I have always attended parties among the people of my own colour dressed in this way—and in New Orleans I always dressed in this way.[43]

Sewally was found guilty of grand larceny and was sentenced to the state prison for three years.[44] In reporting the case, the *Sun* noted that Sewally frequently prowled the streets in the vicinity of the Five Points in order to lure men into dens of prostitution, where he picked their pockets. It is possible Sewally's disguise did not fool all of his customers, some of whom may have knowingly accepted his caresses, even if they were unsuspecting of the theft of their wallets.[45]

Although no statutes outlawed lesbian relationships, females were subject to arrest for wearing male attire.[46] The law could have been directed against a woman's "misrepresenting" herself, but it also may have been a statement of public sexual boundaries. On numerous occasions women were arrested on the streets for masquerading in men's clothing. In one case, a young woman was arrested in an "impure neighborhood" where she had visited a cigar store and a soda fountain in male disguise, and the court released her on promise she would "reform her morals in the future." Another woman claimed she dressed as a man in order to spy on her unsuspecting boyfriend. Most, however, said they dressed as men "on a lark" so they could roam the streets and night spots—the only way they could be out without being arrested as prostitutes.[47]

The stories of Walker and Sewally hint that some homosexuality did exist in nineteenth-century New York, but these relationships probably were rare or very well hidden. Whether lesbian relationships were a part of nineteenth-century prostitution is even more of a mystery. Marion Goldman has pursued the same question for late-nineteenth-century Western prostitutes, and her conclusion applies to New York as well:

The question of whether . . . prostitutes had genital or other physical contact with one another is as unimportant as it is unanswerable. Twentieth-century conceptions which absolutely dichotomize platonic and romantic love distort the rich emotional relationships which occurred between many nineteenth-century women. . . . Some . . . prostitutes created their own social worlds of love and mutuality, although the scope of those worlds remained and remain private matters for the friends who shared them.[48]

Perhaps some of the closest of a prostitute's friends were her sisters and cousins. Census records are among the sources attesting to the fact that many female family relationships remained intact while a woman practiced prostitution. However, since the only relationships recorded by census takers were relationships to heads of households, kinship is not necessarily noted. In many cases in which surnames in a household are the same, birthplaces are identical also, but different places of birth do not preclude the possibility that prostitutes with the same name could be sisters. Moreover, sisters could be together in a brothel but have different names, as in the case of Emma Soule and Grace Walton, in which case kinship would only be known if noted by the census taker. Like surnames could suggest that the women were cousins, aunt and niece, or even sisters-in-law. It is also possible that since many prostitutes changed their names, the names in a household are coincidentally the same, although a prostitute creating a new identity for herself probably would make some effort to be different from other women in a brothel. The following related names were found in the 1850 and 1855 censuses:

Names of Prostitutes (ages)	Brothel Keeper
1850 CENSUS	
Virginia Norwood (22)	Emma Andrews
Harriett Norwood (19)	
Louisa Norwood (17)	
Susan Wells (24)	
Jane Wells (23)	
Alvina Wallace (24)	Mary Howard
Adele Wallace (22)	
Susan Stewart (23)	Maria Adams
Josephine Stewart (18)	
Amanda Cooper (19)	Charlotte Brown
Ellen Cooper (17)	
Kate Rowe (25)	Kate Rowe
Harriet Rowe (22)	
Victoria Clark (23)	Hannah Russell
Charlotte Clark (18)	
Emma Soule (25)	Emma Soule
Grace Walton, sister (20)	
Ann Malloy (36)*	Ann Malloy
Mary Malloy (50)	
1855 CENSUS	
Jane Winslow (29+)	Jane Winslow
Frances Winslow (31)	
Linda Rosella (20)	Clara Godwin
Ida Rosella (19)	

Elizabeth Rome (22)	Nancy Phillips
Louisa Rome (20)	
Georgiana Wood (23)	Charlotte Brown
Fany Wood (20)	
Clara Philips (28)	Maria Adams
Emma Philips (21)	
Anna McReady (38)*	Mary Miller
Sophia McReady (21)	

*Because of the fourteen-year age span of the Malloys and the seventeen-year age span of the McReadys, each set could be mother and daughter instead of sisters or other kin. One finds in comparing censuses, however, that recorded ages are very inexact—for example, names may be repeated in subsequent censuses, but the recorded ages may not always reflect the number of years between censuses.

In 1855 Grace Walton was still living with her sister Emma Soule, but by this time Harriet Rowe was no longer in Kate Rowe's house because she had become the head of her own establishment. Also, Mary Malloy is no longer listed in Ann Malloy's brothel.

Tax records support census data in testifying to the existence of siblings and female kin working together in prostitution. In the 1848 tax record, Elizabeth Lewis and Maria (also Mary or Maggie) Lewis are listed together at 73 Grand, and then for the next ten years one or the other is listed as head of a prostitution house at 6 Thompson.[49] The House of Refuge recorded several sets of sisters admitted for prostitution: Ann and Catherine Butler, Christina and Caroline Hoyt, Margaret and Sarah Lyon, Eliza and Catherine Faulkner, Phebe and Eliza Seigler, and the previously mentioned Ann Jeanette and Mary Ann Utter. Julia Decker, Eliza Van Tassle, Amelia Goldsmith, and Jane Anderson were each said to have practiced prostitution with a sister, though the sisters were not admitted, most likely because they were over eighteen.[50]

That sisters or cousins might remain in close contact with each other in prostitution was more understandable to many in the nineteenth century than that parents would "accept" a daughter's moral transgressions by continuing to associate with her while she was a prostitute. Newspapers like the *Advocate of Moral Reform* reported as fact, though somber fact, that families commonly disowned daughters who had affairs, not to mention those who "fully went on the town." When parents were forgiving, it usually was assumed that the daughter repented and returned home to a moral life.[51] That a parent might accept a daughter's ongoing life of prostitution was incomprehensible to observers. The *Advocate* expressed great dismay over the response of the parents of one young prostitute who were confronted with their daughter's improbity. The Moral Reform Society's visiting committee had been to see a family on Twenty-third Street who had two daughters, eighteen and sixteen. Later, one of the daughters was observed entering a "house of ill fame," and the reformers went immediately and informed the parents. The *Advocate* reported that "the father, who was a foreigner, manifested a cold indifference, and said, 'Oh, lady, I no care for that.'"[52] Another case of parents who accepted and continued associating with a prostitute-daughter is that of Clara Hazard. Hazard noted in a letter to Jewett that: "[I] walk out but very seldom, and when I do, it is only to my mother's."[53] A third example is that noted at the beginning of Chapter 8 of a Mrs. Cornell, who, while managing the operations of a prostitution establishment at the corner of Grand and Mercer streets, "a very private house" attached to a saloon, was said to be "liv[ing] at home with her folks, but attend[ing] to business here in the evenings."[54]

Even more offensive to reformers than parents who passively accepted a daughter's prostitution were parents who actually assisted her in the profession or profited from her illicit sex. This offense Sanger termed a "social crime."[55] To reiterate a few examples: Mary Berry was said to have learned the prostitution profession from her mother, and Charlotte Willis's mother managed the brothel where Charlotte worked as a prostitute. Ann and Catherine Butler were the daughters of a "low, drunken" prostitute who was reported by neighbors to have "traded the girls' sex for rum." Mary Anthony was brought up by prostitute Patience Berger, who claimed to be her guardian, but was believed by some people to be her mother. Although Berger sent her "daughter" away to boarding school for several years, Anthony returned home to the brothel and began a career in prostitution that was intermittent over the next decade.[56]

There are other cases involving parents who were not in the prostitution business themselves but who were not bothered by their daughters' associations with prostitution; in fact, many such parents actually played a role in exposing the daughters to the profession. After observing close-at-hand the life of prostitution, the daughters accepted illicit sex as a practical or familiar way to make money. Margaret Ann Bush was placed by her mother in the brothel of Mrs. Robins at 49 Beaver Street so she could learn to work as a domestic. Jane Leve, a child of Jewish parents, was left at her mother's death with Mrs. Van Allen, keeper of a brothel. Leve helped dress the prostitutes in the brothel and then began sleeping with Van Allen's son before she was brought to the House of Refuge by the police. In the case of Lydia Ann Hawhurst, whose parents seemed not to care about her welfare, it was the police authorities themselves who bound her as a child-keeper to boatman William Harrington and his wife, who kept a bawdy house in Center Street.[57]

Although parents might wish that their daughters were in occupations other than prostitution, the above data on families' relationships with their prostitute daughters suggests that the practice of prostitution was not as alienating a profession as nineteenth-century moral reformers would have one believe. The line separating respectable from disrespectable behavior was much clearer for the middle class than for the laboring class. Working families, like middle-class families, understood differences between moral and immoral actions, but within their milieu, cultural and ethical norms were less rigidly fixed. Some allowance was made for the exigencies of a present situation and the need for choices among limited and unappealing options. A daughter's prostitution may have been instrumental in maintaining a family's economic well-being, in which case rejection was not likely to occur. Certainly, prostitution could be an isolating and difficult occupation for many reasons, but alienation from and lack of emotional support by one's family was not always involved.

A prostitute's relationship with her parental family was often important to her and could be demanding, but the family connection that probably required the most from the prostitute in terms of responsibility and emotional involvement was her role as mother. Sanger's study clearly pointed out how frequently prostitutes assumed this role. Almost half of the interviewees had children—about three-fourths each of the widows and married women, and about 30 percent of the single women. Even though widows and married women had been in legal marital relationships at some point, a little over 40 percent of their children were illegitimate, and thus were children for whom the prostitutes assumed sole responsibility. Sanger also noted a high rate of mortality among prostitutes' children, an overall 62 percent, which was an indication of the difficult life faced by both children and mothers.[58] In spite of the many difficulties encountered as parental providers, however, prostitutes were not so different from other working women as they struggled and worried about how to care for their offspring.

The *Advocate of Moral Reform* noted that the fact of motherhood was one of the "excuses" prostitutes often stated for not leaving their wicked life: "I have no other way of getting a living—I keep my children at boarding schools, and colleges, from the money I receive from [prostitution]."[59] The *Advocate*'s editor also pointed out that prostitutes were "the last in the world to have their daughters follow their footsteps." Thus, by sending children away they could provide a better environment for them. Sanger found that one-third of the prostitute mothers he interviewed boarded their children away from home, and only 10 percent cared for their offspring at home. The remaining children, over 50 percent, presumably lived with relatives or were on their own.[60]

Boarding a child away from home did not solve all of a prostitute-mother's worries. Sarah Buchanan's mother obtained for her twelve-year-old daughter a position as a domestic but then brought Sarah back home when she was raped by her employer. After Susan Matilda Badger turned fourteen and began to mature, her mother, Mary Jane Roberts, placed her in the country to live with a family. When the family learned the profession of the mother, they refused to keep Susan any longer and sent her home. Roberts then resorted to a "public" boarding situation for Susan and "took her before a magistrate and sent [her to the House of Refuge] as a vagrant." And although Patience Berger sent her ward to boarding school for several years and relieved herself of the daily worries of parenting, the experience did not keep the girl out of prostitution.[61]

Many prostitutes lacked the means or the desire to board their children away from home. For a streetwalker with her own living quarters, child care probably was handled much as it would have been by a day worker—older children or relatives helped out, or the children roamed the neighborhood streets, playing and scavenging. For women who lived in brothels or prostitution boarding houses, offspring became part of the brothel family, working at small household tasks or, if too young to be domestically productive, playing with other prostitutes' or servants' children.

Several children who appear to be the offspring of prostitutes are listed in brothels and assignation houses in the censuses of 1850 and 1855.

Since censuses contain no material that elaborates on family histories or the dynamics of childrearing in the brothel, one must speculate on the nature of some relationships. Jane Lord had her four-year-old son John living with her in her assignation house in 1850. No husband is listed with Lord in either that census or the one in 1855, though city directories until 1855 list her husband, Jacob, a seaman, as a resident at the address. The 1855 census stated that Jane Lord was a widow, so it is unclear how much of a role the seaman father had in the family, if he had any at all. Also living as one of seven boarders in the Lord house in 1850 is a Rachel Brown, whose four-year-old daughter Sarah was with her, a probable companion for young John Lord. Elizabeth Darragh and her two sons, ages three and one, moved from Pennsylvania to the brothel of Anna Howell, who was also a native of Pennsylvania and possibly a kinswoman or former friend who offered single-parent Darragh a place to work and rear her children.[62]

In a number of the other brothels, it is clear that one of the prostitute boarders is a mother because a child and woman by the same name are listed together.[63] In some houses, such as those of Rebecca Weyman and Ellen Thompson, children are listed whose names match those of no one else in the brothel, making it impossible to identify their mothers. Perhaps the children were given the mothers' real names or the surnames of the fathers. In Jane Hill's establishment, one of the boarders was a mulatto prostitute named Rhoda Kelly, who had moved from Saratoga two years before and had a six-year-old daughter named Josephine Kelly with her. There is another mulatto child in the house named Anna Smith, who is the only Smith in the house. This child also had moved from Saratoga two years before, the same time as Kelly, so it is possible she was Kelly's daughter and was using her father's name, or she might have been a relative of Kelly, or of Hill, who also was a native of Saratoga. In Eleanor Barrett's house, there is an Ellen Van Fost, age eleven, and a Robert Van Fost, age two, and their surname is different from those of other prostitute boarders. The real estate tax record, however, shows that the property was owned by a "C. J. Vanvorst," possibly the children's father and also possibly Barrett's husband.[64]

Although a prostitute could oversee the rearing of children who remained with her, she could not prevent them from being exposed at some point in their lives to violence, alcohol, drugs, or unsavory company—dangers that might be, but were not necessarily, faced by children of other working parents. When rowdies attacked the brothel of Amanda Smith at 3 Franklin Street, they destroyed a very valuable piano and beat Smith on the head. The men then

wound up their inhumanity by attacking and beating her son, who was at the time crippled through being afflicted with the rheumatism, and whom they beat so violently that he was left on the floor nearly dead.[65]

Smith had the men arrested for assault. In another incident, the four-year-old daughter of prostitute Mary Bowen of 104 Church Street was sent by her mother with a dollar to get crackers at a local store. On the way home, the child was stopped by two older girls, who bullied her and took her money. Accustomed to filing charges against individuals who assaulted her or her brothel, Mrs. Bowen had both girls arrested. Police released them to the custody of their parents, who had to promise they would enforce proper discipline and see that no similar incidents happened again.[66]

Even if a prostitute's children avoided violence, they occasionally witnessed situations that were unsuitable for young children. Reporters for the *Advocate of Moral Reform* were appalled that a middle-aged madam allegedly had seventeen "awful deaths" of prostitutes in her house on Leonard Street in her twelve years in the profession. Compounding the evil was the fact that in addition to the eleven boarding prostitutes in the establishment were two of the madam's own daughters, ages ten and twelve, who were "training for the business" and were exposed to the "unnatural" deaths. The *Advocate* reported that the madam said she also had a three-year-old daughter but admitted she "wouldn't have her in such company."[67]

Sometimes prostitutes' children ran with a group of friends whose activities got them in trouble with the authorities. Eleven-year-old Margaret Fox, daughter of Mrs. Francis Reed, who managed a brothel on Crosby Street, was arrested with four friends for stealing a basket of clothes. The police committed her to the House of Refuge, where she stayed for at least four years and possibly more. Although the Refuge at first thought Margaret was "full of talk but a promising child," by the end of four years they said she had "so ungovernable a temper as to be past management . . . really she is a hard one."[68] Louis Sweet, son of

Susan "Jenny" Sweet of 100 Church Street, got into trouble several times for stealing. Concerned about her son's welfare, Mrs. Sweet

packed him off to New Bedford to ship on a whaling voyage, in order, if possible to relieve him of his bad associates; but the young scamp, before getting on ship ran off, and the day before yesterday returned back to the city again; and that night entered his mother's house, stole [three gold bracelets and other jewelry valued at $60] and soon after pawned them to a Dutch grocer for some liquor. . . . Justice Mountfort gave the young man a severe reprimand and committed him to prison to await further examination.[69]

Although most prostitutes probably tried to care for their children as well as possible, some were unfit for the task. Nine-year-old Maria Frampton's parents were separated, and her father tried to board her in places where she would be "out of reach" of her prostitute mother. Her mother repeatedly found her and took her back to her brothel. When the mother was arrested and sent to the penitentiary for drunken and riotous behavior, Maria was sent to the House of Refuge, where she was found to be "filthy and full of sores from head to the soles of her feet—a real object of pity." Several months after her admittance, the matron recorded that Maria was "knowing far beyond her age . . . and though a long distance off, her mother is bad and gives bad influence."[70] Mary Seymour, who was said to have become "crazy soon after she came to New York," abandoned her baby. She spent five to six weeks "strolling" near Catherine Market and "sleeping in the most filthy cellars among Negroes and in every real sense [she] was a vagrant." Seymour was sent to the House of Refuge because she claimed she was under eighteen, but the admitting officer recorded that she believed Seymour was twenty to twenty-two years old. Officials noted she had "turns of insanity," when she tore her hair and clothes and several times tried to hang herself. On her last suicide attempt, when the matron cut her down she was nearly dead. Refuge officials finally sent Seymour to the "Belle View crazy house," from which she escaped shortly afterward.[71]

For many prostitutes with children, the role of mother was not sought but was a fact of life—women had children, and children had to be cared for. For other women, however, the task of being a mother seemed too onerous, and action was taken to limit future responsibilities by contraception, abortion, and even infanticide or child abandonment.[72] Though there are many reasons why prostitutes would not wish to have children, sources indicate that some welcomed the opportunity. John R. McDowall commented in his *Journal* that "orphans were sometimes taken by bawds and reared to puberty."[73] In 1850 police charged a black couple with "brutal and inhuman treatment" for tying up and nearly starving a five-year-old mulatto girl. The court removed the child from the couple's custody and

she was placed in the kind care of Miss Eliza Fisher, a splendid looking colored woman, carrying a good natured countenance and weighing something like three hundred pounds weight. Eliza very smilingly took charge of the little responsibility, and with a crowd of colored persons, left the court.[74]

Fisher's long history as a prostitute is filled with incidents involving the police, so the authorities must have known her well and believed that she would take good care of the child. Law officials were also aware of the maternal responsibility assumed by prostitute Maria Mitchell, who, as described above, was let go after an arrest for fighting because the magistrates knew she had adopted an "unprotected babe."[75] For Fisher and Mitchell, as for all prostitutes, childrearing was a difficult responsibility—time-consuming as well as a financial and emotional strain. But the emotional rewards of motherhood—of having someone to love, care for, and work for—often seemed rewarding enough for prostitutes to wish to assume the task. Many prostitutes, like other women, including Jewett's friend Clara Hazard, saw motherhood as "the first duty of life" and looked forward to it.

It is impossible to know how most relationships between prostitutes and their children fared over a long number of years, but it is also difficult to know about other relationships between mothers and children in the nineteenth century. In some cases, relationships continued as mother and child aged. Nelson Miller and his wife lived near and had contact with mother Adeline, who had a long career as a brothel madam. Clara Hazard probably continued seeing her mother. If Mary Malloy was the mother of brothel manager Ann Malloy, the fact that they were living together in their fifties and thirties indicates the relationship had continued through most of what would be the average lifespan of a nineteenth-century mother. Other prostitutes sent their children off to create new lives for the offspring, and their anonymity was maintained forever. Still others managed to see that the children grew up, but neither parent nor child invested in a lifetime relationship.

Prostitutes, like other nineteenth-century women, had multiple identities—identities created through a variety of relationships in their private and public lives. Publicly, the prostitute was a harlot, a woman-for-hire, but privately she might be a mother, sister, daughter, and friend, as well as a wife, lover, or business associate. In each of her roles the prostitute had the opportunity for pleasure and enrichment as well as difficulties and disappointments. The prostitute's own evaluation of all these experiences and relationships was crucial, of course, for determining how she felt about herself and her life as a whole. Despondency or depression was one response. The letters of Ann Farmer offer insight into the hopelessness and pessimism felt by some prostitutes. Farmer wrote to Jewett that she wished she had Jewett's temperament and disposition because she then would be "more calculated to go through this ungrateful world." Farmer apparently felt pain and distress because of her profession and because of the unhappy relationships she experienced both with the men in her life and with her family. She noted that even noble-hearted men, when it suited their convenience, would leave prostitutes like herself

unprotected, uncomplemented and uncomforted to buffet the storms of this bleak unfriendly world and leave us to brood over the disgraceful pangs of remorse, until we glide to the grave unnoticed—with perhaps hardly enough to commit us to our mother earth.[76]

Farmer described herself as "extremely unhappy relative to family affairs of a previous nature. I have a silent sorrow here, a grief that rends my heart. O God, I must not think of it."[77] Those less articulate than Farmer sometimes expressed their depression and sense of isolation through alcoholism, drug addiction, and suicide.

Although despondency, if not depression, must have been experienced by most prostitutes sometime in their professional lives, personal relationships, especially with fellow prostitutes, often provided solace and support. As a part of the so-called underworld, prostitutes created a subculture, a sphere of their own which encompassed a social world of brothels, disreputable boardinghouses, saloons, and theaters and was supported by a network of female friendships and relationships established through shared involvements and mutual understanding. Yet even though separated into their own social world, prostitutes were a part of the wider "woman's sphere." As a mother, sister, daughter, wife, lover, or laborer, a prostitute shared the common cares, desires, and constraints of nineteenth-century women, extending her "identity" into the larger female sphere. Some prostitutes could intellectualize about woman's social and emotional position in nineteenth-century society, noting woman's superior sensibilities but limited possibilities—her subordinance in the affairs of the world but predominance in the "affairs of the heart."[78] Helen Jewett, in a letter to her lover, wrote of the differences in the "spheres" and sensibilities of men and women:

Women only can understand woman's heart. We cannot, dare not complain, for sympathy is denied us if we do.

With man it is otherwise. He can with impunity expose all, . . . court sympathy and obtain it, while at the same time poor neglected woman cannot be allowed to share in the many pursuits and pleasures man has to occupy his time; of course he does not need to be pitied, unless it is for his vices and excesses.[79]

Many prostitutes not as articulate as Jewett understood the limitations of nineteenth-century society in terms of their daily lives. But they also understood the options. Prostitution was a profession selected from the limited possibilities available to women. It could be difficult and isolating, but it did not prevent a woman from developing additional identities in life, and it certainly did not prevent her from enjoying rewarding and reinforcing relationships with others.

Epilogue

Two incidents, one often mentioned and another to be described briefly, suggest the argument of this work: that prostitutes need to be viewed in terms of the variety of possibilities and responses their profession allowed, as beings who engaged in a full range of human interests and relations, beset by problems but also by opportunities related to both their profession and their status as women.

In 1834, prostitute Phebe Williamson and her estranged husband went to court. The husband charged his wife with abandonment because she had moved to a prostitution establishment; she charged him with assault and said she would not stay with him any longer. She was there asking the court for assistance in dealing with personal abuse, as she and other prostitutes had successfully done on numerous occasions. He was there asserting his proprietorship in a patriarchal society, where presumptions of male dominance allowed a man to "discipline" his family. The judge ruled that in contrast to other cases in which a prostitute as an individual citizen could enlist the court's assistance in dealing with customer violence in her own home or business, this was "a case over which the law allowed him no control"; he advised the parties to go home and be reconciled.[1] As an abused prostitute, a woman could expect the assistance and protection of the state, but as an abused wife, a woman remained under the control of her husband. Gauging the possibilities of life as a prostitute in relation to those offered as a wife and homemaker with a drunken and abusive husband, Phebe Williamson,

321

like some other women, chose to stay in prostitution, where her socio-legal and economic situation seemed better and where she in fact had more freedom to choose and ability to protect herself than as a house-wife.

That Williamson's choice entailed advantages was apparent to her and to many other prostitutes, but that it also entailed dangers was obvious to all nineteenth-century observers. In April 1836, evidence of both the dangers and the advantages surrounded the charred body of a murdered prostitute, Helen Jewett, found in a brothel at 41 Thomas Street. Describing the scene, a reporter noted the elegant furnishings, the four-poster bed with its linen sheets, the prints hung on the walls, and the writing desk with a number of beautifully bound leather volumes. He also mentioned her velvet dress, feathered bonnets, and leather boots.[2] This description epitomized the hope of most women who entered prostitution: they would have economic opportunities that would allow them a more comfortable way of life, including some luxuries. The coroner's description, however, suggested the other side of prostitution: the body was "externally burned on the arms, back and legs. On the right side of her head were three wounds of the scalp [where] . . . the bone was driven upon the brane [sic] and the brane lacerated." Furthermore, the "uterus was labouring under an old disease."[3] Violence and brutality were ever-present dangers for the prostitute, as were venereal disease and other health problems.

Co-existing with the luxury and the dangers were still other dimensions of Jewett's life, as suggested by her personal correspondence discovered in the bedroom. She had experienced a wide range of positive human relationships that were obviously important to her and that helped her enjoy, as well as cope with, her daily life.

When contemporaries considered the prostitute in relation to genteel Victorians' views of morality and their notions of "woman's nature" and "woman's place," she seemed the antithesis of the true Victorian woman. Everything about her work, whether practiced on a temporary or long-term basis, challenged the traditional assumptions about women's roles. She became a symbol of society's ills or a scapegoat for many of its problems, simultaneously a victimizer and a victim. The labels and abstractions moved her to the center of public discourse, capturing the attention of writers, reformers, and ordinary citizens, but the rhetoric virtually obscured the fact that she remained an ordinary human being, dealing with life in all its human complexity. The moralistic rhetoric also obscured society's prejudices against women who were poor and foreign, and whose lives suggested a social, economic, and sexual independence that was threatening to both social and patriarchal hierarchies.

The life options of New York City prostitutes were not so different from those of many other women at the time, given the constraints, dependence, and often victimization decreed by society. Prostitutes, like other women, were at times able to work around these very considerable limitations to create for themselves reasonably independent and rewarding lives. If nineteenth-century prostitutes were not wholly victims, however, neither were they masters of their own destinies. Just as nineteenth-century women in general were renegotiating gender relations—both poor women laboring outside the family and middle- and upper-class women working in voluntary associations or in women's rights or feminist organizations—so were prostitutes renegotiating their place in society.[4] New York prostitutes displayed a certain independence in their life styles and in their relations with fellow New Yorkers, but they were not assertive of their rights as prostitutes per se. Though some of the early women's rights and feminist advocates noted a parallel between the condition of the prostitute and that of all women, there is no evidence that a self-conscious political sense of sisterhood developed.[5] When New York prostitutes asserted their independence, they did so as citizens, as women, and as workers. As citizens they readily argued their case before public forums such as courts. As daughters they responded to patriarchal strictures and structures by leaving home for more social freedom and control over their own economic resources. As wives they sometimes left abusive, inept, or boring husbands to care for themselves. As workers they left bad-paying and oppressive jobs for an occupation fraught with problems but promising economic opportunity and better working conditions.[6]

Such elements of independence, however, were accompanied by daily compromises, trade-offs necessitated by negotiated relationships with officials and fellow New Yorkers. Prostitutes were able to create a protected though always threatened environment in which to work. As mothers, daughters, and even wives, they accepted the debilitating and degrading aspects of their work in order to provide for families as well as to support themselves. As workers, they responded to clients' sexual demands to raise income or improve lifestyles. As businesswomen they competed but also networked with each other to take advantage of the opportunities of their marketplace. And finally, as friends and co-workers, they mutually depended on each other for social, emotional, and sometimes economic assistance.

For the occupation as a whole, life in mid-century New York City presented a small "window of opportunity." The city's prostitutes enlarged and redefined their place in New York's urban geography, local economy, and social fabric. They moved beyond the geographic and social confines imposed in an earlier period and integrated themselves into the public life and local neighborhoods of the burgeoning metropolis. Furthermore, the social flux accompanying mid-century changes created a situation in which prostitutes were able to establish a significant degree of autonomy and control in their professional lives, both as individual workers and in managerial roles. In spite of being dependent on males as customers, New York's prostitutes were able to sever or lessen their dependence on particular men as they, as females and workers, predominated in the operations of their special sector of the local economy. Some of these gains were temporary. Whereas mid-century New York prostitutes expanded their realm in both a physical and socioeconomic sense, later prostitutes would find opportunities increasingly bounded by geographic restrictions (red-light or vice districts) as well as physical and socioeconomic restraints involving pimps and other third-party interests.

Too much should not be made of the possibilities for New York women in prostitution in the mid-nineteenth century. Women were not empowered by going into prostitution, even though some prostitutes did create personal opportunities out of adversity. Yet the degradation and disadvantages of the occupation were still great for its luckier as well as its less fortunate practitioners. To overemphasize potential opportunities for this group of working women is as misleading or limiting as it was for their contemporaries to view prostitutes as a threatening statistic or as a problem, as victims or victimizers. As nineteenth-century New Yorkers discovered, the prostitutes in their midst were not easily "ordered" or characterized; they were a widely diverse group of women living in a variety of situations—human beings, trapped like others by circumstances, but also using circumstances to create a life and a work culture for themselves and those they cared about.

The story of the life of the mid-nineteenth-century New York City prostitute was the story of hundreds of women, just as it was the story of a Helen Jewett or a Phebe Williamson. The gracious furnishings and the warmly intelligent letters, as well as the brutally battered body at 41 Thomas Street, were all part of the possibilities facing the many women who became prostitutes in New York City. And who could say that Phebe Williamson, in deciding to follow in the footsteps of a Helen Jewett rather than in those of her abusive husband, was either fool or free?

Appendix 1: House of Refuge Collective Intake Profile, 1835

Upon intake, information supplied by the inmate or officials was recorded in narrative form, with brief follow-up entries added later. It does not appear that information was taken in a systematic manner.

Number of girls admitted	59
Number of cases where suspected prostitution indicated in record	34
Ages	9 (1 girl) 12 (2) 13 (3) 14 (5) 15 (9) 16 (8) 17 (4) 18 (2)
Nativity of girl	American: 26 Foreign: 4 (Irish 3, English 1) Not known: 4

Nativity of parents

Both parents native: 15
Both parents foreign: 4 (Irish 2,
    German 1, Dutch 1)
Father foreign/mother native: 5
    (Irish 2, English 2, Scot 1)
Mother foreign/father native: 0
Not clear from intake: 10

Status of parents

Father dead: 8
Mother dead: 3
Both dead: 11
Parents separated: 5

Home life

Father drinks: 2
Mother drinks: 1
Abuse in home: 6
Mother unhappy: 4
Runaway: 7

*Occupational information,
    father*

None/not known: 18
Seaman: 2
All others, 1 each:
    Lamplighter, Works in store,
    Boat builder, Boating, Rigger,
    Grocer/silverplater, Laborer,
    Tailor/fiddler, Public
    house/speculator, Coach
    maker, Segar store, Flour
    merchant, Newspaper carrier,
    Chair painter

*Occupational information,
    mother*

None/not known: 21
Prostitute: 2
Boardinghouse: 2
Service: 2
Works, unsure: 1
Other: Cook 1, Dressmaker 1,
    Tailoress 1, Sickly 1,
    Almshouse 2

Occupational information, girl

None/not known: 9
Prostitute: 7
Servant: 10
Tailoress: 3
Fiddler: 1
Childcare: 1
Servant/seamstress: 1
Fur/capmaker: 1
Factory worker: 1

Causes of prostitution

Raised in brothel: 2
Sister at brothel and stayed
    there: 1
Family associated with
    brothel: 1
Both parents died, so began: 5
Loneliness after death of
    parent: 1
Bad treatment at home: 1
Unhappy living with brother: 1
Problems with parents: 1
Conflict with pious mother: 1
Abuse by parent: 1
Incest: 1
Seduction by family friend: 1
Seduction by cousin: 1
Seduction by employer: 3
Economic loss: 3
Bad company: 8
Mentally ill: 1
Doesn't say: 1

Nature of prostitution

Been in brothels before
    Refuge: 21
Assignation house or
    freelance: 4
Suspected prostitution: 8
Prostitution confirmed after
    leaving Refuge: 1

First sexual encounter with

Friend: 5
Relative: 2
Employer: 3
Doesn't say: 24

*Other personal information
   on girl*

Diseased: 7
Drinks: 1
Suicidal: 1
Pregnant: 1
Previously at Almshouse/
   penitentiary/hospital: 3

Final information listed

Indentured: 12
Ran away from indenture: 6
Sent back from indenture: 1
Returned to parents: 1
Married respectably: 7 (1 before
   Refuge)
Respectable life/occupation: 4
   (milliner and domestic
   service listed)
Sent to hospital and escaped: 1
Died: 2 (1 while at Almshouse)

Appendix 2: Jewett Correspondence

The Helen Jewett correspondence is a collection of eighty-eight letters written over a period of two years, from early 1834 until a few weeks before Jewett's murder in April 1836. Of the letters, 39 are by Jewett, 10 by other prostitutes and a female friend, and 39 by Jewett's clients.

The Jewett correspondence was documented at the time of her death. The trial folder in the District Attorney's papers, Court of General Sessions (NYMA), contains two documents itemizing the letters by senders and receivers. The first document appears to be the initial inventory of the correspondence, and the second is a receipt dated 1 June 1836, the day before the opening of the trial of her accused murderer, verifying that the letters, a diary, and a miniature were delivered to Judge Robert H. Morris by consent of Thomas Phoenix, the district attorney, to be used as evidence.[1]

The collection of correspondence was taken from Jewett's bedroom the morning following her murder, and the existence of the letters immediately became well known to the New York public as well as to court officials. At the coroner's inquest held the day after the slaying, Rosina Townsend testified that about ten days prior to her death, Jewett had told Townsend that Frank Rivers (the brothel alias of Richard Robinson, the man charged in the slaying) had returned Jewett's letters and asked her either to return his or destroy them. Townsend said Robinson was planning to marry another woman. Caroline Paris (Elizabeth Salters) also testified at the inquest that Jewett had told her about ten days before her death that she and Robinson had had a dispute about some correspondence, and, on the afternoon before the murder, Paris had accompanied Jewett on a walk to deliver letters and a book to a person in Pearl Street.[2] At the grand jury hearing held a week after the coroner's inquest, two of the letters were read as evidence, and one of the witnesses, a porter, testified that on many occasions he had delivered correspondence for Jewett.[3]

Nine different articles printed in the *Sun* and *Herald* during the period from the murder until the end of the June trial discuss Jewett's correspondence. The *Herald* noted that Jewett was well known to every pedestrian in Wall Street, and the preceding summer was famous for parading the thoroughfare, "generally with a letter in her hand." Jewett was said to have

carried on an extensive correspondence with every part of the Union. According to the Post Office, last summer she usually received from three to eight letters a day. Her postage bill exceeded that of several brokers in Wall Street. Her private correspondence is of a remarkable character, resembling that of the famous Abelard and Eloise. We are promised a choice selection from this correspondence which are [sic] characterized by great talent, power and brilliancy.[4]

The *Herald* also wrote an article entitled "Her Literary Correspondence," which was devoted exclusively to a description of the letters. It appears that the *Herald*'s writer had been given the opportunity to study the impounded correspondence, which at that time was in the possession of Police Justice Lownds. The letters were said to be "written by her and to her by persons who admired or pretended to admire her talents and beauty." In the letters written by Jewett, there was not a "fulsome expression or unchaste word," and they contained "quotations from Italian, French, and English poets on love and friendship, satirizing playfully the little incidents of her life." Jewett's handwriting was said to be "uncommonly beautiful, something of the character of Bristow's style." The paper stated that some of the letters written to Jewett were from "respectable persons in the city and even married men." A few of the letters were signed with pseudonyms, such as Wandering Willie, Roderic Random, and Frank Rivers.[5]

At the trial in June, several witnesses mentioned the letters, and the packets of correspondence were shown to the court as evidence. Robinson's employer was asked to identify the accused's handwriting in some, and one letter was read into the trial transcript. After the trial ended in Robinson's acquittal, the letters appear to have been forgotten for a number of years.[6]

In January 1849, thirteen years after the trial, the *Police Gazette* began a special series on the Jewett murder in a column called "Lives of Felons." The story ran from January through June. At the end of April, the paper included thirteen letters exchanged between Jewett and Robinson, which the paper explained had been obtained from the police. Given the loose organization of the police and judicial system at the time, it is not surprising that someone was able to obtain official evidence that had been used in a trial. The correspondence met with such interest by readers that the *Police Gazette* continued to publish additional letters in five more editions of the paper through mid-June. After the publication of the first issue containing the correspondence, the original copies of the letters were posted in the *Police Gazette's* Nassau Street office window. The *Brooklyn Daily Advertiser* reported "A New Excitement" over the letters on display, which had attracted crowds so large that the streets in the vicinity of the *Police Gazette* office were "almost blockaded by individuals anxious to get a view."[7]

Because only the printed versions of the letters are available now, it is possible, though unlikely, that the original manuscripts have been altered by editorial changes. The creative embellishments of the newspaper staff appear to have been applied to the life-story narrative that preceded the publishing of the letters and to the editorial commentary that accompanied the correspondence, not to the letters themselves. At times, the emotional or dramatic conclusions drawn by the *Police Gazette* writer in the narrative and commentaries are not consistent with the information provided in the correspondence, which shows little of the sensationalism that was the *Police Gazette's* stock in trade.

Most likely, Jewett initiated much of the correspondence with friends and acquaintances. Many of the letters written to her begin with an acknowledgement of correspondence received: "I received your letter yesterday," or "I received your letter of the 26th."[8] One customer, Charles C., began his letter to Jewett with a statement that a communication had been solicited from him: "I have just received a letter from my friend Harvey, stating that you would like to hear from me if it was convenient, & c."[9] On learning that mail might not be getting through to her or to those she was writing, Jewett wrote that the failed delivery had angered her:

I shall hope to learn to-night from you, that you have received my letter. I think it very strange indeed, do you not, that some of your letters should miscarry and others reach you? A gentleman told me last night, that he had written me twice, and neither of his letters have I received, and this morning I blew up at the post office without finding them. [10]

The correspondence is telling not only about the life of Helen Jewett but also about the general situation of prostitutes at the time. There is a similarity in tone and content in both the notes Jewett wrote and those written to her by other prostitutes. The letters were prevented from being "lost," as most contemporaries' private correspondence was, only because they became public by rare chance circumstances. The letters obviously were private, written without any of the distortions that might come from a sense they might be made public, and though those who write and whose writings get saved are perhaps "atypical," they still speak in part for their group or class. Furthermore, the general patterns found in the correspondence are compatible with public evidence from newspapers and legal records concerning relations of other prostitutes at the time.

Of course, the letters in no way represent a statistically valid sampling of prostitutes' correspondence, nor do they encompass a long enough period of time to reveal much about patterns, cycles, or trends in the profession. There are obvious biases—Jewett exercised some element of selectivity in deciding to whom to write and which letters to keep. And, even though Jewett's position in prostitution was not peculiarly elevated, she was not representative of the majority of prostitutes, who were poor and practiced casual prostitution.

Inventory of the Correspondence

Letters delivered to Robert H. Morris, 1 June 1836, to be used as evidence in the trial of Richard Robinson for the murder of Helen (Ellen) Jewett:

From Mary Berry to H.J.	2
From Robinson to H.J.	9

From Geo. P. Marston to H.J.	19
From H. Jewett to Robinson	43
From Clara Hazzard to H.J.	6
From Emily to H.J.	1
From Edward to H.J.	2
From Chas. Chandler to H.J.	2
From C. of Paterson to H.J.	1
From S. G. Hemphill to H.J.	1
From Ann Farmer to H.J.	2

Letters printed in the *Police Gazette*, 28 April through 9 June 1849:

From Mary Berry to Helen Jewett	2
From Robinson to Helen Jewett	11 (2 repeat)
From Geo. P. Marston to Helen Jewett	6
From H. Jewett to Robinson	39
From Clara Hazzard to H. Jewett	3
From Emily to Helen Jewett	2
From Edward to Helen Jewett	2
From Chas. Chandler to Helen Jewett	2
From Ann Farmer to Helen Jewett	2

The inventory for the district attorney does not report that all of the letters from the trunk were listed; the following may not have been part of the court evidence:

From Wandering Willie to Helen Jewett	3
From J.J.A.S. to Helen Jewett	2
From Robert to Helen Jewett	1
From Stanhope to Helen Jewett	1
From Archibald to Helen Jewett	1
From Bob to Helen Jewett	1
From William to Helen Jewett	1
From Pupil to Helen Jewett	1
From John P. to Helen Jewett	1
From J. to Helen Jewett	1
From N.J. to Helen Jewett	1

Notes

Abbreviations

BCMP	Board of Commissioners, Metropolitan Police
CCHR	County Clerks Office, Hall of Records
CGS	Court of General Sessions
DBA	Documents of the Board of Aldermen
HRCH	House of Refuge Papers, Case Histories
MM	Municipal Manuscripts
NYFBS	New York Female Benevolent Society
NYMA	New York Municipal Archives and Record Center
NYMS	New York Magdalen Society
NYPL	New York Public Library
PCR	Police Court Records
WSHW	Water Street Home for Women

Introduction

1. Judith R. Walkowitz, "'We Are Not Beasts of the Field': Prostitution and the Campaign Against the Contagious Diseases Acts, 1869–1886" (Ph.D. diss., University of Rochester, 1974); idem, *Prostitution in Victorian Society: Women, Class, and the State*; Ruth Rosen, *The Lost Sisterhood: Prostitution in America, 1900–1918*; Christine Stansell, *City of Women: Sex and Class in*

New York, 1789–1860. Two especially interesting works on nineteenth-century American prostitution in the West that have expanded the geographic perimeters of the topic are Marion S. Goldman, *Gold Diggers and Silver Miners: Prostitution and Social Life on the Comstock Lode,* and Anne M. Butler, *Daughters of Joy, Sisters of Misery: Prostitutes in the American West, 1865–90.* Other studies related to the question in New York City are Timothy J. Gilfoyle, "City of Eros: New York City, Prostitution, and the Commercialization of Sex, 1790–1920" (Ph.D. diss., Columbia University, 1987); Barbara Meil Hobson, *Uneasy Virtue: The Politics of Prostitution and the American Reform Tradition;* Barbara Berg, *The Remembered Gate: Origins of American Feminism;* Carroll Smith-Rosenberg, *Religion and the Rise of the American City: The New York City Mission Movement, 1812–1870.*

    2. Rosen, *Lost Sisterhood.*

    3. Stansell, *City of Women,* 221.

    4. Ibid., 191.

Chapter 1

    1. *New York Herald,* 11 April–30 June 1836; Lewis Tappan, *The Life of Arthur Tappan,* 119.

    2. *Herald,* 11 April 1836.

    3. *New York Commercial Advertiser,* 2–11 June 1836; *Herald,* 7–11 June 1836; *The Sun* (New York), 3–4 June 1836; *New York Transcript,* 3–8 June 1836; Oliver Carlson, *The Man Who Made News: James Gordon Bennett,* 143–67; Patricia Cline Cohen, "The Helen Jewett Murder: Violence, Gender, and Sexual Licentiousness in Antebellum America," 374–89.

    4. *Herald,* 12 and 13 April 1836.

    5. *Herald,* 11–15 April 1836; *Morning Courier and Enquirer,* 29 June 1830.

    6. Patrica Cline Cohen has an excellent summary of the various versions of Jewett's life story in "The Helen Jewett Murder." I am indebted to Cohen for sharing her article with me.

    7. There are many sources describing Jewett's background, many of which contain fabricated material. The most accurate information on Jewett appears to be from court documents and the local press at the time of the murder. See *Sun,* April, June 1836; *Herald,* April, June 1836; *Transcript,* 30 June 1834; CGS, *People v. Robinson,* 19 April 1836; Coroner's Inquest, 10 April 1836, in CGS, *People v. Robinson.* At the coroner's inquest, Rosina Townsend said Jewett was born in Hallowell, Maine.

Other sources on Jewett and the murder include *An Authentic Biography of the Late Helen Jewett, A Girl of the Town . . . by a Gentleman Fully Acquainted with her History*; Carlson, *The Man Who Made News*; Joseph Holt Ingraham, *Frank Rivers: or the Dangers of the Town; The Life of Ellen Jewett: Illustrative of Her Adventures . . . Together with Various Extracts from Her Journal, Correspondence, and Poetical Effects*; Richard P. Robinson, *Letter From Richard P. Robinson as Connected With the Murder of Ellen Jewett, Sent in a Letter to his Friend Thomas Armstrong; A Sketch in the Life of Francis P. Robinson, the Alleged Murderer of Helen Jewett, Containing Copious Extracts from his Journal; A Sketch in the Life of Miss Ellen Jewett, Who Was Murdered in the City of New York on Saturday Evening, April 9, 1836; The Truly Remarkable Life of the Beautiful Helen Jewett Who Was So Mysteriously Murdered*; George Wilkes, *The Lives of Helen Jewett and Richard P. Robinson*.

8. *Sun*, 11 April 1836.

9. *Herald*, 12 April 1836; *Commercial Advertiser*, 6 June 1836; *Sun*, 6 June 1836.

10. Though there is no indication of Jewett's weekly earnings except for a comment in the *National Police Gazette* that she "could get $50–$100 a week for Berry's establishment" (24 February 1849), she must have made enough over and above her living expenses and clothing costs to accumulate savings, because on one occasion Mrs. Berry asked her for a loan. "Berry to Jewett," *Police Gazette*, 5 May 1849 (letter dated 14 December 1835). Estimated earnings for an establishment like Berry's are based on information from a variety of contemporary sources. See Chapter 3.

11. There is no evidence that Jewett was ever personally fined or incarcerated. The arrest of the women in her brothel and other court cases are discussed in *Transcript*, 30 June 1834; 12 April, 4 June 1836; *Sun*, 28 June 1834; *Herald*, 13 April 1836; *Commercial Advertiser*, 4 June 1836; *The Life of Ellen Jewett*, 19, 24, 29–30; Wilkes, *The Lives*.

12. *Sun*, 6–8 June 1836; *Herald*, 13 April 1836.

13. "Edward to Helen," *Police Gazette*, 2 June 1849.

14. Ibid., "Helen to Richard," 9 June 1849 (letter dated 24 July 1835). The use of correspondence with clients may not have been unique to Jewett. In the Corless murder case in 1843, a porter testified that he had carried letters between the murdered victim and a prostitute. *Daily Tribune*, 29 March 1843. See Appendix 2 for a full explanation and description of the Jewett correspondence.

15. Information on urban changes in New York City can be found in Robert G. Albion, *The Rise of the New York Port, 1815–1860*; Amy Bridges, *A City in the Republic: Antebellum New York and the Origins of Machine Politics*; Robert Ernst, *Immigrant Life in New York City, 1825–1863*; Douglas T. Miller, *Jacksonian Aristocracy: Class and Democracy in New York, 1830–1860*; Edward Pessen, *Riches, Class and Power Before the Civil War*; Edward Spann, *The New Metropolis: New York, 1840–1857*; Sean Wilentz, *Chants Democratic: New*

York City and the Rise of the Working Class, 1788–1850; James Grant Wilson, ed., *The Memorial History of the City of New York.*

16. On the activities and position of women in the nineteenth century, especially in New York City, see Berg, *Remembered Gate*; Nancy Cott, *The Bonds of Womanhood: "Woman's Sphere" in New England, 1780–1835*; Smith-Rosenberg, *Religion and the Rise*; Stansell, *City of Women*; Barbara Welter, "The Cult of True Womanhood," 151–74.

Many young women and girls found employment in industry or as domestics and seamstresses. Sources noted that women frequently moved from the last two professions into prostitution. House of Refuge case histories include numerous examples of young girls in service having practiced casual prostitution before they were admitted to the Refuge. New York House of Refuge Case Histories (HRCH), 1829–1860, New York State Archives, State Education Department, Albany. See also: NYMS, *First Annual Report of the Executive Committee of the New York Magdalen Society, Instituted January 1, 1830*, 8; William W. Sanger, *The History of Prostitution—Its Extent, Causes and Effects Throughout the World*, 526; Theresa M. McBride, *The Domestic Revolution: The Modernization of Household Service in England and France, 1820–1920*, 22, 99–107; Rosen, *Lost Sisterhood*, 62–63; Stansell, *City of Women*, 167, 178; Margaret Hewitt, *Wives and Mothers In Victorian Industry*, 59. A. J. B. Parent-Duchatelet and Henry Mayhew also noted this as a problem in France and England.

17. The term *social evil* began to be used in the last half of the nineteenth century and became increasingly common in the late nineteenth and early twentieth centuries with the work of Progressive reformers, especially the New York Committee of Fifteen and the Vice Commission of Chicago, both of whom published research reports under the title *The Social Evil*. See James D. McCabe, *Lights and Shadows of New York Life; or, the Sights and Sensations of the Great City*, 579; Matthew Hale Smith, *Sunshine and Shadow in New York*, 371; Rosen, *Lost Sisterhood*, 14, 40.

18. Bertram Wyatt-Brown, *Lewis Tappan and the Evangelical War Against Slavery*, 66; Tappan, *The Life of Arthur Tappan*, 111–12; Smith-Rosenberg, *Religion and the Rise*, 98–103; idem, "Beauty, the Beast, and the Militant Woman: A Case Study in Sex Roles and Social Stress in Jacksonian America," 562–84; *Advocate of Moral Reform*, 1 January 1837; NYMS, *First Annual Report*, 4–9.

19. Philip Hone, *The Diary of Philip Hone, 1828–1851*, 45 (general entry for summer 1831); John R. McDowall, *Magdalen Facts*, no. 1; Tappan, *Life of Arthur Tappan*, 113–18; Wyatt-Brown, *Lewis Tappan*, 68.

20. Wyatt-Brown, *Lewis Tappan*, 70; McDowall, *Magdalen Facts*.

21. John R. McDowall, *McDowall's Journal*, January 1833. Many sources refer to the existence of this list threatened by McDowall, but none documents

where it is found. Only two volumes of *McDowall's Journal* were published, covering the period from January 1833 to December 1834. Some issues contain letters with initials of seducers. See Paul Boyer's discussion of McDowall's threatened list in his analysis of New York moral reformers' attempts at social control, in Paul S. Boyer, *Urban Masses and Moral Order in America, 1820–1920*, 17–21.

22. NYFBS, *First Report of the Female Benevolent Society of the City of New York: Presented January 13, 1834*, 6–7.

23. *Sun*, 15 March 1834.

24. Smith-Rosenberg, *Religion and the Rise*, 102–12; Keith Melder, "Ladies Bountiful: Organized Women's Benevolence in Early Nineteenth-Century America," 231–54.

25. *Advocate of Moral Reform*, 1 January 1837; *Herald*, 11 and 14 April 1836; Tappan, *Life of Arthur Tappan*, 119; [Phebe McDowall], *Memoir and Select Remains of the Late Rev. John R. McDowall, the Martyr of the Seventh Commandment, in the Nineteenth Century*, 1–89, 153–54.

26. A. J. B. Parent-Duchatelet, *De la prostitution dans la ville de Paris*; William Tait, *Magdalenism: An Inquiry into the Extent, Causes, and Consequences of Prostitution*; William Acton, *Prostitution Considered in Its Moral, Social, and Sanitary Aspects in London and Other Large Cities and Garrison Towns, with Proposals for the Control and Prevention of its Attendant Evils*; [Charles Smith], *Madam Restell, An Account of her Life and Horrible Practices, Together with Prostitution in New York, Its Extent, Causes, and Effects Upon Society*; Sanger, *History of Prostitution*. Some of the "popular writers" of the 1840s were George G. Foster, *New York in Slices by An Experienced Carver: Being the Original Slices Published in the New York Tribune* and *New York Naked*; Solon Robinson, *Hot Corn: Life Scenes in New York Illustrated*; Ned Buntline [E. Z. C. Judson], *The Mysteries and Miseries of New York*. See Chapter 7 for a further discussion of popular literature.

27. Sanger has a full discussion of Parent's data in his *History of Prostitution*, 139–54. Judith Walkowitz has an excellent analysis of the best-known nineteenth-century writers on prostitution in "We Are Not Beasts," 44–97. I am indebted to both Walkowitz and Jill Harsin for their discussions of Parent-Duchatelet, for whom there is no translation. Jill Harsin, *Policing Prostitution In Nineteenth-Century Paris*.

28. [Smith], *Madam Restell*, 24; Tait, *Magdalenism*; Acton, *Prostitution Considered*.

29. [Smith], *Madam Restell*, 5–24, 27–48.

30. Sanger, *History of Prostitution*, 27–34, 450–52, 575–676.

31. Most of those interviewed used prostitution as a sole means of support, and many of them probably lived in known houses of prostitution. See ibid., 523.

32. Ibid., 617.

33. The tacit acceptance of prostitutes and their integration into neighborhoods will be discussed in Chapter 6.

Reformer Charles Loring Brace noted that prostitutes understood well the types of explanations for prostitution that would evoke either sympathy or criticism from reformers or police: "They usually relate, and perhaps even imagine, that they have been seduced from the paths of virtue suddenly and by the wiles of some heartless seducer. Often they describe themselves as belonging to some virtuous, respectable, and even wealthy family." He went on to point out: "Their real history is much more commonplace and matter-of-fact. They have been poor women's daughters and did not want to work as their mothers did." Charles Loring Brace, *The Dangerous Classes of New York, and Twenty Years' Work Among Them*, 118.

34. HRCH, 1829–1860. For a collective intake profile for the Houses of Refuge in 1835, see Appendix 1.

35. The Jewett correspondence was printed in the *National Police Gazette* from April–June, 1849. Copies of letters also were referenced or printed in other sources in the 1830s. For a detailed discussion of the Jewett correspondence, see Appendix 2.

36. The discussion of definition will be concerned with female prostitution only. Various nineteenth- and twentieth-century definitions of prostitution are discussed in Acton, *Prostitution Considered*, 2; Walkowitz, "We Are Not Beasts," 93; [Smith], *Madam Restell*, 25; Abraham Flexner, *Prostitution in Europe*, 11; Barbara S. Heyl, *The Madam as Entrepreneur: Career Management in House Prostitution*, 2; Carroll Smith-Rosenberg, "Politics and Culture in Women's History—Response," 62; Vern L. Bullough, *The History of Prostitution*, 1–5.

37. Some of the sources claiming that officials maintained lists of prostitutes or prostitution houses are *McDowall's Journal*, May 1833; *Sun*, October 1834; *New York Daily Times*, 3 January 1855; George W. Walling, *Recollections of a New York Chief of Police: An Official Record of Thirty-Eight Years as Patrolman, Detective, Captain, Inspector and Chief on the New York Police*, 580. Police also were said to have records of all persons who boarded in or moved in and out of a ward. New York City, *Police Department Reorganization Committee Report*, in *Documents of the Board of Aldermen* (DBA), doc. 53 (1844): 808.

38. For information on New York City prostitution in the half century before 1830 see Gilfoyle, "City of Eros," chs. 1 and 2; New York City, *Minutes of the Common Council of the City of New York, 1781–1831*; Magdalen Society of New York, *Second and Third Annual Reports*, 1814–1815. In 1818, the *Columbian* reported that the city watch had found 1,200 prostitutes in New

York City. See Stansell, *City of Women*, 172, 276, n. 2. See also Tappan, *Life of Arthur Tappan*, 110–14.

39. *Courier and Enquirer*, 22 August 1831. According to the *Working Man's Advocate*, the City Watch conducted a ward by ward survey for the Grand Jury and discovered only 1,388 prostitutes. There is a discrepancy of 50 women between the *Courier and Enquirer*'s estimate and that of the *Workingman's Advocate*. *Workingman's Advocate*, 20 August 1831. McDowall's estimate is found in NYMS, *First Annual Report*, 7–9. In calculating his estimates of New York's prostitutes, McDowall referred to the estimates of an alderman and a resident physician at the almshouse, who had both estimated 5,000 prostitutes in New York City. On visits to the Five Points, McDowall had counted 104 notorious places of lewdness. He speculated that each of these places had five females (possibly three times more than that), for a total of 520 lewd women. One could safely double this number and have 1,040 notorious females in the vicinity of the Five Points in the sixth ward. Admitting only 1,000, "a humble estimate," for the entire sixth ward, one could then estimate for the whole city. If each of the other thirteen wards had only one-fourth as many as the sixth, they would together account for 3,250, which added to the 1,000 in the sixth produces a total of 4,250 public women. To this figure, add 400 who are usually in the penitentiary, and the result is 4,650, only 350 less than the alderman had computed. One also should add to these public women those females who reside in houses of higher reputation, who work as domestics, and who take lodgings in private families and boarding houses of respectability. These clandestine prostitutes were "doubtless more numerous than the girls abroad on the town," but if they were estimated at the same number, one would get a total of 10,000! See also [Phebe McDowall], *Memoir and Select*, 153–54.

The one in seventy females identified as prostitutes by the grand jury, as well as McDowall's one in ten, are based on the U.S. Census of 1830. A figure of 101,295 assumes the 1830 female population at roughly 50 percent of the total city population (202,589). U.S., 5th Census, 1830.

40. The estimated figures for prostitution in the period 1830–1847 have come from a variety of sources. See: NYMS, *First Annual Report*, 7–9; *Advocate of Moral Reform*, 15 May 1840; *Daily Tribune* (New York), 14 March 1844; *Herald*, 4, 7, 9, 20 January 1844; Samuel I. Prime, *Life In New York*, 164, 166; *Licentiousness: Its Effects, Extent and Causes*, 7; DBA, *Police Reorganization*, 53 (1844), 104; Foster, *New York in Slices*, 4; Tait, *Magdalenism*. The *Herald* estimated there were 9,000 prostitutes and 3,000 houses of ill fame. Prime stated that there were 10,000 prostitutes, one out of seven women of "sexually active age" (16 to 36), and 400 brothels.

41. *Police Gazette*, 12 June 1847. Smith offered a simple method of checking these calculations. Assuming the population at about 400,000 and the

number of females at about 200,000, one could exclude all females under 14 and all over 40, and the number left *capable* (italics mine) of prostitution was 60,000. Subtract from this all virtuous wives and daughters and all respectable women and girls (a number he must have assumed to be around 57,500) and one would have about the same number as the police returns showed. [Smith], *Madam Restell*, 26.

The female population reported in the 1845 census was 190,751. New York State, Secretary of State, Census, 1845, 29.

42. Sanger, *History of Prostitution*, 616.

43. Ibid., 575–79, 582–84. Sanger calculated the number of prostitutes as follows: To Chief Matsell's number of "not over five thousand," he added a 20 percent increase to adjust for population growth in the years leading up to 1858 and for the economic slump, which he believed caused women to turn to prostitution when they were laid off in other occupations. To test the accuracy of this figure of 6,000, Sanger asked precinct police to estimate the number of prostitutes in their precincts, and their reports totaled 3,857. To this number he added another 1,500 for the "floating prostitute population of station-houses, city and district prisons, hospitals, work-house, alms-house and penitentiary." The resulting total was 5,357, and the difference between that and 6,000 could be accounted for by those who had escaped the eyes of the officers taking the census. To the number of 6,000 he added those whose calling was "effectively disguised"—or approximately 1,260 women who frequented assignation houses for sexual gratification, 400 who visited assignation houses to augment their incomes, and 200 who were assumed to represent half of the kept mistresses (the other half being included in those who visited assignation houses). Taken together, these figures totaled 7,860 public and private prostitutes, or about 2.1 percent of the female population.

In order to compare Sanger's figures with the total female population, I have estimated the number of females as 50 percent of the total population. Thus the female total for 1855 would be 314,952, and for 1860, 416,679. By averaging these two figures together, we get an estimated female population of 365,815 for 1858, for comparison with Sanger's prostitution figure for that year. U.S., 8th Census, 1860, 337; and N.Y., Census, 1855, table 1:2.

44. James D. McCabe, *The Secrets of the Great City: A Work Descriptive of the Virtues and Vices, the Mysteries, Miseries and Crimes of New York City*, 284–85. Female population statistics for 1865 and 1870 are based on an estimated 50 percent of the total population for those years as reported in N.Y., Census, 1875, table 1, p. 2.

45. New York State, Board of Commissioners of the Metropolitan Police (BCMP), *Annual Report of the Board of Commissioners of the Metropolitan Police* (New York: Berger & Tripp, 1867–1870), 86 (1866), 103 (1867), 93 (1868), 106 (1869).

46. Edward Crapsey, *The Nether Side of New York; or, the Vice, Crime, and Poverty of the Great Metropolis*, 24, 146.

47. McCabe, *Lights and Shadows*, 579.

48. Sanger, *History of Prostitution*, 580; *Police Gazette*, 20 January 1849. Also, see Chapter 6.

49. Sanger, *History of Prostitution*, 580. New York City, Municipal Manuscripts (MM), Police Dockets (1849–1851), New York Municipal Archives and Record Center (NYMA).

There are many problems in trying to locate names in the 1855 census. The census has not been indexed, so one must read through pages of old ledgers that do not identify houses by number or street name. In addition, the names are handwritten in ink and often illegible. Furthermore, prostitutes usually went by pseudonyms but may have given census officials their legal names. Despite these difficulties, a survey of wards five and eight did verify the existence of many prostitutes said to have been in New York City at that time. In the 1850 census, 131 prostitutes were identified in ward five and 179 in ward eight for a total of 310. By the 1855 census, there were 46 fewer prostitutes found in these two wards (264, as opposed to 310) but 4 more houses (42, as opposed to 38).

In comparing the number of houses identified in the 1855 census and other sources with the number said by Sanger to exist in wards five and eight, the proportion that can be located is again significant: 44 houses in ward eight (76 percent of Sanger's estimate) and 29 in ward five (41 percent). Because it is difficult to identify assignation houses that were operating discreetly, many have probably been overlooked. New York State, Manuscript Census, 1855, New York City Population Schedules, 5th and 8th Wards, County Clerk's Office, Hall of Records (CCHR); U.S., 7th Census, 1850, New York City Population Schedules, 5th and 8th Wards, NYPL.

50. Rosen, *Lost Sisterhood*, 3; Richard J. Evans, "Prostitution, State, and Society in Imperial Germany," 106–29.

51. Rosen, *Lost Sisterhood*, 3. An appendix to the 1897 edition of Sanger's study noted that if Sanger's ratio of prostitutes to general population had kept pace with the city's growth, the number of prostitutes in that year would be 15,500. According to the editors, "these figures, startling as they are, would seem to fall far short of the calculations of many intelligent investigators of the subject, who place the number as high as 25,000 or even 30,000. The latter was the figure given by a high police official about a year ago. The sensational estimate, tacitly accepted by the committee of the State Senate during its late inquiry, putting the number at 50,000, bears on its face the mark of exaggeration, as it would show one prostitute in every 36 inhabitants, including men, women, and children." The editors accepted the police official's 30,000 as reasonable. Sanger, *History of Prostitution*, Appendix, 677–78.

52. Data related to prostitutes' ages is discussed in detail in Chapter 2 and

its notes. Age structure of the female population of New York in 1850 is based on the 1850 census. See U.S. 7th Census, 1850, 396.

Chapter 2

1. George Templeton Strong, *The Diary of George Templeton Strong,* vol.1, 15 (entry for 12 April 1836).

2. See June 1836 in the *Sun, Advocate of Moral Reform, Herald, Commercial Advertiser,* and *Transcript.* For articles at the time of the murder see the same newspapers for 11 April 1836 and the days following. New York City, Court of General Sessions (CGS), File Papers, NYMA, *People v. Robinson,* 19 April 1836.

Two good sources allow closer glimpses of the lives of prostitutes over time. Documents generated by the most notorious incident involving prostitutes in the era, the Helen Jewett murder case, offer much data about women in the upper levels of prostitution. Case records kept by the House of Refuge provide important facts about some of the more ordinary young prostitutes in New York City. HRCH, 1829–1860. For a collective intake profile for the Houses of Refuge in 1835, see Appendix 1.

3. *Herald,* 12 April 1836.

4. Ibid., 23 June 1836.

5. Ibid., 23, 24 June 1836.

6. *Sun,* 21 June 1836.

7. *Advocate of Moral Reform,* 15 June 1836.

8. Record of Assessments, 1828–1836, Wd. 5; CGS, *People v. Robinson,* 19 April 1836; *Transcript,* 3 June 1836; *Advocate of Moral Reform,* 15 June 1836; *Sun,* 3 June 1836; *Police Gazette,* 4 August 1849.

9. *Herald,* 29 April 1836; *Transcript,* 22 April 1836.

10. According to Edward Pessen, both personal and real property were assessed in the 1830s and 1840s at one-fifth to three-fifths of their actual worth, with the three-fifths evaluation rarely used. By this standard, Townsend's property probably would have been worth $25,000 but possibly as little as $8,300. Pessen also states that it was an "open secret that residents did not reveal the true worth of their possessions in the city." Furthermore, it is not known if Townsend had personal or real property elsewhere in New York, which would not have been listed along with the Thomas Street property in tax records.

To calculate the value of mid-nineteenth-century property in current dollars, a formula can be derived from Pessen's data and indexed for inflation. In light of Pessen's observation that the three-fifths property assessment rate was seldom used, we might obtain a rough approximation of 1840 property values by using an average of the one-fifth and two-fifths rates, or .3. (Assessed valuation divided by .3 = 1840 market value.) Pessen calculated the value of an 1840 dollar as $6.50 in 1970, yielding 1970 values that can be adjusted for inflation since then by multiplying by 2.3 for personal property and 3 for faster-appreciating real property (based on 1989 prices). Thus, the 1836 market value of Townsend's property might be estimated at $16,667 ($17,000), or approximately $250,000 in 1989 dollars. See Edward Pessen, *Riches, Class and Power Before the Civil War*, 12, 17, 19.

A *New York Times* editorial on 6 December 1990 stated that according to "historical indices" a 1990 dollar is worth 24.5 times as much as an 1849 dollar, an inflation rate that would yield about a 40 percent greater valuation on the dollar than the above formula.

11. *Herald*, 19 July 1836.

12. *Sun*, 12 August 1836.

13. *Advocate of Moral Reform*, January 1836; *Sun*, 26 October 1835. Tax records for the mid-1820s mention a Rossana Cisco at 30 Anthony, possibly the mother of Mary (Cisco) Berry. Record of Assessments, 1824–1826, Wd. 6.

14. *Advocate of Moral Reform*, January 1836; *Sun*, 26 October 1835.

15. *Herald*, 30 June 1834; 2 August 1836; *Sun*, 21 June 1836.

16. Record of Assessments, 1835, Wd. 5. A $2,000 assessment suggests her actual worth at approximately $6,700 in 1835.

17. *Police Gazette*, 24 February 1849.

18. "Mary Berry to Helen Jewett," *Police Gazette*, 5 May 1849.

19. Robert Taylor, "Diary," entries for 4 March, 1 August, 20 November 1846; Record of Assessments, 1840, 1845, Wd. 5.

20. A brothel directory published in 1839 stated that: "Mother Miller . . . usually dresses in black, with a plaid handkerchief tied round her head to conceal her grey hairs from view." Her actress daughter was supposedly named Miss Josephine Clifton, and the one "who died mysteriously while under the guardianship of Hamblin" was Miss Missouri Miller (Butt Ender, *Prostitution Exposed*, 5). Other information in U.S., Census, 1830, 1840, 1850; N.Y., Census, 1855; Record of Assessments, 1821–1859, Wards 5 and 6; City Directories, 1830–1860; Taylor, "Diary," entries for 1, 29 August, 16 October, 18, 21–23 November 1846; *Advocate of Moral Reform*, 1 December 1836; *Sun*, 22, 29 November 1836, 19 April 1837; CGS, *People v. Furman*, 13 December 1821, *People v. Lozier*, 14 June 1831; PCR, *Mary Hamilton v. Mary Adams*, no. 7441 (1829).

21. See n. 20. Miller's addresses included 167 Church Street (1821); 32 Orange Street (1822–1826); 53 Crosby Street (late 1820s–early 1830s); 39 Elm Street and 44 Orange Street (1831); and 44 Orange Street, 133 Reade Street, and Mott Street (1835–1836).

22. *Advocate of Moral Reform*, 1 December 1836; CGS, *People v. Lozier*, 14 June 1831.

23. *Sun*, 22, 29 November 1836, 19 April 1837; *Advocate of Moral Reform*, 1 December 1836.

24. Ender, *Prostitution Exposed*, 5; Record of Assessments, 1830s.

25. *Tribune*, 18 July 1842; *Herald*, 11 September 1845.

26. Taylor, "Diary," entries for 1, 29 August, 16 October, 18, 21–23 November 1846; *Police Gazette*, 3 March, 7 April 1849.

27. Record of Assessments, 1855, Ward 5. The $16,500 is under the name Adeline Miller. Another entry lists an Adelaide Miller (William H. Boyd, *Boyd's New York City Tax Book; Being a List of Persons, Corporations, and Co-Partnerships Resident and Non-Resident, Who Were Taxed According to the Assessor's Books, 1856 and 1857*).

28. HRCH, nos. 747, 748 (1830). Prior to the admittance of the Utter sisters to the Refuge, a woman named Eunice Utter was tried and convicted for running a disorderly house. The Refuge case history said the Utters' mother was in prison, so it is possible that Eunice Utter was their mother. See CGS, *People v. Eunice Utter*, 7 July 1830.

29. HRCH, nos. 747, 748 (1830).

30. See, for example, collective intake data for 1835 in Appendix I.

31. HRCH, no. 1596 (1835).

32. HRCH, no. 1559 (1835).

33. Ibid.

34. HRCH, no. 867 (1831).

35. Abby Meade/Meyer was a well-known New York City madam from the 1820s through the 1850s. Several of the young girls at the House of Refuge had stayed at her house. Her name appeared in newspapers in the 1830s and 1840s half-a-dozen times for pressing charges against others, usually servants who allegedly stole from her. An 1839 source asserted that her house at 134 Duane Street was "decidedly A. No. 1, for respectability . . . [and] the proprietor, Mrs. M., lives principally at her country seat on Long Island" (Ender, *Prostitution Exposed*, 9). See also HRCH, no. 867 (1831), no. 1613 (1835); *Sun*, 30 November 1833, 19 September 1835, 30 October 1840; *Tribune*, 31 August 1842; U.S., Census, 1830, Wd. 8; U.S., Census, 1850, Wd. 5:1; City Directories, 1830–1850.

36. HRCH, no. 867 (1831).

37. HRCH, no. 1534 (1835).

38. All quotes and information are from HRCH, no. 1534 (1835).

39. *Advocate of Moral Reform*, December 1835, 15 June 1836; City Directories, 1830–1850 passim; Record of Assessments, 1830–1859, Wd. 5; U.S., Census, 1830, 1840, Wd. 5.

40. HRCH, no. 1641 (1835).

41. HRCH, no. 4687 (1850).

42. Sanger, *History of Prostitution*, 450–548. Parent-Duchatelet found that the average French prostitute was young (overwhelmingly between the ages of 20 and 26), from the laboring class, and poor. If previously employed, she had worked in one of the low-paying employments open to women—as a seamstress, domestic servant, factory worker, or shop girl. William Acton, in his London study, also found that women who practiced prostitution were part of the respectable poor, who had entered the profession when they were young because they had experienced some hardship. These women usually had worked in poorly paid professions where they were "exposed to temptation." Specifically mentioned as likely to become prostitutes were actresses, milliners, shop girls, domestic servants, and women employed in factories or "agriculture gangs." Acton asserted that prostitution was a "transitory state through which an untold number of British women are ever on their passage," and that it was not uncommon for them to marry and become housewives. See: Acton, *Prostitution Considered*, 44–45, 49, 180–85; Parent-Duchatelet, *De la prostitution*, quoted in Sanger, 138–54. See Walkowitz, "We Are Not Beasts," 44–97, for a general summary of nineteenth-century writers.

43. [Smith], *Madam Restell*, 27–28.

44. Current researchers have also found that youth and a working-class or poor background characterized a majority of nineteenth-century prostitutes. Judith Walkowitz noted that most of the English prostitutes registered in the dock towns were single women born in the area where they worked, and the youngest of them (those under nineteen) still lived in the family household. It is not clear how many had had children, but few had offspring living with them, perhaps because they sent children away to live, though it is also possible that they used abortion and infanticide as methods of birth control. The majority of the women remained very much a part of their lower-class communities.

Ruth Rosen's collective profile of the turn-of-the-century urban prostitute emphasized the role played by a prior economic, family, or social hardship. Most prostitutes were native and were urban-born, and contemporary data indicates that native-born women of foreign parentage were more likely to become prostitutes than foreign-born women.

The women of the American West studied by Anne Butler were poor, uneducated, and drawn from all the racial and ethnic groups living in the area—white, black, Chinese, and Mexican. Many prostitutes were married, and some had children, but their marital and domestic relationships were highly unstable. On the frontier, a prostitute's economic situation was at least as precarious as that of the new settlers in general: jobs were scarce, wages poor, and prices inflated. See Walkowitz, "We Are Not Beasts"; Rosen, *Lost Sisterhood*; Butler, *Daughters of Joy*.

45. Using census data for wards five and eight, 310 prostitutes can be

identified in 1850 and 264 in 1855. Police arrest statistics are taken from dockets for the lower wards of Manhattan for the years 1849, 1850, and 1855; U.S., Census, 1850, Wards 5 and 8; N.Y., Census, 1855, Wards 5 and 8; MM, Police Docket, 1849–1855.

46. Sanger, *History of Prostitution*, 452; U.S., Census, 1850, Wards 5 and 8; N.Y., Census, 1855, Wards 5 and 8.

47. Calculations are based on data found in the U.S., Census, 1850, Wards 5 and 8; and N.Y., Census, 1855, Wards 5 and 8. Although brothels and prostitutes were researched in the 1870 census, I did not do a full analysis of data for that year comparable to those for 1850 and 1855. Tim Gilfoyle has noted that his study of the 1870 census supports the same general profile of brothel-keepers found in the 1850s. He located three madams over fifty and two under twenty. See Gilfoyle, "City of Eros," 194.

48. The exact averages of ages for prostitutes for these years were 23.3 for 1850 and 22.3 for 1855.

49. At this time, menarche occurred at approximately fifteen, or possibly even later. See Peter Laslett, *The World We Have Lost*, 87, 285–86 n. 95. Housing juvenile prostitutes put a brothel at greater risk of legal and social repercussions. Since census data and probably Sanger's data are primarily from brothels, juvenile prostitutes are likely to be underrepresented. Sanger's undercounting of child prostitution is discussed in Chapter 1.

50. See HRCH, 1830, 1831, 1835, 1840.

51. MM, Police Docket, 17 September 1849. Mangren (or Mangin) also had two of her own daughters working in her prostitution establishment. See Police Court Records (PCR), Box 7953, *Pease v. Mangren*, 1 August 1855, in NYMA. On Farryall see *Advocate of Moral Reform*, August 1835.

52. [Smith], *Madam Restell*, 28.

53. *Advocate of Moral Reform*, November 1835.

54. *Sun*, 9 October 1835. Other examples of young girls found in houses of prostitution are: *Herald*, 22 October 1842 (house at Mott and Cross streets); *Sun*, 8 March 1843 (house at 138 Church Street).

55. *Sun*, 20 April 1837.

56. *Semi-Annual Report of the Chief of Police*, DBA, vol. 17, pt. 1 (1850), 58–59.

57. Ibid., 63.

58. Pedophilia among Victorian men is discussed in Ronald Pearsall, *The Worm in the Bud: The World of Victorian Sexuality*, 350–63. Stansell has an excellent discussion of child prostitution in New York City at mid-century and notes its relationship to working-class culture, family-reform movements, and Victorian pedophilia (*City of Women*, 180–85). Tim Gilfoyle also emphasizes the juvenile aspect of New York's prostitution as one feature that distinguishes

sexual commerce in this period from that in the preceding and succeeding centuries (Gilfoyle, "City of Eros," chap. 4).

Both Stansell and Gilfoyle have done studies of rape cases and found a significant percentage of child victims. Stansell notes that of a random sampling of 101 rape cases between 1820 and 1860 in New York's Court of General Sessions, 26 (also 26 percent) involved complainants who were under 16 years of age. Of these, 19 were under 12 years old (the youngest was 4), 5 were between the ages of 12 and 16, and 2 were of unknown age (Stansell, *City of Women*, 278 n. 33). Gilfoyle found that of 259 rape cases between 1830 and 1870, 98 victims (38 percent) were between 12 and 16 years of age, and 80 (31 percent) were under 12. See Gilfoyle, "City of Eros," Table XIII, 180. Rapes of children actually may not have represented such a high percentage of total rapes; such cases were more likely than others to be prosecuted because the courts would accept more readily the likelihood of "unwillingness" of girls 12 and under. Child prostitution is discussed further in Chapter 6.

59. Sanger, *History of Prostitution*, 460; *Times*, 10 November 1858. In 1861, Samuel Halliday stated that many of New York's prostitutes were immigrants (*The Little Street Sweeper: or Life Among the Poor*, 235–36).

60. Sanger, *History of Prostitution*, 459. See also: *Evening Tattler*, 17 August 1839, and *Protestant Vindication*, 17 June 1835.

61. Report from Mayor Fernando Wood to Board of Aldermen, DBA, 5 (1855), 18.

62. Ernst, *Immigrant Life*, 187–88; Smith-Rosenberg, *Religion and the Rise*, 173; Albion, *Rise of the New York Port*, 418–419; U.S., Census, 1850; N.Y., Census, 1845, 1855.

63. The daily entries in the lower Manhattan docket for 1849 and 1850 indicate that the overwhelming majority of those arrested for vagrancy/prostitution had Irish names. The same is true of the 220 streetwalkers arrested on five evenings in the spring of 1855, and of New York City prison commitments for all crimes in the 1850s. There were more than three times as many foreigners as native-born persons committed to prison from 1850 to 1858, and the Irish accounted for 76 percent of the foreigners, or more than 50 percent of the total number arrested. MM, Police Docket, 1849–1850; *Times*, March–May 1855; Report of the Warden of the City Prison, Annual Report of The Governor of the Almshouse, quoted in Ernst, *Immigrant Life*, 202–204.

One other arrest statistic that appears to support Wood's association of prostitution and "crime" was for panel-house arrests. A study analyzing panel-house prostitution from 1840 to 1869 has found that of 68 women prosecuted, 65 percent were foreign, and 39 percent of the total were from Ireland. Again, however, court officials' biases could have meant that foreign women were pursued more aggressively (Gilfoyle, "City of Eros," 193 n. 18).

64. Some professions were dominated by the foreign-born. The 1855 census lists 29,470 of the 31,749 domestic servants in New York City as foreign-born. Carol Groneman-Pernicorn states that Irish and German women were preferred as domestics, but some newspaper ads for domestic help in this period reflect a different attitude with statements such as, "Irish need not apply." As I argue in Chapter 3, domestic work was among the lowest paid of women's occupations. Ads are from *Truth Teller*, 28 December 1833, and *Daily Sun*, 11 May 1853, quoted in Ernst, *Immigrant Life*, 67. See also Ernst, 215; Carol Groneman-Pernicorn, "The 'Bloody Ould Sixth': A Social Analysis of a New York City Working Class Community in the Mid-Nineteeth Century," 155. Hasia Diner takes a contrasting point of view, arguing that Irish women in American cities seldom turned to prostitution (*Erin's Daughters in America: Irish Immigrant Women in the Nineteenth Century*, 106–7, 114–18).

65. See Chapter 4 for more on immigrant arrests.

66. Sanger, *History of Prostitution*, 460.

67. Ernst, *Immigrant Life*, 193; U.S., Census, 1850, Wards 5 and 8; N.Y., Census, 1855, Wards 5 and 8.

68. Ernst, *Immigrant Life*, 193; U.S., Census, 1850, Wards 5 and 8; N.Y., Census, 1855, Wards 5 and 8; U.S., Census, 1860.

69. Theodor Griesinger, *Lebende Bilder aus Amerika* (Stuttgart, 1858), 148–56. Barbara Hobson has found in her study of Boston prostitutes that brothel-keepers who were immigrants were overrepresented in the prostitute population. Forty percent of the brothel-keepers in the Boston House of Correction were immigrants. It is also possible that a high foreign percentage indicates police bias in arrests and incarcerations of foreign brothel-keepers (Hobson, *Uneasy Virtue*, 44–45).

70. In 1844, the *Herald* estimated there were 9,000 prostitutes in New York City and 4,000, or almost half, were said to be African-American. This number was determined by the writer's "many years observation of crime," and there is no other data to support the estimate. In fact, 4,000 black prostitutes would have represented over 60 percent of all black females in the city at that time. *Herald*, 4, 9 January 1844. An 1839 brothel directory estimated there were 1,970 black prostitutes. Black prostitutes were listed separately from the 9,291 full-time prostitutes—again, a number that seems exaggerated (Butt Ender, *Prostitution Exposed*).

71. Black women faced the same population imbalance as did Irish women. In 1860, they outnumbered black men in New York by one-third, a statistic that probably reduced their chances for marriage. See Spann, *The New Metropolis*, 27; Paul O. Weinbaum, *Mobs and Demagogues: The New York Response to Collective Violence in the Early Nineteeth Century*, 140–42; Ernst, *Immigrant Life*, 40–41, 67, 104–5, 173, 217; U.S., Census, 1860.

72. There were probably more black prostitutes than records indicate, but they operated discreetly in an effort to avoid incidents of racism and/or legal harassment. Case histories from the House of Refuge illustrate that black women chose prostitution for the same reasons as white women, and that their histories and family backgrounds are comparable. HRCH, no. 1641 (1835), no. 2629 (1840), no. 4895 (1850).

73. H.D. Eastman, *Fast Man's Directory and Lover's Guide to the Ladies of Fashion and Houses of Pleasure in New York and Other Large Cities*, 15.

74. U.S., Census, 1850, Ward 8:31. Nineteenth-century censuses use *mulatto* as a description of race, and I have followed this terminology in discussing census data.

75. Free Loveyer [sic], *Directory to the Seraglios in New York, Philadelphia, Boston and All the Principal Cities in the Union*, 20, 24, 27.

76. Ibid., 20–21.

77. The fact that Sweet is not found in the 1855 census does not mean she had moved. There is no index to this census, and names can be found only by skimming ward listings. Because she is at the same address in the 1854–55 city directory and in the 1859 brothel directory, her name was probably overlooked. U.S., Census, 1850, Wards 5 and 8; N.Y., Census, 1855, Wards 5 and 8.

78. MM, Police Docket, 1849–1850.

79. Eastman, *Fast Man's Directory*, 12, 10.

80. Ibid., 17.

81. *Herald*, 17 January 1846.

82. Newspaper articles repeatedly noted contemporaries' opposition to interracial sex and their blatant expressions of racism. For references to black and white brothels see *New Era and American Courier* (New York), 28 March 1837; *Sun*, 4 June 1834, 27 March, 7 October 1835, 25 May 1836, 4 May, 27 February 1840; *Tribune*, 7 March 1842; *Herald*, 10 June 1836. For additional sources, see discussion of racism and prostitution in Chapter 8 and notes there.

83. *Sun*, 5 October 1840.

84. Ibid., 26 February 1840.

85. U.S., Census, 1850, Wards 5 and 8; N.Y., Census, 1855, Wards 5 and 8. William Sanger discussed black women only as servants in brothels (*History of Prostitution*, 554).

86. *The Gentleman's Directory: The Gentleman's Companion, New York City in 1870*, 24.

87. Ibid., 29.

88. Sanger, *History of Prostitution*, 473–75; N.Y., Census, 1855, Wards 5 and 8; *Times*, 23–24 May 1855.

89. Sanger, *History of Prostitution*, 477–80. It is not possible to say how many of the census prostitutes had had children, since only those children living

in the household were included in the survey. There were, however, a number of children listed as residents of the brothels.

90. Ibid., 477–83. Mortality for children under five was very high for New York as a whole. In 1850 and 1860, 52 percent of children died before they reached age five. Robert Ernst noted that, according to the City Inspector, 67 percent of the city's total mortality for 1857 represented children under five, mostly of foreign parentage (*Immigrant Life*, 53). See also Spann, *The New Metropolis*, 135; John Duffy, *The History of Public Health in New York City*, vol. 1, *1625–1866*, 259, 532–38.

The use of abortion by prostitutes will be discussed in Chapter 7.

91. Smith, *Sunshine and Shadow*, 424; Sanger, *History of Prostitution*, 523–31.

92. *Times*, 24–25 May 1855. It is possible that some of these women were not prostitutes but were arrested merely for being on the street after dark. See Chapter 4 for a discussion of false arrests.

93. Sanger believed that a woman who continued in another occupation after she began working as a prostitute did so to "deceive the world as to her own pursuits, or else to satisfy her conscience that she was not entirely depraved" (*History of Prostitution*, 528, 523–24). In the Sanger study, 75 percent of interviewees had been employed previously. Barbara Hobson has pointed out that 75 percent is very high in light of the low rate of women's participation in the labor force in this era, which she estimates roughly at between 10 percent and 15 percent. The New York Census of 1855, however, stated that 24 percent of women were employed in the workforce. Carol Groneman-Pernicorn's study of New York women in the sixth ward has challenged official estimates on female employment, demonstrating that in this ward, at least, women workers were greatly undercounted. See Hobson, *Uneasy Virtue*, 96; Groneman-Pernicorn, "Bloody Ould Sixth," 149, 162, 169; N.Y., Census, 1855.

94. N.Y., Census, 1855, Wards 5 and 8.

95. Sanger, *History of Prostitution*, 535–36. Approximately one-third of the women were daughters of skilled workers, and almost one-fourth were daughters of farmers. Hobson speculates that these women may have had "expectations of economic and social well-being that could not be fulfilled in a world [where their fathers were facing] narrowing opportunities" (*Uneasy Virtue*, 92–93).

96. Sanger, *History of Prostitution*, 455; NYMS, *First Annual Report*, 9; Tait, *Magdalenism*; Prime, *Life in New York*, 164.

97. [Smith], *Madam Restell*, 28; Parent-Duchatelet, *De la prostitution*; Acton, *Prostitution Considered*, 27, 28–33, 300–302.

98. New York City, Dept. of Health, *Register of Deaths*, 1850–1855; N.Y., Census, 1855.

99. In her research on prostitutes in Boston, Barbara Hobson has sketched a partial portrait of foreign prostitutes. According to Hobson, immigrant women

typically entered the profession later, stayed longer, were more often married, and were usually less literate than native-born prostitutes (*Uneasy Virtue*, 91). No such analysis exists for New York immigrant prostitutes.

Chapter 3

1. Salters was also known as Caroline Paris as well as Catherine Paris. HRCH, no. 819 (1830); *Advocate of Moral Reform*, 15 June 1836; *Police Gazette*, 30 June, 7 July 1849.

2. *Police Gazette*, 30 June 1849.

3. Sanger, *History of Prostitution*, 491.

4. Barbara Heyl, in her recent study, *The Madam as Entrepreneur* (1, 34, 191–95), reviews four theoretical perspectives on why women enter prostitution and summarizes the major explanations of cause exposed by these perspectives. These summary explanations are: (1) The pathological hypothesis: that women with certain personality characteristics enter prostitution in order to meet those personality needs, or because they cannot survive by legitimate means. (2) The social disorganization hypothesis: that women in certain negative social and economic circumstances enter in order to earn a better living. (3) The drift hypothesis: that women find themselves unattached (and perhaps unemployed or poorly paid) and end up, with the help of contacts, finding friends and a source of income in the prostitution world.

5. David M. Schneider, *The History of Public Welfare in New York State, 1609–1866*, 213–14.

6. NYMS, *First Annual Report*, 9.

7. *McDowall's Journal*, March 1833.

8. Water Street Home for Women (WSHW), *Third Annual Report*, vol. 3, 44, 54.

9. From *Advocate of Moral Reform* as quoted in Smith-Rosenberg, *Religion and the Rise*, 121–22.

10. NYFBS, *First Report*; *Advocate of Moral Reform*, 1835–1845. Barbara Hobson argues that female moral reformers recognized the economic roots of prostitution in low wages and poor working conditions. But their ambivalence toward women working outside the home obscured the benefits and opportunities of the labor market and distorted the sexual dangers. As a result, the reformers emphasized lack of protection for women, rather than lack of equal rights, and diverted the focus of reform efforts away from the fundamental reasons for prostitution, i.e., socioeconomic and gender discrimination. See Hobson, *Unequal Virtue*, 49, 64; *Advocate of Moral Reform*, January–February 1835, 1 January 1838, 1 March 1844.

11. *Genius of Temperance*, 29 December 1830, quoted in J. R. Mc-Dowall, *Magdalen Facts*, January 1832, no. 1, 47; Smith-Rosenberg, "Beauty, the Beast;" WSHW, *First Annual Report* (1870), 12, and *Second Annual Report* (1871), 50; Foster, *New York Naked*, 159; Acton, *Prostitution Considered*, 161–69; NYMS, *First Annual Report*, 7–8, 20; *Advocate of Moral Reform*, February 1835; George Ellington, *The Women of New York, or the Underworld of the Great City*, 177. Some recent research on Victorian sexuality points out that one should not confuse prescriptive literature of the nineteenth century with actual nineteenth-century female behavior. Such literature does not reflect what women did, felt, or experienced, but rather what men or society thought women should do. The recent research demonstrates that women were not so sexually passive as the literature would have one believe. See Carl N. Degler, "What Ought to Be and What Was: Women's Sexuality in the Nineteenth Century," 1467–90; Gerda Lerner, "Placing Women in History: Definitions and Challenges," 5–14.

12. Sanger, *History of Prostitution*, 489; Parent-Duchatelet, *De la prostitution*; Acton, *Prostitution Considered*; Tait, *Magdalenism*.

13. Sanger, *History of Prostitution*, 676.

14. Ibid., 525.

15. Woods Hutchinson, "The Economics of Prostitution," 16, 19.

16. Hobson, *Uneasy Virtue*, 101.

17. In addition to the most frequently cited causes discussed in this chapter, some reform literature also cited the evil influences of theaters, romantic novels, balls, ostentatious dress, and even "tight lacings," which critics also believed might lead one into a life of prostitution. See, for example, *Advocate of Moral Reform*, 1830s and 1840s.

18. Sanger, *History of Prostitution*, 492–93.

19. *Sun*, 1 April 1834. See Chapter 7 for a discussion of nineteenth-century infant abandonment.

20. *New Era*, 24 October 1837.

21. Sanger insisted that there were far more who had been seduced than the small percentage who listed it in replies to the questionnaire (*History of Prostitution*, 488, 492).

22. *Advocate of Moral Reform*, August 1835; HRCH, no. 1548, no. 1584 (1835); Ellington, *Women of New York*, 174–76. Joe Farryall was married for a short period in 1833 to a respectable woman. After seven months of marriage, she filed for divorce, citing as causes his consorting with prostitutes, abuse and assault, and abandonment. Court of Chancery, Divorce Proceedings, "Cordelia Farryall v. Joseph Farryall," 5 March 1835, New York County Clerk's Office, Hall of Records.

23. *Advocate of Moral Reform*, 8 February 1836.

24. *Herald*, 23 July 1836; Sanger, *History of Prostitution*, 517; Foster, *New*

York in Slices, 38–39; HRCH, 1830–1860 passim; *Advocate of Moral Reform*, 8 February 1836; NYMS, *First Annual Report*, 8; Ellington, *Women of New York*, 201–2, 306–9.

25. Sanger, *History of Prostitution*, 488.

26. HRCH, no. 865 (1831).

27. HRCH, no. 875 (1831).

28. HRCH, no. 1548 (1835).

29. HRCH, no. 858 (1831); no. 1657 (1835). Sarah Buchanan later married and had a child but died shortly thereafter at age twenty-three.

30. HRCH, no. 728 (1830). See also similar case of Susan M. Badger, no. 4665 (1850); Sanger, *History of Prostitution*, 526.

31. Smith, *Sunshine and Shadow*, 387; Foster, *New York Naked*, 166–68; Marie Flaacke, *Why Women Fall*, 7; Ellington, *Women of New York*, 177; John H. Warren, Jr., *Thirty Years' Battle with Crime; or, the Crying Shame of New York, As seen Under the Broad Glare of an Old Detective's Lantern*, 108; *Madeleine: An Autobiography*, 326; WSHW, *First Annual Report* (1870), 8.

32. Bradford K. Pierce, *Half Century With Juvenile Delinquents or New York House of Refuge and Its Times*, 95.

33. Heyl, *Madam as Entrepreneur*, 191–95.

34. Sanger, *History of Prostitution*, 539–40. Sanger does not tell how many of the prostitutes had lost both parents. He states that 1,349 of their fathers and 1,234 of their mothers were dead.

35. HRCH, no. 1559 (1835). One might expect the House of Refuge to have a high percentage of girls from parentless or single-parent households. A primary reason for admission was that young girls lacked adequate supervision at home, often because they were orphaned or "half-orphaned," with the remaining single parent away from home most of the time working. See HRCH, 1830–1860 passim.

36. HRCH, no. 1603 (1835). See also case no. 1578 (1835).

37. Sanger, *History of Prostitution*, 544; HRCH, 1830, 1831, 1835, 1840.

38. HRCH, no. 2552 (1840).

39. HRCH, no. 1600 (1835), no. 2552 (1840).

40. See Chapter 4 on arrests of women unaccompanied on the streets at night.

41. HRCH no. 1536, no. 1596 (1835); *Sun*, 4, 25 June 1834, 17 August 1836; McBride, *The Domestic Revolution*, 104. Many House of Refuge inmates were committed to that institution either by parents or police because the young women were runaways or because they appeared to lack sufficient parental supervision.

42. Sanger, *History of Prostitution*, 518.

43. HRCH, no. 645 (1829); no. 932 (1831); *Advocate of Moral Reform*, August 1835.

44. HRCH, no. 876 (1831).

45. HRCH, nos. 902–903 (1831).

46. *Advocate of Moral Reform*, 1 July 1836.

47. Sanger, *History of Prostitution*, 488. A number of case histories indicate that Refuge officials suspected but could not prove prostitution by some inmates. In other cases, records show girls practiced prostitution after leaving the Refuge. HRCH, 1830, 1831, 1840, 1850 passim.

48. Heyl, *Madam as Entrepreneur*, 212–13, 195. Like friends and relatives, environment was an important factor influencing girls to enter prostitution. When one grows up surrounded by prostitution, the "opportunity structure" is visible and readily available, and prostitution may seem to be an obvious or natural course of action. See Refuge case histories nos. 624, 625, 645 (1829), 830 (1830), 850, 851 (1831), 1524 (1835).

49. Sanger, *History of Prostitution*, 488. Mary Ann Pitt told House of Refuge officials she "preferred prostitution to work." HRCH, vol. 29 (1866).

50. Sanger, *History of Prostitution*, 488. See also HRCH, no. 329 (1829). Twentieth-century studies also deny sexual motivation or stimulation as a significant cause of prostitution.

51. Sanger, too, believed that giving "light and sedentary" positions, such as store clerk, to women also would be beneficial for men. It would force men "to obtain work situations suitable to their sex and strength, and [would drive] from the crowded cities into the open country some whose effeminacy is fast bringing them to positive idleness and ruin" (*History of Prostitution*, 525). See also Virginia Penny, *The Employments of Women: A Cyclopaedia of Women's Work*, v, vii, 126, 296–97, 486, 488; [Matthew Carey], *Plea for the Poor, Particularly Females. An Inquiry How Far the Charges Alleged Against Them of Improvidence, Idleness, and Dissipation Are Founded in Truth*, 5–6, 39–42. Although the early 1850s was a time of increasing wages for artisans and laborers, women's wages, especially in the needle trades, rose little, and some actually declined. *Tribune*, 8 June 1853; Groneman-Pernicorn, "Bloody Ould Sixth," 150.

52. Sanger, *History of Prostitution*, 524, 528. Stansell, *City of Women*, 226, 228, 155–68, 106–54.

53. Penny, *Employments of Women*, 308–10, 350–52. New York Association for Improving the Condition of the Poor, *Ninth Annual Report* (1852), 26. The U.S. Census of 1860 recorded only 593 hat makers (205 female) and 2700 female shirtmakers, but 16,000 females in other sewing trades. Carol Groneman-Pernicorn and Edith Abbot point out that many women sewed in their homes or worked jointly as tailoresses with husbands and, thus, were not enumerated in official censuses. See U.S., Census, 1860, 379–84; Groneman-Pernicorn, "Bloody Ould Sixth," 95, 140–41; Edith Abbot, *Women In Industry: A Study in American Economic History*, 223, 353–54. Groneman-

Pernicorn, in "Bloody Ould Sixth," tracks changes in wages and prices in the decade after 1850; using an index value of 100 for 1851 prices and wages in New York City, 1861 figures can be calculated at 94.5 for wages but 104.1 for prices, suggesting steadily increasing economic difficulties for poor workers (95).

54. [Carey], *Plea for the Poor*, 5, 39; Smith Hart, *The New Yorkers: The Story of a People and Their City*, 65; *Tribune*, 8 June 1853; Groneman-Pernicorn, "Bloody Ould Sixth," 139–43.

55. *Tribune*, 8 June 1853; Foster, *New York in Slices*, 50–51; Penny, *Employments of Women*, 308–310, 350.

56. Groneman-Pernicorn, "Bloody Ould Sixth," 142; Sanger, *History of Prostitution*, 527, 533; Penny, *Employments of Women*, 308–10. For information on fur sewers and vest, hoopskirt, umbrella, and artificial flower makers see: Penny, 293–94, 301–5; and U.S., Census, 1860, 379–84.

57. *Tribune*, 14 August 1845.

58. Penny, *Employments of Women*, 425–26; Sanger, *History of Prostitution*, 527, 531, 623; *Tribune*, 6 November 1845, 16 September 1846; Groneman-Pernicorn, "Bloody Ould Sixth," 145–46, 155; HRCH, no. 728, no. 758 (1830).

59. Penny, *Employments of Women*, 425–28.

60. *Tribune*, 16 September 1846; Ernst, *Immigrant Life*, 65–68; Groneman-Pernicorn, "Bloody Ould Sixth," 145–46; Sanger, *History of Prostitution*, 527.

61. Sanger, *History of Prostitution*, 524, 527–29.

62. [Carey], *Plea for the Poor*, 6, 11.

63. Ibid. Carey calculated the $48.94 salary by figuring that the woman takes one day a week off for her children and does not work on Sundays; hence 2 x 52 = 104 and 365 less 104 = 261 work days.

64. *Sun*, 13 January 1834; *Tribune*, 19 August 1845; Hart, *The New Yorkers*, 106; Penny, *Employments of Women*, 488. In 1851 Horace Greeley estimated that a working man's family needed $539.24 a year, supported by a salary of $10.37 per week, and in 1853 the New York *Times* estimated a laborer's family of four could live moderately on $600 a year, supported by a weekly salary of $11.54. *Times*, 10 November 1853, quoted in Groneman-Pernicorn, "Bloody Ould Sixth," 91.

65. On reformers' restrictions see: Magdalen Society of New York, *Annual Reports* (1814–1815); NYMS, *Annual Reports*; WSHW, *Annual Reports*. For economic information see: *New Era*, 21 January 1837; Association for Improving the Condition of the Poor Report quoted in Hart, *The New Yorkers*, 117; Groneman-Pernicorn, "Bloody Ould Sixth," 150.

66. Sanger, *History of Prostitution*, 526–27, 533; McBride, *Domestic Revolution*, 99–105. An 1839 brothel directory claimed that at one point in the

1830s, 49 percent of all working women resorted to prostitution to supplement their incomes, a very high figure. Ender, *Prostitution Exposed*.

67. McCabe, *Lights and Shadows*, 583.

68. Nell Kimball, *Her Life as an American Madam*, ed. Stephen Longstreet, 11.

69. HRCH, no. 925 (1831). In the first half of the nineteenth century the term "shilling" was used often and had an approximate value of 12-1/2 cents. Stansell, *City of Women*, 262 n.26.

70. Since each woman had to pay the brothel manager a $1 fee per visitor, one can further assume that the charge per customer would be above $1. Sanger, *History of Prostitution*, 551, 554, 606.

71. The estimated cost to the customer probably included some allowance for buying wine; [Smith], *Madam Restell*, 30; HRCH, no. 1548 (1835); "T.C. to Helen J.," *Police Gazette*, 26 May 1849 (letter dated 26 February 1834). An 1839 brothel directory noted that some establishments might charge customers from $10 to $25 an evening, with breakfast included. Ender, *Prostitution Exposed*.

72. Ellington, *Women of New York*, 201.

73. HRCH, no. 1613 (1835).

74. HRCH, nos. 1556, 1559, 1641 (1835). *Police Gazette*, 7 April 1849, notes $1–$2 as a price for staying with a prostitute.

75. HRCH no. 783 (1830), no. 920, no. 922 (1831), no. 1337 (1834), nos. 1548, 1584, 1623 (1835); *Sun*, 3 October 1835; *Police Gazette*, 3 October 1846; NYMS, *First Annual Report*, 17.

76. Ellington, *Women of New York*, 200. On the 1850s see Sanger, *History of Prostitution*, 550–54. Assignation houses may have been higher at approximately $12 per week. See case in *Police Gazette*, 7 April 1849.

77. Sanger, *History of Prostitution*, 551; Penny, *Employments of Women*, 278. Penny notes that saleswomen also were required to be well dressed. Because they seldom earned more than $6 a week, they were often obliged to eat unwholesome food and live in damp cellars or crowded attics in order to save enough money to dress attractively. See 126 ff.

78. [Carey], *Plea for the Poor*, 5, 15; Sanger, *History of Prostitution*, 549–57.

79. Acton, *Prostitution Considered*, 165–69; Stansell, *City of Women*, 180–90; Hobson, *Uneasy Virtue*, 103–4; and cases in the early years of HRCH, 1830–1840. "Pin money" also was put forth as the reason many women worked in general, and thus served as an excuse for keeping women's wages low. See Penny, *Employments of Women*, 83; Groneman-Pernicorn, "Bloody Ould Sixth," 150.

80. NYMS, *First Annual Report*, 7; Walkowitz, "We Are Not Beasts," 81.

81. James D. McCabe, *New York By Sunlight and Gaslight*, 506–7.

82. See especially Longworth's City Directory, 1855. The uninformed user of city directories in the nineteenth century and now would have no way of knowing if locations were not ordinary boarding establishments. Most census officials did not note the distinction between boardinghouse and prostitution-house keeper if they made any occupational notation at all. (A number of brothels were noted as such in the 1855 census, however.) The position of boardinghouse keeper has not been fully explored as an occupation of nineteenth-century women. Not only is there the problem of defining what constitutes a boardinghouse, but also the position has probably been greatly undercounted in censuses or official surveys. This especially appears to have been the case when the head of a household was a male who listed another occupation while his wife took in boarders. In the 1855 New York census, houses with as many as fifteen boarders are not classified as boardinghouses and the wife's occupation is left blank. On the other hand, a house with as few as three or four boarders might be listed as a boardinghouse, usually when a woman was listed as head of the household. Many nineteenth-century families did take in a few boarders, and the wife and daughters provided the meals and took care of washing and cleaning. By taking in only one boarder, a family could earn as much as if the wife worked as a low-paid seamstress. Groneman-Pernicorn, "Bloody Ould Sixth," 152, 160, 175–76 nn. 48–50.

83. Sanger made a special point of noting when the manager of a particular type of prostitution house was a man, not a woman (*History of Prostitution*, 509, 561, 563). See also Ellington, *Women of New York*, 198. A German visitor in the 1850s also noted that women were managers of New York's brothels (Griesinger, *Lebende Bilder*, 148–56). See Chapters 6 and 7 for related discussions.

Tim Gilfoyle has analyzed, by gender, owners of identified prostitution establishments in the mid-nineteenth century. This analysis included saloons and other leisure establishments that offered entertainments in addition to prostitution.

Years	% Females	% Males	% Couples
1830–39	73	20	7
1840–49	54	43	3
1850–59	61	35	4
1870–79	70	24	6

These establishments were located in brothel directories and court records, but their numbers may distort management figures by indicating an overall underrepresentation of females, especially in the 1840s. Parlor-house brothels, which were mostly female managed, were less frequently harassed by police than other types of prostitution/disorderly houses, so fewer women probably appear in court statistics. Also, even though the extant directories from this era list mostly female-operated brothels and assignation houses, the lack of a directory from the 1840s makes it impossible to identify many female-managed establishments during that decade, leading to the erroneous impression of a decline in female-managed establishments during the 1840s. By the end of the century, female managers no longer dominated the prostitution business in New York. See Gilfoyle, "City of Eros," 186, 523, 541–42; Hobson, *Uneasy Virtue*, 109.

84. J. R. McDowall, in NYMS, *First Annual Report*, 18, uses the word "pimp" and says that in some prostitution houses pimps physically abused the women, especially those wishing to leave the profession. Most other early and mid-nineteenth-century sources (before 1870) do not use the term, and their discussions of the male associates of prostitutes describe them in roles more akin to protectors and watchmen than brokers of sex. Procurers, such as Joseph Farryall, are mentioned earlier in this chapter. Lovers are discussed in Sanger, *History of Prostitution*, 486, 556; [Smith], *Madam Restell*, 34–36; *Police Gazette* on Jewett affair, February–June 1849. See also Chapter 8.

85. Sanger, *History of Prostitution*, 555, 558; Martin, *Secrets*, 286; Ellington, *Women of New York*, 165–66, 199, 235–39; Free Loveyer, *Directory to Seraglios*, 5–20; *Police Gazette*, 7 April 1849; *Tribune*, 18 July 1842.

86. Tracing individuals is most easily done with addresses. Since one had to be a resident of a particular ward to be assessed for personal property but did not have to live on one's property in a ward to be assessed for real estate, personal property is used as a basis for comparison. When known and pertinent, real estate holdings will be noted. It is virtually impossible, however, to trace a person's total real estate holdings, since they might be scattered throughout the city and are grouped and listed by street address, not owner's name. Furthermore, evaluating real estate holdings is problematic because a person may be listed several times on a street, within a ward, and in different wards, leading to a likely overcount of the number of real-estate owners.

Hobson, *Uneasy Virtue*, 108, challenges the idea that prostitutes accumulated assets or invested their capital wisely, thus making considerable sums of money.

87. See Sanger survey for distribution of prostitution in the 1850s. Contemporary newspapers also noted that prostitution existed in all parts of the city (*History of Prostitution*, 580–81). See Chapter 6 for a discussion of New York's community-wide distribution. See Groneman-Pernicorn, "Bloody Ould Sixth," for an analysis of the sixth ward population as family-oriented, hardworking, and respectable.

88. Only 2 percent of the brothels listed were from ward six. Sanger's study, however, showed that ward five led in the number of prostitution and assignation establishments (with seventy), and was followed by wards eight and six, which had fifty-eight each. Ward six's establishments were most likely excluded

from the directories either because they were considered to be "lower class" or because they were not thought to be stable businesses.

After the Civil War the center of brothel activity again shifted to the north. See Chapter 6 for a discussion of prostitute mobility and migration patterns.

89. The remaining wards will not be used in the comparative study. Though ward three had some prostitutes on its northern edge, it was primarily a commercial and financial business district, not a residential/small business area. Its population stabilized and then declined from 1830 to 1850. Wards one and two were already primarily business districts by 1830, and wards four and seven had poorer residents and a large concentration of seamen and other transients. Wards nine, eleven, and thirteen were on the edges of the island, not along the commercial thoroughfares, and wards twelve, sixteen, and eighteen through twenty-two were frontier wards, or were just within the concentrated population limits at the end of the period of comparison. See map, p. 97, for relative placement of wards.

90. The following economic analysis is the result of a selective sampling of tax-record data. Information is taken from five wards at five-year intervals from 1835 to 1855 (although tax records were studied for the entire period from 1830 to 1860). Because of the way in which tax records were kept, numbers of taxpayers had to be determined by a tedious counting of ledger entries. I ascertained the amount of personal property owned by New York women by adding sums of individuals' assessed property. A property holder was determined to be female only if the name was unambiguously a woman's. First names such as Allison, Stacey, and Lowerie were not counted because they might also be nineteenth-century male names, and Francis or Frances is counted as a male name unless a female title is included. Neither were initials regarded as female unless they were preceded by a female designation such as "widow," "Mrs." or "Miss." Furthermore, if a woman was counted as a prostitute, she had to have been clearly identified as one in some source such as a newspaper, census, or brothel directory. Even though a building is known to have been occupied for years as a brothel, the resident or owner is not counted as a prostitute unless the female owner's name or occupant's name in a particular year has been identified in some source as a prostitute. Such a method of determining prostitute property-owners probably undercounts them, but it avoids making exaggerated claims.

In addition to these limitations, there are other reasons why prostitutes and non-prostitute women may not be fully enumerated in the records. A woman usually assumed a new name, a professional name, on becoming a prostitute, but she may have continued to hold property in her legal name. Maria Ashby, who owned 102 Church Street from 1848 through 1859, may be the same person as Mary Ann Burr, who first appeared at this time and operated the property as a brothel for the decade, but one cannot assume this. Neither can

Maria Ashby be assumed to be or to have been a prostitute just because she owns brothel property. A second reason prostitutes and other women property owners may not be fully accounted for is that tax assessing was not a very precise bureaucratic skill in the nineteenth century. Property owners' names are hand written in ledger books and, consequently, are often illegible. Tax assessors also misspelled many names. For example, prostitute DuBois may be listed at various times as Debar, Debair or Depois, and one may miss the fact that all refer to the same person; also, tax assessors sometimes carelessly omitted names from ledger books. For example, Church Street has nine female property-owners in 1830, and from three to nine in every year surveyed from 1840 to 1859. In 1835, however, one of the years selected for study, no female property owners are listed on Church Street.

Church Street serves as an example of another way in which the random five-year selection may not reflect the full extent of property holdings over the entire twenty-year period. Church Street had nine female property owners in both 1845 and 1848. In 1845, a selected year of study, four of the nine assessed property holders were prostitutes, yet in 1848, a year that is not counted, eight of the nine property-owners were prostitutes. A final reason some female property-owners may have been excluded from the tax rolls is that they may not have wished to declare and pay taxes on their property: unless property was visible or known to assessors, they did not disclose their assets. Edward Pessen points out that many nineteenth-century New York residents were known not to declare the true value of their possessions. Records also show that a number of prostitutes appealed their assessments and either had the amounts sworn down or removed from the tax rolls.

Finally, in an effort to determine if there was any correlation between names in tax records and other prostitution records, I cross-checked tax records with the 1850 and 1855 censuses and with the 1853 brothel directory. The results were not conclusive, though the names on tax records correlated a little more closely with censuses than they did with the brothel directory. Both public surveys, census and tax, were taken in the same years, while the directory was printed halfway between the survey dates. The closest correlation between the census and the tax assessments is found in 1850 in ward five. Nineteen prostitutes were assessed for property in ward five, and eleven of them are listed as heads of households in the census. (However, eight prostitute property-owners were not found in the census, and two prostitute heads of households in the census were not assessed for taxes.)

    91. Sanger, *History of Prostitution*, 554.
    92. Ellington, *Women of New York*, 165.
    93. Record of Assessments, 1829–1859, Wd. 5; U.S., 5th Census, 1830; 6th Census, 1840; City Directories, 1830–1851. See Chapter 2 for a brief profile of Berger.

94. See Chapter 2, n. 10 on Pessen's method of calculating current value of assets.

95. Record of Assessments, 1830–1859, Ward 5; *Advocate of Moral Reform*, 15 June 1836.

96. City Directories, 1830–1863; U.S., 5th Census, 1830, 5:277; 6th Census, 1840, 5:23; N.Y., Census, 1855, Ward 8; *Sun*, 30–31 January, 1835; *Commercial Advocate*, 6 June 1836; *Herald*, 15 October 1852.

97. Record of Assessments, 1830–1859, Wards 5 and 8; U.S., 5th, 6th, 7th, Censuses, 1830, 1840, 1850; N.Y., Census, 1855; City Directories 1830–1860; Free Loveyer, *Directory to Seraglios*, 21; Eastman, *Fast Man's Directory*, 6; Ender, *Prostitution Exposed*, 8, 10.

98. Julia Brown also appears to have lived in a house run by Rosina Townsend and then managed a house owned by Adeline Miller before taking over an establishment of her own. Several women were listed in newspapers as "superintendents" of multiple houses of prostitution which meant they, in turn, hired women as brothel keepers, thus giving them a start in the managerial side of the business. Charlotte Briggs ran a house on Thomas Street and superintended another at 159 Church which was managed by her "deputy keeper," Sarah Fisher. *Sun*, 10 March 1840. According to the *Advocate of Moral Reform*, two sisters, Wilson and Harley, superintended fourteen prostitution establishments in different parts of the city, and the editors had heard that another set of sisters supervised thirty houses of assignation. *Advocate of Moral Reform*, 15 March 1837, 15 April 1838.

99. *Life and Death of Fanny White, Being a Complete and Interesting History of the Career of that Notorious Lady*, 16; Record of Assessments, 1851–1859. White's association with Dan Sickles is discussed in Chapter 8.

100. For other information on Tuttle, White, Hastings, Englis, and Gordon see Record of Assessments, 1830–1859, Wards 5 and 8; City Directories, 1830–1860; U.S., 5th, 6th, 7th Censuses, 1830, 1840, 1850, Wards 5 and 8; N.Y., Census, 1855, Wards 5 and 8; Eastman, *Fast Man's Directory*, 5–6, 17; Free Loveyer, *Directory to Seraglios*.

101. Walkowitz and Walkowitz, "We Are Not Beasts," 202–3; Stansell, *City of Women*, 180. The issue of reintegrating into respectable society after practicing prostitution is discussed in Chapter 8.

Chapter 4

1. *Times*, 29 March, 2 April 1855.

2. In 1854 Fernando Wood was elected mayor of New York on a platform promising municipal reform and a crackdown on vice. Citizens had increasingly

voiced their concern about the rise of corruption and vice, including "the shameful disgrace of prostitution." Letters to the editor of the *Times* early in 1855 reflect this heightened citizen concern about the public visibility of prostitution. Writers complained about the constant parade of prostitutes seen on Broadway and other respectable thoroughfares at all hours of the night and day. These letters called for the new mayor to "act to end the disgrace" (*Times*, 3, 20 January, 2 February 1855).

In the months following the public's appeal, on order of the mayor, police arrested large numbers of alleged streetwalkers under the vagrancy law. The first arrests of the mayor's campaign against the streetwalkers occurred on two evenings in the last week of March 1855 in a simultaneous "surprise attack" in four of the city's wards. Seventy-nine women were arrested for walking in the major thoroughfares in wards 3, 4, 8 and 14. The press referred to this as a "limited number of arrests" and attributed the small number to the fact that "word had spread as by telegraph" among the streetwalkers as soon as the first arrests were made (*Times*, 28–30 March 1855). See table 7, Chapter 2.

3. From 1674 until 1895, the mayor's office functioned as a court of law when necessary or when a mayor wished to act in that capacity. See "Appraisal Recommendations for New York County Court Records."

4. Sanger, *History of Prostitution*, 599.

5. *Times*, 2 April 1855.

6. On women's position in society see Stansell, *City of Women*; Cott, *Bonds of Womanhood*; Berg, *Remembered Gate*.

7. *Times*, 2 April 1855.

8. In addition to prostitutes, vagrants included the unemployed or poor who were identified as "beggars, loafers, and the diseased."

9. Strong, *Diary*, vol. 2, 218 (entry for 31 March 1855).

10. *Times*, 23 May 1855.

11. Ibid., 30 March 1855.

12. See James Hurst, *The Growth of American Law: The Law Makers*, for a discussion of law within a cultural context.

13. *Advocate of Moral Reform*, 1 November 1841. For a full discussion of the vagrancy law see *New Era*, 20 July to 15 August, 1838; Sanger, *History of Prostitution*, 25, 634–35, 638–40; *Times*, 29 March–15 June 1855.

14. *New Era*, 20, 28 July, 6, 7 August 1838; *Advocate of Moral Reform*, 1 November 1841; Arthur Barnett Springarn, *Laws Relating to Sex and Morality in New York City*, 10.

15. *McDowall's Journal*, June 1833; *New Era*, 20 July, 6, 7, August 1838; *Times*, 30 March 1855.

16. *Police Gazette*, 24 February 1849; *New Era*, 20 July, 6, 7 August 1838.

17. Ernst, *Immigrant Life*, 191. A greater population increase is shown by Albion in *Rise of the New York Port*, 418–19.

18. *Times*, 30 March 1855. For some examples of arrests, see *Sun*, 31 May 1834; 24 January, 27 March 1835; 27 January, 27 February, 30 April, 4 May 1840; 1 September 1841; *Tribune*, 14, 21 June 1841; *Courier and Enquirer*, 29 June, 26 July 1830; *Herald*, 23 April, 10 June 1836, 23 January 1844; *Police Gazette*, 18 July, 16 December 1846; *Times*, 28 March–15 June 1855.

19. *Semi-Annual Report of the Chief of Police*, DBA, Doc. 3:55–63, 70:1131–45, 54:851–60 (1850); 26:545–47, 42:729–35, 55:1041–44 (1851); 7:116–19 (1852); 14:2 (1854); 22:2, 32:2 (1855); 16:2–13 (1856).

20. It is certain that the two volumes of arrest records in the New York City Archives for this period do not represent all the wards in New York, but it is not certain that they contain all the arrests for the wards they do include. (Apparently only wards 1–6 are covered.) However, by comparing docket statistics with the police chiefs' semi-annual reports for 1850, one can make a relative comparison of the arrests for vagrancy and prostitution, especially in ward 6. For example, the two available dockets list approximately 400 prostitute/vagrants arrested from January to December 1850 in ward 6. The semi-annual police report for April–September 1850 (only six months) lists a total of 1,234 male and female vagrancy arrests in ward 6. (Ward 3 listed 127 vagrants, ward 5 had ninety-nine, and ward 4 had eighty-four in this same six-month period.) For all of New York City during this period, there were 1,889 vagrancy arrests, so ward 6 accounted for over sixty-five percent of all vagrancy arrests in the city.

21. From late March through June 1855, with Mayor Wood's reform program in effect, one could expect a change in vagrancy arrests. At this time police were concentrating on the wards bordering Broadway—wards 3, 5, 8, and 14.

22. Robert H. Morris (1802–1855), the son of a New York merchant, was one of the city's most successful lawyers and a major presence in the local Democratic party. He served as district attorney, state legislator, and city recorder before being elected mayor in 1841. After three one-year terms as mayor, he served as postmaster of New York, and in his last years, as a justice of the State Supreme Court (Spann, *The New Metropolis*, 54).

23. *New Era*, 20 July 1838.

24. Ibid., 20 July–15 August 1838.

25. *Tribune*, 7 August 1841.

26. Ibid., 7 August 1841.

27. *Police Reorganization*, DBA, Doc. 53:975–77 (1844).

28. *Tribune*, 18 August 1843.

29. *Police Reorganization*, DBA, Doc. 53:975.

30. Ibid., 53:976.

31. *Tribune*, 18 August 1843.

32. *Police Reorganization*, DBA, Doc. 53:978–80.

33. *Tribune*, 20–21 November 1843; CGS, *People v. Alexander Hoag and Melinda Hoag*, 24 November 1843.

34. *Tribune*, 21 November, 14, 16, 23 December 1843; *Herald*, 17 January 1844. In November 1845, the *Police Gazette* reported there was no truth in the rumor that Melinda Hoag, "the famous panel thief," had been pardoned from state prison. A few months later, in April 1846, a special justice with the city courts noted in his diary that he had seen Alexander Hoag while on an official visit to Sing Sing. *Police Gazette*, 1 November 1845; Taylor, "Diary," 9 April 1846; CGS, *People v. Hoag*, 24 November 1843; CGS, *People v. Hoag*, 5 August 1844.

That the Hoags were recipients of public comment indicates that they had achieved some degree of notoriety with New Yorkers who seemed fascinated by the prostitute, her paramour, and their involvement in a life of crime. Newspapers reported to curious readers on their status as prisoners and one book included them throughout its discussion of New York's criminals. Several years after they were sent to prison, the press referred to crimes similar to theirs as robberies "a la Hoag" (*Police Gazette*, 17, 24 January 1846; George Wilkes, *The Mysteries of the Tombs*, 16–18, 21–23, 37, 53–58, 64 ff.).

35. *Police Reorganization*, DBA, 53:692–93.

36. *Police Gazette*, 8 August 1846.

37. MM, Police Docket, 7 November 1850.

38. *Herald*, 10 January 1849.

39. See n. 13 above on sources that discuss the vagrancy law and proposed changes in the law.

40. *Times*, 3 April 1855.

41. Ibid., 23, 24 May 1855.

42. Ibid., 23 May 1855.

43. Ibid., 15 June 1855. An 1855 grand jury investigating corruption and misconduct of city government officials brought an indictment against Justice Connelly for allowing prisoners charged with assault and battery to be discharged on their own recognizance (James F. Richardson, *The New York Police: From Colonial Times to 1901*, 74).

44. *Times*, 18 June 1855.

45. Wilber R. Miller, *Cops and Bobbies: Police Authority in New York and London, 1830–1870*, 150–51; Richardson, *New York Police*, 76.

46. MM, Police Docket, 1849–1855.

47. *Semi-Annual Reports of the Chief of Police*, DBA, Doc. 7:119 (1852), Doc. 16:12–13 (1856); BCMP, *Annual Reports*, no. 9:81–82 (1866), no. 13:98–99 (1867), no. 13:88–89 (1868), no. 14:102–103 (1869); Gilfoyle, "City of Eros," 255.

48. Sanger, *History of Prostitution*, 565; *Advocate of Moral Reform*, August 1835.

49. *Advocate of Moral Reform*, 1 March 1840.

50. Sanger, *History of Prostitution*, 565.

51. *Advocate of Moral Reform*, 15 August 1836; *New Era*, 30 January 1837; *Police Gazette*, 28 April 1849.

52. *Sun*, 12 February, 29 June 1842; *Police Gazette*, 4 July 1846, 13 January 1849; *Tribune*, 29 July 1841, 12 February 1842. See also disorderly house cases, CGS, Case Records, 1830–1870, NYMA.

53. CGS, *People v. Rosina Townsend* (Thompson), 13 July 1830.

54. Ibid.

55. CGS, *People v. Rosina Townsend* (Thompson), 13 July 1830; *People v. Valentine*, 11 March 1833; and Jewett murder case, *People v. Robinson*, 19 April 1836.

56. CGS, *People v. Julia Brown*, 13 October 1834.

57. CGS, *People v. Mary Louise Clark, et al.*, 17 October 1834.

58. Ibid.

59. *Herald*, 20 September 1842.

60. Ibid.

61. Ibid.

62. *Advocate of Moral Reform*, 1 March 1840.

63. Ibid., *Sun*, 14 February 1840.

64. *Police Gazette*, 20 January 1849; U.S., Census, 1840; City Directory, 1838; James Monaghan, *The Great Rascal: The Life and Adventures of Ned Buntline*, 184.

65. *Police Gazette*, 20 January 1849.

66. Ibid.; Gilfoyle, "City of Eros," 23; PCR, *People v. Ella*, 1841. Prostitution was considered a legal offense only on public streets. Prostitutes who solicited indoors had legal problems only if they were disorderly.

67. *Police Gazette*, 13, 20 January 1849.

68. See Chapter 3 on changing attitudes. See also *Police Gazette*, 12 May 1849.

69. *Tribune*, 1 April 1843.

70. *Herald*, 22 April, 21 October 1849; *Police Gazette*, 28 April 1849; MM, Police Docket, 20 April, 9 July 1849. On Delaplaine's extensive property holdings that were occupied by prostitutes, see Records of Assessments, 1840s–1850s, and Gilfoyle, "City of Eros," 131.

71. *Herald*, 7 April 1849.

72. In 1857, on behalf of a Committee on Immigration, a bill was presented to Congress to make it a penal offense for an officer or sailor on an immigrant ship to have carnal intercourse with a passenger, with or without the passenger's consent (Sanger, *History of Prostitution*, 462).

73. See Claudia D. Johnson, "That Guilty Third Tier: Prostitution in

Nineteenth-Century American Theaters," 579; Meade Minnigerode, *The Fabulous Forties: 1840–1850; A Presentation of Private Life*, 154–55; Sanger, *History of Prostitution*, 557.

74. *Herald*, 29 October, 1, 6 November 1842.

75. *Police Reorganization*, DBA, 53:799, 844.

76. Sanger, *History of Prostitution*, 557; Johnson, "Guilty Third Tier," 579.

77. Sanger, *History of Prostitution*, 644, 671.

78. *Times*, 5 April 1855.

79. *Police Reorganization*, DBA, 53:692–93; [Smith], *Madam Restell*, 40.

80. *Police Reorganization*, DBA, 53:692–93.

81. [Smith], *Madam Restell*, 40.

82. Walkowitz, "We Are Not Beasts," 49–50; John Griscom, *The Sanitary Conditions of the Laboring Population of New York*, 5.

83. Sanger, *History of Prostitution*, 627–76, 573, 586–89.

84. Aaron Powell, *State Regulation of Vice: Regulation Efforts in America*, 48–52; Lois W. Banner, *Elizabeth Cady Stanton: A Radical for Women's Rights*, 96; Sanger, *History of Prostitution*, 598–99. Sanger noted that: "Every resident of New York will remember the excitement caused in the spring of the year 1855 by the arrest of a large number of prostitutes in the public streets, their committal to Blackwell's Island, and their subsequent discharge on writs of *habeas corpus*, on account of informality in the proceedings; *but it is not generally known that of those arrested at that time a very large proportion, certainly more than one half, were suffering from syphilis in its primary form. . . . We make this assertion from our own knowledge, the result of a professional examination*" (598–99). (Italics mine.)

85. Powell, *State Regulation*, 53–54; Bullough, *History of Prostitution*, 193.

86. Powell, *State Regulation*, 53–63; John C. Burnham, "Medical Inspection of Prostitutes in America in the Nineteenth Century: The St. Louis Experiment and Its Sequel," 203–18.

87. Kate Millett et al., *The Prostitution Papers: A Candid Dialogue*, 146, quoted in Edwin M. Schur, *Labeling Women Deviant: Gender, Stigma, and Social Control*, 169.

88. Millett, *Prostitution Papers*, 143, quoted in Schur, *Labeling Women Deviant*, 170.

89. Not until 1978 did New York pass legislation that ostensibly made patrons liable to the same penalties as prostitutes and that required that customers be fingerprinted, photographed, and booked on arrest (Schur, *Labeling Women Deviant*, 170).

90. L. M. Child quoted in Berg, *Remembered Gate*, 210.

91. *Sun*, 11 February 1842.

92. *Advocate of Moral Reform*, 15 August 1836.

93. See *Advocate of Moral Reform*, 1 March, 15 April, 15 May, 1 June 1840.

94. CGS, *People v. Norman*, 23 November 1843. Norman's [Lydia Brown's] address at 51 West Broadway was on a block where several brothels were located. An 1859 brothel directory lists L. P. Brown as manager of an assignation house (with a few lady boarders) at 82 Green (Free Loveyer, *Directory to Seraglios*, 24).

95. *Herald*, 17, 19 January 1844.

96. CGS, *People v. Norman*, 23 November 1843.

97. Ibid.

98. *Herald*, 19 January 1844.

99. Ibid., 21 January 1844.

100. Ibid., 22 January 1844.

101. Ibid., 27 January 1844.

102. *Police Reorganization*, DBA, 53:844.

103. *Herald*, 10 March 1845; Smith-Rosenberg, "Beauty, the Beast," 576; *Licentiousness*, 8. Adultery was not included in the final bill and did not become a crime in New York until 1907. See Springarn, *Laws Relating to Sex*, xi. See also *Sun*, 11 February 1842, for an example of the difficulties in pursuing a breach of promise and seduction case.

The debate over seduction and adultery was not without its humor. In 1840 editors of the *Sun* argued that people could not be legislated into morality and suggested that the proposed seduction bill be entitled "An Act to Subdue the Passions and Control the Thoughts, Intents and Motives of the Human Heart" (*Advocate of Moral Reform*, 15 April 1840). The *Tribune* quoted a reporter from Albany as saying that the bill would never be accepted unless exceptions were written into it for members of the legislature (*Tribune*, 1 April 1843). A writer at the *Herald* voiced doubt that the legislators would pass the Seduction and Adultery bill because they would be condemning themselves in the past and abolishing their privileges in the future. He continued: "Generally the greatest knaves of the community are picked up and sent to represent the people in legislative bodies," and if the bill were to pass, "several new prisons will have to be built to meet the fashionable wants of the enlightened and Christian" (*Herald*, 20 February 1844). One of New York City's legislative delegates was said to have complained that it was old men who no longer wished to transgress who were responsible for the bill. This legislator believed that the proposed bill was an abridgement of his rights (*Licentiousness*, 8).

104. *Police Gazette*, 20 September 1845; 20 March 1847.

105. *Police Gazette*, 29 September 1849; *Semi-Annual Report of the Chief of Police*, DBA, 1848, 1849.

106. Sanger, *History of Prostitution*, 496.

Chapter 5

1. *Sun*, 19, 21 June 1834.

2. Miller, *Cops and Bobbies*, 45–48; Richardson, *New York Police*, 16–49.

3. Because New York City technically was a creature of the state and had only those governing powers that the state legislature saw fit to grant it, the state could dictate how many marshals there would be. Marshals, constables, and private citizens could arrest without a warrant, though private citizens were more at risk legally if arrest charges were not substantiated.

4. Richardson, *New York Police*, 35–36, 18–22; Miller, *Cops and Bobbies*, 4.

5. Richardson, *New York Police*, 25–30.

6. Ibid.; *Police Reorganization*, DBA, 53:704.

7. *Police Reorganization*, DBA, 53:794; Richardson, *New York Police*, 39, 42–49, 99, 163–64. Other features of the reorganized police were the designation of each ward as a police district with its own stationhouse; appointment of a captain, assistant captains, and police from among the residents of each ward; appointment of a chief of police with limited supervisory powers over the force; one-year terms for the chief and all other policemen; appointment of police by the mayor upon the nomination of the alderman and assistant aldermen of each ward (with the aldermen therefore having the "real" power of appointment); identification of police by a star-shaped badge but no uniform; and refusal by police of all monetary or other rewards except on written permission of the mayor.

8. *Tribune*, 13 March 1844.

9. Walling, *Recollections*, 602.

10. Several sources discuss the general corruption of police in this period. Police Justice Robert Taylor in his diary refers to seeing a daybook and register that "gave proof that corruption exists to an alarming extent with many officials connected with the administration of criminal law in the city" ("Diary," 24 November 1846).

A number of contemporary newspapers complained about corrupt law officials, and in 1836, the *Herald* charged that prostitutes could stay out of jail by bribing policemen with their jewelry (10 August 1836). See also *Tribune*, 13 March 1844.

Charles Lockwood, in *Manhattan Moves Uptown* (1976), says that madams in this period paid police so they would have no problems, but he gives no sources for this claim (146).

Smith Hart, in *The New Yorkers* (1938), argues that police graft was extensive during the 1840s, especially in relation to prostitutes (98, 220–21). His description of this corruption, from George Wilkes, *Police Gazette* editor, is a description of the system of fees and fines that existed at the time. He also says that after the Civil War, madams paid precinct captains an initial protection fee of $500 and $50 monthly dues. When a new captain was appointed, initial fees had to be paid again. According to Hart, one madam testified that she paid over $30,000 to police for protection. Hart also claimed that patrolmen either charged streetwalkers $1 to be on the street and then divided the night's earnings with the prostitutes, or they charged a flat fee of 25 cents for every customer a prostitute serviced. Hart does not specify when this payoff system operated, nor does he document sources for the information.

Tim Gilfoyle claims that in mid-century New York, ward politicians (who controlled the local police) extorted bribes from prostitutes as well as from gambling and drinking establishments. These practices, according to Gilfoyle, led to the extensive system of extortion found in New York City after 1880. His sources are from the later period, however. ("Strumpets and Misogynists: Brothel 'Riots' and the Transformation of Prostitution in Antebellum New York City," 45–65.

11. M. Smith stated that police did not meddle with mid-century prostitutes' businesses unless there was a problem or complaint (*Sunshine and Shadow*, 371). Investigations tended to occur for theft, harboring young girls, or being very disorderly.

12. Prime, *Life in New York*, 169. In the E. Z. C. Judson divorce trial, Officer Dennis Cochran established the defendant's presence in a brothel (Hastings' house at 50 Leonard Street) by testifying that he had observed him leaving the house from the police station next door (*Herald*, 3 October 1849).

13. The concept of "friendship" is challenged by those who question the viability of true friendship in a relationship between people of unequal power; the law enforcer always has the power to coerce the prostitute.

14. *Transcript*, 4 June 1836; *Commercial Advertiser*, 4 June 1836; *Sun*, 4 June 1836.

15. CGS, *People v. Margaret Ryerson*, 13 March 1834; *People v. John Taylor and Susan Shannon*, 19 April 1836.

16. Superior Court, Divorce Record, "Catherine N. Forrest v. Edwin Forrest," 3 January 1852; *Times*, 3–26 January 1852; *Herald*, 6–26 January 1852.

17. *Police Gazette*, 20 January 1849. In the Rebecca Davis disorderly house case, the defendant had a watchman testify to her good character (*Herald*, 20 September 1842).

18. Richardson, *New York Police*, 40, 58.

19. Taylor, "Diary," 5 February 1846–1 August 1847; Richardson, *New York Police*, 58.

20. Taylor, "Diary," quotation from 24 November 1846.

21. Ibid., 23 November, 6 December 1846. Taylor learned the next day that White had not been his visitor. Chapter 7 discusses other prostitutes who assisted police with work: Eliza Fisher, *New Era*, 15 September 1839; and Harriet Smith, *Police Gazette*, 14 February 1846.

22. CGS, *People v. Lozier, et al.*, 14 June 1831.

23. Richardson, *New York Police*, 74–75.

24. *Advocate of Moral Reform*, August 1835, December 1835, January 1836; *Police Gazette*, 20 October 1849.

25. Prime, *Life in New York*, 169.

26. *Sun*, 29 November 1836.

27. Ibid., 16 April 1841, 25 September 1835; CGS, *People v. Ostrander*, 16 June 1831; Ellington, *Women of New York*, 174; *Times*, 5 February 1855; *Herald*, 8 January 1850.

28. *Herald*, 31 March 1850; *Sun*, 21 March, 22 May 1834; 14 January 1835; 20 April 1837; 13 April 1840; Hart, *The New Yorkers*, 97.

29. *Herald*, 6 January 1850.

30. *Police Gazette*, 12 September 1846; *Tribune*, 13 March 1844.

31. *Herald*, 23 June 1848.

32. *Herald*, 26 April 1849.

33. Walling, *Recollections*, 580. My interpretation of the prostitute as "assertive citizen" and as party to "working relationships" with legal officers was made in the 1970s when I first researched and compiled data from police and court documents. Both Anne Butler and Timothy Gilfoyle have articulated similar notions, adding force to this interpretation of the role of the prostitute in the legal community.

34. Record of Assessments, 1848, 1850, Ward 5.

35. MM, Police Docket, 10 February 1850; *Herald*, 7 October 1849.

36. *Police Gazette*, 13 October 1849.

37. Richard O'Connor, *The Scandalous Mr. Bennett*, 7–20; Weinbaum, *Mobs and Demagogues*, 24–27, 41–57.

38. O'Connor, *Scandalous Mr. Bennett*, 21. Twice in 1836 Bennett was attacked with fists and canes by J. G. Webb of the *Courier and Enquirer* after Bennett wrote articles casting aspersions on Webb's integrity. Webb boasted that in addition to hitting Bennett on the head, he had forced Bennett's jaw open and had spit down his throat. Bennett also was horsewhipped by a Wall Street broker in the late 1830s, and in 1850 a defeated Tammany politician and his friends mercilessly beat Bennett to the ground with cowhide whips while Bennett was walking down Broadway with his wife. Hone was delighted to hear about Bennett's misfortune and wrote that he wished it would happen once a week, "so that new wounds might be inflicted before the old ones were healed." George T. Strong found Webb as offensive as Bennett, describing him as "the unblushing and notorious author of more outrages on honesty, morality, and

public decency than any man I at this moment remember" (O'Connor, *Scandalous Mr. Bennett*, 21–22, 33–34; Hone, *Diary*, vol. 2, 908 [entry for 11 November 1850]; Strong, *Diary*, vol. 1, 224 [entry for 21 January 1844]). See also James Monaghan, *The Great Rascal*, 169–70, for a description of the assault on editor Judson.

39. CGS, *People v. Hastings*, 4 April 1849.

40. *Herald*, 7 April 1849.

41. Ibid.

42. *Herald*, 18 April 1849.

43. Ibid.

44. CGS, *People v. Hastings*, 4 April 1849, Exhibit A, "E. Z. C. Judson to Kate Hastings."

45. Ibid., Exihibit B, "One Who Knows Something to Kate Hastings."

46. *Herald*, 18 April 1849.

47. Court of Common Pleas, Divorce Proceedings, "Annie Judson v. Edwin Z. C. Judson," 29 September 1849, CCHR.

48. Record of Assessments, 1840–1860 passim, Wards 5 and 8.

49. Judson: Court of Common Pleas, "Judson v. Judson," 29 September 1849; *Herald*, 30 September, 3 October 1849. Judson was also in court at the same time for his role in the Astor House riots (*Herald*, 30 September 1849). See *Account of the Terrific and Fatal Riot at the New York Astor Place Opera House on the Night of May 10, 1849*.

Forrest: Superior Court, "Forrest v. Forrest," 3 January 1852; *Times*, 3–22 January 1852; *Herald*, 6, 8, 14, 26 January 1852. See also divorces of Childs, *Sun*, 18 January 1842, and Holland, *Police Gazette*, 13 October 1849.

50. *Herald*, 31 May, 1 June 1841; *Tribune*, 21, 27–29 March 1843; *Herald* and *Sun*, June 1836; Walling, *Recollections*, 113–24; Edward Van Every, *Sins of New York as "Exposed" by the Police Gazette*, 135–40. For inquests concerning deaths, see *Sun*, 19 August, 19 September, 13 October 1836; 24 October 1842; *Tribune*, 2 July 1841, 21 July 1842; *New Era*, 10 August 1839; CGS, *People v. Robinson*, 19 April 1836.

51. Goldstreng: *New Era*, 10 December 1836; Fisher: *Tribune*, 18 June 1841, 12 January 1843; Meyer: *Tribune*, 31 August 1842, *Sun*, 30 October 1840; Stewart: *Herald*, 28 April 1849, *Police Gazette*, 13 October 1849. For other examples, see *Tribune*, 16 January 1843; *Sun*, 30 January 1835, 3 March 1840; *Herald*, 19 October 1850.

52. *Sun*, 3 October 1836, 18 March, 19 June 1834.

53. *Sun*, 19 September 1835.

54. CGS, *People v. Valentine*, 11 March 1833; *Sun*, 14 November 1836.

55. Weinbaum, in *Mobs and Demagogues*, describes an incident in which a brothel was destroyed by a group because a woman supposedly contracted cholera on the premises (66). Sanger noted that prostitutes were especially susceptible to assaults by groups and individuals (*History of Prostitution*, 486).

The *Herald*, 22 November 1836, after a vicious attack by a group of men on several brothels in November of 1836, reported that they believed there was a relationship to the fact that Jewett's "murderer" had gone free, stating that since Jewett's case "there are villains who imagine they can do anything with impunity." The *Sun* also editorialized about "citizen" rioters who attack brothels for sport (*Sun*, 21 April 1837).

56. CGS, *People v. Gale, et al.*, 14 June 1831.

57. CGS, *People v. Chichester, et al.*, 7, 11 May 1835. For other cases see *Sun*, 26, 31 December 1833; 8, 22 January 1834; 3, 12 March, 30 September 1835; 29, 30 September, 6 October 1836; 21 April 1837; 5 February 1840; *Tribune*, 17 June 1841; 12 August 1842; 17 August 1844; *Herald*, 17 November 1835; 2 August 1836; *New Era*, 25 November 1836; 11 January, 18, 25 February 1837.

58. See *Sun*, 5–7 January 1840 for a discussion of bullies' targets in the community. The term *brothel bullies* was used at this time to refer to men who attacked brothels, but the *New Era* (6 July 1839) used the term to refer to men who were hired by brothels for protection. George Strong (*Diary*, vol. 4, 113, entry for 18 November 1866) used the term in 1866 to describe some Irish roughs who were part of the "brutal Irishy" in the Democratic party.

59. *Sun*, 22 November 1836, 19 April 1837; *Herald*, 22 November 1836; CGS, *People v. Graham and Cole*, 13 December 1836. Ellen Jewett also got $100 through the court for garments that were destroyed by a client following an argument (*Transcript*, 30 June 1834).

60. *Police Gazette*, 2 January 1847.

61. Maria: *Herald*, 23 April 1836; Gamble: CGS, *People v. Dikeman, et al.*, 14 December 1836; Shannon: *Sun*, 5 February 1840; Williams: *Tribune*, 12 August 1842; CGS, *People v. Mott*, 20 October 1842.

62. *Herald*, 17 January 1844; 5 April 1850; *Police Gazette*, 12 January 1850; *Tribune*, 13 March 1844.

63. *Tribune*, 12 January 1843, *Police Gazette*, 7 July 1849.

64. CGS, *People v. Hyer*, 17 December 1836; *New Era*, 9 January 1837; Logue quote from CGS, *People v. Timpson*, 11 April 1842; *Tribune*, 9 March 1842.

65. CGS, *People v. Ford*, 10 August 1844.

66. CGS, *People v. Nosworthy*, 12 March 1832; *Sun*, 15 May 1834; *Herald*, 4 May 1849; *Police Gazette*, 12 May 1849; *Sun*, 17 May 1834.

67. *Sun*, 9, 26 December 1833. Quote from defense counsel, *Sun*, 21 June 1836.

68. The judge's charge was printed in *Advocate of Moral Reform*, 15 June 1836.

69. Ogden Hoffman was a native New Yorker and the son of a well-known judge. He served as a Democratic member of the legislature but became a Whig

when Andrew Jackson attacked the U.S. Bank. From 1829 through 1835 he was District Attorney of New York and then for a quarter of a century was counsel in almost every celebrated criminal case in the New York City courts. From 1837 through 1841 he served in Congress. Both Hone and Strong admired him, and Strong wrote that he was the "greatest criminal lawyer of the time in New York, a genial, indolent, brilliant man" (Strong, *Diary*, xxx; Hone, *Diary*, xxv).

70. *Advocate of Moral Reform*, 15 June 1836.

71. *Missionary Intelligence*, quoted in *Advocate of Moral Reform*, August 1835; also 1 November 1841.

72. Quote on Shannon from *Sun*, 5 February 1840; on Julia Brown, *Sun*, 20 February 1840.

73. *Police Gazette*, 13, 20 January 1849. For examples of veracity and testimony in other cases, see also *Advocate of Moral Reform*, August 1835, 1 December 1841; *Times*, 23 January 1852, 22 March 1855; *Sun*, 9, 26 December 1833, 29 January 1842; Foster, *New York Naked*, 157.

Chapter 6

1. Sanger, *History of Prostitution*, 29–30.

2. NYMS, *First Annual Report*, 7.

3. *Transcript* quoted in *Advocate of Moral Reform*, August 1835.

4. For the 1840s, see [Smith], *Madam Restell*, 29; for the 1850s, see the distribution of houses in Sanger's survey, *History of Prostitution*, 580–81, also 652, and 1897 edition, Appendix, 677–78; for the 1860s, see Ellington, *Women of New York*, 196–97.

5. In "City of Eros," his study of prostitution from 1790 to 1920, Tim Gilfoyle divides the era into three periods—before 1820, 1820 to 1870, and after 1870—and argues that the middle period offered the greatest freedom in sexual commerce. In the Appendix to the 1897 edition of his *History of Prostitution*, Sanger also notes a change in the post–Civil War period.

6. Weinbaum, *Mobs and Demagogues*, 134, 137–39. Weinbaum uses the New York State censuses of 1825 and 1855 for his calculations. In 1825, 23.9 percent of the immigrant population would have had to relocate in other wards for each ward to have had the same proportion of the city's total immigrant population; in 1855, only 12.6 percent would have had to relocate.

For more information on immigrant populations see Ernst, *Immigrant Life*, 187, 192–96. The Irish represented nearly half of the population of wards 1, 4, and 6, while Germans were primarily concentrated in wards 10, 11, and 17. See also Bridges, *City in the Republic*, 43.

7. Weinbaum, *Mobs and Demagogues*, 140–41; Groneman-Pernicorn, "Bloody Ould Sixth," 35; U.S., Census, 1860.

8. Bridges, *City in the Republic*, 43; Berg, *Remembered Gate*, 43; Hone, *Diary*, 785 (entry for 29 January 1847); Spann, *New Metropolis*, 148.

9. Bridges, *City in the Republic*, 44; Weinbaum, *Mobs and Demagogues*, 134. See also Betsy Blackmar, "Rewalking the Walking City," *Radical History Review*, 131–48.

10. Bridges, *City in the Republic*, 41; Spann, *New Metropolis*, 106–9. Central Park was New York's one great triumph of urban planning. Other attempts, such as housing for the poor, either fell far short of needs or were characterized by failure. See Spann, *New Metropolis*, 139–75.

11. *Herald*, 1 June 1841.

12. McCabe, *Lights and Shadows*, 52.

13. See Gilfoyle, "City of Eros," 66–67 and nn. 40–41 on 90–91 for lists of respectable addresses and their proximity to brothels. James Grant Wilson identifies the following upper-class and fashionable streets: Church, College Place, Barclay, Murray, Park Place, Chambers, Warren, Franklin, and White (*The Memorial History of the City of New York*, vol. 3, 356, 359). Strong also identifies prostitution streets in the same area (*Diary*, vol. 3, 565–66, entry for 18 March 1865).

14. Lockwood, *Manhattan Moves Uptown*, 294. Martin [McCabe], writing in the 1860s, noted that first-class houses of prostitution, often unknown to their immediate neighbors, operated in the best city neighborhoods (*Secrets of the Great City*, 208–9, 285–88).

15. McCabe, *Lights and Shadows*, 697.

16. Lockwood, in *Manhattan Moves Uptown*, 111, attributes the description to the *Courier and Enquirer*; Spann uses the same description, attributing it to the *Tribune*, 7 February 1853 (*The New Metropolis*, 146, 464). See also Hart, *The New Yorkers*, 107.

17. George G. Foster, *New York by Gas-Light: With Here and There a Streak of Sunshine*, 54.

18. N.Y., Census, 1855, Ward 8. For other examples, see CGS, *People v. Strong*, 9 October 1843; *People v. Bodell*, 8 March 1847.

19. Lockwood, *Manhattan Moves Uptown*, 294.

20. Spann notes that after the development of mass transportation and the growth of suburbs in the last half of the nineteenth century, the character of New York's "mixed neighborhoods" began to change (*New Metropolis*, 148–61).

21. Mobility in and out of cities of the Northeast was as characteristic of nineteenth-century populations as was mobility within them. See Stephen Thernstrom and Peter Knights, "Men in Motion: Some Data and Speculations

About Urban Population Mobility in Nineteenth-Century America," 10, 23; Berg, *Remembered Gate*, 51.

22. See Chapters 4, 5.

23. *New Era*, 31 December 1836.

24. Ibid., 11 January 1837. For further discussions of the May Day moving custom, see *Sun*, 27 January 1840, 3 May 1842; *New Era*, 31 December 1836; *Herald*, 1–2 May 1849; Hone, *Diary*, vol. 1, 157–58 (entry for 30 April 1835), and see also 394 (entry for 1 May 1839); and Strong, *Diary*, vol. 1, 231 (entry for 1 May 1844); Ellington, *Women of New York*, 307; Hart, *New Yorkers*, 52–53.

25. William Dunlap, *Diary of William Dunlap: The Memoirs of a Dramatist, Theatrical Manager, Painter, Novelist, and Historian*, ed. Dorothy C. Barck, entry for 1 May 1832.

26. Superior Court, "Forrest v. Forrest," 3 January 1852; *Herald*, 6 January 1852. Prostitute Sarah Clark also noted in the Gage trial that she had moved to her residence at 158 Duane on May 1 (*Sun*, 17 January 1840).

27. Smith, *Sunshine and Shadow*, 378. In a later period prostitutes were said to change brothels monthly and thus the job was said to be very strenuous (Gilfoyle, "City of Eros," 415). It is more difficult to trace ordinary prostitutes because records list only heads of households.

28. See Chapter 1 and related notes for a profile of Jewett. Contrary to the stereotypical view of prostitutes as "bound" to their house madams through economic obligations or intimidation, mid-nineteenth-century prostitutes appear to have exercised considerable personal freedom in deciding when they would move and where they would live. Even so, in many cases it was the madam who decided that the prostitute should leave, either because she felt the prostitute was not attracting enough business or had become diseased, or because the madam felt the need to display "new stock" fairly often.

29. Albion, *Rise of the New York Port*, 398. For information on shipping and ship passengers see also Wilson, *Memorial History*, vol. 3, 335, 445. In 1855, 113 piers extended for thirteen miles of waterfront on both sides of Manhattan on the Hudson and East rivers.

30. Lockwood, *Manhattan Moves Uptown*, 118.

31. James McCague, *The Second Rebellion*, 24.

32. McCabe, *Lights and Shadows*, 582–83; Smith, *Sunshine and Shadow*, 232–34. The general description of the area comes from Ellington, *Women of New York*, 172, 192; Children's Aid Society Report quoted in Gilfoyle, "City of Eros," 73, 93 n. 54; Walt Whitman, *New York Dissected*, ed. Emory Holloway and Ralph Adimari, 6.

33. McCabe, *Lights and Shadows*, 583.

34. Many people attribute the slang term *hooker* to Civil War General

Joseph Hooker, whose troops were notorious for patronizing prostitutes. Lexicographer Stuart Berg Flexner says that the term predates the Civil War and was in use in 1845 at the Hook, or Corlears Hook, in New York (New York *Times*, Westchester, 9 October 1988, p. 3). A number of other cities also take credit for originating the term.

35. [Smith], *Madam Restell*, 31. See also Citizens Association, *Sanitary Conditions of the City of New York*, 1866, noted in Gilfoyle, "City of Eros," 106.

36. Thomas Butler Gunn, *The Physiology of New York Boarding Houses*, 226, 278–80. Also see CGS, *People v. Lawrence*, 12 December 1831, on aggressiveness of some prostitutes in response to neighbors' complaints.

37. The streets that formed the Five Points were Orange (later Baxter), Anthony (later Worth), Cross (later Park), Mulberry, and Little Water (no longer a street).

38. Foster, *New York in Slices*, 22–23; *Sun*, 29 May 1834; 2 May 1840; Groneman-Pernicorn, "Bloody Ould Sixth," 193.

39. Foster, *New York in Slices*, 23; Brown, *Brownstone Fronts*, 20; Gilfoyle, "City of Eros," 60.

40. *Sun*, 27–29 May 1834; Foster, *New York by Gaslight*, 52–62; idem, *New York in Slices*, 22–23. On his visit in 1842, Charles Dickens described the Five Points as housing "hideous tenements which take their names from robbery and murder: all that is loathsome, drooping and decayed is here" (*American Notes*, 89). See also Wilson, *Memorial History*, vol. 3, 437.

41. Hone, *Diary*, vol. 2, 870, 872 (edited general entry for May 1849 and Hone's entry for 28 July 1849).

42. *Sun*, 27–29 May 1834.

43. Ibid., 29 May 1834.

44. MM, Police Dockets, 1849–1855, Ward 6; Groneman-Pernicorn, "Bloody Ould Sixth," 203–5.

45. Groneman-Pernicorn, "Bloody Ould Sixth," 194–95, 199–203. Wilson's *Memorial History*, vol. 3, 436–38, notes the role of the Five Points Mission in transforming the area.

46. Monthly Record of the Five Points Mission, 1860, vol. 4, 16, quoted in Groneman-Pernicorn, "Bloody Ould Sixth," 201.

47. McCabe, *Lights and Shadows*, 398.

48. See Stansell, *City of Women*, for a discussion of the Bowery culture.

49. Ellington, *Women of New York*, 310.

50. Ibid.

51. Spann, *New Metropolis*, 344.

52. In 1835 the leading hotels hosted nearly 60,000 guests in seven months (Jefferson Williamson, *The American Hotel*, 193, 29–30). See also McCabe, *New York by Sunlight*, 52–53, 123–34.

53. For a discussion of Broadway see this chapter, "The Prostitute's Workplace."

54. Eastman, *Fast Man's Directory*, 15. See also Free Loveyer, *Directory to Seraglios*. Wilson notes that 1855–60 was a period when the area changed, and the east side of Church Street was filled with haunts that gave the area a reputation almost as evil as that of the Five Points (*Memorial History*, vol. 3, 456). The *Times*, 23 May 1855, described twenty to thirty brothels on Church Street from Reade to Canal as of the most debased and lewd character.

55. Quotation and other information from *Gentleman's Directory* (1870), 21–22; McCabe, *Lights and Shadows*, 583; Ellington, *Women of New York*, 206–8, 212, 218–19, 232, 300–303; Lockwood, *Manhattan Moves Uptown*, 144–46; Warren, *Thirty Years' Battle*, 109–11; Crapsey, *Nether Side of New York*, 155–59; Griesinger, *Lebende Bilder*, 148–56. Gilfoyle stated that Ward 8 housed few blacks in this period, but the 1860 census shows that Ward 8 had the greatest number of blacks in the city. In 1850 it had the second greatest number, though blacks were not a large proportion of the population ("City of Eros," 78).

56. Ellington, *Women of New York*, 208–9, 211, 231–33; McCabe, *Lights and Shadows*, 190, 583, 590; *Gentleman's Directory*; Gilfoyle, "City of Eros," 372 ff.; Lockwood, *Manhattan Moves Uptown*, 177–78. The Sanitary Commission's Report of 1866 (discussed in Gilfoyle) noted that few brothels were located north of 34th Street at that time.

57. Ellington, *Women of New York*, 232–33.

58. Tim Gilfoyle attempted to count the numbers of brothels and assignation houses in this period and was able to locate far more brothels than assignation houses: for 1830–39, 193 brothels and 13 assignation houses; for 1840–49, 100 and 3; for 1850–59, 241 and 16 ("City of Eros," 112).

59. General information on brothels comes from Smith, McCabe, Ellington, Sanger, censuses, and brothel directories. See Chapter 3 for fees paid in brothels.

60. McDowall divided prostitutes' establishments into two types: boarding houses and assignation houses (*McDowall's Journal*, May 1833).

61. See Chapter 3 for a discussion of boarding houses and their relationship to brothels.

62. [Smith], *Madam Restell*, 32; *McDowall's Journal*, May 1833; Sanger, *History of Prostitution*, 566–68; McCabe, *Lights and Shadows*, 587–89; Ellington, *Women of New York*, ch. 22.

63. The testimony of Caroline Ingersoll at the Forrest divorce trial gives insight into the operations of an assignation house. See Superior Court, "Forrest v. Forrest," 3 January 1852.

64. McCabe, *Lights and Shadows*, 314; Ellington, *Women of New York*, 210–11.

65. See n. 16, this chapter. Sanger, Ellington, McCabe, and Smith all noted the public's "fear" of assignation houses, which they described as the worst form of sex institution because assignations affected the "reputable" sector of the population—meaning reputable women, since so-called reputable men were patronizing brothels. For prostitution proprietors, the fluid structure of the various forms of establishments allowed them to move from a greater involvement in the sex trade to more private and "respectable" positions, for example as assignation or boardinghouse keepers. This meant less management responsibility and risks, an advantage as the women aged (Sanger, *History of Prostitution*, 566; Ellington, *Women of New York*, 173; McCabe, *Lights and Shadows*, 589; [Smith], *Madam Restell*, 32).

66. See the discussion of panel houses with respect to the Melinda and Alexander Hoag cases in Chapter 4.

67. Lockwood, *Manhattan Moves Uptown*, 121; Hone, *Diary*, vol. 1, 13 (entry for 13 April 1829), vol. 2, 746 (entry for 11 October 1845); Strong, *Diary*, vol. 1, 99 (entry for 5 March 1839); Johnson, "That Guilty Third Tier," 575–84.

68. [Smith], *Madam Restell*, 33. George Foster said that by 1849, prostitutes were not allowed in the Broadway Theatre (*New York in Slices*, 90–92). Wilson noted that the Park Theatre, which opened in 1798 and closed in 1848, was for half a century New York's leading theater and the pride of its citizens (*Memorial History*, vol. 3, 146, 370–71).

69. [Smith], *Madam Restell*, 44.

70. "Mary Berry to Helen Jewett," *Police Gazette*, 5 May 1849. Claudia Johnson notes that in some theaters higher-class prostitutes sat in other parts of the house with their escorts ("That Guilty Third Tier"), 577.

71. Johnson, "That Guilty Third Tier," 577.

72. *Herald*, 5 November 1835; *Sun*, 5 November 1835.

73. *Sun*, 2 April 1834.

74. Ibid., 25 April, 28 June 1834; *Transcript*, 30 June 1834.

75. *Sun*, 19 September 1835, 17 August 1836, 26 December 1833; *New Era*, 21 November 1836, 25 February 1837, 25 January 1840. See Chapter 9 for an elaboration of some of these cases.

76. *Advocate of Moral Reform*, 15 November 1838.

77. Foster, *New York in Slices*, 90.

78. Johnson, "That Guilty Third Tier," 580–81.

79. Quoted in ibid., 580.

80. Ibid., 580–81.

81. "W. E. (Bill Easy) to Helen," *Police Gazette*, 26 May 1849; "W. E. (Bill Easy) to Helen," "Helen to Frank," 12 May 1849; "Wm. Easy to Helen," 2 June 1849.

82. Ibid., see 28 April; 5, 12, 26 May; 2, 9 June 1849, passim.

83. Ibid., "Helen to Richard," 26 May 1849.

84. Ibid., "Helen to Richard," 28 April 1849.

85. Ibid. "Helen to Robinson," 2 June 1849. William Chapman was one of nine Chapman family members in the theater. He acted in New York, but he and his family were much more famous for their theatrical tour of the West with a riverboat theater (Mary C. Henderson, *Theater in America: Two Hundred Years of Plays, Players, and Productions*, 20–21).

86. "Helen to Richard," *Police Gazette*, 9 June 1849. James Wallack and his son John were English actors on the New York stage during the 1830s and 1840s. After mid-century they opened a New York theater of their own, Wallack's Theatre (Henderson, *Theater in America*, 15–16).

87. "Helen to Robinson," *Police Gazette*, 28 April 1849.

88. Ibid., "J.J.A.S. to Helen," 5 May 1849 (letter dated December 1835). Edmund Simpson, for most of his career, was associated with the Park Theatre, first as an actor and then as comanager with Stephen Price. He died in 1848 shortly before his beloved Park Theatre burned to the ground (Henderson, *Theater in America*, 11).

89. *Sun*, 2 April 1834.

90. Ibid., 14 May, 18 June 1834. Many House of Refuge case histories list attendance at the theater as a major cause in the downfall of their young prostitute inmates. See HRCH, especially 1830s and early 1840s.

91. *Sun*, 4 June 1834.

92. *Advocate of Moral Reform*, 15 October 1838, 15 May 1841. Other sources on the general corruption of theaters: *Commercial Advertiser*, 11 June 1836; *Herald*, 29 October 1842; *Advocate of Moral Reform*, 1 April 1840, 15 September 1840. See also Ezekiel Porter Belden, *New York As It Is* (New York, 1849).

93. *Commercial Advertiser*, 11 June 1836.

94. Albert M. Palmer, quoted in Johnson, "That Guilty Third Tier," 582. Some people avoided theaters because they tended to attract houses of prostitution to the surrounding area, and many believed it dangerous for families and "ladies" to be in the vicinity.

95. See Chapter 4 for a discussion of this legislation. Johnson says that attendance by prostitutes was necessary for the financial success of theaters at this time ("That Guilty Third Tier," 581).

96. Sanger, *History of Prostitution*, 557.

97. Ellington, *Women of New York*, 166, 211; Johnson, "That Guilty Third Tier," 581.

98. See McCabe, *Lights and Shadows*, 594–97, and Ellington, *Women of New York*, 457–73, for a discussion of concert saloons.

99. McCabe, *Lights and Shadows*, 596.

100. BCMP, *Annual Reports*, 1866–1870.

101. McCabe, *Lights and Shadows*, 597.

102. Foster, *New York in Slices*, 24–25.

103. Gilfoyle, "City of Eros," 453–54.

104. Ellington, *Women of New York*, 297–310; McCabe, *Lights and Shadows*, 589–94; Sanger, *History of Prostitution*, 557–58; Smith, *Sunshine and Shadow*, 424.

105. In *City of Women*, Stansell has an excellent discussion of juvenile huckstering and prostitution (180–92).

106. McCabe, *Lights and Shadows*, 195.

107. *Weekly Journal of Commerce*, 7 June 1849, quoted in Spann, *New Metropolis*, 162.

108. McCabe, *Lights and Shadows*, 195; Wilson, *Memorial History*, vol. 3, 453–54.

109. McCabe, *Lights and Shadows*, 186–87.

110. Strong, *Diary*, vol. 1, 260 (entry for 25 April 1845).

111. McCabe, *Lights and Shadows*, 123.

112. Ibid., 134; Martin, *Secrets of the Great City*, 303–4; Sanger, *History of Prostitution*, 549–50; Spann, *The New Metropolis*, 96; and issues of *Times*, 1855, 1860; *Police Gazette*, 1849; *Tribune*, 1846.

113. [Smith], *Madam Restell*, 33; Smith, *Sunshine and Shadow*, 427; Gilfoyle, "City of Eros," 256; Crapsey, *Nether Side of New York*, 138–39.

114. McCabe, *Lights and Shadows*, 590.

115. Ibid., 591.

116. *Herald*, 30 October 1835.

117. *New Era*, 2 December 1836.

118. *Transcript*, 11 August 1837.

119. In the 1830s streetwalkers were not said to be such a nuisance as they later became, especially in the 1850s and 1860s.

120. *Times*, 20 January 1855.

121. Strong, *Diary*, vol. 2, 57 (entry for 7 July 1851).

122. Ibid., vol. 2, 217 (entry for 31 March 1855).

123. Ibid. Strong disagreed with Mayor Wood's methods because of situations like Matilda Wade's and because of his personal dislike of the mayor (*Diary*, vol. 3, 95 [entry for 31 January 1861].

124. Sanger, *History of Prostitution*, 635.

125. Stansell, *City of Women*, 198–214. In *Lights and Shadows*, McCabe comments on children as streetwalkers in the 1860s and 1870s (134, 590).

126. McCabe, *Lights and Shadows*, 592–93.

127. "J. to Helen," "N.J. to Helen," *Police Gazette*, 2 June 1849.

128. Ibid. See 26 May, 2, 9 June 1849.

129. Quoted in McCabe, *Lights and Shadows*, 614. See also ibid., 611; Warren, *Thirty Years' Battle*, 31; Martin, *Secrets of the Great City*, 294, 301–5.

130. See previously cited brothel directories from 1839, 1853, 1859, and 1870.

131. Strong, *Diary*, vol. 2, 217 (entry for 31 March 1855).

132. Sanger, *History of Prostitution*, 29–30.

Chapter 7

1. [Smith], *Madam Restell*, 47–48, 34.

2. Berg, *Remembered Gate*, 80.

3. Foster, *New York by Gas-Light*, 62.

4. Walkowitz, "We Are Not Beasts," 56. Sanger and others used the term "dangerous classes" although Stansell says it was not a term used widely in the United States until after the Civil War (Sanger, *History of Prostitution*, 484). See also Foster, *New York Naked*, 160; Stansell, *City of Women*, 200.

5. Ellington, *Women of New York* (1869); McCabe, *Lights and Shadows* (1872), *New York By Sunlight* (1882), *Secrets of The Great City* (1868); Crapsey, *Nether Side of New York* (1872); Smith, *Sunshine and Shadow* (1868), *Wonders of a Great City* (1887). See also Griesinger, *Lebende Bilder* (1858).

6. *Herald*, 12, 13 April 1836.

7. Eastman, *Fast Man's Directory*, 5.

8. *Gentleman's Directory*, 36.

9. Sanger, *History of Prostitution*, 557–58.

10. Ellington, *Women of New York*, 208.

11. Sanger, *History of Prostitution*, 560–61.

12. *Sun*, 4 May 1840.

13. *Sun*, 29 May 1834.

14. Ellington, *Women of New York*, 167–72, describes the decline in status and comforts but says most prostitutes entered at the second or third level. In *History of Prostitution*, 557, Sanger notes that many in the second class originally entered in the first.

15. Eastman, *Fast Man's Directory*, 5, 10, 13, 18; Free Loveyer, *Directory to Seraglios*, 21, 22; Sanger, *History of Prostitution*, 554.

16. See U.S., Census, 1850, Wards 5 and 8; N.Y., Census, 1855, Wards 5 and 8. The necessity for business skills is stressed by George Kneeland in *Commercialized Prostitution In New York City*, 92.

17. *Sun*, 25 January 1847; Superior Court, "Ralph Lockwood v. Julia Brown," January 1847.

18. Kate Ridgley had substantial fire damage from heating pipes, and Adeline Miller had to make extensive repairs to her house after rowdies attacked her brothel.

19. Kimball, *Her Life*, 193.

20. Sanger, *History of Prostitution*, 558; *Herald*, 4 January 1850; *Police Gazette*, 12 January 1850.

21. Kneeland, *Commercialized Prostitution*, 92–93; *Sun*, 30 December 1833, 21 March 1834. Ellington says madams were "cold and cynical" (*Women of New York*, 235); see also Hart, *The New Yorkers*, 97.

22. Rosen, *Lost Sisterhood*, 90–91; Walkowitz and Walkowitz, "We Are Not Beasts," 204–5. Both Julia Brown and Rosina Townsend provided for the funerals and burials of prostitutes killed in their houses (*Tribune*, 1 June 1841; *Herald* and *Sun*, April 1836).

23. See Chapter 8 for examples.

24. Superior Court, "Forrest v. Forrest," 3 January 1852, 354–57.

25. Free Loveyer, *Directory to Seraglios*, 18, 23, 27–28; *Sun*, 16 April 1834; 12 March 1835.

26. *Advocate of Moral Reform*, 15 April 1836; *Sun*, 12 June 1834, 22 June 1836.

27. *Sun*, 16 April 1834. See also Sanger, *History of Prostitution*, 541, 551; Foster, *New York in Slices*, 24.

28. See Rosen, *Lost Sisterhood*, 94–98; Gilfoyle, "City of Eros," 415, 459 n. 5. Gilfoyle said it was not uncommon for prostitutes to see over one hundred men in the course of a week, and a conservative number would be ten men per day. He lists several prostitutes who "efficiently entertained a remarkable volume of clients." "Bojtta" saw 185 men in one week, "Lina" saw 273 men in two weeks, and "Darlie" 360 in three weeks.

29. The concept is from E. P. Thompson, "Time, Work-Discipline, and Industrial Capitalism," 56–97.

30. Sanger, *History of Prostitution*, 599.

31. Ibid., 586.

32. Ibid., 554.

33. *Herald*, 10 June 1836, 20 September 1842; *Sun*, 12 February 1842; *Police Gazette*, 11 July 1846, 3 January, 8, 15 August 1846. See Chapter 4 for other case examples and use of law, and see Chapter 6 on the issue of moving and for a discussion of the possible relationship of moving to the small number of cases filed.

34. Walling, *Recollections*, 579–80, gives a description of the 1850s. He notes that it was illegal to harass clients.

35. *Advocate of Moral Reform*, January, February 1835, 15 July 1836, notes both upper- and lower-level houses treated missionaries well. See also McCabe, *Lights and Shadows*, 598–600. Sometimes relations became overly friendly, as when missionary John Gough got "lost" and spent several days in a brothel (*Herald*, 13–16 September 1845; Lockwood, *Manhattan Moves*, 146; Hone, *Diary*, vol. 2, 746 [entry for 15 September 1845]).

36. *Transcript*, 23 April 1836.

37. *Herald*, 23 April 1836.

38. *Herald*, 9 August 1848.

39. See Chapters 5 and 8. For other theft cases, see *Sun*, 5 November 1835, 25 June 1836, 7 May 1840; *Tribune*, 16 January, 25 October, 18 December 1843; *Herald*, 23 January 1844, 7 January, 28 July, 8, 12 September 1845, 12 May, 15 August 1850; *Police Gazette*, 10 January 1846.

40. See *Sun*, 28 February 1834, 26 January 1835, 6 October 1836, 6 January 1842, and other cases in Chapters 5, 8, and 9.

41. *Sun*, 6 October 1836.

42. *Sun*, 3 May 1834, 26 January 1835.

43. *Police Gazette*, 14 February 1846; *Sun*, 14 April 1840.

44. *Herald*, 10 October 1850, and subsequent issues through January 1851.

45. *Police Gazette*, 14 February 1846; *New Era*, 5 September 1839; *Sun*, 21–22 January, 7 March 1840.

46. Sanger, *History of Prostitution*, 485.

47. Ibid., 487.

48. Ibid., 646.

49. *Gentleman's Directory*, 47.

50. Sanger, *History of Prostitution*, 573, 586–89, 646, 672, 675; [Smith], in *Madam Restell*, 40, argued that having syphilis ought to be a misdemeanor and noted that the only reason not to cure venereal disease was that fear of disease deterred some sexual activity. By the end of the century, medical examinations were being performed in many brothels, and prostitutes were paying houses $1–$3 weekly for treatment (Gilfoyle, "City of Eros," 459 n. 5).

51. Goldman, *Gold Diggers*, 130–31.

52. *Gentleman's Directory*, 54.

53. Sanger, *History of Prostitution*, 633–34, 594–97; *Herald*, 6 January 1850; *Sun*, 13 April 1840.

54. *Sun*, 13 April 1840.

55. Studies consulted by Rosen indicated that the percentage of prostitutes contracting disease ranged from 10 to 86.5 (*Lost Sisterhood*, 99).

56. CGS, *People v. Robinson*, 19 April 1836, Coroner's Inquest, 10 April 1836.

57. HRCH, no. 1623 (1835); Sanger, *History of Prostitution*, 454–55; Hart, *The New Yorkers*, 96–97; Walkowitz, "We Are Not Beasts," 83.

58. Venereal disease was a problem for all women, as Strong illustrated in his diary with the story of Jake LeRoy's respectable wife, who died from the disease she got from her husband (*Diary*, vol. 3, 69 [entry for 4 December 1860]).

59. Linda Gordon, "Voluntary Motherhood: The Beginnings of Feminist Birth Control Ideas in the United States," in *Clio's Consciousness Raised: New*

Perspectives on the History of Women," ed. Mary Hartman and Lois Banner, 64; Mohr, *Abortion in America: The Origins and Evolution of National Policy, 1800–1900,* 83–85, 196–97.

60. Linda Gordon, *Woman's Body, Woman's Right: A Social History of Birth Control In America,* 28, 45, 62. Rosen, in *Lost Sisterhood,* 99, says that Progressive prostitutes knew when they were in their fertile period. See John S. and Robin M. Haller, *The Physician and Sexuality in Victorian America,* 114–17.

61. *Gentleman's Directory,* 54.

62. Goldman, *Gold Diggers,* 126; Gordon, *Woman's Body,* 42.

63. *Gentleman's Directory,* 54; [Smith], *Madam Restell,* 5.

64. Mohr, *Abortion in America,* 26–39, 49–50; *Sun,* 18 September 1841. By 1860 the ratio was 1 abortion for every 4 births.

65. *Police Gazette,* 14, 21 February 1846; *Herald,* 10, 14 October 1850; Mohr, *Abortion in America,* 117–27; [Smith], *Madam Restell,* 21.

66. After the war there was a stricter enforcement of the abortion law and a retrenchment in the practice of abortions. Mohr, *Abortion in America,* 46–53, 86–94, 116–70, attributes this partly to a concern by nativist leaders that a majority of the women having abortions were white, native-born, married, and Protestant—those whose offspring would have been "preferred" as future citizens.

67. Sanger, *History of Prostitution,* 478–79.

68. Ibid., 483, 482; Mohr, *Abortion in America,* 79, quoting the 1868 report of the Registrar of Vital Statistics.

69. *McDowall's Journal,* May 1833, 37.

70. Haller, *The Physician and Sexuality,* 216, 284; Goldman, *Gold Diggers,* 127; *Herald,* 12 February 1844; *Sun,* 17–18 January 1840; Mohr, *Abortion in America,* 6–12, 53–69.

71. *Police Gazette,* 28 February 1846; *Sun,* 18 September 1841; *New Era,* 17 August 1839. On trials and convictions, see Mohr, *Abortion in America,* 231.

72. Taylor, "Diary," 14 February 1846; *Police Gazette,* 31 January, 14 February 1846.

73. Ellen Gallagher lived in a number of houses that were associated with prostitution and assignation. She claimed this style of life was a result of her seduction by Davis. The various houses were listed in *Sun,* 17, 18, 20, 22 January 1840.

74. Ibid.

75. On the law, see Mohr, *Abortion in America,* 124; *Police Gazette,* 3 October 1846.

76. Walkowitz, "We Are Not Beasts," 238.

77. Prostitutes had 72.9 percent incidence of sperm-agglutinating anti-bodies, whereas the incidence in a group of single women was 20 percent. Prevention of exposure to semen led to a fall in antibody levels. The pregnancies of women before they became prostitutes resulted in 68.5 percent live births, while afterwards, their pregnancies resulted in 34.3 percent live births (Walter Schwimmer et al., "Sperm Agglutinating Antibodies and Decreased Fertility in Prostitutes," 192–200).

78. See DBA, *City Inspector's Report*, vol. 24, doc. 11 (1857). Abandoned infants were sent to the Almshouse, where few lived beyond one year. In the late nineteenth century, the head physician at the Almshouse said that the 96 percent infant mortality rate at the institution was "not as bad as it looks" because many infants were sickly when they arrived (Duffy, *History of Public Health*, vol. 2, 211). See also *McDowall's Journal*, May 1833; *Advocate of Moral Reform*, 15 January 1836; *Herald*, 27–28 April 1849; *Sun*, 21 June 1836.

In his diary, Philip Hone recorded a poignant story of the discovery of an infant abandoned on his doorstep during a dinner party at which he was entertaining some of New York's most illustrious citizens. The guests were charmed by the "lovely week-old infant," but also cautious, as Hone indicated when he wrote:

My feelings were strongly interested, and I felt inclined at first to take in and cherish the little stranger; but this was strongly opposed by the company, who urged, very properly, that in that case I would have twenty more such outlets to my benevolence. I reflected, moreover, that if the little urchin should turn out bad, he would prove a troublesome inmate; and if intelligent and good, by the time he became an object of my affection the rightful owners might come and take him away. So John Stotes was summoned, and sent off with the little wanderer to the almshouse.

Given the Almshouse statistics quoted above, the infant faced a dismal, and most likely short, future (Hone, *Diary*, vol. 1, 370–71 [entry for 8 December 1838]).

79. *Sun*, 29 October 1841. See Chapter 9 for more on prostitutes as mothers.

80. Sanger, *History of Prostitution*, 542, 541.

81. Ibid., 543.

82. Ibid., 540–41; Ellington, *Women of New York*, 227; McCabe, *Lights and Shadows*, 587–97.

83. Ellington, *Women of New York*, 309–10.

84. Ibid., 220, 227–28, 461, 469; McCabe, *Lights and Shadows*, 587.

85. [Smith], *Madam Restell*, 32–33.

86. McCabe, *Lights and Shadows*, 587.

87. Ellington, *Women of New York*, 223.

88. Strong, *Diary*, vol. 1, 203 (entry for 16 May 1843).

89. Goldman, *Gold Diggers*, 132.

90. McCabe, *Lights and Shadows*, 587; Ellington, *Women of New York*, 223–29.

91. [Smith], *Madam Restell*, 32; Strong, *Diary*, vol. 1, 203 (entry for 16 May 1843); Sanger, *History of Prostitution*, 541–45; Greisinger, *Lebende Bilder*.

92. *Sun*, 9 July 1836. See also the case of Cynthia Stage, *Sun*, 19 September 1836.

93. [Smith], *Madam Restell*, 32–33.

94. Lewis Saum, *The Popular Mood of Pre-Civil War America*.

95. Ellington, *Women of New York*, 328.

96. Ibid., 288; McCabe, *Lights and Shadows*, 587.

97. McCabe, *Lights and Shadows*, 584.

98. *Times*, 8 October 1851. See also *Tribune*, 21 July 1842; *Advocate of Moral Reform*, September 1835. See Chapter 9 for more on depression and suicide.

99. Heyl, *Madam as Entrepreneur*, 197–235; Ellington, *Women of New York*, 190–91.

100. Rosen, *Lost Sisterhood*, 102–4, says that prostitutes in the twentieth century used one name only.

101. See references to the Jewett, Holland, and Gage trials, Chapters 1, 5, 7, 8.

102. *Sun*, 21 October 1842; *Herald*, 17 September, 21 October 1842.

Chapter 8

1. Eastman, *Fast Man's Directory*, 20.

2. Hone, *Diary*, 210–11 (entry for 4 June 1866). General information on Jewett's customers can be found in her correspondence, and other information comes from cases mentioned later in this chapter.

3. On types and classes of clients, see McCabe, *Lights and Shadows*; Ellington, *Women of New York*; Sanger, *History of Prostitution*, sections on hierarchy of prostitution. On mechanics and prostitutes, see *Herald*, 22 June 1836; HRCH, no. 1599 (1835). Ellington said that prostitutes called their clients "Johnny," possibly the origin of the term *john* (*Women of New York*, 302).

4. For racism and biracial prostitution, see the discussion of black prostitution in Chapter 2, and Foster, *New York by Gas Light*, 56–57; Warren, *Thirty Years' Battle*, 110–11; Walling, *Recollections*, 487; *Sun*, 4 June 1834; 27 March, 7 October 1835; 25 May 1836; *New Era*, 28 March 1837; *Herald*, 10 June 1836; *Tribune*, 7 March 1842.

5. Gilfoyle, "City of Eros," 276, and his ch. 7 on "Real Men," 275–92.

6. Goldman, *Gold Diggers*, 122.

7. *Herald*, 12 April 1836. Sanger also discusses prostitutes' hostility (*History of Prostitution*, 496).

8. "William to Helen," *Police Gazette*, 2 June 1849 (letter dated 9 October 1834).

9. Ibid., "Charles H. to Helen," 2 June 1849 (letter dated 5 March 1835).

10. Ibid., "Pupil to Helen," 2 June 1849.

11. Ibid., "Robert to Helen," 26 May 1849.

12. Ibid., "Stanhope to Helen," 26 May 1849.

13. Ibid., "J. to Helen," 2 June 1849.

14. Ibid., "Cambaceres to Helen," 26 May 1849.

15. Ibid., "J.J.A.S. to Helen," 26 May 1849 (letter dated 4 December 1835).

16. Ibid., "Frederick to Helen," 26 May 1849.

17. Ibid., "John P. to Helen," 2 June 1849 (letter dated 9 November 1834).

18. Ibid., "N.J. to Helen," 2 June 1849.

19. Ibid., "Archibald to Helen," 26 May 1849 (letter dated 1 January 1835).

20. Ibid., "T.C. (Henry) to Helen," 26 May 1849 (letter dated 26 February 1834).

21. Ibid., "Charles C. to Helen," 2 June 1849 (letter dated 22 June 1834).

22. Ibid., "Charles Ch . . . to Helen," (letter dated 3 October 1834). Jewett pressed charges against a man for assaulting her at the Park Theatre in June 1834. The reporter who covered the story also did a personal profile article on Jewett's seduction and entry into prostitution.

23. Ibid., "Mary Berry to Helen," 5 May 1849 (letter dated 14 December 1835). Jewett made several trips to visit friends at a brothel in Philadelphia. Letters to her from her Philadelphia friends note the existence of a brothel and client environment similar to that indicated in data on Jewett's New York brothel.

24. Ibid., "W. E. (Bill Easy) to Helen," 12 May 1849.

25. Ibid., "Wm. E. (Bill Easy) to Helen," 12 May 1849.

26. Ibid., preface to letter by "GBM (George B. Marston, alias Bill Easy) to Helen," 28 April 1849. McCabe uses the term *harpies* for men who look for and recruit girls for prostitution (*Lights and Shadows*, 584).

27. *Sun*, 6 June 1836.

28. "GBM (Bill Easy) to Helen," *Police Gazette*, 28 April 1849.

29. Ibid.

30. Ibid., "W. E. (Bill Easy) to Helen," 26 May 1849.

31. Ibid.

32. Ibid., "Wm. E. (Bill Easy) to Helen," 12 May 1849.

33. CGS, *People v. Robinson*, 19 April 1836, Grand Jury Report, 18 April 1836.

34. "Edward to Helen," *Police Gazette*, 2 June 1849 (letter dated 4 May [no year given]).

35. Ibid.

36. Ibid., "Wandering Willie to Helen," 2 June 1849 (letter dated 2 December 1836). See also *Herald*, 13 April 1836.

37. "Wandering Willie to Helen," *Police Gazette*, 26 May 1849 (letter dated 22 January 1836).

38. Ibid. On doing favors see 2 June 1849.

39. HRCH case files describe the social world of young girls before they were admitted to the Refuge.

40. Several newspaper articles complained about police living in brothels; see *Tribune*, 13 March 1844.

41. My position on the late nineteenth-century development of the pimp system is supported by Ruth Rosen and Christine Stansell. Tim Gilfoyle has argued that "by the 1850s a visible, well-established system of pimps existed in New York." I don't find evidence to support this. Gilfoyle's own evidence also points to a much more diverse set of relationships than those that can be truly characterized as "pimp" relationships. "As brothels were attacked with increasing frequency during the 1830s, men for the first time were hired to provide protection. Both brothel keepers and prostitutes admitted that men lived in their houses of prostitution to provide physical protection or perform services such as buying groceries, repairing the house, or serving the guests." Gilfoyle also comments that "the corner of Broadway and Broome Street was a notorious hangout for pimps waiting for prostitutes to hand over their earnings before returning to work," but the reference date is unclear. In discussing late nineteenth- and early twentieth-century prostitution, Gilfoyle describes "pimps" as "responsible for securing a steady supply of women for the brothel," or professional seducers. Some of these men did live off prostitutes' earnings in exchange for protection. But even for this early twentieth-century period, he makes a distinction between these and pimps of a later period: "In contrast to their successors after 1920, pimps were middlemen and brokers of sex, *subject to the control of madams. Only a minority enjoyed the economic and psychological control over prostitutes like they do today* [italics mine]." See Gilfoyle, "Strumpets and Misogynists," 64 n. 48, and "City of Eros," 416; Rosen, *Lost Sisterhood*, 33; and Stansell, *City of Women*, 174.

42. NYMS, *First Annual Report*, 18.

43. *McDowall's Journal*, May 1833; *New Era*, 6 July 1839.

44. W. A. Swanberg, *Sickles The Incredible*, 339.

45. [Smith], *Madam Restell*, 34–35.

46. Ibid., 36.

47. Sanger, *History of Prostitution*, 556.

48. Ibid.

49. *Police Gazette*, 24 February 1849.

50. Sanger, *History of Prostitution*, 486.

51. Ellington, *Women of New York*, 202–3.

52. Ibid., 169.

53. *Sun*, 4 October 1836. See similar case of Charlotte Baldwin beaten by John McChain, *Sun*, 20 February 1835.

54. *Sun*, 27 February 1835.

55. *Sun*, 21 June 1836. Other examples of brutality by paramours include Mary Ann Grover and John Hopkins, *Sun*, 3 March 1834; and Mary Hill and Bill Bigby, *Sun*, 26 January 1835.

56. "Ann Farmer to Helen," *Police Gazette*, 5 May 1849 (letter dated 6 September 1835).

57. *Transcript*, 29 September 1837. See similar case of Hetty Jones, *New Era*, 28 January 1837.

58. *Sun*, 26 December 1833.

59. *Tribune*, 13 March 1844.

60. "Clara to Helen," *Police Gazette*, 5 May 1849 (letter dated 12 June 1835).

61. Ibid., "C. [Clara] Hazard to Helen," 5 May 1849 (letter dated 26 July 1835).

62. Ibid., "Clara Hazard to Helen," 5 May 1849 (letter dated 20 October 1835).

63. *Sun*, 10 February 1842.

64. *Times*, 14 June 1855.

65. *Commercial Advertiser*, 11 July 1836.

66. "Agnes J. Thompson to Helen Jewett," *Police Gazette*, 5 May 1849 (letter dated 2 November 1835).

67. *Sun*, 16 September 1835.

68. CGS, *People v. Robinson*, 19 April, Grand Jury Report, 18 April 1836.

69. "Helen to Frank Rivers," *Police Gazette*, 9 June 1849 (letter dated 24 July 1835).

70. Ibid., "Frank to Helen," 2 June 1849.

71. Ibid., "Helen to Frank," 9 June 1849.

72. Ibid., "Helen to Frank," 28 April 1849.

73. Ibid., "Helen to Frank," 26 May 1849.

74. Ibid., "Helen to Frank," 28 April 1849.

75. Ibid., "Helen to Frank," 2 June 1849. See also 9 June 1849, and several other letters.

76. Ibid., "Helen to Frank," 9 June 1849.

77. Ibid.

78. Ibid.

79. Ibid.

80. Ibid., "Helen to Frank," 26 May 1849. See also 2, 9 June 1849.

81. Ibid., 9 June 1849. Apparently, Jewett's suspicions were not unfounded. In August 1835, Robinson was seeing a woman at the brothel of Elizabeth Stewart on Reade Street (*Commercial Advertiser*, 6 June 1836; *Sun*, 6 June 1836). Other women he was said to have been involved with earlier were Emma Chancellor and a Miss Browne (*Sun*, 14 June 1836; *Police Gazette*, 14 April 1849).

82. "Helen to Frank," *Police Gazette*, 9 June 1849.

83. Ibid.

84. CGS, *People v. Robinson*, 19 April 1836; *Commercial Advertiser*, 7 June 1836. A letter written on 11 November 1835 concerning the return of the miniature was read on 8 June 1836 at the trial.

85. *Herald*, 22 June 1836.

86. *Sun*, 3 March 1835.

87. HRCH, no. 1599 (1835), reference to 7 January 1837.

88. Sickles was a lawyer and served as corporation counsel for New York City, a state legislator, and secretary to Buchanan at the U.S. Legation in London. Later he served in Congress, 1856–1861, and then as a Union general, commander of one of the five military districts during Reconstruction, and minister to Spain. See Edward Longacre, "Damnable Dan Sickles," 16–25; Strong, *Diary*, vol. 2, 438–39 (editor's note with entry for 28 February 1859) and 330 (entry and note for 10 April 1857); vol. 4, 138, 249, 502, 507 (entries for 29 May 1867, 12 July 1869, 21 November and 27 December 1873); Thomas Balderston, "The Sad Shattered Life of Teresa Sickles," 41–45.

89. Swanberg, *Sickles*, 61, 75, 83–98, 285, 359; Balderston, "Sad Shattered Life." The controversy over whether White had helped with campaign funds was referred to by Strong in his *Diary*, vol. 4, 248 (entry for 12 July 1869) and 422 (entry for 20 April 1872).

90. The personal property tax record for 119 Mercer (Fanny White's brothel) lists "M. Bagiolix, $1000" which is crossed out and replaced with the phrase, "appears 92 Prince Street." At 92 Prince Street, following a notation that the previous owner has died, is a listing for "Antonio Baggioli, $1000." The owner of the Mercer Street property before White was John Graham, a Tammany friend of Sickles. Sickles's family also owned property that housed prostitutes in the 1820s.

Among other rumors "granted and generally believed," Strong mentions reports that Sickles had seduced his mother-in-law, blackmailed his father-in-law, and seduced his wife before their marriage. Strong also noted that Teresa Sickles was said to have had an affair with Buchanan, the reason Buchanan remained loyal to Sickles. Strong greatly disliked Sickles and gleefully noted the

New York *World's* response to a libel suit threatened by Sickles: "[We] might as well try to spoil a rotten egg as to damage Dan's character" (quoted in *Diary*, vol. 4, 422, entry for 20 April 1872). Other information from vol. 2, 77, 330, 438, 440–41, 449, 456 (entries for 20 December 1851, 10 April 1857, 28 February, 5 March, 26 April, 20 July 1859); vol. 3, 323, 328, 350 (entries for 17 May, 4 July, 21 August 1863); vol. 4, 138, 248–49, 422, 502, 507 (entries for 29 May 1867, 12 July 1869, 20 April 1872, 21 November and 27 December 1873).

91. Quote from Strong, *Diary*, vol. 2, 377 (entry for 24 December 1857). See n. 89 above for other information on White and Sickles.

92. *Life and Death of Fanny White*, 9–16; Strong, *Diary*, vol. 2, 377 (entry for 24 December 1857). George Strong recorded in his diary in 1860 that "a retired strumpet," formerly with Fanny White, had become the "housekeeper" for old Jake LeRoy and remained with LeRoy after he married an upstate woman several decades younger than himself. The housekeeper, Mary Ann, who was married to LeRoy's body servant, supposedly told the new wife "that she must not presume on her position, and that if she did, she should be turned out of doors" (vol. 3, 68–69 [entry for 4 December 1860]). The young wife became pregnant and very ill with venereal disease and died. Because of rumors that she had been poisoned, her body was exhumed, and an autopsy and inquest were held. Strong found it ironic that the same doctors performed the autopsy on Jake LeRoy's wife and on his former concubine Mrs. Blankman, Fanny White, who had died a few weeks before. "The coincidence is partly funny, partly hideous and revolting" (vol. 3, 73, entry for 12 December 1860).

93. Hone, *Diary*, 98 (entry for 3 July 1833). Herbert S. Parmet and Marie B. Hecht, *Aaron Burr: Portrait of an Ambitious Man*; Leonard Faulkner, *Painted Lady, Eliza Jumel: Her Life and Times*.

94. Dunlap, *Diary*, vol. 3, 796 (entry for 19 June 1834).

95. Strong, *Diary*, vol. 4, 22 (entry for 19 July 1865).

96. Ibid., vol. 1, 114 (entry for 16 November 1839).

97. Ibid., vol. 1, 132–33 (entry for 6 April 1840).

98. Acton, *Prostitution Considered*, 27, 33, 47, 49; Walkowitz, "We Are Not Beasts," 67–69. Walkowitz cites Frances Place and E. P. Thompson as supporting documentation.

99. Christine Stansell, "Women of the Laboring Poor in New York City, 1850–1860," 170–72. See also Stansell's note on the role of sexual mores in the laboring classes in the eighteenth and nineteenth centuries (*City of Women*, 254 n. 35).

100. WSHW, *Second Annual Report* (1871), 34.

101. See HRCH, nos. 728, 747, 783 (1830); nos. 858, 865, 924 (1831); nos. 1343 (1834); nos. 1524, 1570, 1613, 1655 (1835); nos. 2559, 2496, 2520 (1840); no. 5015 (1850).

102. See Chapter 2, Personal Profiles, 40–41.

103. *Herald*, 13 September 1849; Court of Common Pleas, CCHR, "John Waters v. Felicite Waters," no. 1506, 5 October 1849. See a similar case of "Peter Duryea v. Marietta Duryea," 30 March 1850, discussed in A. A. Reidy, "A Peek at Divorce in Old New York."

104. *Sun*, 21 July 1836; *Advocate of Moral Reform*, 15 August 1836.

105. HRCH, no. 1342 (1834). See also *Sun*, 18 June 1834.

106. *Madeleine*, 326, notes that there is "little difference between an unhappy marriage and prostitution."

107. Sanger, *History of Prostitution*, 475.

108. *Herald*, 21 May 1848.

109. Ibid.

110. HRCH, no. 932 (1831).

111. Sanger, *History of Prostitution*, 473, 475.

112. HRCH, no. 728 (1830).

113. Ibid., no. 2540 (1840).

114. Ibid., no. 924 (1831). The 1850 Census lists a Caroline Dean, age 20, in Cinderella Marshall's house and notes that Dean had been married within the past year, indicating she either had left her husband or was helping to support the new union by working in the brothel. U.S., Census, 1850, Wd. 5.

115. *Herald*, 30 May 1848.

116. Superior Court, "Mary Browning v. Jacob Browning," 24 June 1863; also discussed in Reidy, "A Peek at Divorce."

117. Walkowitz and Walkowitz, "We Are Not Beasts," 211. Some may have feared prostitutes would use a claim of marriage as an escape from prostitution/vagrancy charges. This is a possible explanation for a note that was sent to the district attorney during a court hearing on charges against Julia Brown. The note said: "Esq. Hoffman—Sir I wish you wold cawl on Miss Julia Browns Trial & see if she will cawl Mr. Harrison her husband the man she lives with now. for hur one husband is hear from Albany now in the Cort house & is agoing to leave this after noon. Yours—S. Rathbone" CGS, *People v. Julia Brown*, 13 October 1834.

118. *Police Reorganization*, DBA, 53: 975–80, case of Melinda and Alexander Hoag. See also Acton, *Prostitution Considered*, 47; Walkowitz, "We Are Not Beasts," 69–70.

119. CGS, *People v. Taylor and Shannon*, 19 April 1836; *Advocate of Moral Reform*, August 1835; *Police Gazette*, 13 March 1847. See Free Loveyer, *Directory to Seraglios*, 17; N.Y., Census, 1855, Ward 5; *Sun*, 7–8, 20 January 1840; *New Era*, 10 August 1839.

120. *Tribune*, 13 March 1844; Ellington, *Women of New York*, 214–15; *Tribune*, 18 July 1842.

121. Gilfoyle, "City of Eros," 120–35.

Chapter 9

1. See [Smith], *Madam Restell*, 33, 48; Foster, *New York by Gas Light*, 62; idem, *New York Naked*, 154; Ellington, *Women of New York*, 169–70, 242; Sanger, *History of Prostitution*, 518; *McDowall's Journal*, May 1833, 36; *Police Gazette*, 27 October 1849. The *Herald* believed professional jealousy may have caused Jewett's death. *Herald*, 12 April 1836.

2. Sanger, *History of Prostitution*, 547–48, 552, 555; *Police Gazette*, 3 March 1849; [Smith], *Madam Restell*, 34, 48; Ellington, *Women of New York*, 242.

3. *New Era*, 21 November 1836, 26 January 1840, 25 February 1837; *Sun*, 17 August 1836.

4. *Sun*, 6 May 1841, 28 February 1840, 9 March 1835. For other cases, see *Tribune*, 11 June 1841; *Sun*, 26 June 1839, 7 May 1840; *Transcript*, 26 September 1837.

5. *Sun*, 7–8 January 1840; *New Era*, 10 August 1839.

6. *Sun*, 2–3 February 1835.

7. Goldman, *Gold Diggers*, 120, has an excellent discussion of the personal relationships of Western prostitutes.

8. "Clara to Helen," *Police Gazette*, 5 May 1849 (letter dated 26 July 1835).

9. Ibid. (letter dated 12 June 1835).

10. Ibid.

11. Ibid. (letter dated 20 October 1835)

12. Ibid., "Helen to Frank," 9 June 1849.

13. Ibid., "Clara to Helen," 5 May 1849 (letter dated 12 June 1835).

14. Ibid.

15. Ibid. (letters dated 12 June and 26 July 1835).

16. Ibid. (letter dated 26 July 1835).

17. Ibid.

18. Ibid., "Ann Farmer to Helen," 5 May 1849 (letter dated 6 September 1835).

19. Ibid. (letter dated 10 September 1835). See discussion of Mary Gallagher and her property relationships in Chapter 3.

20. Ibid.

21. Ibid. (letter dated 6 September 1835).

22. Ibid., "Mary Berry to Helen," 5 May 1849 (letter dated 12 December 1835).

23. Ibid.

24. Ibid.

25. Ibid., "Mary Berry to Helen" (letter dated 14 December 1835).

26. Ibid.

27. Ibid.

28. See *Sun*, 18 June 1834, and HRCH, case nos. 747, 748, 749 (1830); 902, 903 (1831); 1342, 1343 (1834); 1551, 1554, 1569, 1596 (1835).

29. U.S., Census, 1850, Wards 5 and 8; N.Y., Census, 1855, Wards 5 and 8. Eastman, *Fast Man's Directory*; Free Loveyer, *Directory of Seraglios*. For other brothel relationships, see Chapter 3, property relationships.

30. Ellington, *Women of New York*, 324; "Mary Berry to Helen," *Police Gazette*, 5 May 1849 (letter dated 14 December 1835); Griesinger, *Lebende Bilder*, 148–56. Ellington also notes that postwar prostitutes had their own special gambling houses, and certain coffee and cake saloons served as their "club houses" (218, 239, 277).

31. Ellington, *Women of New York*, 326.

32. "Clara to Helen," *Police Gazette*, 5 May 1849 (letter dated 12 June 1835).

33. Ibid., "Emily to Helen," 26 May 1849 (letter dated 7 March [no year given]).

34. Ibid. (letter dated 26 February [no year given]).

35. Ibid. (letters dated 26 February and 7 March [no year given]).

36. Prime, *Life in New York*, 178.

37. *Sun*, 9 May 1834.

38. CGS, *People v. M. L. Clark*, 17 October 1834. Letter from neighbor.

39. Ibid.

40. *Sun*, 2 September 1834.

41. Heyl, *Madam As Entrepreneur*, 201 ff.

42. *Sun*, 15 August 1836.

43. CGS, *People v. Sewally*, 16 June 1836.

44. *Herald*, 17, 20 June 1836; *Sun*, 16 April 1835, 17 June 1836.

45. *Sun*, 17 June 1836. The reports of the trial reveal the coarse racism of court officials and observers.

46. Marion S. Goldman makes the same point in discussing prostitution in the West (*Gold Diggers*, 120).

47. *New Era*, 27 July 1839; *Sun*, 13 August 1836; *Herald*, 15 September 1842; *Police Gazette*, 12 December 1846, 26 December 1846.

48. Goldman, *Gold Diggers*, 121.

49. Record of Assessments, 1848–1859, Ward 8; *Advocate of Moral Reform*, 15 March 1837, 15 April 1838.

50. A few examples from the HRCH include nos. 747, 748, 829 (1830); nos. 850, 851, 920, 932 (1831); nos. 2520, 2521, 2555 (1840); nos. 4789, 4790, 4736, 4737, 4933, 4934 (1850).

51. *Advocate of Moral Reform*, 15 January 1840; Sanger, *History of Prostitution*, 515; *Sun*, 12 June 1834.

52. *Advocate of Moral Reform*, 15 February 1838.

53. "Clara to Helen," *Police Gazette*, 5 May 1849.

54. Eastman, *Fast Man's Directory*, 20. The use of the word *folks* instead of husband or family is taken to mean a more extended family, but it may indicate her husband only, especially since Cornell is referred to as "Mrs." Most brothel keepers, however, went by the title "Mrs." unless very young. The Reversed City Directory for 1851 lists 106 Grand, corner of Mercer and Grand, as the establishment of James Cornell, confectioner. The 1850 census lists a James Cornell (22), saloon operator, with Mary Cornell (30) and four other women, a waiter, and two servants. The 1854/55 City Directory lists James Cornell at 106 Grand, confectioner; home, 27 Greene. James Cornell may have been a husband, eight years younger than Mary, but the two may also have been siblings, living at home with their "folks."

55. Sanger, *History of Prostitution*, 502, 511, 516.

56. *Sun*, 26 October 1835; HRCH, no. 645 (1829), no. 850, 851 (1831); no. 1524 (1834).

57. HRCH, no. 624, 625 (1829); no. 830 (1830). After the death of her father, Jane Kane's mother sent her to work in an Elm Street brothel (*Police Gazette*, 28 October 1848).

58. Sanger, *History of Prostitution*, 477–83.

59. *Advocate of Moral Reform*, January 1835.

60. Ibid.; Sanger, *History of Prostitution*, 483.

61. HRCH, no. 858 (1831); no. 4665 (1850).

62. N.Y., Census, 1855, Wards 5 and 8; U.S., Census, 1850, Wards 5 and 8.

63. Ibid.

64. Ibid.

65. *New Era*, 18 February 1837.

66. *Sun*, 14 November 1834.

67. *Advocate of Moral Reform*, September 1835.

68. HRCH, no. 2170 (1838).

69. *Herald*, 5 January 1850.

70. HRCH, no. 1538 (1835).

71. HRCH, no. 1648 (1835).

72. *McDowall's Journal*, May 1833; *Advocate of Moral Reform*, 15 January 1836; *Herald*, 27 April 1849; *Sun*, 21 June 1836. See Chapter 7.

73. *McDowall's Journal*, May 1833, 35.

74. *Herald*, 9 October 1850.

75. *Sun*, 17 August 1836.

76. "Ann Farmer to Helen," *Police Gazette*, 5 May 1849 (letter dated 10 September 1835).

77. Ibid.

78. See Cott, *Bonds of Womanhood*; Linda Kerber, "Separate Spheres, Female Worlds, Woman's Place: The Rhetoric of Women's History," 9–39.

79. "Helen to Frank," *Police Gazette*, 28 April 1849.

Epilogue

1. *Sun*, 15 March 1834. The similar story of Ann Burke reinforces the details of this case. See *Sun*, 27 February 1835.

2. *Herald*, 12 April 1836.

3. CGS, *People v. Robinson*, 19 April 1836, Coroner's Inquest Report of 10 April 1836.

4. For an interpretive framework for understanding nineteenth-century women's history, see: Kerber, "Separate Spheres," 9–39. For a discussion of the activities and position of women in the nineteenth century see Cott, *Bonds of Womanhood*; Stansell, *City of Women*; Smith-Rosenberg, *Religion and the Rise*; Suzanne Lebsock, *The Free Women of Petersburg: Status and Culture in a Southern Town, 1784–1860*; and Mary P. Ryan, *Cradle of the Middle Class: The Family in Oneida County, New York, 1790–1865*.

5. Barbara Berg, *Remembered Gate*, 199, 267–69, notes that a sense of sisterhood, or a sense of common socio-legal condition shared with prostitutes, existed in the antebellum New York female moral reform movement. For a discussion of the political activities of English prostitutes in response to the Contagious Diseases Acts, see Walkowitz and Walkowitz, "We Are Not Beasts," 208–20.

Not until the twentieth century would American prostitutes themselves find a collective voice to press for their legal and social rights, with their organization of COYOTE in the United States and their participation in the World Whores Conference in Europe. See Rosen, *Lost Sisterhood*, 177; Hobson, *Uneasy Virtue*, 216–17; and Penny Skillman, "Life 'In the Life,'" 11.

6. Stansell, in *City of Women*, uses the concept of independence in a similar way.

Appendix 2

1. CGS, *People v. Robinson*, 19 April 1836, contains the inventory of Jewett correspondence held by police as evidence.

2. Robinson worked on Maiden Lane, which crossed Pearl Street. The

testimony of Emma French also referred to Jewett's letters. CGS, *People v. Robinson*, 19 April 1836, Report of Coroner's Inquest, 10 April 1836.

3. CGS, *People v. Robinson*, 19 April 1836, Grand Jury Report, 18 April 1836.

4. *Herald*, 12 April 1836.

5. *Herald*, 13 April 1836. Of these three names, only Frank Rivers is listed in the official inventory, but letters from Wandering Willie are found in the copies of correspondence. A copy of one of Wandering Willie's letters was printed in the *Herald* on 13 April 1836. It is accompanied by an explanation that he was a writer for a rival publication (the *Transcript*), who met Jewett in 1834 at the Police Office. The *Transcript*'s 1834 article on the police case is reprinted with the letter.

6. *Sun*, 6–9 June 1836.

7. *Brooklyn Daily Advertiser*, reprinted in the *Police Gazette*, 5 May 1849. The letters appeared in the following issues of the *Police Gazette*: 28 April; 5, 12, 26 May; 2, 9 June 1849.

8. "Anne Farmer to Helen Jewett," and other letters, *Police Gazette*, 5 May 1849. A number of the letters are reprinted in Chapters 6, 8, and 9. See personal profile in Chapter 1 and accompanying notes for biographical references on Helen Jewett and further interpretation of the correspondence.

9. Ibid., "Charles C. to Helen," 2 June 1849.

10. Ibid., "Helen to Richard," 26 May, 28 April 1849.

Bibliography

Primary Sources

MANUSCRIPTS

New York City. Almshouse Records. 1830–1870. New York City Municipal Archives and Records Center.

———. "Appraisal Recommendations for New York County Court Records." Norman Goodman, Director. County Clerk's Office, Hall of Records.

———. Bureau of Social Hygiene. Miscellaneous Papers. Rockefeller Foundation Archives Center, Pocantico Hills, North Tarrytown, New York.

———. Court of Chancery Records. 1830–1847. New York County Clerk's Office, Hall of Records.

———. Court of Common Pleas Records. 1830–1870. New York County Clerk's Office, Hall of Records.

———. Court of General Sessions. 1830–1870. New York City Municipal Archives and Records Center.

———. Municipal Manuscripts. Police Docket. 1849–1855. New York City Municipal Archives and Records Center.

———. Police Court Records. 1829–1860. New York City Municipal Archives and Records Center.

———. Record of Assessments. 1829–1860. New York City Municipal Archives and Records Center.

————. Superior Court Records. 1828–1870. New York County Clerk's Office, Hall of Records.

New York State. Census, 1855. New York City Schedules. County Clerk's Office, Hall of Records.

————. Census, 1870. New York City Schedules. County Clerk's Office, Hall of Records.

————. House of Refuge Case Histories. 1829–1860. New York State Library. Albany, New York.

Robert Taylor Diary. 5 February 1846–1 August 1847. New York Public Library.

United States. Census Office. 5th Census, 1830. New York City Schedules. New York Public Library.

————. 6th Census, 1840. New York City Schedules. New York Public Library.

————. 7th Census, 1850. New York City Schedules. New York Public Library.

PUBLISHED REPORTS
AND DOCUMENTS

American Female Guardian Society. *Constitution and Circular of the New York Female Moral Reform Society; With the Addresses Delivered at Its Organization.* New York: J. N. Bolles, 1834.

Florence Crittenton League, New York. *Annual Reports.* 1886–1890.

Inwood House [New York Female Benevolent Society]. *Annual Reports.* 1834–1862.

Magdalen Society of New York. *Annual Reports.* 1814, 1815.

————. *Constitution and By-Laws of the Magdalen Society of New York.* New York: J. Seymour, 1812.

New York City. Board of Aldermen. *Police Department Reorganization Committee Report.* Doc. 53. New York, 1844.

————. Board of Aldermen. *Semi-Annual Reports of the Chief of Police.* 1847–1856.

————. Board of Alderman, Board of Assistant Aldermen. *Documents.* 1840–1870.

————. Committee of Fifteen. *The Social Evil: With Special Reference to Conditions Existing in the City of New York.* New York: G. P. Putnam's Sons, 1902.

————. Court of General Sessions. *White Slave Traffic.* Reprint of Presentment of the Grand Jury. New York, 1902.

————. Department of Health. *Register of Deaths.* 1845–1858.

————. *Minutes of the Common Council of the City of New York: 1781–1831.* New York: M. B. Brown Printing & Binding Co.,1917.

New York Female Moral Reform Society. *First Annual Report of the Executive Committee of the New York Magdalen Society, Instituted January 1, 1830.* New York, 1831.

New York Magdalen Society. *First Annual Report 1830–1831.*

New York State. Board of Commissioners of the Metropolitan Police. *Annual Reports.* New York, 1864–1872.

————. Secretary of State. Census, 1845. Albany.

————. Secretary of State. Census, 1865. Albany.

————. Secretary of State. Census, 1875. Albany.

United States. Office of the President. *Economic Report of the President, 1989.* Washington, D.C.: Government Printing Office, 1988.

————. Census Office. 8th Census, 1860.

————. Census Office. 9th Census, 1870.

Washington Square Home for Friendless Girls. *Annual Reports.* 1866–1875.

Water Street Home for Women. *Annual Reports.* 1870–1875. New York: Egbert, Bourne and Co.

NEWSPAPERS AND JOURNALS

Advocate of Moral Reform. 1835–1845.

Daily Tribune (New York). 1841–1845.

McDowall's Journal. 1833–1834.

Morning Courier and Enquirer (New York). 1830–1836.

National Police Gazette. 1845–1849.

New Era and American Courier (New York). 1836–1840.

New York Commercial Advertiser. 1836.

New York Daily Times. 1851–1860.

New York Herald. 1835–1852.

New York Transcript. 1835–1837.

The Subterranean. 1845–1847.

The Sun (New York). 1833–1848.

NEW YORK CITY DIRECTORIES AND MAPS

Doggett's New York City Street Directory for 1851. New York: Doggett, 1851.

Illuminated Pictorial Directory of New York. New York: Jones and Newman, 1848.

Longworth, Thomas. *Longworth's City Directory.* 1830–.

Perris, William. *Maps of the City of New York Surveyed Under Directions of Fire Insurance Companies*. New York: William Perris, 1850–1859.

Rude's Directory. New York: Charles Rude, 1850–1860.

OTHER CONTEMPORARY
PRINTED SOURCES

Abbot, Edith. *Women In Industry: A Study in American Economic History*. New York: D. Appleton & Co., 1910.

Account of the Terrific and Fatal Riot at the New York Astor Place Opera House on the Night of May 10, 1849 with the Quarrels of Forrest and Macready, Including All of the Causes Which Led to That Awful Tragedy. New York, 1849.

Acton, William. *Prostitution Considered in Its Moral, Social, and Sanitary Aspects in London and Other Large Cities and Garrison Towns, with Proposals for the Control and Prevention of its Attendant Evils*. London: John Churchill & Sons, 1857, 1870; reprint, London: Frank Cass & Co., 1972.

An Authentic Biography of the Late Helen Jewett, A Girl of the Town Who Was Murdered on the 10th of April 1836: Together with a Full and Accurate Statement of the Circumstances Connected with the Event by a Gentleman Fully Acquainted with Her Story. New York, 1836.

Andrews, Edmund. *Prostitution and Its Sanitary Management*. St. Louis, 1871.

Bannard, Moses. *Discourse on the Moral Aspects and Destitution of the City of New York*. N.p., 1851.

Belden, Ezekiel Porter. *New York As It Is*. New York, 1849.

Blackwell, Elizabeth. *Essays in Medical Sociology*. London: Ernest Bell, 1902; reprint, New York: Arno Press, 1972.

Blanc, Marie T. *The Condition of Women in the U.S.: A Traveller's Notes*. Boston, 1895; reprint, New York: Arno Press, 1972.

Bobo, William M. *Glimpses of New-York City, by a South Carolinian*. Charleston: J. J. McCarter, 1852.

Boyd, William H. *Boyd's New York City Tax Book; Being a List of Persons, Corporations, and Co-Partnerships Resident and Non-Resident, Who Were Taxed According to the Assessor's Books, 1856 and 1857*. New York: William H. Boyd Pub., 1857.

Brace, Charles Loring. *The Dangerous Classes of New York, and Twenty Years' Work Among Them*. New York: Wynkoop & Hallenbeck Pub., 1872.

Buntline, Ned [E. Z. C. Judson]. *The Mysteries and Miseries of New York*. New York: Berford & Co., 1848.

Burns, William. *Life in New York: In Doors and Out of Doors*. New York: Bunce and Bros., 1851.

Campbell, Helen. *Darkness and Daylight; or, Lights and Shadows of New York Life*. Hartford: A. D. Worthington & Co., 1892.

——. *Prisoners of Poverty: Women Wage-Workers, Their Trades and Their Lives*. Boston: Roberts Bros., 1887.

——. *The Problems of the Poor: Women Wage Earners*. 1893. New York: Arno Press, 1973.

[Carey, Matthew]. *Plea for the Poor, Particularly Females: An Inquiry How Far the Charges Alleged Against Them of Improvidence, Idleness, and Dissipation Are Founded in Truth*. Philadelphia, 1836.

Costello, A. E. *Our Police Protectors*. New York, 1880.

Crapsey, Edward. *The Nether Side of New York; or, the Vice, Crime, and Poverty of the Great Metropolis*. New York: Sheldon & Co., 1872.

Darling, William. *List of Persons, Copartnerships, and Corporations, Who Were Taxed on Seventeen Thousand Five Hundred Dollars and Upwards in the City of New York in the Year 1850*. New York: John F. Whitney Pub., 1851.

Dayton, Abram C. *Last Days of Knickerbocker Life in New York*. New York: G. P. Putnam's Sons, 1897.

Dickens, Charles. *American Notes*. 1842; reprint London: J. M. Dent and Sons Ltd., 1970.

Dunlap, William. *Diary of William Dunlap: The Memoirs of a Dramatist, Theatrical Manager, Painter, Novelist, and Historian*. Edited by Dorothy C. Barck. 3 vols. New York: New-York Historical Society, 1930.

Eastman, H. D. *Fast Man's Directory and Lover's Guide to the Ladies of Fashion and Houses of Pleasure in New York and Other Large Cities*. New York, 1853.

Edholm, Mary G. Charlton. *Traffic In Girls and the Florence Crittenton Missions*. Chicago: William Templeton Pub., 1893.

Ellington, George. *The Women of New York; or, the Underworld of the Great City*. New York: The New York Book Co., 1869; reprint, New York: Arno Press, 1972.

Ender, Butt. *Prostitution Exposed; or, a Moral Reform Directory, Laying Bare the Lives, Histories, Residences, Seductions & c. of the Most Celebrated Courtezans and Ladies of Pleasure of the City of New York*. New York, 1839.

[Five Points Mission]. *The Old Brewery, and the New Mission House at the*

Five Points: By Ladies of the Mission. New York: Stringer and
Townsend, 1854.

Foster, George G. *Celio; or, New York Above-Ground and Under Ground*.
New York: Robert M. DeWitt, Pub., 1850.

———. *Fifteen Minutes Around New York*. N.p., 1850.

———. *New York by Gas-Light: With Here and There a Streak of
Sunshine*. New York: Dewitt & Davenport, 1850.

———. *New York in Slices by An Experienced Carver: Being the Original
Slices Published in the New York Tribune*. New York: W. F. Burgess,
1849.

———. *New York Naked*. New York: R. M. DeWitt, [1850].

Francis, John W. *Old New York; Or, Reminiscences of the Past Sixty Years*.
New York: Charles Roe, 1858.

Free Loveyer [sic]. *Directory to the Seraglios in New York, Philadelphia,
Boston and All the Principal Cities in the Union*. New York, 1859.

*The Gentleman's Directory: The Gentleman's Companion, New York City in
1870*. New York, 1870.

Gerard, James. *The Impress of Nationality Upon the City of New York*.
New York: Columbia Spectator Pub., 1883.

Griesinger, Theodor. *Lebende Bilder aus Amerika*. Stuttgart, 1858.

Griscom, John. *The Sanitary Conditions of the Laboring Population of New
York*. New York: Harper and Bros., 1845.

Gunn, Thomas Butler. *The Physiology of New York Boarding Houses*. New
York: Mason Bros., 1857.

Halliday, Samuel B. *The Little Street Sweeper; or, Life Among the Poor*.
New York: Phinney, Blakeman, and Mason, 1861.

Hardie, James. *The Description of the City of New York*. New York: Samuel
Marks, 1827.

[Hastings, Thomas Sr.]. *Missionary Labors Through a Series of Years
Among Fallen Women*. New York, 1870.

Headley, Joel T. *Great Riots of New York, 1712 to 1873*. New York: E. B.
Trent, 1873.

Hone, Philip. *The Diary of Philip Hone, 1828–1851*. Edited by Allan
Nevins. New York: Dodd, Mead, & Co., 1927.

Howe, William F., and A. H. Hummel. *In Danger! or Life in New York:
A True History of a Great City's Wiles and Temptations: True Facts and
Disclosures*. Red Cover Series. New York: J. S. Ogilvie, 1888.

Hutchinson, Woods. "The Economics of Prostitution." *American
Medico-Surgical Bulletin*, August 1895. Reprint.

*Income Record: A List Giving the Taxable Income for the Year 1863, of
Every Resident of New York*. New York: American News Co., 1865.

Ingraham, Joseph Holt. *Frank Rivers; or, the Dangers of the Town.* New York, 1843.

International Abolitionist Federation. *An Address to Members of the American Legislature.* N.p., 1877.

Inwood House. *Charges Preferred Against the New York Female Benevolent Society, and the Auditing Committee in 1835.* New York, 1835.

Kimball, Nell. *Nell Kimball: Her Life as an American Madam, by Herself.* Edited by Stephen Longstreet. New York: Macmillan Co., 1970.

Leonard, Ellen. "Three Days Reign of Terror or the July Riots of 1863 in New York." *Harper's Magazine,* January 1867. Reprint.

Licentiousness: Its Effects, Extent and Causes. Boston: B. Marsh, 1846.

Life and Death of Fanny White, Being a Complete and Interesting History of the Career of that Notorious Lady. New York, 1860.

The Life of Ellen Jewett Illustrative of Her Adventures with Very Important Incidents from Her Seduction to the Period of Her Murder, Together with Various Extracts from Her Journal, Correspondence and Poetical Effects. New York, 1836.

Lippard, George. *New York: Its Upper Ten and Lower Million.* Cincinnati: E. Mendenhall, 1854.

Madeleine: An Autobiography. Introduction by Judge Ben B. Lindsey. New York: Harper Brothers, 1919.

Martin, Edward Winslow [James D. McCabe]. *The Secrets of the Great City: A Work Descriptive of the Virtues and the Vices, the Mysteries, Miseries and Crimes of New York City.* Philadelphia: National Pub. Co., 1868.

Martineau, Harriet. *Society in America.* 2 vols. New York: Saunders and Otley, 1837.

Mathews, Cornelius. *Pen and Ink Panorama of New York City.* New York: John S. Taylor, 1853.

Mayer, Joseph R. *Regulation of Commercial Vice from Segregation to Repression in the United States.* N.p., 1922.

McCabe, James D. *Lights and Shadows of New York Life; or, the Sights and Sensations of the Great City.* Philadelphia: National Pub. Co., 1872.

———. *New York by Sunlight and Gaslight.* Philadelphia: Hubbard Bros., 1882; reprint, New York: Greenwich House, 1984.

———. *Secrets of the Great City: A Work Descriptive of the Virtues and Vices, the Mysteries, Miseries and Crimes of New York City.* Philadelphia: National Pub. Co., 1868.

McDowall, John R. *Magdalen Facts.* New York, 1832.

[McDowall, Phebe]. *Memoir and Select Remains of the Late Rev. John R.*

McDowall, the Martyr of the Seventh Commandment, in the Nineteenth Century. New York: Leavitt, Lord & Co., 1838.

Miller, James. *Prostitution Considered in Relation to its Causes and Cure.* Edinburgh: Sutherland & Knox, 1859.

New York Press. *Vices of a Big City, An Expose of Existing Menaces to Church and Home in New York City.* New York: J. E. Clark Pub., 1890.

Parent-Duchatelet, Alexandre Jean-Baptiste. *De la prostitution dans la ville de Paris.* 2nd ed. 2 vols. Paris, 1857.

Penny, Virginia. *The Employments of Women: A Cyclopaedia of Woman's Work.* Boston: Walker, Wise, & Co., 1863.

Pierce, Bradford K. *Half Century with Juvenile Delinquents; or, New York House of Refuge and its Times.* N.p., 1869.

Powell, Aaron. *State Regulation of Vice: Regulation Efforts in America.* New York: M. L. Holbrook, 1878.

Prime, Samuel Irenaeus. *Life in New York.* New York: Robert Carter, 1847.

Robinson, Richard P. *A Letter From Richard P. Robinson as Connected with the Murder of Ellen Jewett, Sent in a Letter to His Friend Thomas Armstrong.* New York, 1837.

Robinson, Solon. *Hot Corn: Life Scenes in New York Illustrated.* New York: DeWitt & Davenport, Pub., 1854.

Ross, Joel H. *What I Saw In New York.* Auburn, N.Y.: Derby and Miller, 1852.

Sanger, William W. *The History of Prostitution—Its Extent, Causes and Effects Throughout the World.* New York: Harper and Bros., 1858; reprint, New York: The Medical Publishing Co., 1927.

A Sketch in the Life of Francis P. Robinson, the Alleged Murderer of Helen Jewett, Containing Copious Extracts from his Journal. New York, 1836.

A Sketch of the Life of Miss Ellen Jewett Who Was Murdered in the City of New York on Saturday Evening, April 9, 1836. Boston, 1836.

Skillman, John B. *Skillman's New York Police Reports, 1828–1829.* New York: Ludwig and Tolefree, 1830.

[Smith, Charles]. *Madam Restell: An Account of her Life and Horrible Practices, Together with Prostitution in New York, Its Extent, Causes, and Effects Upon Society.* New York, 1847.

Smith, Matthew Hale. *Sunshine and Shadow in New York.* Hartford, Conn.: J. B. Burr, 1868.

Snares of New York; or, Tricks and Traps of the Great Metropolis. New York, 1880.

Strong, George Templeton. *The Diary of George Templeton Strong.* Edited by Allan Nevins and Milton Halsey Thomas. 4 vols. New York: Macmillan & Co., 1952.

Stryker, Peter. *Lower Depths of the Great American Metropolis*. New York, 1866.

Tait, William. *Magdalenism: An Inquiry into the Extent, Causes, and Consequences of Prostitution*. Edinburgh, 1840.

Tappan, Lewis. *The Life of Arthur Tappan*. N.p., 1874.

The Truly Remarkable Life of the Beautiful Helen Jewett Who Was So Mysteriously Murdered. Philadelphia: Barclay & Co., 1880.

W——, George. *Sketch of the Life of Miss Ellen Jewett By One Who Knew Her, Who Was Murdered in the City of New York, on Saturday Evening April 9, 1836*. Boston: J. Q. Adams, n.d.

Walling, George W. *Recollections of a New York Chief of Police: An Official Record of Thirty-Eight Years as Patrolman, Detective, Captain, Inspector and Chief on the New York Police*. New York: Caxton Book Concern, 1887.

Wardlaw, Ralph. *Lectures on Magdalenism: Its Nature, Extent, Effects, Guilt, Causes, and Remedy*. New York: J. S. Redfield, 1843.

Warren, John H., Jr. *Thirty Years' Battle With Crime; or, the Crying Shame of New York, As Seen Under the Broad Glare of an Old Detective's Lantern*. Poughkeepsie, N.Y.: A. J. White, 1874.

Whitman, Walt. *New York Dissected*. Edited by Emery Holloway and Ralph Adimari. Garden City, N.Y.: Doubleday and Co., 1936.

Wilkes, George. *The Lives of Helen Jewett and Richard P. Robinson*. New York, 1849.

————. *The Mysteries of the Tombs*. New York, 1844.

Wilson, Henry Joseph, and James P. Gladstone. *Report of A Visit to the United States as Delegates from the British, Continental and General Federation for the Abolition of Government Regulation of Prostitution*. Sheffield, England: Leader and Sons, 1876.

Wood, George W. *The Growth of New York*. New York, 1865.

Secondary Sources

Addams, Jane. *A New Conscience and An Ancient Evil*. New York: The Macmillan Co., 1912.

Albion, Robert G. *The Rise of the New York Port, 1815–1860*. New York: Charles Scribner's Sons, 1939.

Balderston, Thomas. "The Sad Shattered Life of Teresa Sickles." *American History* 17 (September 1982): 41–45.

Banner, Lois W. *Elizabeth Cady Stanton: A Radical for Women's Rights.* Boston: Little, Brown & Co., 1980.

Barnhart, Jacqueline Baker. *The Fair But Frail: Prostitution in San Francisco, 1849–1900.* Reno: University of Nevada Press, 1986.

Batterberry, Michael, and Ariane Batterberry. *On the Town in New York: From 1776 to the Present.* New York: Charles Scribner's Sons, 1973.

Berg, Barbara. *The Remembered Gate: Origins of American Feminism.* The Woman and the City Series. New York: Oxford University Press, 1978.

Blackmar, Betsy. "Rewalking the Walking City." *Radical History Review* 21 (Fall 1979): 131–48.

Boyer, Paul S. *Urban Masses and Moral Order in America, 1820–1920.* Cambridge: Harvard University Press, 1978.

Bridges, Amy. *A City in the Republic: Antebellum New York and the Origins of Machine Politics.* Cambridge: Cambridge University Press, 1984.

Brown, Henry Collins. *Brownstone Fronts and Saratoga Trunks.* New York: E. P. Dutton & Co., 1935.

Brownmiller, Susan. "Speaking Out on Prostitution." In *Radical Feminism,* ed. Ann Koedt, Ellen Levine, and Anita Rapone, 72–77. New York: Quadrangle Books, 1973.

Bullough, Vern L. *The History of Prostitution.* New Hyde Park, N.Y.: University Books, 1964.

Burnham, John C. "Medical Inspection of Prostitutes in America in the Nineteenth Century: The St. Louis Experiment and Its Sequel." *Bulletin of the History of Medicine* 45 (May–June 1971): 203–18.

———. "The Progressive Era Revolution in American Attitudes Toward Sex." *Journal of American History* 59 (March 1973): 885–908.

Butler, Anne M. *Daughters of Joy, Sisters of Misery: Prostitutes in the American West, 1865–90.* Urbana: University of Illinois Press, 1985.

Carlson, Oliver. *The Man Who Made News: James Gordon Bennett.* New York: Duell, Sloan & Pearce, 1942.

Chesney, Kellow. *The Anti-Society: An Account of the Victorian Underworld.* Boston: Gambit, 1970.

Cohen, Barbara, Seymour Chwast, and Steven Heller, eds. *New York Observed: Artists and Writers Look at the City, 1650 to the Present.* New York: H. N. Abrams, 1987.

Cohen, Patricia Cline. "The Helen Jewett Murder: Violence, Gender, and Sexual Licentiousness in Antebellum America." *National Women's Studies Association Journal* 2 (Summer 1990): 374–89.

Cott, Nancy. *The Bonds of Womanhood: "Woman's Sphere" in New England, 1780–1835.* New Haven: Yale University Press, 1977.

Degler, Carl N. "What Ought to Be and What Was: Women's Sexuality in the Nineteenth Century." *American Historical Review* 79 (October 1974): 1467–90.

Diner, Hasia R. *Erin's Daughters in America: Irish Immigrant Women in the Nineteenth Century.* Baltimore: Johns Hopkins University Press, 1983.

DuBois, Ellen, Mari Jo Buhle, Temma Kaplan, Gerda Lerner, and Carroll Smith-Rosenberg. "Politics and Culture in Women's History: A Symposium." *Feminist Studies* 6 (Spring 1980): 26–64.

Duffy, John. *The Healers: The Rise of the Medical Establishment.* New York: McGraw-Hill, 1976.

———. *The History of Public Health in New York City.* Vol. 1, *1625–1866.* Vol. 2, *1866–1966.* New York: Russell Sage Foundation, 1968, 1974.

Dunshee, Kenneth Holcomb. *As You Pass By: Directory of Forgotten Streets.* New York: Hastings House, 1952.

Ernst, Robert. *Immigrant Life in New York City, 1825–1863.* New York: King's Crown Press, 1949.

Evans, Richard J. "Prostitution, State and Society in Imperial Germany." *Past and Present* 70 (1976): 106–29.

Faulkner, Leonard. *Painted Lady, Eliza Jumel: Her Life and Times.* New York: E. P. Dutton & Co., 1962.

Feldman, Egal. "Prostitution, the Alien Woman and the Progressive Imagination, 1910–1915." *American Quarterly* 19 (Summer 1967): 192–206.

Flaacke, Marie. *Why Women Fall.* New York, 1901.

Flexner, Abraham. *Prostitution In Europe.* New York: Century Press, 1920.

Gardner, Charles W. *The Doctor and the Devil; or, Midnight Adventures of Dr. Parkhurst.* New York: Gardner & Co., 1894; reprint, New York: Vanguard Press, 1931.

Gibson, Mary. *Prostitution and the State in Italy, 1860–1915.* New Brunswick, N.J.: Rutgers University Press, 1986.

Gilfoyle, Timothy J. "City of Eros: New York City, Prostitution, and the Commercialization of Sex, 1790–1920." Ph.D. diss., Columbia University, 1987.

———. "Strumpets and Misogynists: Brothel 'Riots' and the Transformation of Prostitution in Antebellum New York City." *New York History* (January 1987): 45–65.

———. "The Urban Geography of Commercial Sex: Prostitution in New York City, 1790–1860." *Journal of Urban History* 13 (August 1987): 371–93.

Goldman, Emma. *"The Traffic in Women" and Other Essays on Feminism.* New York: Times Change Press, 1971.

Goldman, Marion S. *Gold Diggers and Silver Miners: Prostitution and Social Life on the Comstock Lode.* Ann Arbor: University of Michigan Press, 1981.

Gordon, Linda. "Voluntary Motherhood: The Beginnings of Feminist Birth Control Ideas in the United States." In *Clio's Consciousness Raised: New Perspectives on the History of Women,* ed. Mary Hartman and Lois Banner, 54–71. New York: Harper & Row, 1974.

———. *Woman's Body, Woman's Right: A Social History of Birth Control in America.* New York: Penguin, 1977.

Griffin, Clifford. *Their Brother's Keepers: Moral Stewardship in the United States, 1800–1865.* New Brunswick, N.J.: Rutgers University Press, 1960.

Grimsted, David. "Rioting in Its Jacksonian Setting." *American Historical Review* 77 (1972): 361–97.

Groneman-Pernicorn, Carol. "The 'Bloody Ould Sixth': A Social Analysis of a New York City Working-Class Community in the Mid-Nineteenth Century." Ph.D. diss., University of Rochester, 1973.

Haller, John S., and Robin M. Haller. *The Physician and Sexuality in Victorian America.* Urbana: University of Illinois Press, 1974.

Harlow, Alvin F. *Old Bowery Days: The Chronicles of a Famous Street.* New York: D. Appleton & Co., 1931.

Harsin, Jill. *Policing Prostitution in Nineteenth-Century Paris.* Princeton: Princeton University Press, 1985.

Hart, Smith. *The New Yorkers: The Story of a People and Their City.* New York: Sheridan House, 1938.

Henderson, Mary C. *Theater in America: Two Hundred Years of Plays, Players, and Productions.* New York: Henry N. Abrams, 1986.

Henriques, Fernando. *Prostitution in Europe and the New World.* 2 vols. New York: The Citadel Press, 1963.

Hewitt, Margaret. *Wives and Mothers in Victorian Industry.* Westport, Conn.: Greenwood Press, 1958.

Heyl, Barbara Sherman. *The Madam as Entrepreneur: Career Management in House Prostitution.* New Brunswick, N.J.: Transition Books, 1979.

Hill, Joseph A. *Women in Gainful Occupations 1870 to 1920: A Study of the Trend of Recent Changes in the Numbers, Occupational Distribution, and Family Relationship of Women Reported in the Census as Following a Gainful Occupation.* Census Monograph. Washington, D.C.: U.S. Government Printing Office, 1929.

Hobson, Barbara Meil. *Uneasy Virtue: The Politics of Prostitution and the American Reform Tradition.* New York: Basic Books, 1987.

Hughes, Glenn. *A History of the American Theatre, 1700–1950*. New York: Samuel French, 1951.

Hurst, James W. *The Growth of American Law: The Lawmakers*. Boston: Little, Brown, 1950.

Johnson, Claudia D. "That Guilty Third Tier: Prostitution in Nineteenth-Century American Theaters." *American Quarterly* 27 (December 1975): 575–84.

Kerber, Linda K. "Separate Spheres, Female Worlds, Woman's Place: The Rhetoric of Women's History." *The Journal of American History* 75 (June 1988): 9–39.

Kneeland, George J. *Commercialized Prostitution in New York City*. New York: Century Co., 1917.

Komroff, Manuel. *A New York Tempest*. New York: Coward-McCann, Inc., 1932.

Kouwenhoven, John A. *The Columbia Historical Portrait of New York: An Essay in Graphic History in Honor of the Tricentennial of New York City and the Bicentennial of Columbia University*. Garden City, N.Y.: Doubleday & Co., Inc., 1953.

Laslett, Peter. *The World We Have Lost*. New York: Scribner, 1971.

Lebsock, Suzanne. *The Free Women of Petersburg: Status and Culture in a Southern Town, 1784–1860*. New York: W. W. Norton Co., 1985.

Lerner, Gerda. "Placing Women in History: Definitions and Challenges." *Feminist Studies* 3 (Fall 1975): 5–14.

Lipman-Blumen, Jean. "Towards A Homosocial Theory of Sex Roles: An Explanation of the Sex Segregation of Social Institutions." *Signs* 1 (Spring 1976): 16–28.

Lockwood, Charles. *Manhattan Moves Uptown*. Boston: Houghton Mifflin, 1976.

Longacre, Edward. "Damnable Dan Sickles." *Civil War Times* 23 (May 1984): 16–25.

Lubove, Roy. "The Progressive and the Prostitute." *The Historian* 24 (1962): 308–30.

McBride, Theresa M. *The Domestic Revolution: The Modernization of Household Service in England and France, 1820–1920*. New York: Holme & Meier, 1976.

McCague, James. *The Second Rebellion: The Story of the New York City Draft Riots of 1863*. New York: The Dial Press, 1968.

Marcus, Steven. *The Other Victorians: A Study of Sexuality and Pornography in Mid-Nineteenth-Century England*. New York: Basic Books, 1966.

Mayer, Joseph R. *Regulation of Commercial Vice: From Segregation to Repression in the United States*. New York: The Klebold Press, 1922.

Melder, Keith. "Ladies Bountiful: Organized Women's Benevolence in Early Nineteenth-Century America." *New York History* 48 (July 1967): 231–54.

Miller, Douglas T. *Jacksonian Aristocracy: Class and Democracy in New York, 1830–1860.* New York: Oxford University Press, 1967.

Miller, Wilber R. *Cops and Bobbies: Police Authority in New York and London, 1830–1870.* Chicago: University of Chicago Press, 1973.

Millett, Kate. *The Prostitution Papers: A Candid Dialogue.* New York: Avon Books, 1973.

Minnigerode, Meade. *The Fabulous Forties: 1840–1850; A Presentation of Private Life.* Garden City, N.Y.: G. P. Putnam's Sons, 1924.

Mohl, Raymond. *Poverty in New York 1783–1825.* New York: Oxford University Press, 1971.

Mohr, James C. *Abortion in America: The Origins and Evolution of National Policy, 1800–1900.* New York: Oxford University Press, 1978.

Monaghan, James. *The Great Rascal: The Life and Adventures of Ned Buntline.* Boston: Little, Brown & Co., 1952.

Morris, Lloyd. *Incredible New York: High Life and Low Life of the Last Hundred Years.* New York: Random House, 1951.

Murtaugh, John M., and Sarah Harris. *Cast the First Stone.* New York: McGraw-Hill, 1957.

North, Douglas C., and Roger LeRoy Miller. *The Economics of Public Issues.* New York: Harper & Row, 1971; 3rd ed., 1973.

O'Connor, Richard. *The Scandalous Mr. Bennett.* Garden City, N.Y.: Doubleday & Co., Inc., 1962.

Parmet, Herbert S., and Marie B. Hecht. *Aaron Burr: Portrait of an Ambitious Man.* New York: Macmillan, 1967.

Parkhurst, Charles P. *My Forty Years in New York.* New York: Macmillan, 1923.

———. *Our Fight with Tammany.* New York: Charles Scribner's Sons, 1895.

Pearsall, Ronald. *The Worm in the Bud: The World of Victorian Sexuality.* London: Weidenfeld & Nicolson, 1969.

Pessen, Edward. *Riches, Class and Power Before the Civil War.* Lexington, Mass.: D. C. Heath & Co., 1973.

Peters, John P. "The Story of the Committee of Fourteen of New York." *Social Hygiene* 4 (July 1918): 347–88.

Pickett, Robert S. *House of Refuge: Origins of Juvenile Reform in New York State, 1815–1857.* Syracuse: Syracuse University Press, 1969.

Pivar, David J. *Purity Crusade: Sexual Morality and Social Control, 1868–1900.* Westport, Conn.: Greenwood Press, 1973.

Reed, James. *From Private Vice to Public Virtue: The Birth Control*

Movement and American Society Since 1830. New York: Basic Books, 1978.

Reidy, A. A. "A Peek At Divorce In Old New York." *New York Law Journal*, 17 January 1980.

Richardson, James F. *The New York Police: From Colonial Times to 1901*. New York: Oxford University Press, 1970.

Riegel, Robert E. "Changing American Attitudes Towards Prostitution, 1800–1920." *Journal of the History of Ideas* 29 (1968): 437–452.

Rosen, Ruth. *The Lost Sisterhood: Prostitution in America, 1900–1918*. Baltimore: The Johns Hopkins University Press, 1982.

Rosen, Ruth, and Sue Davidson, eds. *The Maimie Papers*. Bloomington: Indiana University Press and the Feminist Press, 1977.

Ryan, Mary P. *Cradle of the Middle Class: The Family in Oneida County, New York, 1790–1865*. New York: Cambridge University Press, 1983.

Sachs, Emanie. *"The Terrible Siren": Victoria Woodhull, 1838–1927*. New York: Harper & Bros., 1928.

Saum, Lewis O. *The Popular Mood of Pre-Civil War America*. Westport, Conn.: Greenwood Press, 1980.

Schneider, David M. *The History of Public Welfare in New York State, 1609–1866*. Chicago: University of Chicago Press, 1938.

Schur, Edwin M. *Labeling Women Deviant: Gender, Stigma, and Social Control*. Philadelphia: Temple University Press, 1984.

Schwimmer, Walter B., K. A. Ustay, and S. J. Behrman. "Sperm Agglutinating Antibodies and Decreased Fertility in Prostitutes." *Obstetrics and Gynecology* 30 (1967): 192–200.

Scott, Joan, and Louise Tilly. "Women's Work and the Family in Nineteenth-Century Europe." *Comparative Studies in Society and History* 7 (January 1975): 36–64.

Sheehy, Gail. "The Economics of Prostitution: Who Profits, Who Pays?" *Ms. Magazine* (June 1973): 59–109.

Sicherman, Barbara. "American History." *Signs* 1 (Winter 1975): 461–85. Review.

Simon, Kate. *Fifth Avenue: A Very Social History*. New York: Harcourt, Brace, Jovanovich, 1978.

Skillman, Penny. "Life 'In the Life.'" *Belles Lettres* (1990): 11.

Smith, Daniel Scott. "Family Limitation, Sexual Control, and Domestic Feminism in Victorian America." In *Clio's Consciousness Raised: New Perspectives on the History of Women*, edited by Mary S. Hartman and Lois Banner, 119–136. New York: Harper and Row, 1974.

Smith, Timothy. *Revivalism and Social Reform: American Protestantism on the Eve of the Civil War*. New York: Harper & Row, 1957.

Smith-Rosenberg, Carroll. "Beauty, the Beast, and the Militant Woman: A

Case Study in Sex Roles and Social Stress in Jacksonian America." *American Quarterly* 23 (1971): 562–84.

———. *Disorderly Conduct: Visions of Gender in Victorian America.* New York: Alfred A. Knopf, 1985.

———. "The Female World of Love and Ritual." *Signs* 1 (1975): 1–29.

———. "Politics and Culture in Women's History—Response." *Feminist Studies* 6 (Spring 1980): 55–64.

———. "Puberty to Menopause: The Cycle of Femininity in Nineteenth-Century America." *Feminist Studies* 1 (Winter/Spring 1973): 58–72.

———. *Religion and the Rise of the American City: The New York City Mission Movement, 1812–1870.* Ithaca: Cornell University Press, 1971.

Spann, Edward. *The New Metropolis: New York, 1840–1857.* New York: Columbia University Press, 1982.

Springarn, Arthur Barnett. *Laws Relating to Sex and Morality in New York City.* New York, 1915.

Stansell, Christine. *City of Women: Sex and Class in New York, 1789–1860.* New York: Alfred A. Knopf, 1986.

———. "The Origins of the Sweatshop: Women and Early Industrialization in New York City." In *Working-Class America: Essays on Labor, Community, and American Society,* edited by Michael H. Frisch and Daniel J. Walkowitz, 78–103. Urbana: University of Illinois Press, 1983.

———. "Women, Children, and the Uses of the Streets: Class and Gender Conflict in New York City, 1850–1860." *Feminist Studies* 8 (1982): 309–35.

———. "Women of the Laboring Poor in New York City, 1820–1860." Ph.D. diss., Yale University, 1979.

Stokes, I. N. Phelps. *Iconography of Manhattan Island 1498–1909.* 6 vols. New York, 1915.

Sturgis, Frederic Russel. *Prostitution: Its Suppression and Control.* N.p., n.d.

Swanberg, W. A. *Sickles The Incredible.* New York: Charles Scribner's Sons, 1956.

Thernstrom, Stephen, and Peter Knights. "Men in Motion: Some Data and Speculations About Urban Population Mobility in Nineteenth-Century America." *Journal of Interdisciplinary History* 1 (Autumn 1970–Spring 1971): 7–37.

Thompson, E. P. "Time, Work-Discipline, and Industrial Capitalism." *Past and Present* 38 (December 1967): 56–97.

Van Every, Edward. *Sins of New York as "Exposed" by the Police Gazette.* New York: Frederick A. Stokes, 1930.

Verbrugge, Martha H. "Women and Medicine in Nineteenth-Century America." *Signs* 1 (Summer 1976): 957–72.

Walkowitz, Judith R. "The Making of an Outcast Group: Prostitutes and Working Women in Nineteenth-Century Plymouth and Southampton." In A *Widening Sphere: Changing Roles of Victorian Women*, edited by Martha Vicinus, 72–93. Bloomington: Indiana University Press, 1977.

———. "Notes on the History of Victorian Prostitution." *Feminist Studies* 1 (Summer 1972): 105–113.

———. *Prostitution In Victorian Society: Women, Class, and the State.* Cambridge: Cambridge University Press, 1980.

———. "'We Are Not Beasts of the Field': Prostitution and the Campaign Against the Contagious Diseases Acts, 1869–1886." Ph.D. diss., University of Rochester, 1974.

Walkowitz, Judith R., and Daniel J. Walkowitz. "'We Are Not Beasts of the Field': Prostitution and the Poor in Plymouth and Southampton Under the Contagious Diseases Acts." *Feminist Studies* 1 (Winter/Spring 1973): 73–106.

Walsh, Robert F. *Dr. Parkhurst's Crusade, or New York After Dark.* New York: Commonwealth, 1892.

Warner, John DeWitt. "The Raines Law Liquor Tax Law." *Municipal Affairs.* N.d., reprint.

Waterman, Willoughby Cyrus. *Prostitution and Its Repression in New York City, 1900–1931.* New York: Columbia University Press, 1932.

Weinbaum, Paul O. *Mobs and Demagogues: The New York Response to Collective Violence in the Early Nineteenth Century.* Ann Arbor: UMI Press, 1979.

Welter, Barbara. "The Cult of True Womanhood." *American Quarterly* 28 (Summer 1966): 151–74.

Werner, Morris Robert. *It Happened in New York.* New York: Coward-McCann, 1957.

Whiteaker, Larry. "Moral Reform and Prostitution in New York City, 1830–1860." Ph.D. diss., Princeton University, 1980.

Wilentz, Sean. *Chants Democratic: New York City and the Rise of the American Working Class, 1788–1850.* New York: Oxford University Press, 1984.

Wilson, Dorothy Clarke. *Lone Woman: The Story of Elizabeth Blackwell, the First Woman Doctor.* Boston: Little, Brown & Co., 1970.

Wilson, James Grant, ed. *The Memorial History of the City of New York.* 4 vols. New York, 1893.

Wilson, Otto, and Robert S. Barrett. *Fifty Years' Work With Girls,*

1883–1933. Alexandria, Va.: The National Florence Crittenton Mission, 1933.

Woolston, Howard B. *Prostitution in the United States Prior to the Entrance of the United States into the World War*. New York: The Century Co., 1921.

Wyatt-Brown, Bertram. *Lewis Tappan and the Evangelical War Against Slavery*. Cleveland: Case Western Reserve University Press, 1969.

Wyman, Margaret. "The Rise of the Fallen Woman." *American Quarterly* 3 (1951): 167–176.

Index

Compositor: Braun-Brumfield, Inc.
Text: 10.5/13.5 Electra
Display: Electra
Printer: Braun-Brumfield, Inc.
Binder: Braun-Brumfield, Inc.